31-23

74-76

83-91

106-110

137

159-60

☆173,

177

194-95

230-231

basic pt: affections = soul
not emotions. Not mere feelings,
but, summarizing much 20 lit,
beauty / good-ksd. – p. 229

early
Good division GA
post-GA

(1) Overview to make a pt:
affections ≠ feelings & emotions
But SOUL / won't say it, but
NOAD CASNS

(2) unclear how

T & T CLARK STUDIES IN SYSTEMATIC THEOLOGY

UNDERSTANDING AFFECTIONS IN THE THEOLOGY OF JONATHAN EDWARDS

"The High Exercises of Divine Love"

by
Ryan J. Martin

t&t clark
LONDON • NEW YORK • OXFORD • NEW DELHI • SYDNEY

T&T CLARK
Bloomsbury Publishing Plc
50 Bedford Square, London, WC1B 3DP, UK
1385 Broadway, New York, NY 10018, USA

BLOOMSBURY, T&T CLARK and the T&T Clark logo are trademarks of Bloomsbury Publishing Plc

First published in Great Britain 2019

A catalogue record for this book is available from the British Library.

A catalog record for this book is available from the Library of Congress.

ISBN: HB: 978-0-5676-8224-6
ePDF: 978-0-5676-8225-3
eBook: 978-0-5676-8229-1

Series: T&T Clark Studies in Systematic Theology

Typeset by Deanta Global Publishing Services, Chennai, India

Printed and bound in Great Britain

For the beautiful Jennifer,
my dearest companion,
with the sweetest affection
SDG

CONTENTS

Foreword ix
Acknowledgments x
Note on Text xii
The Yale University Press Edition of *The Works of Jonathan Edwards* xiii
List of Abbreviations xiv

INTRODUCTION 1

Chapter 1
LOST IN TRANSLATION: THE PROBLEM OF EDWARDS, AFFECTIONS, AND EMOTIONS 3
- The Problem of Jonathan Edwards and Affections 4
- *Emotions* and Other Definitions 16
- The Problem of Jonathan Edwards and Emotions 23

Chapter 2
HUMAN AFFECTIONS IN PATRISTIC AND MEDIEVAL THEOLOGY 29
- Patristic Thought 31
- Medieval Thought 46

Chapter 3
HUMAN AFFECTIONS IN POST-MEDIEVAL THOUGHT 59
- Reformation Figures 59
- The Puritan Tradition and Early Enlightenment Moral Philosophy 66
- Conclusion 88

Chapter 4
YOUNG JONATHAN EDWARDS'S EDUCATION IN AFFECTIONS 91
- Edwards's Educational Background 92
- Jonathan Edwards and John Locke 96

Chapter 5
JONATHAN EDWARDS'S EARLY PSYCHOLOGY 111
- "The Mind" 112
- Personal Writings 118
- Early Sermons and Revival Writings 137
- *A Faithful Narrative* 146
- *Charity and Its Fruits* 148
- Conclusion 159

Chapter 6
ENTHUSIASM, PASSIONS, AND THE GREAT AWAKENING
DISPUTES OVER THE ROLE OF AFFECTIONS IN RELIGION 161
Historical Background 162
Charles Chauncy on the Place of Affections in Religion 164
Jonathan Edwards on the Affectionate Part of Man 171
Conclusion 194

Chapter 7
AFFECTIONS AND CHRISTIAN APOLOGY: THE LATER
PSYCHOLOGY OF JONATHAN EDWARDS 197
Historical Survey 198
Affections in the Later Years 201
Conclusion 229

Chapter 8
TOWARD A THEOLOGY OF AFFECTIONS 233

Bibliography 239
Yale Works of Jonathan Edwards 239
Other Works by Jonathan Edwards 240
Other Primary Sources 241
Biography 246
Secondary Sources: Books and Dissertations 246
Secondary Sources: Journal Articles and Essays 255

Index 259

FOREWORD

Jonathan Edwards flourished during the Age of Enlightenment; indeed, he has been dubbed a "Dordtian Philosophe." Yet he has also often been pointed to as anticipating the Age of Sentiment and the Age of Romanticism for the ways in which he contributed to a modern, subjective sense of the self. Ryan J. Martin pertinently suggests that in this respect Edwards has been lost in translation.

From early in his life, Edwards worked from an inherited Reformed notion of affections as primarily synonymous with passivity or receptiveness. Thus, as a young man he considered it proper for orators and preachers to move the passions in order to show earnestness, and thereby convince the judgments of their auditors. The affections or passions were "lively exercises of the will" that involved "the animal nature." As he matured, Edwards developed a more sophisticated notion of affections as involving the whole being, will and judgment, heart and head, a conception most on display in his masterwork, *A Treatise Concerning Religious Affections*. There, he convincingly demonstrates, among other things, the fallacy of equating true religious affections with mere emotions. The work you hold in your hands grapples with the persistent misapplication of Edwards's categories, and sorts out the difference between affections and emotions as he conceived them.

Edwards reminds us of the venerable connection between "passion" and "passive," analogous to "action" and "active." In modern and post-modern times, we tend to think of passion, not as involuntary, as the etymology of the word indicates, but as the opposite of passive—as earnestly, even violently, reacting to or involved in something. But for Edwards, action and passion were not modes of existence but of relation.

In the post-modern world, it seems, all emotions are self-justified, all sensations legitimate as ends in themselves or as proof of the reality of an experience. Many trace this legacy to Edwards, but what is needed is an appreciation of Edwards's complexity: that affections are not simply emotions or "feelings," and that they are not all to be affirmed unquestioningly. An effort such as the one made in this study to understand Edwards's concept of affections in all its aspects can be helpful—may even be essential—in examining and critiquing modern assumptions not only about the nature of religious experience but about the nature of the self.

Kenneth P. Minkema
Jonathan Edwards Center, Yale University

ACKNOWLEDGMENTS

Expressio unius est exclusio alterius is a Latin expression that seems fitting as I begin. It means, "to express one is to exclude another." I cannot truly name all the people who helped me with this book. Yet, I am a debtor to many, and I sense an obligation to try to name at least a few of them.

The lights that make up the galaxy of Edwardsean scholars shine very brightly. The heft of the intellectual heavyweights that seek to explicate and mine the mind of Jonathan Edwards is not lost on any who venture into studying this great thinker. In writing this book, I have sifted through some of the keenest and most encyclopedic minds in scholarship to great personal profit. No one can read Perry Miller, Norman Fiering, Michael McClymond, Mark Noll, Gerald McDermott, Michael Haykin, Ken Minkema, William Morris, Paul Ramsey, Wallace Anderson, Anthony Levi, William Danaher, Stephen Wilson, and Doug Sweeney (to name a few!) without a real appreciation taking hold. I have greatly benefited from the great labors and scholarship of these august scholars.

I am grateful for the faculty of and interim professors for Central Baptist Theological Seminary, from Jeff Straub to Jon Pratt. They have encouraged me in my research and writing, and their off-hand commendations have always gone further than they know. Deborah Forteza happily "shared" with me her access to a "real library" during a season where my ability to obtain important resources was rather limited. Rachel Lott was huge help in my study of Mastricht and Thomas Aquinas. I am also grateful to Joel Zartman, Chris Tuttle, Steve Diachenko, David de Bruyn, Chuck Bumgardner, Michael Riley, Eric White, and my wife, Jennifer, who took up the unhappy chore of editing different drafts. Thanks should be especially given to Liisa Sullivan, an editor who substantially helped my work.

I am also grateful to Adriaan Neele, who helpfully pointed me in the direction of Mastricht's discussion of God's affections. Ken Minkema has always shown himself a patient and hospitable guide, both in opening the Yale Center for Jonathan Edwards and in agreeing to write the foreword to this book. I owe him a great deal, as do so many of us who have ventured into the study of this singular American pastor.

Two churches as a whole were instrumental to my writing this book, and I owe them a hearty thanks. Bethany Bible Church of Hendersonville, North Carolina (and especially Greg and George Stiekes), I thank you all for your cheerful encouragement, patience, uncommon love, and your intercessions on my behalf to our "Prayer-Hearing God." Also, to First Baptist Church of Granite Falls, I thank you for your encouragement and friendship as you sit under my weekly pulpit ministry.

I owe much to my friend and mentor Kevin Bauder. I remember, in my MDiv days, as I was first plodding through *Religious Affections* (reading just a page or two a day), I would eagerly come to him with some theological point I had discovered. His careful admonishments and encouragements aided my getting to this point in a hundred ways, small and great. Thank you, Kevin, for your commitment to excellence, for your radical monotheism, and for continuing to teach us about the affections.

Gratefulness should be extended to my parents, Randy and Jan Martin, for all the ways they have helped me get this done. Long ago you taught me to persevere. Throughout this process, you, along with my brothers Rory, Regan, and Ross, have shown interest and offered joyful support.

I am also deeply indebted to Anna Turton, Sarah Blake, and their colleagues at Bloomsbury and T&T Clark for their patience and willingness to publish this work. I am especially grateful to the editors of this series, Ian A. McFarland, Ivor J. Davidson, Philip G. Ziegler, and John Webster, for including me in the roster of volumes making up the *Studies on Systematic Theology*.

To my children, Jared, Judson, Sebastian, Jonathan, Anna Magdalena, and Evangeline, thank you for the many sacrifices you (often unwittingly) made to help me complete this book. I love all of you dearly. My faithful wife, Jennifer, has nearly as much an investment in this book as I do. She has always given unusual affection and advocacy, despite the many additional hardships and responsibilities it brought her personally. She is, for all these reasons and more, a rare and precious woman. I did not do this for her, but I could not have done it without her, and in the end her patient provocations and love was an inscrutable and profound necessity toward the completion of this book. Thank you, Jen.

Finally, the acknowledgments for a book like this would not be complete without pointing to the loving Triune God who gives the grace and means to write a book. This little volume must seem like the tiniest achievement in his eyes. Yet I could not have done this without his help. God deserves no blame for the many failings of this book, but I return thanks to him for his gracious provision of the requisite time, finances, opportunity, and abilities. Jesus's death for sinners makes the theological task a rare delight. The spiritual grace that comes from the Holy Spirit's ministry truly makes inspired Scripture's truth shine with a sublime beauty. Can there be any greater privilege, joy, and responsibility than when God is the object of our study? God be thanked for all he did to grant me the humbling and terrifying task of writing about him. To him be glory, both now and forever.

NOTE ON TEXT

This book uses the same method of referencing the printed Yale *Works of Jonathan Edwards* that is used in Sang Hung Lee, ed., *The Princeton Companion to Jonathan Edwards* (Princeton, NJ: Princeton University Press, 2005). Unless otherwise noted, all references to Jonathan Edwards's published writings are to the printed Yale edition.

Parenthetical references consist of volume numbers and page numbers. For example (2:98) references volume 2 of the Yale edition, *Religious Affections*, page 98. When a reference is made to one of Edwards's "Miscellanies," the "Miscellanies" number or entry number is also indicated. For example ("Misc. 782," 18:452) references "Miscellanies," number 782 in volume 18 of the Yale edition, page 452. References to Yale's *Online Works of Jonathan Edwards* will be made in the footnotes. For complete bibliographical information on the printed Yale edition, see below.

THE YALE UNIVERSITY PRESS EDITION OF

THE WORKS OF JONATHAN EDWARDS

General Editor: Harry S. Stout
Executive Editor: Kenneth P. Minkema

Vol.	Date Published	Volume Title	Volume Editor(s)
1	1957	*Freedom of the Will*	Paul Ramsey
2	1959	*Religious Affections*	John E. Smith
3	1970	*Original Sin*	Clyde A. Holbrook
4	1972	*The Great Awakening*	C. C. Goen
5	1977	*Apocalyptic Writings*	Stephen J. Stein
6	1980	*Scientific and Philosophical Writings*	Wallace E. Anderson
7	1985	*The Life of David Brainerd*	Norman Pettit
8	1989	*Ethical Writings*	Paul Ramsey
9	1989	*The History of the Work of Redemption*	John F. Wilson
10	1992	*Sermons and Discourses, 1720–1723*	Wilson H. Kimnach
11	1993	*Typological Writings*	Wallace E. Anderson and Mason I. Lowance, Jr., with David H. Watters
12	1994	*Ecclesiastical Writings*	David D. Hall
13	1994	The "Miscellanies" (entry nos. a–500)	Thomas A. Schafer
14	1997	*Sermons and Discourses, 1723–1729*	Kenneth P. Minkema
15	1998	*Notes on Scripture*	Stephen J. Stein
16	1998	*Letters and Personal Writings*	George S. Claghorn
17	1999	*Sermons and Discourses, 1730–1733*	Mark Valeri
18	2000	The "Miscellanies" (entry nos. 501–832)	Ava Chamberlain
19	2001	*Sermons and Discourses, 1734–1738*	M. X. Lesser
20	2002	The "Miscellanies" (entry nos. 833–1152)	Amy Plantinga Pauw
21	2003	*Writings on the Trinity, Grace, and Faith*	Sang Hyun Lee
22	2003	*Sermons and Discourses, 1739–1742*	Harry S. Stout and Nathan O. Hatch
23	2004	The "Miscellanies" (entry nos. 1153–1360)	Douglas A. Sweeney
24	2006	*The "Blank Bible"*	Stephen J. Stein
25	2006	*Sermons and Discourses, 1743–1758*	Wilson H. Kimnach
26	2008	*Catalogues of Books*	Peter J. Thuesen

LIST OF ABBREVIATIONS

Affections	Jonathan Edwards, *A Treatise Concerning Religious Affections*
ANF	*The Ante-Nicene Fathers*, ed. Roberts and Donaldson
CH	*Church History*
Civ.	Augustine, *The City of God*
C. Jul. op. imp.	Augustine, *Against Julian: Opus Imperfectum*
Conf.	Augustine, *Confessions*
CTJ	*Calvin Theological Journal*
HTR	*Harvard Theological Review*
JEAE	*Jonathan Edwards and the American Experience, ed. Hatch and Stout*
JECSS	*Jonathan Edwards Classic Studies Series*
JEE	*The Jonathan Edwards Encyclopedia*
JHBS	*Journal of the History of Behavioral Sciences*
JRE	*Journal of Religious Ethics*
JSCE	*Journal of the Society of Christian Ethics*
LCC	Library of Christian Classics, Westminster Press
"Misc."	"The Miscellanies"
MT	*Modern Theology*
Nat. hom.	Nemesius of Emesa, *The Nature of the Soul*
NPNF[2]	*The Nicene and Post-Nicene Fathers*, Series 2, ed. Schaff and Wace
Nupt.	Augustine, *Marriage and Concupiscence*
OCP	*The Oxford Companion to Philosophy*
OED	*The Compact Edition of the Oxford English Dictionary*
OHRE	*The Oxford Handbook of Religion and Emotion*
PCJE	*Princeton Companion to Jonathan Edwards*, ed. Lee (after initial citation)
PG	*Patrologiae Graeca*, ed. Migne
PL	*Patrologia Latina*, ed. Migne
ST	Thomas Aquinas, *Summa Theologiae*
Strom.	Clement of Alexandria, *Stromata* (*Miscellanies*)
Trin.	Augustine, *The Trinity*
WH	*The Works of Jonathan Edwards*, ed. Edward Hickman, Banner of Truth Trust
WJE	*The Works of Jonathan Edwards*, Yale Univ. Press (after initial citation)
WJEO	*The Works of Jonathan Edwards Online*, Yale Univ. Press (after initial citation)
WMQ	*The William and Mary Quarterly*
WTJ	*Westminster Theological Journal*

INTRODUCTION

The study of emotion—especially emotion and religion—has become a thriving field, even since I first began my research. But the focus is often (though certainly not always) on our own definitions and ideas of how human emotions work. These ideas move about in a building designed according to a certain intellectual architecture which presupposes what it means to be human, the nature of our physicality, and any possible relation between body and "soul." But is there a better way of thinking about human affections?

When I first began reading Edwards as a young man, I tried to understand his idea of affections and passions in relation to my own garbled ideas of emotion, but kept finding that the score of Edwards's thought presented a discordant, arrhythmic sound. His artistry unveiled itself when I let the man speak for himself. Rather than hear Edwards as some new popular composer or crossover artist, I learned to listen to how *Edwards* spoke of the affections, will, and passions. What I heard from his own voice was a harmonic, unified symphony portraying the inner workings of the human person far differently than the cacophony of contemporary explanations around me. I hope that this book helps you hear that symphony for yourself.

This book is not so much about a singular theologian or a particular articulation of Reformation theology. I concede that this study is very concerned with Jonathan Edwards's understanding of the Christian religion and the way that understanding shaped his view of human affections. Indeed, half of the eight chapters, and the great majority of the book's content, sets out to discuss Edwards in one respect or another. Still, this book is more an endeavor to comprehend on their own terms older understandings of human (and divine) affections.

I am acutely aware that there is no shortage of works on Edwards. At this point, the bibliography on Edwards has itself become a substantial volume.[1] Of the many volumes and articles on Edwards, many address the affections to some extent. Yet I think the argument of this book is important. Building upon the thought of scholars like Thomas Dixon, I shine a scrutinizing light on the tendency of scholars and authors to equate Edwards's idea of affections with the more

1. M. X. Lesser, *Reading Jonathan Edwards: An Annotated Bibliography in Three Parts, 1729-2005* (Grand Rapids, MI: Eerdmans, 2008).

contemporary, popular idea of emotions.[2] At the same time, I evaluate the extent to which Edwards's ideas of human affectivity were influenced by the emerging Enlightenment thought. I also demonstrate how tightly and cohesively Edwards (much like Augustine and Aquinas) wove his understanding of human affectivity into his whole theological system.

The study begins with an introduction of the question. I explain the different approaches to the question of how Edwards's notion of affections relates to today's idea of emotions (Chapter 1). Then I trace the traditional Christian understanding of affections and passions throughout church history, especially highlighting the Reformed and post-Reformed traditions (Chapters 2, 3). Turning to Edwards himself, I describe his theology of affections and passions as a young student at Yale (Chapters 4, 5), during the years of the Great Awakening (Chapter 6), and in his later efforts to defend his understanding of the Reformed faith from "Arminian" foes (Chapter 7). A conclusion ties together the research and urges that popular and pastoral attempts to contextualize Edwards's understanding of affections be more chastened (Chapter 8).

In unearthing older ways of understanding human affections, this is my own meager attempt, in the words of C. S. Lewis, to "keep the clean sea breeze of the centuries blowing through our minds."[3] The views of past thinkers best assist our own thought, not when we immediately appropriate them to our own questions and controversies, but first understand them (as best we are able) as they explain their views themselves.

Is there a better way of thinking about human affections? Perhaps. I hope to expound and prove that in the heritage of the Christian past are at least *other* ways of thinking about human affections. And, by considering such models, we may well learn more about ourselves and what it means to be human.

2. Thomas Dixon, *From Passions to Emotions: The Creation of a Secular Psychological Category* (Cambridge: Cambridge University Press, 2003).

3. Introduction to St. Athanasius, *On the Incarnation: The Treatise* De Incarnatione Verbi Dei, trans. a religious of C. S. M. V. (Crestwood, NY: St. Vladimir's Seminary Press, 1993), 5. As Lewis went on to explain: "This can be done only by reading old books."

Chapter 1

LOST IN TRANSLATION: THE PROBLEM OF EDWARDS, AFFECTIONS, AND EMOTIONS

> Come down, O Love divine,
> Seek Thou this soul of mine,
> And visit it with Thine own ardor glowing;
> O Comforter, draw near,
> Within my heart appear,
> And kindle it, Thy holy flame bestowing.
> O let it freely burn,
> Till earthly passions turn
> To dust and ashes in its heat consuming;
> And let Thy glorious light
> Shine ever on my sight,
> And clothe me round, the while my path illuming.
>
> — Bianco da Siena, tr. Richard Frederick Littledale

Jonathan Edwards's theology has been compared to a symphony and to the sacred masterpieces of Johann Sebastian Bach. He has been called "the greatest philosopher yet to grace the American scene," at least among those living before the twentieth century. Christians the world over study his preaching, politics, rhetoric, and revivals.[1]

1. For Edwards's theology as symphony, see Michael J. McClymond and Gerald R. McDermott, *The Theology of Jonathan Edwards* (New York: Oxford University Press, 2012), 3–9; for Edwards and Bach, see George Marsden, *Jonathan Edwards: A Life* (New Haven, CT: Yale University Press, 2003), 79, 129, 473. For Edwards as philosopher, some attribute the above quote to Perry Miller, but its source seems to be Paul Ramsey, "General Editor's Note," in *Freedom of the Will*, vol. 1 of *WJE*, ed. Paul Ramsey (New Haven, CT: Yale University Press, 1957), viii. Ramsey, "Editor's Introduction," in *WJE* 1:2. Edwards was seen as a philosopher as early as the nineteenth century; see Dugald Stewart, *Dissertation, Exhibiting a General View of the Progress of Metaphysical, Ethical, and Political Philosophy since the Revival of Letters in Europe*, in vol. 6 of *The Works of Dugald Stewart* (1829), 384; and George P. Fisher, "The Philosophy of Jonathan Edwards," *The North American Review* 128 (1879): 284–303. Also see William H. Squires, "Glimpses into Edwards' Life,"

For many historians, Jonathan Edwards represents the headwaters of American religious thought. Near the heart of this man's deep and contoured theology lies the importance of the affections. Edwards's protégé Samuel Hopkins pointed to Edwards's work in separating true and false religion as his most important legacy. Referencing Hopkins's observation nearly two centuries later, John Smith suggests that the "whole of [Edwards's] thought" is "one magnificent answer to the question, *What is true religion?*" In their magisterial summary of Edwards's theology, Michael McClymond and Gerald McDermott, citing Smith's remark, add that the affections are a crucial aspect of the nature of true religion in Edwards's thought.[2]

This leads to an important question. When Jonathan Edwards wrote of affections, what was he talking about? If Edwards is important, and if the nature of true religion and (thereby) the affections are important to Edwards, determining what affections are is a significant inquiry. It becomes more important still when one sees the different ways the question has been answered.

The Problem of Jonathan Edwards and Affections

The problem of interpreting Edwards's understanding of affections is illustrated by numerous explanations of his thought, both in the scholarly and popular literature. Consider the appropriations of Edwards's emphasis on religious affections by his evangelical heirs. Some evangelicals use Edwards's psychology to

The Edwardean 1 (1903): 4–12; Morton White, *Science and Sentiment in America: Philosophical Thought from Jonathan Edwards to John Dewey* (New York: Oxford University Press, 1972), 30–54; Wallace E. Anderson, "Editor's Introduction," in *Scientific and Philosophical Writings*, vol. 6 of *The Works of Jonathan Edwards* (New Haven, CT: Yale University Press, 1980), 1–143; Norman Fiering, *Jonathan Edwards's Moral Thought and Its British Context* (Chapel Hill: University of North Carolina Press, 1981), 3–14; Bruce Kuklick, "Jonathan Edwards and American Philosophy," in *Jonathan Edwards and the American Experience*, eds. Nathan O. Hatch and Harry S. Stout (New York: Oxford University Press, 1988), 246–59; Bruce Kuklick, *A History of Philosophy in America, 1720–2000* (Oxford: Clarendon Press, 2001), 5–25; W. Gary Crampton, *Meet Jonathan Edwards: An Introduction to America's Greatest Theologian/Philosopher* (Morgan, PA: Soli Deo Gloria, 2004), v–47; Stephen H. Daniel, "Edwards as Philosopher," in *The Cambridge Companion to Jonathan Edwards*, ed. Stephen J. Stein (Cambridge: Cambridge University Press, 2007), 162–80; and Gerald McDermott, *The Great Theologians: A Brief Guide* (Downers Grove, IL: InterVarsity Press, 2010), 113.

2. Samuel Hopkins, *The Life and Character of the Late Reverend, Learned, and Pious Mr. Jonathan Edwards* (Boston: S. Kneeland, 1765), [iv]; John E. Smith, "Editor's Introduction," in Jonathan Edwards, *Religious Affections*, vol. 2 of *The Works of Jonathan Edwards* (New Haven, CT: Yale University Press, 1959), 2; McClymond and McDermott, *Theology of Jonathan Edwards*, 311.

stress that religion should be emotional. Others use affections to defend a version of Charismatic theology.

In more scholarly settings, many historians attribute Edwards's psychology to the influence of the Enlightenment empiricist John Locke. Besides this, numerous scholars and popular practitioners assume that affections in Edwards's thought are synonymous with emotions.

The Affections of Jonathan Edwards in Defense of Emotional Evangelicalism

Since 1980 American evangelicals—who have been using Edwards's thought for a long time—have cited Edwards as a proponent of an emotional Christianity and worship. John Piper, "America's most famous Edwardsean minister," arguably began this trend. Those evangelicals influenced by Piper stress with him that Edwards said true religion must have high emotions.[3]

In *Desiring God*, Piper argues that Jonathan Edwards advocates that true Christianity binds emotion with intellect. This union means that Christian worship must be emotional: "Without the engagement of the heart, we do not really worship. The engagement of the heart in worship is the coming alive of the feelings and emotions and affections of the heart."[4] By the terms *emotion* and

3. Douglas A. Sweeney, "Evangelical Tradition in America," in *The Cambridge Companion to JE*, 230. Compare Sean Michael Lucas, "Jonathan Edwards between Church and Academy: A Bibliographic Essay," in *The Legacy of Jonathan Edwards*, eds. D. G. Hart, Sean Lucas, and Stephen Nichols (Grand Rapids, MI: Baker Academic, 2003), 233. On the influence of Edwards on American evangelicals, see Joseph A. Conforti, *Jonathan Edwards, Religious Tradition, & American Culture* (Chapel Hill, NC: University of North Carolina Press, 1995); Mark A. Noll, "The Contested Legacy of Jonathan Edwards in Antebellum Calvinism," in *Reckoning with the Past*, ed. D. G. Hart (Grand Rapids, MI: Baker Books, 1995), 200–17; Douglas A. Sweeney and Allen C. Guelzo, *The New England Theology: From Jonathan Edwards to Edwards Amasa Park* (Grand Rapids, MI: Baker Academic, 2006); and Sweeney, "Evangelical Tradition in America," 217–38; McClymond and McDermott, *Theology of Jonathan Edwards*, 647. For an account of Edwards's legacy, including his global legacy, see David W. Kling and Douglas A. Sweeney, eds., *Jonathan Edwards at Home and Abroad: Historical Memories, Cultural Movements, Global Horizons* (Columbia, SC: University of South Carolina, 2003). For an interesting comparison of Edwards to evangelicals of the last half of the twentieth century, see Neil Postman, *Amusing Ourselves to Death: Public Discourse in the Age of Show Business* (New York: Penguin, 1985), 52–56. Also see Kenneth P. Minkema, "Jonathan Edwards in the Twentieth Century," *JETS* 47 (2004): 659–87 and Lesser, *Reading Jonathan Edwards*.

4. John Piper, *Desiring God: Meditations of a Christian Hedonist* (Sisters, OR: Multnomah Books, 1996), 81. Piper adds, "Truth without emotion produces dead orthodoxy and a church full . . . of artificial admirers (like people who write generic anniversary cards for a living). On the other hand, emotion without truth produces empty frenzy and cultivates shallow people who refuse the discipline of rigorous thought. But true worship comes

feeling, Piper says he means the same thing Edwards does by *affections*. He agrees with Edwards that affections are seated in the soul, working with the body in a complex way.[5]

Citing Edwards, Piper says that true Christianity fuses "emotion and thought, affection and reflection, doxology and theology."[6] For Piper, Edwards's goal was to raise the affections to the highest degree possible, leading Piper to conclude that Edwards "was utterly convinced of the crucial importance of powerful affections in worship." He echoes Edwards's warning to avoid "light without heat."[7] The "heat" of affections should come from the "light" of biblical truth. Thereby Christians avoid dividing "deep thought and deep feeling."[8] For Piper, Edwards's notion of affections is synonymous to that of emotions.

In his careful and influential interpretation of Edwards, Gerald McDermott presents Edwards in contrast to the both Great Awakening extremists and Old Light clergy. According to McDermott, Great Awakening supporters emphasized religious feelings to the exclusion of beliefs and actions. The Old Light clergy emphasized the importance of doctrine in religion.[9] Edwards refused to stress

from people who are deeply emotional and who love deep and sound doctrine. Strong affections for God rooted in truth are the bone and marrow of biblical worship." Ibid., 76. In some respects Piper resembles James M. Gustafson., who also (re)defines emotions based on Edwards's idea of affections. Nevertheless, Gustafson acknowledges the confusion regarding emotions to a greater extent than Piper does. See James M. Gustafson, *Can Ethics Be Christian?* (Chicago: University of Chicago Press, 1975), 42–44.

5. Ibid., 79, 298–99 n1. Compare John Piper, *When I Don't Desire God: How to Fight for Joy* (Wheaton, IL: Crossway Books, 2004), 179–82.

6. Piper, *Desiring God*, 90.

7. Jonathan Edwards, "The True Excellency of a Gospel Minister," in *Sermons and Discourses, 1743–1758*, vol. 25 of *The Works of Jonathan Edwards*, ed. Wilson H. Kimnach (New Haven, CT: Yale University Press, 2006), 96.

8. Piper, *Desiring God*, 90–92. Compare "Sweet Sorrow: The Happy Root of Holy Living," [lecture, The Jonathan Edwards Institute, Annapolis, Maryland, July 2, 2003], Desiring God Ministries, https://www.desiringgod.org/messages/sweet-sorrow-the-happy-root-of-holy-living/ (accessed November 24, 2017). Elsewhere Piper presents a similar interpretation of the Great Awakening. *Religious Affections* says "*yes* to the place of appropriate emotions springing from perceptions of truth, but *no* to the frenzies, private revelations, irrational swoonings, and false assurances of godliness." John Piper, *God's Passion for His Glory* (Wheaton, IL: Crossway Books, 1998), 93–94. Explaining why he wrote *Desiring God*, Piper elaborates on a similar theme. Edwards taught that the affections of the truly regenerate were transformed. "I find this supported throughout Scripture. We are commanded to feel, not just to think or decide." He admits that Christians' emotions are often sluggish. God's Word must still be obeyed, though the believer should repent for her weak love. Piper, *Desiring God*, 247–48.

9. This largely discussion is limited to McDermott's *Seeing God: Twelve Reliable Signs of True Spirituality* (Downers Grove, IL: InterVarsity Press, 1995), a paraphrase of *Religious*

either mind or heart. He understands Edwards's idea of affections to "lie at a deeper level of the human person than either thoughts or feelings, and in fact are the source and motivating power of thoughts and feelings."[10]

McDermott defines affections as "*strong inclinations of the soul that are manifested in thinking, feeling and acting*."[11] Holy affections incline the person toward God, unholy affections away from God. According to McDermott, true affections go further than mere belief in doctrine; they are "a passionate affair of the soul—one's innermost being—that is reflected in every part of one's life."[12] Affections are more than emotions; emotions are often a part of affections, but they are not the same. Sometimes emotions conflict with affections, and emotions are often "more fleeting and superficial." Affections also differ from passions, which are "sudden, violent emotions that overpower the mind."[13]

McDermott differs from Piper in distinguishing affections from emotions and acknowledging Edwards's distinction between passions and affections. In later studies McDermott adds: "These [affections] are not emotions, as many scholars have erroneously reported, but something akin to what earlier traditions called the 'soul,' from which emotions arise."[14] Still, his dictum that affections are not emotions—yet more than emotions—would influence other interpreters, such as Talbot and Storms.

Mark Talbot also cites Edwards as a defender of emotional Christianity. McDermott's influence on Talbot is evident in the latter's definition of affections:

> Modern dictionaries often take [*affections*] to refer merely to what we call the emotions—and perhaps only to the more moderate emotions at that. But for Edwards our *affections* involve a lot more than just our emotions. They have

Affections. Other works by McDermott will be taken up later. The influence of *Seeing God* is widespread. For example, see Duffy Robbins, "Jonathan Edwards, Religious Affections, and Spirituality in the Third Millennium," in *This Way to Youth Ministry Companion Guide*, eds. Duffy Robbins and Len Kageler (El Cajon, CA: Youth Specialties Books, 2004), 167–70. McDermott says the contemporary heirs of the Old Light ministers are those who focus on preaching. McDermott, *Seeing God*, 29–30.

10. Ibid., 31.

11. Ibid., 31, emphasis in original. More recently, McDermott puts it this way: "Edwards . . . conceived of godly affections as an inseparable unity of knowing (by the mind) and choosing (with the will) and feeling (in the emotions)." "Jonathan Edwards on the Affections and the Spirit," in *The Spirit, the Affections, and the Christian Tradition*, eds. Dale M. Coulter and Amos Young (Notre Dame, IN: University of Notre Dame Press, 2016), 280. Also see ibid., 283.

12. Ibid., 35.

13. Ibid., 33.

14. "Jonathan Edwards: America's Theologian," in *The Great Theologians: A Brief Guide* (Downers Grove, IL: IVP Academic, 2010), 117.

> to do with the whole side of us that values and desires and chooses and wills as well as feels.[15]

Talbot contrasts affections with cognition. When desires are stronger, the soul acts strongly and sensibly, and in this, Talbot explains: "We feel our inclinations as emotions. Our affections, Edwards tells us, are these 'more vigorous and sensible exercises of the inclination and will of the soul.'" Talbot stresses that inclinations must be strong to be genuine. When "Godly desires and emotions" continue it is a sign of genuine faith.[16]

More recently, Sam Storms's paraphrase of Edwards's *Religious Affections* closely follows Edwards's classic.[17] Yet in his chapter summarizing Edwards's definition of affections, he offers a lengthy paragraph that has no corresponding part in *Affections*. He explains (in the voice of Edwards):

> We should also distinguish affections from "emotions" or "feelings." Certainly there is what may rightly be called an emotional dimension to affections. Affections, after all, are sensible and intense longings or aversions of the will. Perhaps it would be best to say that whereas affections are not less than emotions, they are surely more. Emotions can often be no more than physiologically heightened states of either euphoria or fear that are unrelated to what the mind perceives as true. Affections, on the other hand, are *always* the fruit or effect of what the mind understands or knows.
>
> One can experience an emotion or feeling without it properly being an affection, but one can rarely if ever experience an affection without it being emotional and involving intense feelings that awaken and move and stir the body.[18]

Thus the affections are always emotional, but not all emotions are affections, especially when emotions are "physiological" feelings unrelated to the cognitive powers.

15. "Godly Emotions (*Religious Affections*)" in *A God Entranced Vision of All Things: The Legacy of Jonathan Edwards*, eds. John Piper and Justin Taylor (Wheaton, IL: Crossway Books, 2004), 230–31. "Emotions . . . can indicate whether our hearts are right with God, as Jonathan Edwards argues in his great book, *A Treatise Concerning the Religious Affections*." Ibid., 222.

16. Ibid., 234. Talbot here begins a discussion of "godly desire and emotion." He distinguishes *beliefs*, what we understand to be true, and *concerns*, the "more persistent or insistent inclinations or desires." He says that emotions arise out of beliefs and concerns, and change when one receives new information related to these beliefs and concerns. These two aspects produce emotions. Ibid., 235, 237.

17. Storms prefers to call it an interpretation rather than a paraphrase. Sam Storms, *Signs of the Spirit: An Interpretation of Jonathan Edwards' Religious Affections* (Wheaton, IL: Crossway Books, 2007), 14.

18. Storms, *Signs of the Spirit*, 45.

Brian Borgman also uses Jonathan Edwards in his defense of "godly emotions" in his book *Feelings and Faith*.[19] He writes: "To have a theologically robust perspective on the proper use of the emotions is to enter into the greenhouse of spiritual growth, for, as Jonathan Edwards argued in his classic, *Religious Affections*, 'The nature of true religion consists in holy affections.'"[20] Borgman's definition of emotions will be explained later, but the point here is that he equates affections with emotions. Borgman sprinkles lengthy quotations by Edwards throughout his monograph to defend his view of emotions.[21]

The influence of Piper's reading of Edwards should not be underestimated. In his defense of "Contemporary Music-Driven Worship" in *Exploring the Worship Spectrum*, Joe Horness refers to John Piper's emphasis on emotions in worship, which is, as Don Williams noted, built on Piper's reading of Edwards.[22]

That affections and emotions are the same is easily found in popular literature, as the following six examples will illustrate. Gerrit Immink and Reinder Bruisnma say of Edwards's idea of affections: "Affections have an intense emotional component that we experience as something coming over us: we are being moved."[23] Andrew Lester makes a similar point.[24] Elsewhere Dale and Sandy Larsen quip that "Jonathan Edwards, the supreme rationalist, found emotion inseparable from true religion."[25] Roger Olson argues to the same effect.[26] Although Robert Crapps is careful to note some of Edwards's distinctions (i.e., between affections and passions), he nevertheless says Edwards "believed that emotion was a necessary ingredient of genuine religion."[27] Lastly, Dane Ortlund, while offering some helpful

19. Brian S. Borgman, *Feelings and Faith: Cultivating Godly Emotions in the Christian Life* (Wheaton, IL: Crossway Books, 2009). Borgman cites Talbot's definition of emotions in "Godly Emotions." Borgman, *Feelings and Faith*, 6.

20. Ibid., 23.

21. Ibid., 45–46, 56–57, 173–74, 184, 186.

22. Joe Horness, "Contemporary Music-Driven Worship," in *Exploring the Worship Spectrum: Six Views*, eds. Paul E. Engle and Paul A. Basden (Grand Rapids, MI: Zondervan, 2004), 101. Don Williams, "A Charismatic Worship Response," in *Exploring the Worship Spectrum*, 125.

23. Gerrit Immink and Reinder Bruinsma, *Faith: A Practical Theological Reconstruction*, trans. Reinder Bruinsma (Grand Rapids, MI: Eerdmans, 2005), 100.

24. He says, "Edwards wrote his famous *Religious Affections* in part to defend the importance of emotion in religious experience" in *The Angry Christian: A Theology for Care and Counseling* (Louisville, KY: Westminster John Knox Press, 2003), 47.

25. Dale Larsen and Sandy Larsen, *Jonathan Edwards: Renewed Heart* (Downers Grove, IL: InterVarsity, 2002), 36.

26. Roger Olson, *Westminster Handbook to Evangelical Theology* (Louisville, KY: Westminster John Knox Press, 2004), 20.

27. Robert W. Crapps, *An Introduction to Psychology of Religion* (Macon, GA: Mercer University Press, 1986), 234. See also Andrew D. Lester, *The Angry Christian: A Theology for Care and Counseling* (Louisville, KY: Westminster John Knox Press, 2003), 47.

distinctions between popular notions of emotions and Edwards's "affections," nevertheless suggests that affections are what "today we would probably call the 'emotions.'"[28] The tendency among popular literature to equate affections and emotions is noteworthy.

This trend is also seen in paraphrases of Edwards's works on a popular level besides Storms's *Signs of the Spirit*. At times, James Houston's 1984 paraphrase of *Religious Affections* appears to distinguish affections from emotions, but at other times treats them as synonyms.[29] In the introduction to his 1991 abridgment of *Affections*, Nicholas Needham argues that "emotions," "seems the best modern equivalent of what Edwards meant by 'affections,'" and proceeds to replace every instance of *affections* with "emotions."[30] Archie Parrish's modernized text of *The Distinguishing Marks of a Work of the Spirit of God* replaces *affections* with *emotions* in several places.[31]

Some evangelical authors acknowledge that affections are different from emotions, but follow McDermott in saying that affections are always emotional. Piper and Borgman equate the affections with emotions and feeling, and Talbot also emphasizes affections as feelings. Storms and McDermott insist that affections have an emotional component. In sum, for the modern American evangelical, Edwards defends emotions in religion.

The Affections of Jonathan Edwards in Defense of the Charismatic Movement

Despite their openness to spiritual gifts and tendencies toward non-Calvinist theology, advocates of the Charismatic movement nevertheless marshal the Calvinist Jonathan Edwards to criticize their more "Stoic" evangelical counterparts. This unusual use of a Reformed cessationist to defend the continuation of sign gifts can be partially attributed to Edwards's reputation as a premier American theologian on revival. Several of Edwards's seminal works, including *Affections*, are used in defense of the Charismatic movement.[32]

John White's defense of the Vineyard movement is an early example of a Charismatic use of Edwards. White wonders if conservative Christians are "scared

28. Dane Ortlund, *A New Inner Relish: Christian Motivation in the Thought of Jonathan Edwards* (Ross-shire, Scotland: Christian Focus, 2008), 62; compare 163.

29. James M. Houston, *Religious Affections: A Christian's Character before God* (Minneapolis, MN: Bethany House, 1996), xx, 38, 161, etc.

30. Nicholas R. Needham, introduction to *The Experience that Counts!* (London: Grace Publications Trust, 1991), 10. For more on Needham's justification of this move, see note 121.

31. R. C. Sproul and Archie Parrish, *The Spirit of Revival: Discovering the Wisdom of Jonathan Edwards with the Complete, Modernized Text of* The Distinguishing Marks of a Work of the Spirit of God (Wheaton, IL: Crossway Books, 2008), 57–59, 66–69, 90–93, 115.

32. On the relationship of Jonathan Edwards and such interpreters on revival in general, see McClymond and McDermott, *Theology of Jonathan Edwards*, 690–94.

of emotion." He explains: "Well aware that heat and light must go together, [Edwards] urged that we need more than mere knowledge. We also need 'holy affections,' by which he means emotions within God's will." Edwards said those unmoved had a "stony" heart. "His pastoral experience compelled him to conclude that nothing of religious significance ever took place in a human heart if it wasn't deeply affected by such godly emotions."[33]

In *Surprised by the Power of the Spirit*, Jack Deere (who cites John White) uses Edwards's *Distinguishing Marks* to defend some of the Vineyard movement's physical manifestations of the Spirit's work. Repudiating his former "Stoic" approach to religion, Deere laments: "I had embraced a form of Christianity that radically separated obedience and feelings. Obedience without emotion is nothing more than discipline or will power. It is not love. . . . Affection and passion are indispensable aspects of love for God." Deere says: "Edwards took great pains to prove from the Scriptures that true Christianity is a religion of the emotions as well as the will."[34]

John White's appeal to Edwards also informed Guy Chevreau's defense of Charismatic theology, who claims the Reformed divine's legacy on behalf of the Toronto Blessing and its own physical manifestations.[35] Chevreau says: "Again and again, Edwards writes of 'extraordinary affections,' accompanied by physical demonstrations of fear, sorrow, love, joy; of 'tears, trembling, groans, loud outcries, agonies of the body, and the failing of bodily strength,' of 'fits, jerks, and convulsions.'"[36] Referencing Edwards's *Some Thoughts*, Chevreau says that Edwards

33. John White, *When the Spirit Comes with Power: Signs & Wonders among God's People* (Downers Grove, IL: InterVarsity Press, 1988), 51–52.

34. Jack Deere, *Surprised by the Power of the Spirit* (Grand Rapids, MI: Zondervan, 1993), 185–86. Deere explains, "I like the word *passion* because it stresses the emotional side of love. Passion can be defined as 'any kind of feeling by which the mind is powerfully effected or moved: a vehement, commanding, or overpowering emotion.' Passion is a feeling that moves the mind and the will to action." Ibid., 192.

35. The Charismatic movement that sprang from the Toronto Airport Christian Fellowship in the mid-1990s became known as the "Toronto Blessing." The normal Pentecostal-like physical manifestations were present, like healing, miracles, and speaking in tongues. But what made the "Toronto Blessing" into a noteworthy movement was its additional unusual manifestations "of the Spirit": uncontrollable laughter, "floor time," and even animal-like noises. See Martyn Percy, "Adventure and Atrophy in a Charismatic Movement: Returning to the 'Toronto Blessing,'" *Journal of Contemporary Religion* 20 (2005): 71–74. See also Kenneth L. Woodward, "The Giggles are from God," *Newsweek* 125 (February 15, 1995): 54; John D. Hannah, "Jonathan Edwards, The Toronto Blessing, and the Spiritual Gifts: Are the Extraordinary Ones Actually the Ordinary Ones?" *TrinJ* 17 (1996): 167 n2; and *The Jonathan Edwards Encyclopedia* (hereafter *JEE*), ed. Harry S. Stout (Grand Rapids, MI: Eerdmans, 2017), s.v. "Enthusiasm."

36. Guy Chevreau, *Catch the Fire: The Toronto Blessing: An Experience of Renewal and Revival* (Toronto: Harper Perennial, 1994), 90.

sought "a balanced position" between "reason and emotion, while avoiding the extremes of unfeeling, speculative rationalism on the one hand, and unchecked, anti-intellectual 'enthusiasm' on the other."[37] According to Chevreau, Edwards warns against an overemphasis on experience: "*Affection* is the term [Edwards] chooses to describe the motivating, driving, inclining forces that are the source of our willing and acting. He maintains that the affections are the motivator in human life."[38] True religion must have "lively actings" of the will and affections, and not mere doctrinal knowledge. Chevreau continues: "Building on this foundation, he moves on to give consideration to the bodily manifestations: 'True religion lies much in the emotions. There is great power in them and no reason exists why bodily sensations should not follow as a matter of course.'"[39]

Charismatic apologists use Edwards to defend the idea that physical manifestations come from God. More significantly, according to them, Edwards understood the affections as heightened and vehement feeling ("passion") for God. Deere and Chevreau especially contrast the affections with the mind or doctrinal knowledge. Edwards's other psychological categories are completely overlooked.

Edwards, Affections, and the Academy

In the academy, many believe that Edwards invented his psychology in response to the challenges of the Great Awakening. Others equate affections with emotions. Despite the importance of affections in Edwards's thought, even scholars do not agree concerning their source and nature.

Edwards as Inventor of a New Psychology Edwards has been accused of rewriting traditional Puritan psychology because of his admiration for Locke and determination to defend the Great Awakening.

In his famous biography of Edwards, Perry Miller presented him as a secret admirer of John Locke, espousing a "radical and foreign psychology" against Charles Chauncy.[40] Miller said that Chauncy used faculty psychology to oppose the Awakening. Faculty psychology taught, "reason, imagination, and will were

37. Chevreau, *Catch the Fire*, 115. On *Some Thoughts*, see Chapter 6.

38. Ibid., 134.

39. Ibid., 139. It should be noted that Chevreau uses quotations marks but does not precisely cite Edwards. More important, Chevreau misses Edwards's point. In the passage cited, Edwards said: "It is no sign that affections have the nature of true religion, or that they have not, that they have great effects on the body" (*WJE* 2:131). That is, bodily responses are for Edwards no proof positively or negatively that affections come from God. Yet Chevreau uses Edwards to prove these outward manifestations have a divine source.

40. Perry Miller, *Jonathan Edwards* (1949; repr., Lincoln: University of Nebraska Press, 2005), 178. Compare Clarence H. Faust and Thomas H. Johnson, *Jonathan Edwards: Representative Selections, with Introduction, Bibliography, and Notes*, rev. ed. (New York: Hill and Wang, 1962), xxiv–xxxix.

distinct 'faculties' and the affections a separate and autonomous power."[41] Chauncy marginalized the passions, forcing Edwards to defend his novel view of affections. Miller enjoyed the irony that the theological progressive argued using the obsolete faculty psychology of the Reformed Scholastics to fight the Calvinist who delighted in Locke's cutting-edge philosophy. From his reading in Locke, Edwards viewed humanity, not under the rubric of faculties, but as a living organism (even though Edwards retained the language of faculties). Thereby, he merged the will and the emotions.[42] "Edwards' problem, therefore, was to distinguish, scientifically, between emotions which are mechanical reflexes, one in kind with collision among stones, and those which signify something other than the juices of the glands."[43]

Conrad Cherry accepted this part of Miller's thesis. Although the American Puritans were able to hold in tenuous balance a Christianity of both reason and emotion, the Great Awakening drove a wedge between them. According to Cherry, Chauncy believed that the Spirit influenced the intellect, not the passions, while Edwards believed the Spirit influenced both intellect and emotion. Cherry said: "Edwards' dissent from Chauncy's rationalistic appraisal of the revivals is dictated to a large extent by his adoption and adaption of the Lockean psychology."[44]

For J. Rodney Fulcher, the affections created a problem for American Puritans. In subjugating the passions to reason in their faculty psychology, the divines restricted the legitimate operation of affections, a problem not finally resolved until "the more innovative proposals of Jonathan Edwards."[45]

In a 2003 collection of essays, D. G. Hart also casts Edwards as a psychological innovator. Older Puritans strictly divided mind and will, while Edwards understood the two as an "organic one."[46] The heart no longer represented feeling, but included

41. Ibid., 177.

42. Ibid., 180–83.

43. Ibid., 184.

44. Conrad Cherry, *The Theology of Jonathan Edwards: A Reappraisal* (1966; repr., Bloomington: Indiana University Press, 1990), 164, 168. Cherry cites Miller's *Jonathan Edwards*. On Puritanism, see Joel R. Beeke and Randall J. Pederson, *Meet the Puritans: With a Guide to Modern Reprints* (Grand Rapids, MI: Reformation Heritage Books, 2006), xv–xix. On Edwards and Puritanism, see J. Rodney Fulcher, "Puritans and the Passions: The Faculty Psychology in American Puritanism," *JHBS* 9 (1973): 127; Iain Murray, *Jonathan Edwards: A New Biography* (Carlisle, PA: Banner of Truth Trust, 1987), 66–70; Harry S. Stout, "The Puritans and Edwards," in *JEAE*, 141–59; David D. Hall, "The New England Background," in *Cambridge Companion to JE*, 61–79; Douglas A. Sweeney, *Jonathan Edwards and the Ministry of the Word: A Model of Faith and Thought* (Downers Grove, IL: IVP Academic, 2009), 21–29, especially 23 n4; McClymond and McDermott, *Theology of Jonathan Edwards*, 40–49. Ibid., 168.

45. Fulcher, "Puritans and the Passions," 132.

46. D. G. Hart, "Jonathan Edwards and the Origin of Experimental Calvinism," in *The Legacy of Jonathan Edwards: American Religion and the Evangelical Tradition*, eds. D. G. Hart, Sean Michael Lucas, and Stephen J. Nichols (Grand Rapids, MI: Baker Academic, 2003), 168.

an intellectual and dispositional component. In the same book, K. Scott Oliphint explains that faculty psychology held reason to be primary, controlling the imagination and the will. In *Affections*, however, "Edwards sought to show not only that the longstanding medieval Scholastic psychology was unwarranted but also that his own position of the organic unity of a person was both biblical and explanatory of the nature of revival."[47]

Thus Edwardsean scholars for several decades have been repeating the charge that, in adopting the premise of Lockean psychology that a human being was an organic whole, Edwards was able to introduce affections as a crucial element in genuine religion.

Edwards and Emotions Some scholars have also equated Edwards's idea of affections or passions with emotions. Jeremiah Day seems to have been the first to use the word *emotion* as a stand-in for *affections* in expositing Edwards.[48] Henry Tappan made similar statements.[49] Alexander Allen explicitly identified "affections" and "emotions."[50] Williston Walker's *Ten New England Leaders*, Haroutunian's *Piety*, and Clarence Faust and Thomas Johnson's *Jonathan Edwards* treated the terms as synonymous.[51] Perry Miller alternated between *affections*, *passions*, and *emotions* as if there is no difference among them.[52] Ola Winslow described *Religious Affections* as "an argument for the central place of the emotions in all religious experience."[53]

Numerous more recent interpreters have expressed the same or similar opinions.[54] James Blight makes Edwards's understanding of humanity as "rational-emotive unity,"

47. K. Scott Oliphint, "Jonathan Edwards on Apologetics: Reason and the Noetic Effects of Sin," in *Legacy of Jonathan Edwards*, 132. Oliphint cites Alan Heimert and Perry Miller.

48. Jeremiah Day, *An Inquiry Respecting the Self-Determining Power of the Will or Contingent Volition* (New Haven: Herrick & Noyes, 1838), 38–40, 84–85.

49. Henry Tappan, *A Treatise on the Will* (Glasgow: Lang, Adamson, & Co., 1857), 253–61.

50. Alexander Viets Griswold Allen, *Jonathan Edwards* (New York: Houghton, Mifflin and Company, 1889), 221.

51. Williston Walker, *Ten New England Leaders* (New York: Silver, Burdett and Company, 1901), 241; Joseph Haroutunian, *Piety versus Moralism: The Passing of the New England Theology* (1932; repr., Hamden, CT: Archon Books, 1964), 43; and Faust and Johnson, *Jonathan Edwards*, xxxix.

52. For example, see *Jonathan Edwards*, 177, 180–81, 183, 194; Perry Miller, *Errand into the Wilderness* (Cambridge, MA: Harvard University Press, 1984), 180–81.

53. Ola Elizabeth Winslow, *Jonathan Edwards, 1703–1758* (New York: Collier Books, 1961), 215. Later, she adds: "Jonathan Edwards and John Wesley stood together in their insistence on the inner witness, not of the mind, but of the emotions." Ibid., 217.

54. For example, see Ralph G. Turnbull, *Jonathan Edwards: The Preacher* (Grand Rapids, MI: Baker Book House, 1958), 96–97; James G. Blight, "Jonathan Edwards's Theory of the Mind," in *Explorations in the History of Psychology in the United States*, ed.

a key part of his study of Edwards's psychological theory.[55] Eugene White's study lucidly shows the New England trends in psychology that culminated in Edwards's own thought, but he essentially treats affections and emotions as synonyms. For White, Edwards is not only "the first to apply the principles of modern psychology . . . to homiletics," but also a trailblazer for whom "the emotions are

Josef Brožek (Cranburg, NJ: Associated University Presses, 1984), 79; Conrad Cherry, *Theology*, 170–71; C. C. Goen, *Revivalism and Separatism in New England, 1740–1800: Strict Congregationalists and Separate Baptists in the Great Awakening* (Middletown, CT: Wesleyan University Press, 1987), 17–18; Murray, *Jonathan Edwards*, 253; William Breitenbach, "Piety *and* Moralism: Edwards and the New Divinity," in *JEAE*, 181; Karen Lystra, *Searching the Heart: Women, Men, and Romantic Love in Nineteenth-Century America* (New York: Oxford University Press, 1989), 239; Paul Lewis, "'Springs of Motion': Jonathan Edwards on Emotions, Character, and Agency," *JRE* 22 (1994): 275–97; Henry H. Knight III, "True Affections: Biblical Narrative & Evangelical Spirituality," in *The Nature of Confession: Evangelicals & Postliberals in Conversation*, eds. Timothy R. Phillips and Dennis L. Okholm (Downers Grove, IL: InterVarsity Press, 1996), 193–95; Leon Chai, *Jonathan Edwards and the Limits of Enlightenment Philosophy* (New York: Oxford University Press, 1998), 22–35; John Corrigan, John Kloos, and Eric Crump, *Emotion and Religion: A Critical Assessment and Annotated Bibliography* (Westport, CT: Greenwood Press, 2000), 12; Stephen R. Holmes, *God of Grace and God of Glory: An Account of the Theology of Jonathan Edwards* (Grand Rapids, MI: William B. Eerdmans, 2000), 4; Dwight Edwards, *Revolution Within: A Fresh Look at Supernatural Living* (Colorado Springs, CO: Waterbrook Press, 2002), 123; Richard A. Bailey, "Driven by Passion: Jonathan Edwards and the Art of Preaching," in *The Legacy of Jonathan Edwards*, 70; Oliphint, "Jonathan Edwards on Apologetics," 132; William C. Spohn, "Spirituality and Its Discontents: Practices in Jonathan Edwards's *Charity and Its Fruits*" *JRE* 31 (2003): 266; Gordon T. Smith, *The Voice of Jesus: Discernment, Prayer and the Witness of the Spirit* (Downers Grove, IL: InterVarsity Press, 2003), 49–50; William J. Danaher, Jr., *The Trinitarian Ethics of Jonathan Edwards*, Columbia Series in Reformed Theology (Louisville, KY: Westminster John Knox Press, 2004), 123; David L. Weaver-Zercher, "Theologies," in *Themes in Religion and American Culture*, eds. Philip Goff and Paul Harvey (Chapel Hill: University of North Carolina Press, 2004), 13; Robert A. Emmons, "Sacred Emotion," in *Soul, Psyche, Brain: New Directions in the Study of Religion and Brain-Mind Science*, ed. Kelly Bulkeley (New York: Palgrave MacMillan, 2005), 96; Philip F. Gura, *Jonathan Edwards: America's Evangelical* (New York: Hill and Wang, 2005), 124; Matthew Arnold, *Faithful Feelings: Rethinking Emotion in the New Testament* (Grand Rapids, MI: Kregel, 2006), 15, 140; and Robert C. Roberts, *Spiritual Emotions: A Psychology of Christian Virtues* (Grand Rapids, MI: William B. Eerdmans, 2007), vii.

55. James George Blight, "Gracious Discoveries: Toward an Understanding of Jonathan Edwards' Psychological Theory, and an Assessment of his Place in the History of American Psychology," (PhD diss., University of New Hampshire, 1974).

primary and pervasive."[56] Although Terrance Erdt usefully places the language of "sense of the heart" with the Calvinist tradition, he says that same Puritan tradition "generally identified the heart with the will, the source of emotions, or *affections*."[57] Brad Walton, despite his helpful work highlighting Edwards's dependence on the Puritan theology of the heart, also collapses affections and emotions.[58] While Robert Davis Smart understands affections in Edwards to be "more than emotion," he nevertheless insists that Edwards's doctrine does not place "'emotion' and 'reason' . . . at odds with each other."[59] Paul Helm asserts that Edwards's *Treatise on Religious Affections* "is a book about the importance of emotion, expressed in a public, visible way, being the measure of true religion."[60]

But not all scholars agree. Some have suggested, to varying degrees, that Edwards's notion of affections should not be considered emotions outright.[61] So in what sense is it proper to speak of affections as emotions? To what extent was Edwards in his discussion of psychological faculties an innovator or a traditionalist? The answers to these questions are further complicated by the complexity in understanding emotions.

Emotions *and Other Definitions*

What are emotions? Before one can begin to understand the relationship of affections and passions to emotions in Edwards's theology, one must have an idea what emotions are. Yet this makes the task at hand even more difficult. Scholars do not agree on what emotions are, and in popular thought the meaning of the word is vague at best.

56. Eugene E. White, *Puritan Rhetoric: The Issue of Emotion in Religion* (Carbondale: Southern Illinois University Press, 1972), 41. Also see 40–48 and 119. White says the key difference between Edwards and other Calvinists is the shift in emphasis "*from divine truth to divine beauty.*" Ibid., 41–42.

57. Terrence Erdt, *Jonathan Edwards: Art and the Sense of the Heart* (Amherst: University of Massachusetts Press, 1980), 5.

58. Brad Walton, *Jonathan Edwards,* Religious Affections, *and the Puritan Analysis of True Piety, Spiritual Sensation, and Heart Religion*, Studies in American Religion 74 (Lewiston: E. Mellen Press, 2002), 144, 148, 182, etc.

59. Robert Davis Smart, *Jonathan Edwards's Apologetic for the Great Awakening with Particular Attention to Charles Chauncy's Criticisms* (Grand Rapids, MI: Reformation Heritage Books, 2011), 265, 266. Compare Smart's explanation of Chauncy's opposition to Edwards: "Chauncy's pneumatological understanding of revival would not allow for emotion and religious experience." Ibid., 222.

60. Paul Helm, "Edwards on True Religion," Helm's Deep, entry posted April 1, 2011, http://paulhelmsdeep.blogspot.com/2011/04/edwards-on-true-religion.html (accessed December 4, 2017).

61. See the discussion in the following text.

What are Emotions?

Perhaps the most accepted aspect in the discussion of emotion is the difficulty in defining it.[62] A word that originally spoke of "moving out" or agitation could refer to the migration of a people on the one hand or restless horses on the other.[63] The present use of the word dates only to the nineteenth century. Today its nature is disputed across and within academic disciplines. Some philosophers despair of ever-reaching agreement on a definition. Others suggest discarding the word altogether.[64] Despite the elusiveness of agreement, the interest in emotions has increased significantly over the last few decades.[65]

The Modern Rise of Emotions Thomas Dixon has documented the recent rise of the use of the term *emotions*. Dixon argues that Christian theologians understood the soul to have different movements: passions arose out of the lower soul, and affections arose out of the higher rational soul.[66] Not until the early nineteenth century does one find the contemporary psychological understanding of emotions as "a mental 'feeling' or 'affection' . . . as distinguished from cognitive or volitional states of consciousness."[67]

In the English-speaking world David Hume was one of the earliest thinkers to use *emotions* widely, as the category grew out of his program to situate moral virtue in passion rather than reason.[68] Around 1820–50, *emotions* began to displace the terms *affections* and *passions* with the Scottish philosopher Thomas Brown's (1778–1820) *Lectures on the Philosophy of the Human Mind.*[69] Brown's main project

62. Richard Shweder puts it well: "The phrase 'essentially contested concept' was not coined with the 'emotions' in mind, but it might have been. Everything from their substance to their distribution to their logical form is a subject of debate." From "'You're Not Sick, You're Just in Love': Emotion as an Interpretative System," in *The Nature of Emotion: Fundamental Questions*, eds. Paul Ekman and Richard J. Davidson (New York: Oxford University Press, 1994), 33. Also see Arnold, *Faithful Feelings*, 43; Robert Solomon, *The Passions: Emotions and the Meaning of Life* (Indianapolis, IN: Hackett, 1993), 73; and John Corrigan, introduction to *Religion and Emotion: Approaches and Interpretations* (New York: Oxford University Press, 2004), 3–31.

63. *The Compact Edition of the Oxford English Dictionary*, s.v. "Emotion."

64. Richard A. Shweder, "'You're Not Sick"; *Encyclopedia of Philosophy*, 2nd ed., s.v. "Emotion."

65. On the recent surge of interest in emotions, see Ronald de Sousa, "Emotion," in *The Stanford Encyclopedia of Philosophy*, Spring 2010 ed., ed. Edward N. Zalta, http://plato.stanford.edu/archives/spr2010/entries/emotion/ (accessed December 4, 2017).

66. Dixon, *From Passions to Emotions.* Dixon touches on the thought of Jonathan Edwards, describing his thought as within the accepted Christian tradition with minor adjustments. See *From Passions to Emotions*, 72–81.

67. *OED*, s.v. "Emotion."

68. Dixon, *From Passions to Emotions*, 104–09.

69. Ibid., 26–61; 109–27.

was to transform the knowledge of human emotions into a hard science, confining the study of the movements of the soul to empiricism and natural laws. For Brown, emotions were merely passive feelings, not actions of the intellectual powers.[70]

Brown's concept of *emotion* is noteworthy for at least two more reasons. First, Brown (following Hume) embraced the idea that reason was an illusion, and, as Dixon explains it, "the springs of action were brute forces rather than reasoned judgments."[71] The will was reduced to whatever passion or emotion prevailed. Therefore, the will was subject to the forces of emotions following the laws of nature. Second, Brown himself acknowledged that defining the emotions was difficult. He optimistically held that everyone innately knew what they were. Of even greater significance, older distinctions (such as appetites, sentiments, affections, and passions) collapsed. Thomas Brown's own ambiguity is indicative of subsequent confusion in the study of emotions.[72]

The development of a doctrine of emotion in the nineteenth century further moved away from Christian dualism toward physicalism. Alexander Bain, Herbert Spencer, and Charles Darwin were among those who advocated that the mind be studied through scientific inquiry. Emotions were increasingly attributed to animals, as Dixon explains: "The demise of the passions-affections distinction meant that to say that human emotions were like animal emotions (rather than that passions alone resembled animal states) was to reduce a much broader range of feelings to our animal nature."[73] More and more, thinkers considered emotions to be non-cognitive feelings.[74] Charles Darwin believed that emotions were originally mental processes expressed through physical responses, and the most helpful of these effects became innate through normal evolutionary processes.[75]

William James built on this foundation, leading to a surge of interest in the science of psychology, especially in America. James affirmed the physicality of emotions, and inverted the interplay between them and the brain. He famously said: "*[T]he bodily changes follow directly the* PERCEPTION *of the exciting fact, and that our feeling of the same changes as they occur* IS *the emotion.*"[76] As a result of such thought, traditional psychologies, which continued to affirm humankind as spiritual, eventually faded from prominence as their foundational beliefs directly opposed the new methods of the physicalist psychologies of scientism.

70. Thomas Brown, *Lectures on the Philosophy of the Human Mind* (Hallowell: Glazier, Masters and Smith, 1839), 1:156–66. See Dixon, *From Passions to Emotions*, 124–25.

71. Dixon, *From Passions to Emotions*, 125. Brown, *Lectures*, 2:85; 87–88; 260–66.

72. Brown, *Lectures*, 165; Dixon, *From Passions to Emotions*, 125–26.

73. Ibid., 146.

74. Ibid., 156–58. Also see John Corrigan, "Appendix 2: Emotion as Heart, Blood, and Body," in *Business of the Heart: Religion and Emotion in the Nineteenth Century* (Berkeley: University of California Press, 2002), 281–93.

75. Ibid., 171–72.

76. William James, "What Is An Emotion?" in *The Nature of Emotion: Selected Readings*, ed. Magda B. Arnold, Penguin Modern Psychology (New York: Penguin, 1968), 19.

Psychologists dismissed out of hand any remotely spiritual understanding of emotion (or humanity) because physiology was the only legitimate way to understand emotions.[77]

Dixon helpfully observes that the way individuals study psychological categories shapes the very knowledge gained in the study.[78] Choosing to study human beings by recording the cortex's electrical activity, by measuring body fat, or by observing their table manners would result in very different understandings of the person. The study of human beings as physical specimens, while limiting reliable information to that which can be observed, will yield a certain understanding of human nature. A different notion of human nature results when metaphysical questions are considered.

In conclusion, Dixon proposes that "emotions" are a distinctly modern category in two ways:

> Modern-day uses of "emotions" have both different extensions and intensions from older uses of "passions." Of course neither term has ever had a fixed meaning or fixed extension, but there have been general tendencies, and some degree of consensus. The extension of "emotions" (the items included in that category), for example, tends to include many feelings that might previously have been categorized not as passions but as appetites (e.g. lust), or affections (e.g. religious feelings), or sentiments (e.g. sympathy).[79]

Dixon continues:

> The intension of "emotion" (the definition of the term) has differed very significantly from the intension of 'passion': the former has tended to be defined in an amoral way as an autonomous physical or mental state characterised by a vivid feeling and physical agitation, the latter has been defined in more morally and theologically engaged ways as a disobedient and morally dangerous movement of the soul (as well as being used in a vague and general way to refer to a variety of lively mental states).[80]

77. Dixon, *From Passion to Emotion*, 223–27.

78. Dixon writes, "It surely makes a difference, for instance, to our experience and understanding of ourselves, whether we think of our anger as being produced by our inner demons or by our inner baboon; of our love as the movement of a soul or the firing of neurons; of our conscience as an inherited emotion or the voice of God; of our frustration and despair as signs of sin and the Fall or of suppressed and unconscious desires." "Revolting Passions," *MT* 27 (2011): 308.

79. Dixon, *From Passions to Emotions*, 18. Compare Eric D'Arcy, introduction to Thomas Aquinas, *The Emotions (1a2ae. 22–30)*, vol. 19 of *Summa Theologiae* (New York: McGraw-Hill Book, 1967), xxiii.

80. Dixon, *From Passions to Emotions*, 18.

Competing Theories of Emotions Today The recent rise of *emotion* as a psychological category has failed to produce any agreement concerning what emotions are. Although scientific investigations have greatly influenced the scholarly discussion of emotions, "linguistic and conceptual" matters have generated the most important conversations. Consequently, many recent philosophers have tended to agree that emotions are cognitive to some extent. The "standard view" is that beliefs and dispositions cause emotions.[81]

Robert Solomon and Martha Nussbaum illustrate this approach to emotion. In Solomon's theory of emotions, "passions" are the "entire range of those phenomena . . . that may be said to 'move' us," and under the head "passions" are the species "emotions," "moods," and "desires."[82] As Solomon explains it, emotions are distinguished from their expressions or *necessary* physiological concomitants.[83] The Neo-Stoic Martha Nussbaum is another prominent example of this view.[84] Nussbaum says, "[E]motions are appraisals or value judgments, which ascribe to things and persons outside the person's own control great importance for that person's own flourishing."[85] Emotions include evaluation, an idea of what is good, and how external objects relate to that good. For Nussbaum, *all* mental processes, including emotions, are bodily, yet they are intentional and do not necessarily entail a "definite bodily state."[86] Nussbaum argues that feeling is not a part of emotion: "[T]he cognitive elements are part of what the emotion *is*."[87] The views of Solomon and Nussbaum are not identical, but they represent similar concepts of emotion.[88]

81. Dixon, "Revolting Passions," 298. *Encyclopedia of Philosophy*, 2nd ed., s.v. "Emotion."

82. Solomon, *The Passions*, 68, 70. Compare M. B. Arnold and J. A. Glasson: "An emotion or an affect can be considered *as the felt tendency toward an object judged suitable, or away from an object judged unsuitable, reinforced by specific bodily changes according to the type of emotion.*" "Feelings and Emotions as Dynamic Factors in Personality Integration," in *The Nature of Emotion*, ed. Arnold, 203.

83. Ibid., 75.

84. Martha Nussbaum, *Therapy of Desire: Theory and Practice in Hellenistic Ethics* (Princeton, NJ: Princeton University Press, 1994) and idem, *Upheavals of Thought: The Intelligence of Emotions* (Cambridge: Cambridge University Press, 2001). Nussbaum uses the terms "emotions" and "passions" as nearly synonymous, without "salient distinction." She believes this is warranted because both terms serve as the "genus" for movements such as fear, love, grief, and so on. Ibid., 319 n4.

85. Nussbaum, *Upheavals of Thought*, 4.

86. Ibid., 25.

87. Ibid., 35.

88. Nussbaum believes emotion attempts to find true valuation in the outside world where in Solomon's account (as Nussbaum portrays him) emotion imputes a subjective and existential value to the outside world. Nussbaum, *Upheavals of Thought*, 48 n45.

In his attempt to construct a Christian psychology, Robert C. Roberts has made similar attempts to redefine emotions. He rejects definitions of emotion based on physicalist assumptions. He says: "To Christians [emotions] seem more like attitudes toward things, ways a person's heart is oriented toward something." Therefore emotions are "concern-based construals."[89]

The views of Nussbaum and Solomon, however, are disputed by scholars in other fields. Those coming from physicalist, scientific, or neuroscience perspectives often believe that emotion should be defined and studied only through physiological investigation. Social constructionists emphasize the social and cultural forces that determine particular emotive states.[90]

The fundamental issue between the competing definitions of emotions is how human nature ought to be conceived. Should human beings be seen as developed persons, or should they be viewed as complex biological organisms? The current discussion has reached an impasse over this issue.[91]

Outside the academy, popular ideas of emotions further complicate the matter. The *American Heritage Dictionary* (1985) defines *emotions* as a "complex and usually strong subjective response" that can involve "physiological changes." The word can also refer to that "part of the consciousness that involves feeling

89. Roberts, *Spiritual Emotions*, 11 and 22–26. Compare William C. Spohn, "Passion and Principle," *TS* 52 (1991): 71.

90. For examples of the physicalist, scientific, or neuroscience perspectives on emotion, see Paul Ekman, "All Emotions are Basic," in *The Nature of Emotion: Fundamental Questions*, 15–19; Antonio Damasio, *Descartes' Error: Emotion, Reason, and the Human Brain* (New York: Penguin Books, 1994); Paul Griffiths, *What Emotions Really Are: The Problem of Psychological Categories* (Chicago: The University of Chicago Press, 1997), cited in Robert C. Solomon, ed. *What Is an Emotion? Classic and Contemporary Readings*, 2nd ed. (New York: Oxford University Press, 2003), 284–90. Solomon calls this the "*hydraulic model*" of emotions. Solomon, *The Passions*, 77–88. For examples of the social constructionist approach to emotion, see Richard A. Shweder, "Emotion as an Interpretative System" and Catherine A. Lutz, *Unnatural Emotions: Everyday Sentiments on a Micronesian Atoll & Their Challenge to Western Theory* (Chicago: University of Chicago Press, 1988). John Corrigan writes, "Scholarship has focused in many instances on demonstrating that the components of emotionality—the way a group conceives of emotion in relation to thinking and doing, its understanding of particular emotions, its strategies for conveying emotion and for obscuring it, its networking to language—vary from context to context. Nevertheless, most researchers continue to embrace, in some measure, the notion that certain aspects of emotional life are consistent across cultural boundaries." "Introduction," in *The Oxford Handbook of Religion and Emotion*, ed. John Corrigan (New York: Oxford University Press, 2008), 7.

91. Shweder, "Emotion as an Interpretative System," 33–37. Compare Magda Arnold, "Introduction," in *The Nature of Emotion*, ed. Arnold, 9–14.

or sensibility."[92] This is noted by de Sousa, who says: "The simplest theory of emotions, and perhaps the theory most representative of common sense, is that emotions are simply a class of feelings, differentiated from sensation and proprioceptions by their experienced quality."[93] Similarly, the "Wiktionary" defines "emotion" as "[a] person's internal state of being and involuntary physiological response to an object or situation, based on or tied to physical state and sensory data."[94] Indeed, popular culture uses the idea of emotion in numerous ways: emotional intelligence, emotional abuse, emotional eating, and myriad professional athletes "getting emotional."[95] Emotions have become associated with physiological changes or "feelings" with reference to nonlocalized sensations.[96]

Unfortunately, few who discuss the relationship of affections to emotions in Edwards's thought define *emotions*. Some exceptions do exist. For example, Matthew Elliot, following Nussbaum and Arnold (among others), stresses that emotions are cognitive.[97] Elliot adds: "It is important to stress that the cognitive theory of emotion does not neglect physiological change." Such changes are significant parts of emotion.[98] Elliot influences Borgman, who says, "[*T*]*he emotions are . . . the values and evaluations of a person and influence motives and conduct*."[99] Meanwhile Michael McClymond turns to his desk dictionary, where "emotion" is defined as a "feeling," an awareness apart from a particular sensation, perception, or thought.[100] Yet, significantly, these authors are anomalies. Most commentators assume some form of the popular idea that emotions are vaguely quasi-cognitive sensations.

92. *American Heritage Dictionary*, 2nd college ed., s.v. "emotion."

93. *The Stanford Encyclopedia of Philosophy*, s.v. "Emotion." Compare Brian S. Borgman, *Feelings and Faith*, 23–27.

94. Wikimedia Foundation, "emotion—Wiktionary," Wiktionary, http://en.wiktionary.org/wiki/emotion (accessed December 4, 2017).

95. A quick search on espn.com offers 311 results for the term "emotional" in the year 2010 alone. http://search.espn.go.com/results?startDate=01%2F01%2F2010&endDate=12%2F31%2F2010&searchString=emotional&soccernetSearch=false&dims=0&dateFilter=GO (accessed December 9, 2011).

96. Solomon, *The Passions*, 85–86, 97n. Solomon argues to the contrary. Ibid., 97.

97. Matthew A. Elliot, *Faithful Feelings*, 31–32. For Magda Arnold's view, Nussbaum, *Upheavals of Thought*, 4.

98. Elliot says, "What is clear is that the physiological change experienced in emotion is a result of cognition and evaluation and not a direct response to a stimulus." Here Elliott quotes Edwards and his extended remarks in *Affections* regarding the distinction between affections and their bodily effects. Elliot, *Faithful Feelings*, 41.

99. Borgman, *Feelings and Faith*, 26.

100. Michael McClymond, "Jonathan Edwards," in *The Oxford Handbook of Religion and Emotion*, ed. John Corrigan (New York: Oxford University Press, 2008), 405–06.

A Definition of Emotions For this study, emotions will be defined following de Sousa above, as a "class of feelings, differentiated from sensation or proprioceptions by their experienced quality." Although the clarity of cognitive theories has done much good, those definitions are not commonly understood. Presently, the concept of *emotions* as judgments or cognitive acts remains obscure. In preferring this definition, I am not merely trying to sever Edwards and modern thought. Even if one accepted the definition of *emotion* suggested by Nussbaum or Solomon or Roberts to be an accepted standard, problems remain, as I will show, in assuming that Edward's idea of affections is synonymous with emotions.[101]

Other Terms

The word *psychology* was coined before the eighteenth century to refer to the study of the soul, and so it will be used here of any theory concerning the soul.[102] With respect to the human soul, a *faculty* refers to one of its inborn or cultivated powers. *Faculty psychology* designates the way Scholastic philosophers and theologians thought of these powers as more or less distinct operations.[103] In cognitive science, affective psychology is a branch of psychology distinct from cognitive psychology, concerned with motivation, personality, and attitudes. In this book, however, *affective psychology* refers to a particular understanding of the relationship of affections, passions, and the soul within the larger discussion of faculty psychology. The word *sentimentalism* will refer to the eighteenth-century British movement emphasizing humanity's moral sense as a way of determining good and evil.[104]

The Problem of Jonathan Edwards and Emotions

The tendency among many evangelicals and scholars to read the idea of affections in Edwards's writings as *emotions* has already been established. Some scholars, however, challenge this approach. A few examples should demonstrate the complexity of the issue.

101. See Dixon, "Revolting Passions," 199.

102. *OED*, s.v. "Psychology." For example, see David Hartley, *Observations on Man*, in Joseph Priestly, *Hartley's Theory of the Human Mind, on the Principle of the Association of Ideas; with Essays relating to the Subject of It* (London: J. Johnson, 1775), 188.

103. On the faculties and the so-called Puritan "faculty psychology" see, for example, Perry Miller, *The New England Mind: The Seventeenth Century* (New York: Macmillan, 1939), 239–79; Lewis, "Springs of Motion," 281; Ramsey, "Editor's Introduction," in *WJE* 1:48–53; Norman Fiering, *Moral Philosophy at Seventeenth-century Harvard: A Discipline in Transition* (Chapel Hill: University of North Carolina Press, 1981), 104–10; and Oliphint, "Edwards on Apologetics," 131–35.

104. Ted Honderich, ed., *The Oxford Companion to Philosophy* (New York: Oxford University Press, 1995), s.v. "moral sense."

In his 1980 monograph, Don Sailer recognizes a distinction between Edwards's category of affections and emotions. He opposes "the substitution of sentiment and the interior consolations of experience for the more enduring affections which are the wellspring of emotion, thought, and action." Citing Edwards's *Religious Affections*, he criticizes the emphasis on "zealous experiential religion," and therefore desires "a language" for the "connections between self, world, and God." That language void is filled by Edwards's phrase "religious affections," as opposed to "mere sentiment or . . . passing enthusiasms." For Sailer, affections, which lie at the core of the individual, are the basis of how one views the world, and the cause of deep emotions. Edwards positioned himself between those who disparaged emotion and the enthusiasts, believing that "the degree of truthfulness in religious faith is not found in the experiential *abundance* of emotion and feeling." The passions, Sailer argues, were often viewed as the violent, irrational tempests that people suffer. "This classical notion of human passions," he continues, "has carried over into many of our modern views of emotion."[105]

Gordon Clark, perceiving the conflict between the language of modern psychology and the Bible, noted that Scripture often mentions the "heart," but never the word *emotion*. Clark rejected the notion that Edwards was emphasizing "emotion, feeling, passion" as essential to all religion: "Edwards' word *affections* does not mean *emotions*." Clark buttressed this argument with citations from *Religious Affections*, especially Edwards's situating the affections in the soul (rather than the body).[106]

Other authors have also noted the difference between emotions and Edwards's concept of affections. Robert Jensen says that American Christians have misunderstood the complex relationship of Edwards's anthropology to his Trinitarianism, and so have failed to appreciate the "consciousness" of affections.[107] Mark Noll says that Edwards's idea of affections could be called the "habitual inclinations at the core of a person's being."[108] John Smith interprets affections in Edwards as the fruit of the Spirit; they are not based on a head-heart dichotomy. Passions overpower a person's understanding, but affections always "involved ideas and perceptions." He says: "An affection is a *response* of the person accompanied by understanding." For Smith, confusing affections and emotions

105. Don E. Sailer, *The Soul in Paraphrase* (New York: The Seabury Press, 1980), 4–14. Sailer prefers affection because the term *emotion* has problems, typically referring to "feelings, moods, sudden sensations, and a wide range of other states." Ibid., 7.

106. Gordon Clark, *The Biblical Doctrine of Man* (Jefferson, MD: The Trinity Foundation, 1992), 78–81.

107. Robert Jensen, *America's Theologian: A Recommendation of Jonathan Edwards* (Oxford: Oxford University Press, 1988), 76.

108. Mark Noll, *America's God: From Jonathan Edwards to Abraham Lincoln* (Oxford: Oxford University Press, 2002), 23.

is a "fundamental error."[109] John Hannah echoes Smith, as does Michael Haykin, who urges that affections not be "equated with emotions or experience."[110]

Nicole Eustace agrees. She says that the modern definition of emotion is not the same as the eighteenth-century category of affections.[111] Edwards's taxonomy of affections and passions further substantiates this for her.[112] "While present definitions of the word regard *emotion* as separate from the mind and from the will, 'from cognitive or volitional states,' people of the eighteenth century made no such assumptions."[113]

Like Sailer, Sean Michael Lucas distinguishes affections and emotions and equates Edwards's idea of passions with the contemporary understanding of emotions. He explains: "In eighteenth-century philosophical parlance, passions were irrational and out-of-control emotions that were to be avoided at all costs; and affections were not irrational, but rational, deeper springs to action."[114]

Thomas Dixon argues that the idea behind the term *emotions* cannot be found in pre-modern authors. He traces the distinction between affections and passions in Augustine and Aquinas, both of which believed "that some human feeling or affection is proper and necessary in this life, but also that God, the angels and perfected humans are free from the turmoil and perturbations of sin and the passions."[115] Dixon insists that emotions are not the same as passions;

109. "Jonathan Edwards and the Great Awakening," 16–17. Compare Timothy Hessel-Robinson, "Jonathan Edwards: Religious Affections" in *Christian Spirituality: The Classics*, ed. Arthur Holder (New York: Routledge, 2010), 269–80.

110. Hannah, "Jonathan Edwards," 175–76. Michael A. G. Haykin, *Jonathan Edwards: The Holy Spirit in Revival: The Lasting Influence of the Holy Spirit in the Heart of Man* (Webster, NY: Evangelical Press USA, 2005), 125. Compare James M. Nelson, *Psychology, Religion, and Spirituality* (New York: Springer, 2009), 140. Haykin cites McDermott and John Smith. Hannah is not always precise with his terms. Compare "Jonathan Edwards," 178.

111. Nicole Eustace, *Passion is the Gale: Emotion, Power, and the Coming of the American Revolution* (Chapel Hill, NC: University of North Carolina Press, 2008), 597–98 n2.

112. Eustace, *Passion is the Gale*, 598 n5.

113. Ibid., 481.

114. Sean Michael Lucas, *God's Grand Design: The Theological Vision of Jonathan Edwards* (Wheaton, IL: Crossway, 2011), 92. Compare Scott Aniol, who, citing Edwards, argues that "Pre-modern" thought included both affections and passions as species of *emotion*. Affections "involve the mind," while "passions" are "surface-level feelings," or "physical, chemical responses to some sort of stimulus." The affections of the soul were considered superior to the body's passions. He adds, "Biblical affection intricately involves the mind, the will, and the emotions." Scott Aniol, *Worship in Song: A Biblical Approach to Music and Worship* (Winona Lake, IN: BMH Books, 2009), 52–54. Also see Kendra G. Hotz and Matthew T. Mathews, *Shaping the Christian Life* (Louisville, KY: Westminster John Knox, 2006), 13–14, 24.

115. Thomas Dixon, *From Passions to Emotions*, 61.

the traditional model considered both passions and affections to be properly connected to the soul, and not the body.[116] He adds that Jonathan Edwards espoused such a view in the tradition of Christian psychology he inherited.[117] The idea of emotions as they are popularly conceived today would not come about until Thomas Brown (1778–1820) introduced the idea in direct opposition to traditional Christian psychological categories, attempting to explain human affection by the scientific method.[118]

Michael McClymond also argues that in Edwards's thought affections are not the same as emotions. McClymond points out that affections for Edwards always have an object, while emotions, as considered today, can often be without an object. "Emote" is "an intransitive verb," and "affect" is not. Citing *Webster's International Dictionary*, he says that emotion is a "feeling," where a person is in a state of awareness apart from a particular sensation, perception, or thought. Noting Edwards's well-known distinction between understanding and will, he adds, "Though there are many shades and nuances in the affections, a basic contrast exists between attraction and aversion, or inclination and disinclination." McClymond understands the will to have more control over affections than passions. Edwards "hints at . . . a biological basis for human emotion," but does not speak at length on the relationship: "Edwards says little on the metaphysical issue of how soul and body interact, though he seems to imply that changes in either the soul or the body may affect the other." The body can affect (sometimes through the influence of Satan) the mind. McClymond situates Edwards in the Augustinian tradition, where people's volitions have more significance than their perceptions.[119]

On the other hand, McClymond and McDermott's *Theology of Jonathan Edwards* insists that affections have an intellectual component and cautions against equating affections and emotions. They continue:

> Both sides, then, and many scholars since, have wrongly assumed that Edwards's affections were the same thing as "emotions." But emotions for Edwards were

116. Ibid., 20; 56–59; 76–79.

117. Ibid., 72–81.

118. Dixon calls Thomas Brown the "inventor of the emotions." Ibid., 109. Brown argued in his *Lectures on the Philosophy of the Human Mind* that the principles of "Newtonian philosophy" should be rigorously applied as much as possible to the study of human nature. Brown's "mental science" understood a strong tie between the physics of matter and the physics of mind; no longer did the mind have faculties, but only "states." As Dixon explains it: "The mind disappeared from the picture and the reader was left with free-standing thoughts and emotions." Ibid., 122. Brown rejected outright the distinction between understanding and will. Why begin using the term *emotions*? Brown explains: "A difference of words is, in this case, more than a mere verbal difference. Though it be not the expression of a difference of nature, it very speedily becomes so." *Lectures*, 1:162.

119. "Jonathan Edwards," in *The Oxford Handbook of Religion and Emotion*, ed. John Corrigan (New York: Oxford University Press, 2008), 405–06.

> only one dimension of human experience shaped by affections, along with thinking and choosing. Edwards argued that true religious affections sometimes choose against emotional feeling, such as when Jesus chose not to yield to his feelings of fear in the Garden of Gethsemane. When "passions" overwhelm one's better judgment, as in a fit of rage, emotions are in fact opposed to true religious affections. Furthermore, Edwards always linked affections to an object, while emotions may or may not have an object.[120]

Those who equate pre-modern passions and affections with modern emotions do so for different reasons, although a rationale is not always given. Some argue from species to genus, as do scholars such as Martha Nussbaum, Simo Knuttila, and Matthew Elliot.[121] In other words, because ancients threw affects such as love, anger, joy, and the like into a bucket called "affections," while moderns throw the same species into a bucket called "emotions," it is assumed that the two can be equated without "salient distinction."[122] Other scholars believe that affections and emotions can be equated simply because they refer to relatively parallel categories. Because there is some faculty in humanity that is different from or even opposed to cognition, and both emotions and passions tend to present themselves as this different faculty, some have concluded that they are synonymous. This perspective is taken for granted so often that its defense goes unstated.[123]

The central question is whether Edwards is being read rightly. Edwards rarely speaks of emotions, and it is not altogether clear that his category of affections can be taken to be synonymous with emotions in the modern sense. The question of what Edwards meant by his terms calls for a careful investigation into the psychology of Edwards, tracing its development throughout his life.[124]

I hope to demonstrate that using the term *emotions* as a synonym for affections or passions is at best confusing and unhelpful. Edwards not only perpetuated the traditional Christian distinction between affections and passions, but he used that

120. *Theology of Jonathan Edwards*, 313.

121. Nussbaum, *Therapy of Desire*; Simo Knuuttila, *Emotions in Ancient and Medieval Philosophy* (Oxford: Clarendon Press, 2004); Elliot, *Faithful Feelings*. Compare Roberts, *Spiritual Emotions*, 8–9 and D'Arcy, introduction to *The Emotions*, xix–xxiii. John Piper seems to argue for near identity in emotions and affections from species to genus in *Desiring God*, 298 n1. See Needham, introduction to *The Experience that Counts!*, 10–11, where he cites the *OED*.

122. Nussbaum, *Therapy of Desire*, 319 n4.

123. For example, see Borgman, *Feelings and Faith*, 23–25.

124. I am optimistic that an answer can be reached, although I acknowledge Stephan A. Wilson's sobering point, "that one cannot even formulate the rudiments of Edwards's position on baseline issues in Reformed theology without privileging some texts or ideas and relegating others to less consequential peripheries." Stephen A. Wilson, *Virtue Reformed: Rereading Jonathan Edwards's Ethics*, Brill's Studies in Intellectual History 132 (Leiden: Brill, 2005), 348.

distinction often throughout his ministry to illustrate the difference between the spiritual inclinations of the soul and those beastly and instinctual desires that arise from sensual pleasures. In defending the central place of affections in genuine Christian piety, Edwards was not trying to defend emotions in Christianity, but the necessity in true religion of a Spirit-wrought love for God revealed in Christ. This book is not an argument that affections lie at the core of Edwards's theology, but an argument concerning his concept of the nature of affections and passions.

In light of this goal, a few caveats are in order. First, although a large representation of Edwards's use of *affections*, *passions*, and *emotions* should be surveyed, every occurrence of these terms need not be cited. Moreover, in sorting out the difference between affections and emotions, it should not be assumed that the lack of a term (e.g., *emotion*) means the absence of a concept.[125] Still further, *affections* and *passions* are not always used as technical terms for Edwards, and proper respect must be paid to the distinction between word and concept. Throughout this study, Edwards's own dictum must be kept in mind "that language is here somewhat imperfect, and the meaning of words in considerable measure loose and unfixed, and not precisely limited by custom, which governs the use of language."[126]

The category of affections, which Edwards used in a theological sense to stress the importance of Christian piety and traditional Christian ethics during a time of both religious revival and Enlightenment skepticism, is key to his entire body of work. Therefore, understanding more precisely how he used such psychological categories is essential to understanding Edwards's theology. The aim of this study is to describe Edwards's own affective psychology, to find its points of contact and discordance with modern emotions, and to develop that affective psychology through the thought of this singular American theologian and pastor.

125. Edwards does use the term *emotion*, but, as I will argue, in different ways than it is used today. On the "Word-Concept" fallacy, see Carl R. Trueman, *Histories and Fallacies: Problems Faced in the Writing of History* (Wheaton, IL: Crossway Books, 2010), 156–58.

126. *Religious Affections*, *WJE* 2:97. See Danaher, *Trinitarian Ethics*, 120–24. As Gregory S. Clapper says in his study of John Wesley's use of "affections": "Awareness of the potential for distortion by forcing a commensurability of all uses has guarded my work throughout. An analysis focusing on particular words need not be distortive if carefully done, and can, in fact, be very helpful for the task of understanding a concept, as long as the distinction between 'word' and 'concept' is honored." *John Wesley on Religious Affections: His Views on Experience and Emotion and Their Role in the Christian Life and Theology*, Pietist and Wesleyan Studies 1 (Metuchen, NJ: The Scarecrow Press, 1989), 44.

Chapter 2

HUMAN AFFECTIONS IN PATRISTIC AND MEDIEVAL THEOLOGY

Is there a thing beneath the sun
That strives with Thee my heart to share?
Ah! Tear it thence, and reign alone,
The Lord of every motion there;
Then shall my heart from earth be free,
When it has found repose in Thee.

— Gerhard Tersteegen, tr. John Wesley

Comprehending how the concepts of affections and passions functioned in Christian theology before Edwards is essential to understanding Edwards's own concepts. Premodern or even early modern Christian theology knew nothing of emotions in the modern, scientific sense. Christian theology not only uses different terminology for human affectivity, but considers human affectivity in strikingly different ways.

The following discussion surveys different understandings of human affections and passions throughout the first seventeen centuries of Christian theology. This survey not only proves but augments the theses of Thomas Dixon.[1] It begins with Augustine (354–430) and other church fathers and then moves to Medieval thought, focusing on the contributions of Thomas Aquinas (1224–74). The following chapter will discuss patristic and medieval categories of human affectivity, categories which will inform the thought of later Reformation theologians, Puritans, and early Enlightenment figures.

Throughout Christian history, different theologians and traditions have stressed either the intellect or the will. These two approaches have been called *intellectualism* and *voluntarism* respectively. Broadly, intellectualism (commonly understood as Aquinas's legacy) tends to emphasize the intellect; the will follows reason or the dictates of the understanding. Voluntarism accentuates the will and is commonly understood to be an Augustinian tradition. Intellectualism tends to emphasize contemplation of God as the ultimate good, while voluntarism emphasizes love for God. To be clear, neither intellectualism nor voluntarism

1. Dixon, *From Passions to Emotions*; Dixon, "Revolting Passions," *MT* 27 (2011): 298–312.

addresses the importance of reason in life or the freedom of the will. Even allowing for such differences, intellectualists and voluntarists often share an understanding of what affections are, and how they are distinct from lower inclinations.[2]

In order to properly understand older ways of thinking about human affectivity, it is first important to clear away any assumption that earlier categories directly correlate to modern notions. At the most basic level, traditional Christian psychology understood affections as the inclinations and aversions of the soul. In general, Christian schemes of human affectivity held that the higher and lower parts of the soul experience distinguishable appetites. The appetite of the higher soul corresponds to reason, understanding, and the will. The appetite of the lower soul analogously corresponds to the body and its senses. The present discussion will adopt the terms Aquinas occasionally gave these different movements, using *affections* to refer to the movements of the soul that answer to the rational appetite and *passions* to refer to those movements of the soul that answer to the sensitive appetites. Not all theologians gave different names for the different movements; some authors considered all movements affections, and others considered them all passions. Nevertheless, Christian theologians for some 1,700 years consistently distinguished those inclinations and aversions of the soul that arose from sense pleasure and pain from those inclinations and aversions of the soul that arose from the good and evil of the "higher," rational faculties.[3] This basic outline is essential for understanding how the ideas of affections and passions in Christian antiquity differ from modern notions of emotions.

The distinction between higher and lower appetites significantly influenced the thought of Christian theologians, as can be seen in the near-universal agreement that God, while impassible, is also a God who loves.[4] Furthermore, Christian theologians have always been suspicious of passions, but have simultaneously affirmed the necessity of love and joy. On these points, the modern category of emotions simply will not do justice to the historical testimony. Something more is at work, and fuller explanation is possible.

The testimony of Christian theologians concerning human affectivity bears strong marks of similarity on other key points. Nevertheless, theologians articulated the Bible's teaching in different ways. Differences over human affectivity abound, not only between different historical epochs of the church, but between different

2. These remarks follow the helpful summary of Richard A. Muller, *The Unaccommodated Calvin: Studies in the Foundation of a Theological Tradition* (Oxford: Oxford University Press, 2000), 162. Also see Fiering, *Moral Philosophy*, 104–46. On this debate coming to a head in Jonathan Edwards's own day against Charles Chauncy, see George Marsden, *Jonathan Edwards*, 282–83.

3. Dixon, *From Passions to Emotions*, 26–61.

4. The doctrine of divine impassibility does not rest solely on a distinction between appetites and their corresponding movements of the soul, but it is an important part of the conversation. For more on divine impassibility among the church fathers, see Thomas G. Weinandy, *Does God Suffer?* (Notre Dame, IN: University of Notre Dame Press, 2000), 83–107.

theologians within the same epoch.[5] As already noted, not every Christian thinker consistently distinguished affections and passions by name. Some stressed the distinction between the affections of a renewed and unrenewed will more than a distinction between movements of various appetites. Still, other key ideas were held in common. Many agreed that affections and passions are seated in the soul. Christian theologians commonly held that affections and passions are connected with the will and its operations. Finally, Christian ethics often touched directly on the object, nature, and subjects of affections and passions. These themes will be developed over the next two chapters.

Patristic Thought

This survey of ancient Christianity will look at the thought of four church fathers on the affections and passions. Put most simply, all four understood affections and passions to be inclinations and aversions of the soul. Although the four together show the influence of Greek philosophy on their concepts of the affections, they all strive to submit to Scripture as the greater authority. Since Augustine represents the most important and influential player in the patristic understanding of human affectivity, this discussion of primitive Christian theology devotes the most space to his views.

First, however, three theologians—two preceding and one contemporary with Augustine—illustrate the similarity of early Christian thought. Clement of Alexandria (*c.* 150 to *c.* 215), or Titus Flavius Clemens, taught the catechumens school in Alexandria and has been called "the pioneer of Christian scholarship."[6] His *Stromata* (*Miscellanies* or *Carpets*) strings together disorganized teachings on varied subjects. In several essays he discusses human passions.[7] Nemesius of Emesa (d. *c.* 359) is known only as a successor of Eusebius of Emesa and as the author of the fourth-century work *On the Nature of Man*.[8] This work, used by both Peter Lombard and Thomas Aquinas, defends the Christian notion of humanity as incorporeal soul and material body, borrowing heavily from the knowledge of Greek physicians like Galen.[9] The third, Gregory of Nyssa (*c.* 335 to *c.* 394) was one

5. Dixon, *From Passions to Emotions*, 26–29.

6. Johannes Quasten, *The Ante-Nicene Literature after Irenaeus*, vol. 2 of *Patrology* (Utrecht: Spectrum Publishers, 1953), 6.

7. Clement of Alexandria, *The Stromata, or Miscellanies* (*ANF* 2:299–568).

8. See Johannes Quasten, *The Golden Age of Greek Patristic Literature from the Council of Nicaea to the Council of Chalcedon*, vol. 3 of *Patrology* (Utrecht: Spectrum Publishers, 1963), 351–55 and William Telfer, "General Introduction," in *Cyril of Jerusalem and Nemesius of Emesa*, LCC 4 (Philadelphia, PA: The Westminster Press, 1955), 203–11.

9. Some consider *On the Nature of Man* to be unfinished notes Nemesius was preparing for publication, but it still provides a valuable testimony to early Christian understandings of affections and passions. Quasten, *Patrology*, 3:353; Telfer, "General Introduction," 211.

of the three famous Cappadocian fathers. He spent his early life in a monastery with his brother Basil until he was pressured into serving as a bishop in Nyssa and eventually Sebaste. In addition to doctrinal works, he left sermons, exegetical works, and ascetic writings.[10]

Clement of Alexandria, Nemesius of Emesa, and Gregory of Nyssa

Four themes are worth noting in Clement, Nemesius, and Nyssa. The first is that they offer clear definitions for the movements of the soul. The second is that they submit their understanding of human nature to Scripture. The third is that each recognizes the distinction between affections and passions, and the fourth is their ideas concerning the eschatological contours of these movements.

The Definition of the Passions All three of these fathers offered clear definitions of his key psychological terms. For example, Clement, in the second book of the *Stromata*, explained that the impulse to sin comes from the relationship of appetites and passions: "Appetite is then the movement of the mind to or from something. Passion is an excessive appetite unbridled and disobedient to the word. Passions are a perturbation of the soul contrary to nature, in disobedience to reason" (*Strom.* 2.13). The passions of the soul are desires that are often disordered. In most contexts, Clement frowned upon the "irrational impulses" of the passions (*Strom.* 2.13). Nemesius of Emesa similarly understood a passion to be "a movement of the faculty of appetite upon perceiving an image of something good or bad," or "an irrational movement of the soul due to apprehending something good or bad."[11] The passions are necessary for life, but come from outside the soul. Nemesius also used *passions* to refer to a movement that violates reason and morality. These movements are actions, but as "inordinate and unnatural," they are thus *passions* (*Nat. hom.* 16).

In *On the Soul and the Resurrection*, Gregory of Nyssa portrayed a dialogue with his sister Macrina following the death of their brother Basil. In this dialogue Gregory and Macrina discussed at length the soul's passions, wondering how desire and anger relate to the soul.[12] In particular, the question is whether these

10. Quasten, *Patrology*, 3:254–96. Catharine P. Roth, Introduction to *On the Soul and the Resurrection*, by Gregory of Nyssa, Popular Patristics Series 12 (Crestwood, NY: St. Vladimir's Seminary Press, 1993), 7–25.

11. Telfer notes that here Nemesius follows Galen. Telfer observed that *pathos* refers to suffering, "and does not necessarily imply feeling, as the English word does" (*Cyril and Nemesius*, 349 n6, 348 n5).

12. Citations of *On the Soul and the Resurrection* come from Roth's translation. Since there are no agreed upon chapters, page numbers are given. Also see Gregory of Nyssa, *On the Soul and the Resurrection* (*NPNF2* 5:430–68). Also see *De Anima et Resurrectione Dialogus* (*PG* 46:11–160). Knuuttila briefly discusses Gregory's thought in this work in *Emotions*, 131–32.

two faculties are proper to the rational soul. Reason and understanding are the properties exclusive to human nature, but appetites and passions are properties shared with plants and animals.[13] But even those qualities shared with plants and animals, "proper to the irrational nature," are now "mixed" with the soul and its reasoning powers.[14]

Patristic Psychology under the Scriptures Clement and Gregory especially desired to submit to Scripture's authority in their understanding of the morality of passions. For example, Clement offered a qualified affirmation of the passions. While espousing God's impassibility, Clement acknowledged that God not only loves but also rejoices. Although God's affections should not be compared to those of humans, Clement believed that the Bible attributes affections to the Deity, and so confessed that God "rejoices, without suffering change."[15] Nevertheless, God is impassible. That is, by nature God has no anger or desire, and so experiences no need to control desires he does not have (*Strom.* 4.23). Yet Clement often taught that "God is love."[16] Love is in many respects the anti-passion in Clement.

As for Gregory of Nyssa, his declared intention in *On the Resurrection* is to "fix our eyes on the mark of inspired Scripture."[17] Therefore, he admitted that passions can be good, as seen by Daniel's desire and Phineas's anger. The Scriptures praise fear and godly grief. For Gregory, the Bible teaches that such passions are not "disorders," because "disorders would not be employed to assist in the establishment of virtue."[18]

13. Compare *On the Making of Man* 18.1 (*NPNF2* 5:407).

14. *On the Soul and the Resurrection*, 57. According to J. Warren Smith, Gregory used the word *pathē* confusingly. Passions controlled by reason are necessary for morally positive decisions. Yet, when *epithymia* and *thymos* are used for good, Gregory said they should not be called *passions*, for passions are unfit for Christians. Though Gregory's construct of passions is too simplistic for Smith, Gregory used it urge Christians to overcome sensual appetites. Smith adds that passion is driven by, in Martha Nussbaum's words, an "intentional awareness." Passions are not simply inclinations toward or aversions from sense stimuli. Passions also interpret the sensory world. See J. Warren Smith, *Passion and Paradise: Human and Divine Emotion in the Thought of Gregory of Nyssa* (New York: Crossroad Publishing, 2004), 92–94.

15. *Strom.* 2.16. Compare *Strom.* 3.16.

16. *Strom.* 4.16, 4.18, 5.2.

17. *On the Soul and the Resurrection*, 51. Compare ibid., 58. See Smith, *Passion and Paradise*, 102.

18. *On the Soul and the Resurrection*, 54. The Greek Bible ἀνὴρ ἐπιθυμιῶν referred to Daniel as an ἀνὴρ ἐπιθυμιῶν ("a man of desires") in Dan. 9:23, 10:11, and 10:19. See *On the Soul and the Resurrection*, 54 n12.

Patristic Distinctions between the Movements of the Soul All three church fathers distinguished different kinds of affections. Clement lauded affections like love and hope, but insisted that passions were to accord with reason and "holy beauty." Christians should cultivate impassibility to the greatest extent possible because it is an imitation of God himself.[19] Through their reason people can control their appetites and passions. This is a great struggle, because the passions are "impressions on the soul that is soft and yielding, and, as it were, the signatures of the spiritual powers with whom we have to struggle" (*Strom.* 2.20). Clement referred specifically to the fleshly desires for comfort and pleasure in the present. What makes humanity unique among other creatures is the ability to reason, and this reason must be used to shun passions and seek true, reasonable pleasures:

> [H]aving beguiled those incapable of distinguishing the true from false pleasure, and the fading and meretricious from the holy beauty, [the passions] lead them into slavery. And each deceit, by pressing constantly on the spirit, impresses its image on it; and the soul unwittingly carries about the image of the passion, which takes its rise from the bait and our consent.[20]

Virtue, or humanity's chief good, consists in becoming like Christ to the greatest extent possible in righteousness and holiness. This virtue is the end of faith (*Strom.* 2.20). In another *Stroma*, Clement contrasted lustful passions with love, which "joins us to God" and perfects the elect (*Strom.* 4.18). He also said that faith and hope, having invisible objects, are properly connected with the mind (*Strom.* 4.3). The virtuous, whose lives accord with reason and nature, contemplate and do good for its own sake. This is tantamount to living in accordance with the soul, which is better than the body: "The good actions, as better, attach to the better and ruling spirit; and voluptuous and sinful actions are attributed to the worse, the sinful one."[21]

19. Clement wrote, "[T]he Divinity needs nothing and suffers nothing; whence it is not, strictly speaking, capable of self-restraint, for it is never subjected to perturbation, over which to exercise control; while our nature, being capable of perturbation, needs self-constraint, by which disciplining itself to the need of little, it endeavors to approximate in character to the divine nature" (*Strom.* 2.18; compare *Strom.* 2.19, 6.19, 7.4). "Those that are superior to Pleasure, who rise above the passions, who know what they do—the Gnostics, who are greater than the world." "God's greatest gift to us is self-constraint" (*Strom.* 2.20). Again, "The variety of disposition arises from inordinate affection to material things" (*Strom.* 4.22).

20. *Strom.* 2.20. Later Clement added, "For peace and freedom are not otherwise won, than by ceaseless and unyielding struggles with our lusts" (*Strom.* 2.20).

21. *Strom.* 4.26. Clement clarified that the superiority of the soul over the body does not mean that the soul is good and the body bad by nature.

Nemesius of Emesa also distinguished the higher and lower movements of the soul.[22] He found the term *pleasure* ambiguous, referring to objects desired sometimes by the body or the soul. "Some are noble and some are base, some false and some true."

> Therefore a true man of God must pursue only the pleasures that are both necessary and natural [e.g., clothes and food], while, at his rear, the man in virtue's second rank may indulge other pleasures besides, which, while natural, are not necessary [e.g., marital intercourse], provided always that they are fitting, moderate, mannerly, seasonable, and in their right place. (*Nat. hom.* 18)

Every other pleasure should be shunned. On the other hand, the truest pleasures—those that "are *not* called passions"—are "susceptibilities," pleasures "that belong to the soul itself," coming from "contemplation" and "doing good."[23] Nemesius's ideal is to be "completely unmoved" by passions such as grief, for the "contemplative . . . has severed himself from present things, and cleaves to God." Nevertheless, a lesser but still worthy man could be moderately affected by grief or even righteous anger.[24] The acts of the appetite are connected with the will: "The criteria of the voluntary are . . . pleasure in the attaining, and grief in being disappointed; whence it is clear that anyone acting in lust or anger acts voluntarily." If passions are unwilled, then so are the acts of virtue.[25] All acts of will mix desire, discernment, and deliberation.

Gregory did not consider passions to be evil *per se*. Macrina explained: "Instead, by the particular use of our free choice such impulses of the soul[26] become instruments of virtue or wickedness."[27] When controlled by reason, passions are tools for good; when they control reason, "the impulses are turned into passions, as indeed we can see also in the irrational animals."[28] Macrina lamented that

22. Like Augustine and his four "perturbations," Nemesius of Emesa divided concupiscence into four: pleasure (present good), grief (present evil), desire (future good), and fear (future evil). Anger or concupiscence becomes an "evil" passion when individuals are disposed wrongly toward good or evil objects or when they mistakenly judge the objects before them as good or bad (*Nat. hom.* 17). Nemesius said, "The evil passions arise in the soul in these three ways; from a bad upbringing, from perversity, or through a poor constitution" (*Nat. hom.* 17).

23. *Nat. hom.* 18. Earlier in the book, Nemesius explained that the faculties of the soul differ; some rule and others serve. The passions are among those natural faculties subordinate to the ruling faculties like thought and knowledge (*Nat. hom.* 6).

24. On righteous grief, see *Nat. hom.* 19. On righteous anger, see ibid., 16, 20.

25. *Nat. hom.* 32.

26. τῆς ψυχῆς κινήματα (*PG* 46:61a).

27. *On the Soul and the Resurrection*, 57.

28. Ibid. τότε εἰς πάθος αἱ ὁρμαὶ καταστρέφονται. (*PG* 46:61c). Macrina added, "So also in us, if these faculties are not directed by reason towards what is right, but if instead

wicked people have abused love and anger, yet noted that if desire, love, and anger were removed from people, they would be worse off. After all, love is how human beings are "joined with the divine."[29] For Macrina (and Gregory), such "impulses of the soul"[30] are neither good nor evil in themselves. What mattered was how individuals use them. When men and women use them for good, they warrant praise, "as desire for Daniel, anger for Phineas, and grief for the one who mourns rightly." Macrina continued: "If, on the other hand, their inclination is toward the worse, then they become passions and are named accordingly."[31]

Eschatological Passions in the Fathers Before concluding, Clement and Gregory's vision of eschatological impassibility is worth noting. Clement said that humanity's ideal is ever-increasing proximity to divine impassibility. Jesus was entirely impassible, as were his apostles, who "mastered, through the Lord's teaching, anger, and fear, and lust, and were not liable even to such of the movements of feeling, as seem good, courage, zeal, joy, desire, through a steady condition of mind, not changing a whit" (*Strom.* 6.9). Again, such affections are good, but they are simply impossible in a "perfect man," for courage is impossible when terror cannot afflict and anger is impossible with undistracted love for God. Clement continued:

> Nor, consequently, does [the perfect man] fall into any desire and eagerness; nor does he want, as far as respects his soul, aught appertaining to others, now that he associates through love with the Beloved One, to whom he is allied by free choice, and by the habit which results from training, approaches closer to Him, and is blessed through the abundance of good things. (*Strom.* 6.9)

Thereby the virtuous person is like Jesus Christ, impassible and "godlike in form and semblance as respects his soul" (*Strom.* 6.9).[32]

the passions rule over the power of the mind, our humanity is changed from intelligence and godlikeness to irrationality and mindlessness. We are turned into beasts by the force of these passions." *On the Soul and the Resurrection*, 57–58.

29. *On the Soul and the Resurrection*, 59.

30. κινήματα τῆς ψυχῆς. (*PG* 46:65c).

31. *On the Soul and the Resurrection*, 60. Compare Gregory of Nyssa, *On the Making of Man* 18.5 (*NPNF2* 5:408). On the importance of hope in Nyssen's account of virtue, see Smith, *Passion and Paradise*, 99–100.

32. Is true impassibility reached when such good persons desire the good? Clement suspected such cavils are raised by those who are not acquainted with divine love. No desire perturbs love; love "is a relation of affection [στερκτικὴ . . . οἰκείωσις]. . . . But he who by love is already in the midst of that in which he is destined to be, and has anticipated hope by knowledge, does not desire anything, having, as far as possible, the very thing desired" (*Strom.* 6.9). From knowledge comes practice, which works a habit, which in turn "produces impassibility, not moderation of passion" (*Strom.* 6.9; *PG* 9:293d).

Similarly, for Gregory, when the soul is united to a resurrected body, it will be purified of passions. Yet how can movements like desire, so important to the virtuous life now, be absent in the resurrection? Resurrected saints retain faculties like contemplation and discernment, proper to the "godlike part of the soul."[33] When cleansed of sin, the soul will exist in pure beauty and have no need to desire the good. He explains, "Thus it imitates the superior life, being conformed to the properties of the divine Nature, so that nothing else is left to it but the disposition of love, as it becomes in its nature to the beautiful."[34]

Summary In sum, Clement emphasized the evil of passions, especially when inordinately attached to worldly appetites. Worldly pleasures are empty and misleading. As the only creature with a rational soul, humans should live in accordance with their nature, but passions draw them away. Clement urged people to conform to their Creator as much as possible. Thereby the happy life is found in impassibility—in having such a disposition of love that no earthly desire ever troubles them.[35]

Nemesius of Emesa believed in two kinds of passions. Passions generally are those movements of the appetite toward the good and away from the bad. Such movements are good when necessary and natural. In another sense, passions are evil when the individual allows appetites to have control apart from reason. Nemesius meanwhile held that passions were different from the Christian soul's movement toward God.

Gregory of Nyssa also taught that any virtue in the soul's movements depends upon those who use them. Sometimes he called these movements *passions*, but at other times he reserved the term *passions* for movements that subvert reason's control. The soul's movements merit praise when controlled by reason. These movements are not proper to the soul's essence, which bears God's image. God is impassible, and this impassibility is the goal for humans in the eschaton. Eschatological impassibility is without desire or anger, yet it is consistent with infinite love in possessing Divine beauty.

Augustine of Hippo

Augustine's writings are second only to those of Thomas Aquinas in their influence over Christian ideas of human affectivity. His thought is similar to that of other

33. Ibid., 77.

34. Ibid., 79–80. Compare Gregory of Nyssa, *On the Making of Man* 5.2 (*NPNF2* 5:391). Smith notes that God, as incorporeal, has a beauty that is not physical but virtuous. Smith, *Passion and Paradise*, 100.

35. Knuuttila adds, "Although Clement and Origen stressed the complete mortification of the mundane emotional habits, they could employ very affective terms in describing the mystical union of the soul with the Logos and God." *Emotions*, 125.

church fathers. Augustine most clearly articulated his understanding of affective psychology in *Confessions* and *The City of God*.[36]

Augustine said that humans have a material body and an immaterial soul, and that the soul has both lower and higher powers. The lower or earthly powers include sensation, imagination, or sense memory. The higher powers include *scientia* and *sapientia*. On the one hand, the rational knowledge of earthly things, *scientia* makes right knowledge of the temporal world possible. *Sapientia*, on the other hand, is the highest power of the soul, and that for which the soul was created; *sapientia* contemplates divine or eternal truth. These two powers comprise the *mens*, or the "inner man."[37] Tragically fallen and disordered, the soul seeks happiness in sensual things.[38]

The soul's various movements correspond to the different faculties. Proper affections of the soul take spiritual realities as their objects, such as fearing eternal damnation, sorrowing over sin, loving God, and desiring eschatological glory. People often still turn away from spiritual good. Through the lower appetites, passions powerfully draw people toward the sense world in rebellion against the rational soul.[39]

36. Augustine, *Confessions*, ed. W. H. D. Rouse, 2 vols., Loeb Classical Library 26–27 (Cambridge, MA: Harvard University Press, 1977); Augustine, *The City of God*, trans. Marcus Dods (New York: The Modern Library, 1993); *De civitate Dei* (PL 41). On the life of Augustine, see Peter Brown, *Augustine of Hippo: A Bibliography*, rev. ed. (London: Faber and Faber, 1967).

37. Edmund Hill, "Forward to Books IX–XIV," in *The Trinity* (De Trinitate), vol. 5 of *The Works of Saint Augustine*, ed. John E. Rotelle (Hyde Park, NY: New City Press, 1991), 258–65. Also see Dixon, *From Passions to Emotions*, 32.

38. For example, see *Trin.* 11.2.6. Also see Robert J. O'Connell, *St. Augustine's Early Theory of Man, A.D. 386–391* (Cambridge, MA: Harvard University Press, 1968), 217–18. Augustine said, "[The soul] finds delight in bodily shapes and movements, and because it has not got them with it inside, it wraps itself in their image which it has fixed in the memory. In this way it defiles itself foully with a fanciful sort of fornication by referring all its business to one or the other of the following ends: curiosity, searching for bodily and temporal experience through the senses; swollen conceit, affecting to be above other souls which are given over to their senses; or carnal pleasure, plunging itself in this muddy whirlpool" (*Trin.* 12.3.14).

39. See Dixon, *From Passions to Emotions*, 26–51. Augustine found from the senses a "confused multitudes of phantasies, which contradict one another." Therefore, the knowledge of the unchangeable was more sure than that which is changeable. "And now came I to have a sight of those invisible things of thee, which are understood by those things which are made" (*Conf.* 7.17).

Affections in Confessions Throughout the *Confessions*, Augustine contrasted a proper affection for God, seated in the heart or soul, with improper affections or desires, usually for carnal pleasure connected with the body and its lusts. Augustine compared the wandering soul to the prodigal son, who "went from thee out of a voluptuous affection,[40] that is to say, a darkened one"[41] (*Conf.* 1.18). In Augustine, sinful affections often carry a modifier such as "impure" (*inmunditia*), "misty" (*tenebroso*), "voluptuous" (*libidinoso*), or even "carnal" (*carnales*). The audience at the theater loves the writers who better move them to "passion," all of which is a "pernicious pleasure" (*perniciosae voluptatis*) (*Conf.* 3.2). At other times, he spoke of the *dolor* or inner pain of these sinful desires.[42]

In the final book of the *Confessions*, Augustine turned the creation account into an allegory of spiritual truth. The work of grace in believers moves their affections away from the world (*Conf.* 13.22). So the "spiritual man" has affections "tamed" "in chastity, in fasting, and in holy meditations"—his affections are turned away from that which appeals to the body's senses (*Conf.* 13.24). God himself formed these spiritual affections (*Conf.* 13.34). Since the soul is nobler than the body, the affections directed toward an unchanging God are superior to those directed toward a changing world.[43]

Throughout *Confessions*, the term *affectus* is ambiguous. Yet the text draws a distinction between the affections of the Christian and the unbeliever. Those

40. *affectu . . . libidinoso.*

41. *tenebroso.*

42. Compare Dixon, "Revolting Passions," 300. Rhetoricians used "*dolor*" for the Greek παθος or "passionate, warm expression." S.v., "dolor," Charlton T. Lewis and Charles Short, *A New Latin Dictionary* (New York: American Book Company, 1907), 607.

43. *Beat.* 1.4. Also see Ludwig Schopp, "Introduction," in *Writings of Saint Augustine, Volume 1*, ed. Ludwig Schopp, FC 5 (New York: CIMA Publishing, 1948), 32–33; also see O'Connell, *Theory of Man*, 155–61, 187–88. In the tenth book, Augustine reflected on past affections of his mind. He observed that the recollection of past happiness, sadness, fear, or even desire (*cupiditatem, laetitiam, metum, tristitiam*), differs from their original experience. He spoke of "four perturbations": desire, joy, fear, and sorrow, and marveled that the mind is able to conjure up these affects without actually re-experiencing the affects: "And yet could we never speak of them, did we not find in our memory, not the sounds of the names alone according to their images imprinted in it by the senses of the body, but even the very notions of the things themselves, which we never received in by any of the cinqueports of our body, but which the very mind itself, perceiving by the experience of its own passions [*sed eas ipse animus per experientiam passionum suarum sentiens*], hath committed unto the memory; or else which the memory hath of itself retained, being never committed unto it" (*Conf.* 10.14). Thus passions belong to the mind, and the notion of passion was never received through the body's senses. As the mind experiences passions, it stores the experience in its memory, which it can retain in some sense at a later time.

not in a state of grace are carnal and unruly.[44] Their affections inordinately desire the world and its impermanent happiness. Yet Augustine affirmed Christians' affections when well-ordered and directed toward God, as in 7.20, where Augustine spoke of drinking a wholesome affection in the Scriptures (*affectu quem salubrem inbiberam*) (also see *Conf.* 9.8).[45]

Affections, Passions, and the City of God The labor of fourteen years, Augustine's *City of God* stands among his most significant works, uniting strands of his political, theological, and philosophical thought in twenty-two books. The work refutes false religion and vindicates Christian teaching. In *De civitate Dei* Augustine presented two cities founded on two loves, self-love and love for God.[46] As it relates to Augustine's psychology, *City of God* shows the basic spirituality of passions, their relationship with the will, and the disordered condition in humans because of original sin. For Augustine, passions and affections were strong inclinations or aversions of the soul toward or from other things or persons.[47]

Later in *City of God* Augustine argued that no demon is able to make people blessed; this privilege is given to Christ alone. His argument turns first on a demonstration that all demons are evil. In so arguing, Augustine made several observations about the passions. Although spirit beings, demons are nevertheless driven by passions. If demons have passions, then passions are spiritual. Indeed, the Manichees' doctrine that the flesh itself was evil was too superficial.[48] Even if rational creatures, evil demons are still buffeted by "unreasonable passions," like "foolish men." Passions therefore cannot be restricted to "some inferior part of their spiritual nature." Rational demons are nevertheless "tossed with passion like the stormy sea." Even wise people surpass demons, having an "undisturbed mind" that resists "these perturbations." The demonic mind "is a sea tossed with tempest, having no rallying point of truth or virtue in their soul from which they can resist their turbulent and depraved emotions"[49] (*Civ.* 9.3). As Augustine saw it, even purely rational creatures like demons can experience passions. Augustine continued: "Among the philosophers there are two opinions about these mental emotions, which the Greeks call πάθη, while some of our own writers, as Cicero, call them perturbations, some affections, and some, to render the Greek word

44. *Conf.* 4.6, 4.14, 4.15, 5.7, 9.8.

45. Augustine also used different terms for love (*amor*, *dilectio*, and *caritas*) ambiguously. See Hannah Arendt, *Love and Saint Augustine*, eds. Joanna Vecchiarelli Scott and Judith Chelius Stark (Chicago, IL: University of Chicago Press, 1996), 38–39.

46. Agostino Trapé, "Saint Augustine," in *The Golden Age of Latin Patristic Literature from the Council of Nicea to the Council of Chalcedon*, vol. 4 of *Patrology*, ed. Angelo di Berardino, trans. Placid Solari (Westminster, MD: Christian Classics, 1991), 363.

47. "Although passion is often identified with emotion, the two are not the same." See *OCP*, s.v. "passion."

48. Dixon, *From Passions to Emotions*, 33.

49. *qua turbulentis et pravis affectionibus repugnatur.*

more accurately, passions."[50] Although Augustine did not draw here a distinction between affections and passions, it is important to observe that these are *animi motibus* or "motions of the soul."

Augustine turned to a discussion of the morality of the passions. Augustine explained that Platonic and Aristotelian philosophers permit these perturbations when controlled by reason, while Stoics reject them all. Citing Cicero, Augustine believed that the difference between the Stoics and Platonists was semantic; in both schemes, the mind, when resolved that righteousness is better than bodily pleasure or comfort, allows reason to overcome perturbations in the weaker parts of the soul (*Civ.* 9.4).[51] Scripture instructed Christians to yield their mind to God and moderate passions for righteousness. He continued, "In our ethics, we do not so much inquire whether a pious soul is angry, as why he is angry; not whether he is sad, but what is the cause of his sadness; not whether he fears, but what he fears" (*Civ.* 9.5). Christian ethics, according to Augustine, is not a matter of denying all motions of the soul, but of the will behind them. A just man may be rightly angry at moral evil or sad at suffering. Furthermore:

> [T]he holy angels feel no anger while they punish those whom the eternal law of God consigns to punishment, no fellow-feeling with misery while they relieve the miserable, no fear while they aid those who are in danger; and yet ordinary language ascribes to them also these mental emotions,[52] because, though they have none of our weakness, their acts resemble the actions to which these emotions move us;[53] and thus even God Himself is said in Scripture to be angry, and yet without any perturbation.[54] For this word is used of the effect of His vengeance, not of the disturbing mental affection.[55] (*Civ.* 9.5)

Augustine returned to the morality of passions and affections. The demons are subject to passions, and so how can they be wise? How can demons be good

50. "Perturbationes, quidam affectiones, vel affectus, quidam vero, sicut iste de graeco expressius, passiones vocant." The contrast between pre-modern and modern psychological terminology is noticeable when the same passage is read in a 1610 translation of the *City of God:* "Concerning motions of the minde which the Greekes call πάθη, and some of us, (with *Tully*) *Perturbations* others *Affects*, or affections, and some more expressly from the Greeke, *Passions.*" *St. Augustine, of the Citie of God: with the Learned Comments of Ioannes Lodovicus Vives* (n.p.: George Eld, 1610), 340–41.

51. James Wetzel contrasts Augustine's concepts with Stoic thought. "Augustine," in *OHRE*, 349–63.

52. "Et tamen istarum nomina passionum consuctudine locutionis humanae etiam in eos usurpentur."

53. "Propter quamdam operum similitudinem, non propter affectionum infirmitatem." A better translation would be, "because of the similarity of certain acts, not because of affections of infirmity."

54. *nec tamen ulla passione turbatur.*

55. *non illius turbuleatus affectus.*

mediators for humans if they (like humans) are so weak in their souls, which are the better part of men? Demons' minds are, as it were, "tossed by a hurricane of passions" (*Civ.* 9.6).[56] In Augustine's view, morality consists not in the absence of all affections and passions, but in a right will directed toward God.

In book fourteen, Augustine addressed original sin, the cause of evil human passions. Lust has justly become the punishment of Adam's first sin. Citing the "apostolic authority" of Scripture, Augustine said both lusty Epicureans and ascetic Stoics live after the flesh, since the fleshly lusts include more than the mere bodily sins:[57]

> For among the works of the flesh which he said were manifest and which he cited for condemnation, we find not only those which concern the pleasure of the flesh, as fornications, lasciviousness, drunkenness, revellings, but also those which, though they be remote from fleshly pleasure, reveal the vices of the soul. For who does not see that idolatries, witchcrafts, hatred, variance, emulations, wrath, strife, heresies, envying, and vices rather of the soul than of the flesh? (*Civ.* 14.2)

Therefore, both the body and the soul are the seat of vice. The body is not burdensome in itself, but in its corruption. The corruption of the flesh is the fount of some vice. Scripture overturns all ethics rooted in soul, body, or even both. The carnal man is the fleshly or animal man who lives for humanity and not for God (*Civ.* 14.4).[58] For Augustine, desire, fear, joy, sorrow could be moved either in the flesh or spirit (*Civ.* 14.5).[59] What matters is the will: "the character of the human will is of moment; because, if it is wrong, these motions of the soul will be wrong, but if it is right, they will be not merely blameless, but even praiseworthy. For the will is in them all; yea, none of them is anything else than will" (*Civ.* 14.6). The will is at the center of all affections and therefore all morality. Augustine asked: "For what are desire and joy but a volition of consent to the things we wish? And what are fear and sadness but a volition of aversion from the things we do not wish?

56. Augustine continued: "But if, . . . it must needs be that all men, so long as they are mortal, are also miserable, we must seek an intermediate who is not only man, but also God, that, by the interposition of His blessed mortality, He may bring men out of their mortal misery to a blessed immortality" (*Civ.* 9.15).

57. For a distinction between sense and concupiscence, see *Answer to the Pelagians III* 4.69.

58. Augustine said that even Platonists are "fleshly" in that they do not live for God (*Civ.* 14.5).

59. "Unde etiam, illis [i.e., the Platonists] fatentibus, non ex carne tantum afficitur anima, ut cupiat, metuat, laetetur, aegrescat; verum etiam ex se ipsa his potest motibus agitari. [Hence also, they themselves acknowledge, not only of the flesh is the soul moved to desire, fear, joy, sorrow, but also of itself can these movements often be agitated.]" (*Civ.* 14.5).

But when consent takes the form of seeking to possess the things we wish, this is called desire; and when consent takes the form of enjoying the things we wish, this is called joy." The will is central to these affections, "and generally in respect of all that we seek or shun, as a man's will is attracted or repelled, so it is changed and turned into these different affections" (*Civ.* 14.6).

Furthermore, loving God and one's neighbor is the demonstration of a good will, and those who live to God love good and hate evil. The right will has love directed to the proper end. Augustine said all four basic affections flow from love. Desire is actually love seeking to have the beloved; joy is having the beloved; fear is fleeing what is against the beloved; sadness is love recognizing that what opposes the beloved has overtaken it. Augustine's larger point is that evil love makes the affections evil and good love makes the affections good.[60]

Augustine upheld the philosophers' distinctions between movements of the soul, but qualified the discussion. He insisted that passions are necessary for human flourishing in this world, that affections can both be as evil as passions, and that true virtue lies in a renewed will toward God. He noted that Cicero calls good motions (in the wise) *constantiae* and bad motions (in fools) *passions*. Greeks call them εὐπαθεία and πάθη.[61] Augustine, after surveying both Scripture and secular works, found an abundance of equivocation; an evil or good man can be content; either can rejoice. "Good and bad men alike will, are cautious, and contented" (*Civ.* 14.8). Scripture approves desire, love, joy, fear, and sadness when they take place in those who love God. He added: "And because their love is rightly placed, all these affections of theirs are right" (*Civ.* 14.9). Citing several passages including Rom. 8:23, 1 Cor. 15:54, Mt. 24:12, and Mt. 10:22, Augustine showed that the Bible lauds affections both for oneself and toward others.

Augustine also distinguished affections and passions. He said:

> If these emotions and affections,[62] arising as they do from the love of what is good and from a holy charity, are to be called vices, then let us allow these emotions which are truly vices to pass under the name of virtues. But since these

60. *Civ.* 14.7. On the connection between the Platonists and Augustine's idea of love, see Wetzel, "Augustine," *OHRE*, 355; and Nussbaum, *Upheavals of Thought*, 527–56.

61. Hannah Arendt noted that Augustine, by affirming desire, differed from the Stoics who tried to suppress desire. The difference between *cupiditas* and *caritas* was one of will. All people seek happiness outside themselves—those marked by *cupiditas* are consumed with desire for this world and its happiness, while the will of those marked by *caritas* is turned toward God himself and the world to come. Love will be fulfilled eschatologically as "the manifest expression of man's attachment to God," where restless craving ends. While Arendt observed the conflict arising in Augustine's thought through his affirmation of finding happiness both outside oneself and inside oneself, her observations on the place of love and desire in his thought helpfully illustrate the distinction between affections and passions. Arendt, *Love and Saint Augustine*, 31.

62. *Hi motus, hi affectus.*

affections [*affectiones*], when they are exercised in a becoming way, follow the guidance of right reason, who will dare to say that they are diseases or vicious passions [*vitiosas passiones*]? (*Civ.* 14.9)[63]

Even Jesus knew such "perturbations."[64] Nevertheless, passions—even those conforming to God's will—are only for this life. They will not be found in eternal glory. Affections come from human weakness (though not so for Jesus). Yet people are helped by them, and the life with passions is better than the life without them. Those who attempt to live entirely free from passions are "blunted sensibilities both of mind and body."[65] Therefore, impassibility—taken in the sense of freedom from the passions that are "contrary to reason and disturb the mind"—is desirable, but unattainable in this life. "When there shall be no sin in a man, then there shall be this ἀπάθεια." In other words, in the eschaton Christians will be free from mind-disturbing passions such as fear and sadness, but love and joy will be part of that state of *apatheia* in blessedness. Because a good life is required for a blessed life, "a good life has all these affections right, a bad life has them wrong." Here Augustine added a warning for philosophers: "And if some, with a vanity monstrous in proportion to its rarity, have become enamoured of themselves because they can be stimulated and excited by no emotion, moved or bent by no affection,[66] such persons rather lose all humanity than obtain true tranquility" (*Civ.* 14.9).

But this leads to another question, from the parallel nature of original and eschatological blessedness: did Adam and Eve know fear or sadness before the Fall? Augustine said no. Adam and Eve trusted God and did not desire the illicit fruit. The first parents were not "agitated by . . . mental perturbations" (*Civ.* 14.10). God created the will good, but it fell through pride. In Adam's sin, human nature was altered, now "subject to the great corruption we feel and see, and to death, and is distracted and tossed with so many furious and contending emotions,[67] and

63. Elsewhere, Augustine was even more explicit as to the negative force of passions: "the Latin equivalent *passio* [to the Greek ἐν παθει ἐπιθυμιας], especially in the ecclesiastical use, is usually understood as a term of censure" (*Nupt.* 2.55). *The Anti-Pelagian Works of Saint Augustine, Bishop of Hippo*, trans. Peter Holmes (Edinburgh: T. & T. Clark, 1874).

64. Augustine cited 1 Jn 4:18 on the point that fear will not be present in the afterlife. In order to reconcile this with Ps. 19:9's statement that fear endures forever, Augustine said the latter "fear" "is not a fear deterring us from evil which may happen, but preserving us in the good which cannot be lost. For where the love of acquired good is unchangeable, there certainly the fear that avoids evil is, if I may say so, free from anxiety" (*Civ.* 14.9). Compare Clement of Alexandria, *Strom.* 6.9.

65. The *Confessions* in several places shows Augustine's negativity toward the bodily pain or *dolore* of the passions. For example, he referred to his "intolerable sorrow [*dolore intolerabili*]" (*Conf.* 9.3), lamented the Manichees' "vehement and bitter sorrow" (*Conf.* 9.4), confessed his impious pain at his mother's death (*Conf.* 9.7), and scrutinized his mind's memory of past pain (*Conf.* 10.14–15).

66. *nullo flectantur atque inclinatur affectu.* "By no emotion" is not in the original.

67. *perturbaretur et fluctuaret affectibus.*

is certainly far different from what it was before sin" (*Civ.* 14.12). Consequently, humanity's punishment is best seen in their unbridled disobedience and broken will. Now the embodied soul abuses its corporeal pleasure and pain by yielding to the passions.

Summary As Augustine saw it, passions and affections were fundamentally inclinations and aversions of the soul. Here Corrigan rightly observes that for Augustine "feeling was best understood in connection with volition."[68] Augustine maintained but did not stress a distinction between affections, as movements of the rational soul and will, and passions, those inclinations and aversions related to sense experience. Although Augustine believed the future human blessedness will include a state of simultaneous love and *apatheia*, he was more interested in stressing the sinfulness of affections (illustrated by the passion-driven demons) and the necessary role passions play in the present. Nevertheless, Augustine did not condone a life given over to passion. The soul's higher faculties should regulate passions, which is only possible when people give their will to God. Augustine regarded the effects of passions on the body to be painful perturbations. Affections are good when the will is directed toward God, but the movements of the unbeliever's soul are evil, whether that passion is toward bodily pleasure or in sinful acts of the mind. Augustine affirmed that passions are necessary for life, and, even in the future state of *apatheia*, love will remain.[69] All affections are connected with this life and its weakness, but in the age to come only love and joy will remain. Even so, fear and sorrow can be good affections in this life, provided they flow out of a love for God. Dixon helpfully observes that for modern readers Augustine appears inconsistent, sometimes dismissing "emotions" and at other times approving of them. He cautions: "But such a reading, employing the modern English-language category of the 'emotions,' cannot capture Augustine's intent since he knew no such category (despite the use of the term in modern translations of his work). We cannot expect to find in Augustine (or any other premodern author) any attitude towards the 'emotions.'"[70]

Augustine distinguished affections and passions in several ways. Sometimes the distinction is moral as Augustine divided vicious passions and virtuous affections. Other times, while employing the same word (*passiones* or *affectus*) the distinction was made with regard to the part of the soul moved, the difference consisting in

68. "Introduction," in *OHRE*, 4. In lumping Augustine's entire affective thought under emotions, Corrigan fails to appreciate the distinctions Augustine made between the soul's various movements.

69. Trapé says that Augustine boiled down the passions to a shared ground in "love," allowing for three occasions of them: "absence of passion, ordered passion which is subject to reason, and disordered passion or concupiscence." Agostino Trapé, "Saint Augustine," 414. The final of these three is evil. Trapé further posits from Augustine's *Unfinished Work in Answer to Julian* that the bishop "distinguished between passion and feeling." Compare *C. Jul. op. imp.* 4.29 and 4.69.

70. Dixon, "Revolting Passions," 300.

the state of the will. The movement of the higher soul toward God is good and honorable; sourced in divine love, all such movements are blessed. The movement of the lower soul toward temporal things is often evil and vicious; a distorted will is seen in confused and fleshly desires. The latter movements are perturbations lacking the serenity of affections. Spiritual persons tame their affections through grace, reorienting them toward God.

Despite some differences, this sampling of early and later patristic thought on human affectivity shows that Christian theologians shared some beliefs about the affections and passions of the soul. First, these movements are seated in the soul. Second, God (unlike humans) is not only impassible but also has an immutable will of love. Third, the passions of the soul are movements of the sense appetite toward the temporal world of sense and bodies. These passions are necessary for the present life, but are largely viewed from a disposition of suspicion and even scorn; in the life of the virtuous, passions will be strictly controlled by reason. Fourth, affections like love are entirely different from passions. The church fathers sometimes described such affections as lacking the disturbance of desire, but in full enjoyment of the possessed beloved object.

Medieval Thought

Developing the thought of patristic thinkers such as Nemesius of Emesa and Augustine, Christian theologians of the Middle Ages perpetuated the distinction between movements of the soul's higher and lower faculties. These authors continued to scrutinize the relationship of affections and passions both to the will and to virtue and vice.[71] This summary will begin with Anselm of Canterbury (1033–1109) and Bernard of Clairvaux (1091–1153), followed by a longer treatment of Thomas Aquinas (1225–74).[72] While medieval Christian explanations of human affectivity were not uniform, certain themes remained constant.

Anselm of Canterbury affirmed affections in the life of the devout. He described his book of prayers as an aid to "stir up the affections to prayer."[73] So he petitioned the Lord: "In my heart I know and worship you, love you and ask for your affection, not because of my imperfect desires, but because it belongs to your Son to make and to save, to redeem and bring back to life."[74] Anselm most clearly illustrates the difference between affections and passions in his doctrine of God. In the *Proslogium*, Anselm's *a priori* argument for God's existence, Anselm noted the paradox of God's simultaneous impassibility and compassion: "But how art

71. Knuuttila, *Emotions*, 177–95.

72. This is a severely limited sample of authors. Many others could be studied at great profit. See Knuuttila, *Emotions*, 177–255.

73. Anselm of Canterbury, *The Prayers and Meditations of St Anselm*, trans. Benedicta Ward (New York: Penguin Books, 1973), 90.

74. *The Prayers and Meditations of St Anselm*, 116.

thou compassionate and, at the same time, passionless?" God, Anselm concluded, is utterly different from humans:

> For, when thou beholdest us in our wretchedness, we experience the effect of compassion, but thou dost not experience the feeling [*sentis affectum*]. Therefore, thou art both compassionate because thou dost save the wretched, and spare those who sin against thee; and not compassionate, because thou art affected by no sympathy for wretchedness [*quia nulla miseriae compassione afficeris*].[75]

The compassion of the impassible God does not consist in an affection felt by God but in human enjoyment of the effect of his compassion. Anselm also affirmed without qualification the love that Father and the Son share for each other in the Holy Spirit. Anselm said that he searched for God through his "sinful senses" in vain, but found true happiness in that source of all that is: "And now, my soul, arouse and lift up all thy understanding, and conceive, so far as thou canst, of what character and how great is that good. . . . If there are many great delights in delectable things, what and how great is the delight in him who has made these delectable things."[76] He continued:

> Why, then, dost thou wander abroad, slight man, in thy search for the goods of thy soul and thy body? Love the one good in which are all goods, and it sufficeth. Desire the simple good which is every good and it is enough. For, what dost thou love, my flesh? What dost thou desire, my soul? There, there is whatever ye love, whatever ye desire.[77]

Bernard of Clairvaux not only emphasized affection for God, but the distinction between intellect and affections. Echoing Augustine's fourfold division of passions of distress, joy, fear, and desire, Bernard sometimes equated the affections with the will, which in turn he distinguished from lower movements of the soul.[78]

In *On Loving God*, Bernard's discussion moved through four degrees of love by which one ascends to pure love for God. The first and most carnal love is the love humans have for themselves for their own sake. Though natural, this love

75. *Proslogium* 8, in Anselm of Canterbury, *St. Anselm: Basic Writings*, trans. S. N. Deane (LaSalle, IL: Open Court, 1962), 59–60; *Proslogion seu Alloquium de Dei existentia* (*PL* 158:231).

76. Ibid., 17–18; 24. On God's compassion, see ibid., 10. On Trinitarian love, see ibid., 23.

77. Ibid., 25.

78. Knuuttila, *Emotions*, 195–99. Of Song 2:6, Bernard said, "In this way the Bridegroom's left hand is rightly under the bride's head, so that, as she leans back, her head is supported on it, meaning the intention of her mind, lest bending down it should be enticed by carnal and worldly desires." *On Loving God*, 4.13. All citations of *On Loving God* come from Bernard of Clairvaux, *Treatises II*, vol. 5 of *The Works of Bernard of Clairvaux*, trans. Robert Walton, Cistercian Fathers Series 13 (Washington, DC: Consortium Press, 1974). On Bernard's use of *affections* in hermeneutics, see Knuuttila, *Emotions*, 198.

should always be moderate.[79] The second degree is love of God for one's own benefit. Those loving in this way will find themselves unable to love God rightly, which leads them to understand that love for God is possible only through God's grace. The regular pursuit of God results in divine love's third degree: loving God for God's own sake. Here Christians "taste and discover how sweet the Lord is."[80] Such love for God is free, pure, and chaste. This love for God adores God not for his benefits, but for who God is in himself. Loving God for God's own sake leads to the fourth degree of love, the climax of the loves, where a person loves self for God's own sake.[81] The fourth degree of love is rare, yet God intended all of creation to experience it. The apex of love results in divine grace replacing the human will with God's will. Such a will is an "affection" that is "sweet and pleasant."[82]

Bernard contrasted love for God with the passions. According to Bernard, love for Jesus Christ destroyed "the false attractiveness of the carnal life."[83] The Scriptures, Bernard noted, compare those who delight in earthly things and refuse to regulate appetite to the beasts.[84] Because of sin, human reason is deceived, memory is confused, and the will was "torn and troubled by passion."[85] Bernard used the distinction between passions and affections to illustrate the difference between loving Christ with a lower, fleshly love (though still spiritually helpful), and loving Christ with a higher, spiritual love. There are three grades of love: carnal love, rational love, and spiritual love.[86] Christians must not direct "carnal love" to the "essentially carnal" world.[87] The disciples "loved [Jesus] in a carnal way, not

79. *On Loving God*, 8.23–5. Bernard explained that this love becomes social as a person learns to moderate his desires and out of his denial share with others. Then, in a statement that sounds remarkably similar to Jonathan Edwards in *The Nature of True Virtue*, he added, "Nevertheless, in order to love one's neighbor with perfect justice, one must have regard to God." Ibid., 8.25.

80. *On Loving God*, 9.26.

81. Ibid.

82. Ibid., 10.29.

83. Bernard of Clairvaux, "Of the Three Ways in Which We Love God (Sermon XX on the Song of Songs)," in *Late Medieval Mysticism*, ed. Ray C. Petry, LCC 8 (Philadelphia: Westminster Press, 1957), 69.

84. Bernard of Clairvaux, *Sermons on the Canticles*, in *The Life and Works of Saint Bernard*, ed. Dom John Mabillon, trans. Samuel J. Eales (London: John Hodges, 1896), 4:505. Compare ibid., 4:18 and 497.

85. Bernard of Clairvaux, "Fragments from a Fragment by St. Bernard," in *Saint Bernard on the Love of God*, trans. Marianne Caroline and Coventry Patmore (London: C. Kegan Paul, 1881), 70–71.

86. Thus Bernard explained the love of "heart, soul, and strength" in Deut. 6:5: "It seems to me, if no other sense occurs to you better to give to that threefold distinction, that the love of the heart answers to the earnestness of affection; the love of the soul, to the purpose or judgment of the reason; the love of the strength, to the constancy and vigor of the mind." Bernard of Clairvaux, "Three Ways," 69.

87. "Three Ways," 72.

reasonably," and Jesus rebuked them for it in Jn 14:28. Nevertheless, a carnal love for Christ is good, but it ought to lead to higher love for Christ. The heart goes after Christ in a carnal way when "the heart of a man is affected toward Christ according to the flesh."[88] Bernard believed this to be a reason for the incarnation: "To draw, in the first place, to the salutary love of his sacred flesh all the affections of carnal men who were unable to love otherwise than in a carnal manner, and so by degrees to draw them to a pure and spiritual affection."[89] A fleshly love for Christ is nevertheless able to draw persons from carnal love of the world. Higher love, "that other affection," does not love the "Word" as flesh, but "the Word as wisdom, as righteousness, as truth, as holiness, goodness, virtue, and all other perfections of whatever kind."[90] Higher love is "rational," but when perfected it becomes "spiritual."[91] Comparing carnal and spiritual love, he asked: "If you compare these two types of affection, does it not appear to you that the second is plainly the superior? And that in comparison with it the former is in a manner carnal?"[92]

Thomas Aquinas

For most his life, Thomas Aquinas (1225–74) divided his time between the University of Paris and the papal courts. His writings, including the monumental works *Summa Theologiae* and *Summa Contra Gentiles*, would influence all subsequent theology. What follows is a summary of his understanding of human passions. Especially in the *Summa Theologiae*, Thomas discussed the affectivity of the human soul.[93] Thomas Aquinas is usually classified in the intellectualist tradition, whose adherents taught that the intellect has priority over the will.[94]

88. Ibid., 70–71.

89. Ibid., 71.

90. Ibid. Bernard's emphasis on the rationality of the higher love with his repetition of the word *verbum* is more clearly seen in the original Latin than in Petry's English translation: "illius . . . amoris respectu, quo non tam Verbum caro jam sapit, quam Verbum sapientia, Verbum justitia, Verbum veritas, Verbum sanctitas, pietas, virtus." Bernard of Clairvaux, *Sermones in Cantica* (*PL* 183:871).

91. Ibid., 73.

92. Ibid., 72–73.

93. Thomas Gilby, introduction to *St. Thomas Aquinas: Philosophical Texts*, by Thomas Aquinas (New York: Oxford University Press, 1960), xiii–xxii; Mark W. Elliott, "Thomas Aquinas," in *Shapers of Christian Orthodoxy*, ed. Bradley G. Green (Downers Grove, IL: IVP, 2010), 341–88; Gerald McDermott, *Great Theologians*, 63–78; Anton C. Pegis, introduction to *Introduction to Saint Thomas Aquinas*, by Thomas Aquinas (New York: The Modern Library, 1948), xi–xiii. Citations of the *Summa Theologiae* will begin with *ST* with following references: part, question, and article (e.g., *ST* 1a 75.3). If referencing a reply to an objection, "ad" with the appropriate number will be supplied (e.g., *ST* 1a 75.3 ad 3). Unless otherwise noted, the English edition cited is Thomas Aquinas, *The Treatise on Human Nature: Summa Theologiae 1a, 75–89*, ed. Robert Pasnau (Indianapolis, IN: Hacket, 2002).

94. Anri Morimoto compares Jonathan Edwards's soteriology to Thomas Aquinas with the express hope that his readers "will find in Edwards the potential for . . . mutual

The Soul and Its Appetites Like the Christian teachers who preceded him, Aquinas's understanding of human affections arose from his understanding of the soul. He believed the soul, as the substantial form of human beings, exists in itself, while together the immaterial soul and the material body comprise the human person (*ST* 1a 75.2 ad 2; 75.4).[95] Although the soul has different capacities, every individual has only one soul (*ST* 1a 76.3).[96] Aquinas also maintained the distinction between the soul's sensitive and intellective capacities.[97] The soul's capacities are ordered by the degree of "pure soul" involved (*ST* 1a 77.4). The abilities (like mind and will) that do not exercise an organ of the body are properties of the soul, while the abilities that require both soul and body are properties of both soul and body (*ST* 1a 77.5). Upon this understanding of the soul Thomas explained human affectivity.[98]

The capacities of the soul with which the theologian was concerned were the intellective and appetitive, for "it is here that the virtues are found" (*ST* 1a 78). Aquinas understood appetite to correspond to the capacity operating it.[99] The intellective capacity, as agent or active, "actualizes intelligible things by means of abstraction" (*ST* 1a 79.3 ad 3). The intellect (memory, reason, and intelligence) receives the particulars from the senses and abstracts them into real knowledge (*ST* 1a 79.7, 79.8, 79.10).[100]

enrichment" across theological boundaries. *Jonathan Edwards and the Catholic Vision of Salvation* (University Park, PA: Pennsylvania State University Press, 1995), 2.

95. Dixon explains, "Aquinas steered a middle path between a Platonic belief in the natural immortality of the soul and a radical Aristotelian commitment to the impossibility of a disembodied form (or soul)." Dixon, *From Passions to Emotions*, 38.

96. Aquinas defined "capacity" as "the proximate principle of an operation belonging to the soul" (*ST* 1a 78.4).

97. *ST* 1a 75.3 ad 3. The five kinds of capacities of the soul are vegetative, sensory, appetitive, locomotive, and intellective (*ST* 1a 75.5). See Pasnau's commentary on this division in *Human Nature*, 272.

98. Joseph P. Wawrykow, *The SCM Press A–Z of Thomas Aquinas* (London: SCM Press, 2005), 4–8.

99. Aquinas defined "natural appetite" as "the inclination of any given thing, of its own nature, for something. Thus any capacity desires, by natural appetite that which is agreeable to it" (*ST* 1a 78.2 ad 3).On Aquinas's distinction between the appetites, see Robert Miner, *Thomas Aquinas on the Passions: A Study of* Summa Theologiae *1a2ae 22–48* (Cambridge: Cambridge University Press, 2009), 19–21.

100. See Miner, *Aquinas on Passions*, 21–25. On Thomas's statement that the passions are morally neutral, see Michael R. Miller, "Aquinas on the Passion of Despair," *New Blackfriars* 93 (2012): 387–96.

Cognition and Appetite in the Intellect and Senses Aquinas distinguished appetite from apprehension. Appetite is a distinct capacity of the soul, separate from cognition (*ST* 1a 80.1). Appetite is inclination.[101] Every created thing has some inclination determined by its form. "The senses, for example, receive the species of all sensible things, and the intellect the species of all intelligible things" (*ST* 1a 80.1). Appetite not only differs from intellect, but itself may be further divided into sensory and intellective appetite. For Aquinas, as the ability to perceive through sense and through intellect was clearly different, so the sensitive and intellective appetites were different (*ST* 1a 80.2). Apprehension, being completed at the moment it happens, is not a movement like appetite (*ST* 1a 81.1).[102]

Sensuality, or sense appetite, is the appetite for sense objects. The sense appetite has both irascible and concupiscible capacities. The concupiscent capacity is when the soul moves toward sense good or away from sense evil. On the other hand, the irascible capacity resists whatever prevents sense good or inflicts harm (*ST* 1a 81.2).[103] Both the concupiscible and irascible capacities can obey "the higher part containing intellect (or reason) and will" (*ST* 1a 81.3). For example, the obedience of these appetites to reason is seen when people rationally quiet themselves from fear. In brute animals, sense appetite necessarily demands the response—for example, a sheep will de facto flee from the wolf. A human, on the other hand, waits for the will to command. The sense appetite only moves a person when the will consents (*ST* 1a 81.3). The soul has a despotic rule over the body. Reason has a political rule over sense, because the sensory appetite has something of its own rule and can disobey reason's command.[104]

The soul has a necessary appetite for happiness, despite the different notions of how happiness comes.[105] The will, which is found in both God and human beings, is the intellectual appetite (*ST* 1a 19.1). In an absolute sense the will is inferior to intellect, for the objects of intellect (the *nature* of what is good for appetite)

101. Pasnau observes, "[T]he use of 'appetite' here is technical and is very far from the normal English usage." *Human Nature*, 299.

102. See Miner, *Thomas Aquinas on the Passions*, 13–21.

103. Craig A. Boyd, "Aquinas on Sanctifying the Affections," in *The Spirit, the Affections*, 144–47.

104. *ST* 1a81.3 ad 2. Compare Thomas Aquinas, *On Evil*, trans. Richard Regan, ed. Brian Davies (New York: Oxford University Press, 2003), 3.9 (170–71). References to *On Evil* will provide the question and article, followed by the page number in the OUP edition.

105. *ST* 1a82.1. Pasnau, *Human Nature*, 311–12. Miner explains, "Appetite for goods that are either pleasant or useful does not, according to Aquinas, require the possession of general concepts of pleasure and utility. On the contrary, non-rational animals lack these concepts altogether. They do not know 'what pleasure is.' But their appetites conform to a pattern; they are drawn *only* to things perceived as pleasant or useful." Irrational beings cannot desire good distinct from pleasure or utility. Miner, *Aquinas on Passions*, 24.

excels that of the objects of will (what is good for appetite). Relatively, on the other hand, the will is superior to the intellect when the will is inclined toward things above the soul. "Thus the love of God is better than the cognition of God, whereas the cognition of corporeal things is better than the love of such things" (*ST* 1a 82.3).

Affections and Passions Distinguishing the intellectual appetite from the sensory appetite, Aquinas argued, following his interpretation of Nemesius of Emesa, that the irascible and concupiscible should not be considered parts of the will.[106] The sensory appetite has a certain good in view, and so the concupiscible and irascible capacities correspond to the nature of sense good or evil. The intellectual appetite is drawn to good alone under a certain perception of the good, and therefore such distinctions that apply to the sensory appetite are unnecessary.[107] Aquinas distinguished such movements from passions, explaining that they are sometimes considered affections:

> Love, concupiscence, and the like are taken in two ways. Sometimes they are taken as a sort of passion, the sort that appears along with a certain arousal of the spirit. . . . Taken this way, which is how they are generally taken, they are found solely in the sensory appetite. Taken another way, they signify a simple affect [*Alio modo significant simplicem affectum*], without any passion or arousal of the spirit. Taken this way, they are acts of the will, and also attributed to the angels and to God. But when so taken, they do not pertain to different capacities, but to just one capacity, which is called the will. (*ST* 1a 82.5 ad 1)[108]

The will's affections are without passion and drawn to good. Aquinas earlier defined passions as the "actions of sensory appetite, insofar as they involved an associated

106. Aquinas actually cites Nemesius of Emesa as Gregory of Nyssa, a common error. See *ST* 1a 82.4, and Pasnau, *Human Nature*, 124 n24.

107. *ST* 1a82.5. See Pasnau, *Human Nature*, 316–17.

108. Thomae Aquinatis, *Summa Theologica Editio Altera Romana ad Ementatiores Editiones Impressa et Noviter Accuratissime Recognita: Pars Prima* (Rome: Ex Typographia Forzani, 1894). In *Summa Contra Gentiles*, Thomas wrote, "There are no affections associated with passions in God. . . . For there is no passion associated with an intellectual affection, but only with a sensory one . . . Now there can be no affection of the latter sort in God. . . . Thus, there is no affection associated with passion in God." *ST* I 89, cited in Shawn D. Floyd, "Aquinas on Emotions: A Response to Some Recent Interpretations," *History of Philosophy Quarterly* 15 (1998): 166. See Dixon, *From Passions to Emotions*, 45–47; Daniel Westberg, "Emotion and God: A Reply to Marcel Sarot," *The Thomist* 60 (1996): 118; and Boyd, "Aquinas on Sanctifying the Affections," 144.

bodily transformation."[109] Thomas further explained that the will, when opposed to evil, "can be called irascible," but in a different sense from "passionate impulse." The will's capacity for irascibility occurs "through judgment." Some even regard it concupiscible in its inclination toward good. Charity and hope, theological virtues separate from sensory appetite, are properly seated in the will (*ST* 1a 82.5 ad 2; compare *ST* 1a 19.1).[110]

Following Aristotle, Aquinas distinguished between activity and passivity. On highest end of scale of being is God, the prime mover of activity. For an object to be passive meant that it could change and even require further improvement. Humans are both active and passive beings. The goal for human beings was then "rest in the eternal unmoved activity of God."[111] For one to be acted upon implied imperfection—some other thing was necessary for fulfillment. Creatures nearest God are most perfect, and have the least amount of potency in them, and therefore less passion (*ST* 1a2ae 22.2 ad 1).[112]

Aquinas drew a distinction between the will and passions.[113] Passions, as connected with sensuality, always and necessarily change the body (*ST* 1a2ae 22.2).[114] Even so, passions should not be identified with movements of the body.[115] The bodily change happens as the sensory appetite functions, which presents the crucial difference between affections and passions. No physical operation is connected to the intellectual appetite because it is not a faculty of the physical body. Passions belong to the sensitive appetite, not the intellectual (*ST* 1a2ae 22.3). Therefore the passions, in contrast with the will (i.e., the intellectual appetite), are seated in the sense appetite. As Miner observes, Aquinas "uses *affectiones* (and, less frequently, *affectus*) for acts that may or may not belong to the sensitive appetite."[116] "Hence," Aquinas explained, "the phrase *a passion for the things of God* means here a passionate desire for the things of God, and union with them through love; but this involves no physiological modification" (*ST* 1a2ae 22.3 ad 1). From this it follows that spirit beings like God and the

109. *ST* 1a 20.1 ad 1, cited in Pasnau, *Human Nature*, 317. See Miner, *Aquinas on Passions*, 29–35.

110. According to Boyd, Aquinas taught that the Holy Spirit must move the human soul to have the love God requires. "Aquinas on Sanctifying the Affections," 154–57.

111. Dixon, *From Passions to Emotions*, 36.

112. Unless otherwise noted, all citations of *ST* 1a2ae 22–30 are from Thomas Aquinas, *The Emotions*, ed. Eric d'Arcy.

113. Knuuttila, *Emotions*, 239–55.

114. Aquinas explained, "Thus, in defining the various [movements] of the sensory [appetite], one mentions the modification of the relevant bodily organ: anger, for instance, is said to be *the overheating of the blood around the heart*" (*ST* 1a2ae 22.2).

115. Miner, *Aquinas on Passions*, 44. Miner argues that for Aquinas events of the soul produced "distinct bodily events," but that any "distinction is not separation." Ibid., 45.

116. Miner, *Aquinas on Passions*, 35.

angels have no passions *per se*. "When love, joy, and the like, are attributed to God or the angels or man's intellectual orexis [*appetitum*], they refer simply to acts of will which produce indeed the same sort of result as does action prompted by emotion, but not in fact accompanied by emotion [*passione*]" (*ST* 1a2ae 22.3 ad 3).[117] The two appetites have different formal objects, and so the passions themselves are different species (*ST* 1a2ae 22.4). As the sensory appetite is connected to the will, passions are voluntary and moral. This vital distinction between will and passion runs through Aquinas's discussion of the passions of soul.

Citing Augustine, Aquinas believed that the morality of a passion depends upon the condition of the will of its subject (*ST* 1a2ae 24). When they function as "a true servant of reason," passions enhance the goodness of an act. Aquinas explained: "As the Psalmist says, *My heart and my flesh cry out for the living God:* the word 'heart' suggesting the intellectual orexis [*appetitu intellctivo*], and the word 'flesh' the sensory" (*ST* 1a2ae 24.3). Because Thomas considered the will to be above the passions, he said the will ought to move the sense appetite, not the other way around. When a passion does accompany an act of the will, it may do so as an "overflow," where "the higher part of the soul is so strongly bent upon some object that the lower part follows it." This gives the act a greater moral quality (*ST* 1a2ae 24.3 ad 1). Similarly, one might deliberately allow a passion to accompany an act of will. Such circumstances are impossible for spiritual beings like God or the angels (*ST* 1a2ae 24.3 ad 2).[118] Likewise, Aquinas preferred *dilectio*, which is love with a prior element of choice, to *amor*, a more general love, simply because the former is seated in the intellectual appetite (*ST* 1a2ae 26.3).

117. On this point, Aquinas includes a citation of Augustine's *City of God* 9.5. Compare *ST* 1a 20.1.

118. Aquinas said some passions are only metaphorically attributed to God: "When certain human passions are predicated of the Godhead metaphorically, this is done because of a likeness in the effect. . . . There is, however, this difference between will and anger, that anger is never attributed to God properly, since in its primary meaning it includes passion; whereas will is attributed to Him properly. Therefore in God there are distinguished will in its proper sense, and will as attributed to Him by metaphor. Will in its proper sense is called the will of good pleasure" (*ST* 1a 19.11). Thomas Aquinas, *The Summa Theologica of St. Thomas Aquinas*, 2d ed., trans. Fathers of the English Dominican Province (1920), under "Question 19. The Will of God," http://newadvent.org/summa/1019.htm#article11 (accessed December 4, 2017).

The Formal and Material Aspects of Passions In addition to his distinction between affections and passions, Aquinas also distinguished the formal and material aspects of passions. In context, he said a passion can possibly inflict harm upon the soul (*ST* 1a2ae 28.5). Formally considered, as connected with appetite, a passion may benefit or harm the individual, depending upon its suitability. Inappropriate loves harm the soul. A love for God benefits above all; love for sin harms above all. But these comments pertain specifically to the formal aspect of the passions, as connected with appetite. "The material aspect," on the other hand, "is the physiological modification produced by the emotion of love [*in passione amoris*], and this may be harmful when it is excessive" (*ST* 1a2ae 28.5). Not only can passions inflict physical harm, but they may also restrict reason and encourage evil acts.[119] Thomas also said that these two aspects are mutually proportioned so that the bodily transformation resembles the nature of the movement of the appetitive.[120]

The Divine Appetite Finally, Aquinas's teachings on the will of God illustrate his teachings on human affectivity. God has a will (intellectual appetite), even though God is not subject to the sensory appetite (*ST* 1a 19.1; 19.11). God has an appetite, not in the sense that anything actualizes a potency in God whereby he completes his being, but in a secondary sense, in that he delights in or is inclined toward what is already his.[121] Thomas also said that love, a regard for good universally, exists in God, as love is the first principle of all movements of appetite (*ST* 1a 20.1).[122] Acts of the sensory appetite, having with them bodily change, are passions, but the will's acts are not so designated. Love, joy, and delight may be called passions if they follow the sensory appetite or if they act upon the mover to move toward a more desirable state, but they are not passions if they are connected with the intellectual appetite.[123]

Knuuttila, who is himself inclined to refer to Aquinas's *passiones* as *emotions*, acknowledges, "Even though Aquinas refers to feelings, this is not a central subject in his theory of emotions. Following thirteenth-century philosophical approaches, he analyses emotions as motive acts and classifies them from the point of view of

119. Aquinas, *On Evil*, 3.9 (171).

120. *ST* 1a2ae 44.1. For a helpful discussion of Aquinas's understanding of passions as motions, see Miner, *Aquinas on Passions*, 38–46. Likewise, while noting that sorrow is the most harmful passion, Thomas emphasized the proportioned relationship between the formal and material aspects of the soul's passions. Compare *ST* 1a 20.1 ad 2. Also see Knuuttila, *Emotions*, 239–42.

121. Miner, *Aquinas on Passions*, 16.

122. Compare *ST* 1a2ae 25.2.

123. See Diana Cates, *Aquinas on the Emotions: A Religious-Ethical Inquiry* (Washington, DC: Georgetown University Press, 2009), 194–201. Compare *ST* 1a2ae 26.3 ad 3.

behavioral changes."[124] Diana Cates correctly shows that Aquinas's idea of sensory appetite is not "pure body," but includes apprehension.[125] Indeed, Aquinas saw sensory apprehension and appetite to be powers of the human *soul*. Still, Cates impedes a correct understanding of Aquinas as she renders the word *passiones* as *emotions* throughout her work. The same could be said for Eric D'Arcy's translation of *ST* 1a2ae 22–30. Thomas Dixon and Robert Miner disapprove, the latter observing that "the practice of translating *passiones* by 'emotions,' rather than 'passions,' is misleading, since it necessarily obscures the question about the relation between passions and emotions."[126] For Aquinas, passions were functions of the sensory appetite and distinct from movements of intellectual appetite. The modern category of emotions makes no such distinction and is much broader than acts of inclination or aversion.

Summary

Although medieval Christian explanations of human affectivity differed from one another, certain themes remained constant. Although Thomas's predecessors were arguably more Platonic, he and they still held much in common. Fundamentally, affections and passions were discussed as rooted in appetite rather than cognition. Medieval Christians also distinguished the soul's higher movements from its lower and often baser (but necessary) counterparts. These authors viewed human affectivity strictly as inclination and aversion. The higher affection of love is praiseworthy, but the passions are to be moderated.

Dixon rightly observes that Augustine and Aquinas agreed on the distinction between the higher, rational soul and the lower, sensitive soul and on the conflict between the higher and lower movements of the soul.[127] The distinction is evident in all the theologians surveyed to this point, both patristic and medieval. Moreover, all four medieval scholars represented here understand affections and passions to be movements of the soul and under the control of human beings—although not all people do control them. These authors maintained the distinction between the affections of the higher, rational soul and the passions of the lower, sensitive

124. *Emotions*, 252. Despite his learned treatment of Aquinas, Knuuttila spends little time treating the significance of the intellectual appetite in Aquinas's account of human psychology. As was discussed above, he takes passions to be the same as emotions. In my opinion Knuuttila should have acknowledged the discontinuity between emotions and passions as well as the difference between intellectual and sensory appetite in Aquinas.

125. Cates, *Aquinas on the Emotions*, 130–31. Cates argues against Shawn Floyd, who believes that Aquinas's passions and modern emotions should not be equated because modern emotions are cognitive to some degree, while Aquinas's passions were completely bodily. Floyd, "Aquinas on Emotions," 161–75.

126. Miner, *Aquinas on Passions*, 4; Dixon, *From Passions to Emotions*, 35–48.

127. Dixon, *From Passions to Emotions*, 35.

soul (although they did not always apply the terms consistently). In fact, Aquinas described these distinctions with great specificity. He noted that passions have a corresponding material response in the body, but he seated passion itself in the sensitive soul. All these thinkers viewed the passions with suspicion, rebuking people who allowed themselves to be controlled by them and insisting passions be regulated by reason. At the same time, the authors emphasized love for God to the highest possible degree.

Chapter 3

HUMAN AFFECTIONS IN POST-MEDIEVAL THOUGHT

Come, Holy Spirit, heavenly Dove,
With all Thy quickening powers,
Kindle a flame of sacred love
In these cold hearts of ours.

— Isaac Watts

Human affections were important in the thought of Reformation, Puritan, and early Enlightenment figures as well. Though they modified older views, key ideas from traditional Christian thought were perpetuated, including a distinction between the different appetites of the soul and the notion that human affectivity is defined by inclination and aversion. Although the Reformers and their followers did not stress a distinction between the quality of the movements of the higher and lower appetites, they did emphasize the heart as the seat of all affections. This emphasis continued through the Reformation up to the late Puritan period and into early Enlightenment moral philosophy.

Reformation Figures

Many scholars today rightly understand that the Renaissance and Reformation theology produced profound changes that fractured the West, toward individualism and autonomy. Yet the Reformers saw their work to be in the stream of medieval piety. Indeed, "none of the Reformers ever intended to create a new world-view."[1]

1. Quentin Faulkner, *Wiser than Despair: The Evolution of Ideas in the Relationship of Music and the Christian Church*, Contributions to the Study of Music and Dance 40 (Westport, CT: Greenwood Press, 1996), 136. Roland H Bainton has argued, "At the start Luther envisaged no reform other than that of theological education with the stress on the Bible rather than on the decretals and the scholastics." *Here I Stand: A Life of Martin Luther* (New York: Mentor, 1950), 51. Also see John Herman Randall, Jr., *The Making of the Modern Mind: A Survey of the Intellectual Background of the Present Age*, rev. ed. (Cambridge, MA: Houghton Mifflin, 1954), 142–71; Rudolph W. Heinze, *Reform and Conflict: From the*

This brief treatment hopes to show that in two prominent Reformers, while their "Reformation" inevitably modified earlier views, they nevertheless maintained great continuity with traditional Christian understandings of human affectivity.

Philipp Melanchthon

The *Loci Communes Theologici* of Philipp Melanchthon (1497–1560), the first theological system of the Reformation, influenced the thought of John Calvin (1509–64) on the affections.[2] Appointed Wittenberg's first Greek professor at the age of twenty-one, he was already maligning the Scholastics in favor of humanism. Only three years later he published his *Loci*, what he described as "a common outline of the topics that you can pursue in your study of Scripture."[3] Therein, the affections become a special point of emphasis, especially in Melanchthon's discussion of sin and the will. He lauds faith as an affection of the heart.

In his discussion of will Melanchthon sought simplicity and submission to Scripture. He thought that the Bible's teaching on the will had been distorted by attempts to placate human philosophy. Philosophers had added too many divisions into their concepts of human nature. For Melanchthon, a cognitive and an appetitive faculty suffice. Within the appetitive faculty the distance between will, affection, and appetite is in some ways slight: "[t]he faculty from which the affections [*affectus*] arise is that by which we either turn away from or pursue the things known, and this faculty is sometimes called 'will' (*voluntas*), sometimes

Medieval World to the Wars of Religion, A.D. 1350–1648, Baker History of the Church 4 (Grand Rapids, MI: Baker Books, 2005), 96–97; and Owen Chadwick, *The Reformation* (Grand Rapids, MI: Wm. B. Eerdmans, 1964), 40–75.

2. Bernd Wannenwetsch's summary of Martin Luther's theology of affections shows that Melanchthon well represents Luther's own views (i.e., "präziser Interpret Luthers"). He continues, "Der Zusammenhang von Affekt und Gebot, den wir in Luthers exegetischen und katechetischen Schriften nachgezeichnet haben, ist von Melanchthon im zweiten und dritten Kapitel der *Loci Communes* 1521 in großer analytischer Klarheit systematisiert worden." "Affekt und Gebot. Zur ethischen Bedeutung der Leidenschaften im Licht der Theologie Luthers and Melanchthon," in *Passion, Affekt und Leidenschaft in der Frühen Neuzeit*, 2 vols., Johann Anselm Steiger, ed. (Wiesbaden, Germany: Harrassowitz Verlag, 2005), 1:213. Similarly, Simeon Zahl observes, "Luther's interest in the affections, especially in the 1519–25 period, is deeply and complexly interwoven with Melanchthon's." "The Bondage of the Affections: Willing, Feeling, and Desiring in Luther's Theology, 1513–1525," in *The Spirit, the Affections*, 200 n9.

3. Melanchthon, *Loci Communes Theologici*, in *Melanchthon and Bucer*, 70. Unless otherwise noted, all subsequent English citations of Melanchthon's *Loci* will come from Pauck's edition. The source for Latin citations will be Philipp Melanchthons, *Die Loci Communes*, ed. D. Th. Kolde (Erlangen: George Böhme, 1890). On Melanchthon and the *Loci*, see Wilhelm Pauck, "Editor's Introduction," in *Melanchthon and Bucer*, LCC 19 (Philadelphia: Westminster Press, 1969), 3–17.

'affection,' and sometimes 'appetite.'"[4] Though Melanchthon seemed to distinguish higher and lower appetites, his doctrine of the will emphasized the higher, because he believed that affections arose from it. The will or "heart" is the "fount" of affections, not only of the sensitive appetite, but also of spiritual movements like love, hate, and blasphemy.[5]

For Melanchthon, the will and affections are by nature wholly corrupt and confused. The heart represents the will and affections, and herein sin resides. Since the heart is depraved, the affections are outside a person's power. "[T]he Schools are in error when they imagine that the will (*voluntas*) by its very nature opposes the affections, or that it is able to lay an affection aside whenever the intellect so advises or warns."[6] Philipp judged the Scholastic doctrine that a person can will something despite the opposition of affections to be self-contradictory.[7] External acts without purity of heart are evil; vicious affections maligned humanity's best good works.[8] Melanchthon stressed this conflict between internal inclinations and external acts. When the heart's affections oppose external acts, it is mere "simulation and deceit." The natural person, loving only what pleases self, is unable to love God. Melanchthon described the human plight frankly: "you do not love God no matter how good he is, unless you think that he is useful for your plans and for yourself."[9] Depravity engulfs the whole person. Through an inordinate devotion to philosophy the Scholastics wrongly restricted the extent of sinful corruption to the sensory appetite.[10] Melanchthon understood the "natural man" to entirely depraved and under "natural affections and emotions [*motibus obnoxius*]."[11]

4. Ibid., 23. Melanchthon explained, "I wanted to warn about this distinction which the Scholastics make lest they deceive anyone. They distinguish between the 'appetite of the intellect' and the 'sensitive appetite' (the appetite related to the senses), and they attribute depraved affections to the appetite of the senses, whereas they maintain that the appetite of the intellect is free of any defect (*vitium*)." Ibid., 48.

5. Ibid., 27, 47. See Michael B. Aune, "'A Heart Moved': Philip Melanchthon's Forgotten Truth About Worship," *Lutheran Quarterly* 12 (1998): 395–418; and Simeon Zahl, "Bondage," in *The Spirit, The Affections*, 186. Zahl also shows how Luther likewise ties affections to the will. Ibid., 184–85 and 188–89.

6. Melanchthon, *Loci*, 27.

7. Ibid., 28. In his own words, Melanchthon said, "Thus, although we are by nature godless and downright despisers of God, . . . those fellows teach that the will (*voluntas*) can cause nature to love God."

8. Ibid., 29–30.

9. Ibid., 41. Graham Ward contrasts Melanchthon's thought with Augustine's. See Graham Ward, *How the Light Gets In: Ethical Life I* (New York: Oxford University Press, 2016), 97–98. Ward defines *affectus* as "a broad term covering emotions, moods, dispositions, and attitudes"; it "governs all human thinking and acting." Ibid., 97.

10. Melanchthon, *Loci*, 46. Melanchthon also stressed the lack of freedom in both appetites. Ibid., 48.

11. Ibid., 131. Melanchthon added, "By 'flesh' are meant the natural human feelings, not only being hungry and thirsty, but loving wealth and glory and other things of this kind."

On the other hand, Melanchthon defined faith itself as an "affection of the heart."[12] Here Melanchthon specifically responded to Scholasticism's reduction of faith to mere assent. Using the example of King Saul in the Old Testament, Melanchthon observed that, despite Saul's knowledge of the judgment and mercy of God, the king did not have "faith," or seek after God. Saul's *heart* did not correspond to the *opinion*. Melanchthon compared this to his readers' own "uncleanness of heart," demonstrated in their devotion to worldly "desires." "Are you not worried," Melanchthon asked, "about your livelihood, reputation, life, children, and wife because you trust God too little, because you do not weigh the abundance of divine mercy?"[13] True faith in Christ stills the heart and moves the believer to thankfulness and good works.[14] The love of God required in the First Commandment pertains to the affections and can only be produced by the Spirit.[15] Elsewhere he wrote, "Faith therefore is an affection, which certainly clings to the promises and threatenings of God."[16]

John Calvin

On many points, John Calvin's understanding of human affections resonates with that of Melanchthon. While Calvin may not often be known for his warmth of affection, he was an ardent man who believed that affection for God was a crucial part of genuine *pietas*.[17] While employing the medieval Christian understanding

Note the depravity of both appetites—hunger and thirst refer to sense appetite, while greed and pride refer to the higher appetite.

12. Ibid., 90.

13. Ibid.

14. Ibid., 92. Simeon Zahl observes that, while many theologians today disparage the Protestant doctrine of justification by faith to be "cold" or "forensic," Melanchthon repeatedly described the doctrine to be one that brings great comfort and warm affections to the believer. "On the Affective Salience of Doctrines," *Modern Theology* 31 (2015): 428–44.

15. Ibid., 54."[L]ove for God is the fruit of faith." Ibid., 147. Also see Ward, *How the Light Gets In*, 98. Susan C. Karant-Nunn argues that "evangelical forms of belief were made aware . . . that along with late-medieval Catholic Christianity, emotion-oriented piety was at an end, or at least to be severely curtailed and redirected." She says that nascent Lutheran piety emphasized "quiet submission to the workings of faith within the individual Christian and, externally, as gentle, less emotive (however feeling), non-flaunting submission to authority and the service of one's neighbor." *The Reformation of Feeling: Shaping the Religious Emotions in Early Modern Germany* (New York: Oxford University Press, 2010), 65.

16. Melanchthon, *De Arte Concionandi Formulae ut Breves, Ita Doctae & Piae* (Basil, 1540), 57. "Fides igitur est affectus, qui certo affentit promissionibus Dei, & comminationibus." Author's translation.

17. On Calvin, see Theodore Beza, *The Life of John Calvin*, trans. Henry Beveridge (Philadelphia: Westminster Press, 1909); John T. McNeill, *The History and Character of*

of affections and passions as a basic framework for his own understanding of human affectivity, Calvin was not content to leave the framework untouched, but offered an Augustinian critique of some aspects of the medieval Scholastic model.

In the first book of his *Institutes of the Christian Religion*, Calvin explained the Bible's teaching concerning human nature. Humans consist of a body and a soul. The soul is "an incorporeal substance."[18] Although he acknowledged theories about the faculties of the soul that were espoused by "philosophers," Calvin saw little in the theories that would promote godliness. The information obtained by the five senses pools into the common sense, which is then distinguished by fancy. Reason "embraces universal judgment," and the understanding studiously contemplates what reason produces. Calvin saw three appetitive faculties: the will, the irascible appetite, and concupiscence.[19] Nevertheless, Calvin believed that it was best to conceive of two simple, fundamental faculties of the soul: the understanding and the will. The will follows the judgment of the understanding, which includes sense.[20] As a result of his study of Scripture, Calvin argued that the mind and heart correspond to the understanding and will: "Scripture is accustomed to divide the soul of man, as to its faculties, into two parts, the mind and the heart. The mind means the understanding, while the heart denotes all the dispositions or wills."[21]

Calvin assumed the basic Scholastic framework for understanding the soul, yet he explicitly rejected some views of the medieval Christian "philosophers," especially with respect to their moral philosophy. For example, Calvin argued that

Calvinism (London: Oxford University Press, 1954), 93–234; and William J. Bouwsma, *John Calvin: A Sixteenth Century Portrait* (New York: Oxford University Press, 1988), 9–31. On Calvin and *pietas*, see Elsie Anne McKee, introduction to John Calvin, *Writings on Pastoral Piety*, Classics of Western Spirituality (Mahwah, NJ: Paulist Press, 2001), 2–5, and Joel R. Beeke, *Puritan Reformed Spirituality: A Practical Theological Study from our Reformed and Puritan Heritage* (Darlington, England: Evangelical Press, 2006), 1–33. On Calvin and emotions, see McNeill, *Calvinism*, 116.

18. *Institutes* 1.15.2; 1.15.6. All English citations of the *Institutes* are from John Calvin, *Institutes of the Christian Religion*, ed. John T. McNeill, trans. Ford Lewis Battles (Philadelphia, PA: Westminster Press, 1960). Latin citations of the *Institutes* are from Ioannis Calvini, *Institutio Christianae Religionis*, ed. August Tholuck (Berlin: Gustav Eichler, 1834).

19. *Institutes* 1.15.6. *Pace* Kyle Fedler, who says that "Calvin rejects the notion that emotions are located in and derived from an independent faculty, like the 'oretic' [*sic*] faculty posited by Aquinas." "Calvin's Burning Heart: Calvin and the Stoics on the Emotions" *JSCE* 22 (2002): 137.

20. Ibid., 1.15.7. I agree with Muller that Calvin was a voluntarist, but with statements like that in *Institutes* 1.15.7, Calvin sounds inconsistent. Muller, *Unaccommodated Calvin*, 164–67; 170–73.

21. *The Epistles of Paul the Apostle to the Galatians, Ephesians, Philippians and Colossians*, trans. T. H. L. Parker, Calvin's Commentaries 11 (Grand Rapids, MI: William B. Eerdmans, 1965), 290. Also see Muller, *Unaccommodated Calvin*, 167–70.

the difference between virtue and vice does not lie in following reason instead of the senses. Christian philosophers had forced a reconciliation between Christian dogma and philosophy and had thereby overlooked human depravity.[22] He explained their view: "They hold that the appetite, if it undertakes to obey the reason and does not permit itself to be subjected to the senses, is borne along to the pursuit of virtues, holds the right way, and is molded into the will."[23] Calvin objected to the idea that reason alone can guide toward the virtuous life through free will.[24] For Calvin, without grace the will and senses are inclined toward evil. An unregenerate will is corrupt and unable to choose the good.

Calvin believed that pious affections are necessary for true saving faith, a doctrine that later Reformed teachers would also emphasize. By nature people are tainted by corrupt thoughts and affections.[25] Without heart affections, humans cannot even begin to approach God, for faith itself "is more of the heart than the brain, and more of the disposition [*affectus*] than of the understanding."[26] Christian affections do not bypass the understanding; they are not animal passions. Such affections flow from the heart; they are "neither lifeless nor bestial," but the result of the Spirit's grace in the heart and understanding.[27] The Holy Spirit is the source of the Christian's affections.[28] Therefore, doctrines should be held, not only by the understanding and memory, but in "the whole soul," including the heart's affections.[29] Without such pious affections, God cannot even be worshiped aright.[30] Christians should also lay aside affections for earthly things.[31] For Calvin, the sum of the Christian life is self-denial, which includes a subjection of the affections to God.[32]

22. *Institutes*, 1.15.8.

23. Ibid., 2.2.2. Compare ibid., 2.1.9.

24. Ibid., 2.2.2–4; 2.2.12.

25. Ibid., 3.3.19.

26. Ibid., 3.2.8. Also see ibid., 3.3.16 and Calvin's remarks on repentance in ibid., 3.3.6. See Muller, *Unaccommodated Calvin*, 161–64. Calvin said, "It follows that faith can in no wise be separated from a devout [affection] [*Consequitur, fidem a pio affectu nllo modo esse distrahendam*]." Calvin was careful to emphasize that the assent of faith "rests upon such pious [affection]." *Institutes*, 3.2.8.

27. John Calvin, *Foreword to the Psalter*, trans. Charles Garside, in *Writings on Pastoral Piety*, 92.

28. Calvin, *Institutes*, 3.3.8. Also see ibid., 3.6.4.

29. Ibid., 3.7.4.

30. Calvin said, "[T]he beginning of right living is spiritual, where the inner [affection] of the mind is unfeignedly dedicated to God for the cultivation of holiness and righteousness [*ubi interior animi affectus sine fictione ad sanctitatem et iustitiam colendam Deo addicitur*]." Ibid., 3.7.5.

31. Ibid., 3.6.3.

32. Ibid., 3.7.8.

Calvin most often used the word *affections* to refer to the soul's appetitive movements. Sometimes he used the word *passions*, but as a synonym for *affections*.[33] One can nevertheless see evidence that Calvin accepted the distinction between higher and lower movements of the soul. For example, he regarded it a sin to yield to "unbridled appetites" and passions.[34] He was also concerned with disordered affections and, when describing such movements, occasionally used the words *libido* or *cupiditates*.[35] Virtue is not a matter of following the soul's higher movements, for the whole soul is depraved and needs grace. The ungodly who control their passions externally are simply "the more strongly . . . inflamed" within.[36] By nature all human faculties are depraved, including the affections and desires.[37] Although Calvin rarely distinguished the terms *affections* and *passions*, he did make a conceptual distinction between the soul's movements.

Calvin maintained both divine impassibility and God's capacity for love and hatred.[38] God's affections, like his will and counsel, do not change.[39] The incarnate Christ experienced affections like other people because affections are not sinful *per se*. Human passions are sinful when immoderate and misdirected.[40] Jesus

33. Ibid., 2.2.23. Also see Calvin's commentary on Jn 11:33. Ioannis Calvini, *In Evangelium Ioannis*, vol. 3 of *Novum Testamentum Commentarii*, ed. August Tholuck (Berlin: Gustav Eichler, 1833), 220–21.

34. John Calvin, *Commentaries on the First Twenty Chapters of the Book of the Prophet Ezekiel*, trans. Thomas Myers (Grand Rapids, MI: Baker Book House, 1979), 115 (Commentary on Ezek. 16:17). Calvin said in 2 Pet. 2:10 that the phrase to "*walk after the flesh* . . . means to be given up to the flesh just as brute beasts do not behave rationally or responsibly but are guided entirely by their fleshly desires." John Calvin, *The Epistle of Paul The Apostle to the Hebrews and The First and Second Epistles of St Peter*, trans. William B. Johnston, Calvin's Commentaries 12 (Grand Rapids, MI: William B. Eerdmans, 1963), 351 (Comm. on 2 Pet. 2:10).

35. Calvin, *Institutes*, 2.2.13; 2.5.14; 2.7.10; 3.10.3.

36. Ibid., 2.7.10. Calvin observed that in Jude 19, "The soul is here set against the Spirit, that is, the renewal effected by grace; hence, the senses in their depraved condition, such as in men not yet born again. In our degenerate nature, which we derive from Adam, there is only the base and earthly material, no part of us aspiring to God, until we are renewed by His Spirit." John Calvin, *A Harmony of the Gospels: Matthew, Mark and Luke Volume III and the Epistles of James and Jude*, trans. A. W. Morrison (Grand Rapids, MI: William B. Eerdmans, 1972), 333–34 (Comm. on Jude 19).

37. Calvin, *Institutes*, 3.3.12.

38. Ibid., 1.15.5; 2.16.1–4.

39. Ibid., 1.17.13.

40. Calvin said, "I say that there is excess because none rejoices or grieves only sufficiently or as God permits, and many even shake off the bridle altogether. The vanity of our mind makes us sorrow or grieve over trifles, or for no reason at all, because we are too much devoted to this world. Nothing like this was to be found in Christ. No passion of His ever went beyond its proper bounds. He had none that was not right and founded on reason

assumed the weakness of passions, but those movements were strictly moderate, proper, and sinless.[41] Only with shared passions can Christ truly have a shared human nature. God created Adam and Eve with affections, but their affections in innocence always submitted to reason. So Christ's affections were "without ἀταξία."[42]

Scholastic theology framed the discussion of human affections for both Melanchthon and Calvin. The Reformers saw affections to be inclinations or aversions, and they recognized the affections to be closely connected with the will. They strongly opposed the idea that only the passions were depraved. Depravity affected the whole person, both the higher and lower appetites. Total depravity in turn supported their denial of free will. Both, however, viewed affection for God as a necessary part of saving faith.[43] For them, the most important affections—affections for God—came only through a gracious work of the Spirit. Both taught that improper affections to the world of sense and pleasure were to be curbed and avoided. Therefore, although the emphasis on higher and lower faculties is not found in either Melanchthon or Calvin, medieval Scholastic thought on human affectivity informed both their teaching on the wholly depraved person as well as their understanding of faith as including a Spirit-wrought love and desire for God.

The Puritan Tradition and Early Enlightenment Moral Philosophy

The foregoing survey has shown that a general consensus existed concerning the passions and affections from the patristic period to the middle of the sixteenth century. Although important differences existed between the individual theologians, they understood affections and passions to be seated in the soul, defined them as inclination and aversion, and often distinguished between the movements of the body and of the soul. The purpose of this history has been to show the intellectual background for Jonathan Edwards's own understanding of affections and passions.

Now the discussion must turn to observe the thought of the direct predecessors and contemporaries of Edwards. The Puritan and Reformed Scholastic tradition

and sound judgment." Comm. on Jn 11:33. Calvin, *The Gospel according to St John 11–21 and The First Epistle of John*, trans. T. H. L. Parker (Grand Rapids, MI: Wm. B. Eerdmans, 1959), 12. See Fedler, "Calvin's Burning Heart," 151–52 and Charles Taylor, *Sources of the Self: The Making of the Modern Identity* (Cambridge, MA: Harvard University Press, 1989), 218–27.

41. Calvin, *Institutes*, 2.16.12.

42. Comm. on Jn 11:33. Calvin added, "If you compare his passions with ours, they are as different as pure, clear water flowing in a gentle course from muddy and thick foam." Fedler explains ἀταξία to mean "disorderly, undisciplined, irregular, or inordinate." "Calvin's Burning Heart," 153.

43. The legacy of this emphasis will be seen in the Puritan authors surveyed below.

perpetuated the outlines of traditional Christian understandings of human affectivity. All the authors examined to this point taught to some extent the importance of love for God. The Puritan tradition combined the Augustinian emphasis on love, the distinction between affections and passions, and, of even greater significance, the Reformed insistence on a graciously changed heart and will. These ideas were gathered into something like an obsession with affections. In some respects the result sounds like Aristotelian Augustinianism.

Despite larger intellectual trends, the Reformed tradition perpetuated the idea of affections as inclinations of the soul distinct from lower movements and maintained the centrality of affections in Christian life. Meanwhile, René Descartes (1596–1650), the Cambridge Platonists, and other early Enlightenment figures made their own contributions to the period's understanding of human affectivity.[44]

Affective Psychology in the Early Enlightenment

The Passions of the Soul by René Descartes (1596–1650) is an important work that introduced the concept of passions as perceptions of the body acting upon the soul. Perhaps more significantly, Descartes explored these perceptions as natural philosopher rather than moral philosopher.[45] In approaching the passions in this manner, Descartes suggested a more literal meaning to the soul-body distinction.[46] The passions are no longer the inclinations of the lower soul; the passions are explained physically.

Descartes proposed a simple way of distinguishing the domains of the soul and body: what could not be ascribed to inanimate objects must belong to the soul, and all else belongs to the body. The passions are "perceptions or sensations or excitations of the soul which are referred to it in particular and which are caused, maintained, and strengthened by some movement of the spirits."[47] Descartes ascribed understanding and volition to the soul. The will is the soul's *action*. Perception and knowledge is the soul's *passion*; with these the soul obtains information. The passions move upon the soul via the animal spirits (themselves

44. Brumm Ursula, "Passions and depressions in early American puritans," in *La passion dans le monde anglo-américain aux XVIIe et XVIIIe siècles* (Paris: Universite de Bourdeaux, 1978), 85–96. Compare Miller, *The New England Mind*. Although Miller saw the distinction between the rational and sensitive soul, he wrongly read both passions and affections as movements of the sensitive soul.

45. Geneviève Rodis-Lewis, introduction to René Descartes, *The Passions of the Soul*, trans. Stephen Voss (Indianapolis, IN: Hackett, 1989), xvi.

46. See Dixon, *From Passions to Emotions*, 76–77. Also see Anthony Levi, *French Moralists: The Theory of the Passions 1585 to 1649* (London: Oxford University Press, 1964), 268–69.

47. Descartes, *Passions*, §27. References to Descartes, *The Passions of the Soul*, designate the article, not the page number.

corporeal movements), and the soul controls the body via the "pineal" gland near the center of the brain. The heart is not the seat of the passions.[48]

Because passions are perceptions, in Descartes the passions have little to do with the will. Volitions are self-referential and self-caused "excitations of the soul."[49] Reason, on the other hand, cannot will to avoid passions. "The most the will can do while this excitation is in its full strength is not to consent to its effects and to restrain many of its movements to which it disposes the body."[50] Descartes plainly rejected older views:

> And all the struggles that people customarily imagine between the lower part of the soul, which is called sensitive, and the higher, which is rational, or between the natural appetites and the will, consist only in the opposition between the movements which the body by its spirits and the soul by its will tend to excite simultaneously in the gland. For there is only a single soul in us, and this soul has within itself no diversity of parts; the very one that is sensitive is rational, and all its appetites are volitions.[51]

Passions excite involuntary actions in the body, and the soul attempts to stop them when they begin. This is the perceived struggle. Therefore, the proper weapons for fighting against the passions are strong "judgments" about right and wrong.[52] Some people are captive to passions because of error, but no soul is weak enough to be entirely captive to passions. The forty passions enumerated by Descartes (the total is indefinite) result from sense perception and corporeal movements of the animal spirits. The six simple and primitive passions are admiration, love and hate, desire, and joy and sadness.[53]

With his concepts of passions, pineal gland, and the soul, Descartes dispensed with traditional understanding of higher and lower soul. The soul alone is volitional. The war between passions and the will takes place at that pineal gland as it perceives the tension between the animal spirits and the will. The passions alone do not influence the will, but "judgments incline the soul to join itself in volition with the things it deems good and to separate itself from those it deems bad."[54] The will's inner excitations can join themselves with passions at the pineal gland.[55]

48. Ibid., §10; §33; §34.
49. Ibid., §29.
50. Ibid., §46.
51. Ibid., §47.
52. Ibid., §48.
53. Ibid., §§69–95.
54. Ibid., §79.
55. Ibid., §147. Levi explained, "The old contrast between reason and passion reappears in Descartes in the guise of a distinction between the passion and the 'pensée raisonnable' which is an interior emotion of the soul produced independently of the body." Levi, *French Moralists*, 277.

The will is morally superior to the passions. The soul has its own pleasures, but the pleasures it shares with the body come from the passions. Descartes said, "But Wisdom is useful here above all: it teaches us to render ourselves such masters of them, and to manage them with such ingenuity, that the evils they cause can be easily borne, and we even derive Joy from them all."[56]

Blaise Pascal (1623–62) represents a different early Enlightenment perspective that emphasized the morality of love and passions in continuity with the Christian theology. Important for Jansenists like Pascal was the Augustinian concept of *amour-propre*, an inordinate self-love and the source of evil passions.[57] For Pascal specifically, self-love stood opposed to true charity born of divine grace.

Pascal believed that people in a state of nature are under the power of their own base passions, which he consistently interpreted to be inclinations and aversions of the soul. Humans have been created to love. On the one hand, passions hinder humanity's apprehension of the truth, being distorted by self-love.[58] Yet Pascal believed that the heart and feelings, though opposed to reason, form a necessary means of human knowing.[59] Pure thought without passion would only weary humankind; therefore, "it is necessary that he should sometimes be agitated by those passions the deep and vivid sources of which he feels within his heart."[60] Passions are seated in the mind, though they are "occasioned by the body."[61] People find such delight in bodily pleasure that they often yield to it irrationally.[62] Yet reason is insufficient itself to subdue passions.[63] Through self-love and concupiscence they plunge people into vice: "[E]verything which drives us to

56. *Passions*, §212. For more on the relationship of the will and passions, see Levi, *French Moralists*, 275–77. Also see Fiering, *Moral Philosophy*, 271–75.

57. See Levi, *French Moralists*, 225–27.

58. Blaise Pascal, *Pensées*, trans. A. J. Krailsheimer (Harmondsworth, Middlesex, England: Penguin Books, 1966), §119 (423). References to *Pensées* are given by the number of Lafuma edition followed by the number in parenthesis to the Brunschvicg edition. For a brief history of the text, see Roger Ariew, Introduction to Pascal, *Pensées*, trans. Roger Ariew (Indianapolis, IN: Hackett, 2004), xi–xiv. On self-love, see Pascal, *Pensées*, §978 (100).

59. See, for example, Pascal, *Pensées*, §§ 751 (3); 112 (344); 131 (434); 410 (413); 406 (395); and 821 (252). Compare §119 (423).

60. *Passion of Love*, 411.

61. Ibid., 412. Pascal noted, concerning the idea that some nations love more than others, "Love consisting only in an attachment of thought, it is certain that it must be the same over all the earth. It is true that, considering it otherwise than in the thought, the climate may add something, but this is only in the body." Ibid., 420.

62. *Discourse on the Passion of Love*, in *Blaise Pascal: Thoughts and Minor Works*, Harvard Classics 48, trans. O. W. Wright (New York: P. F. Collier and Son, 1938), 414. There is some disagreement concerning the authenticity of this discourse. Compare Pascal, *Pensées*, §795 (160).

63. Pascal, *Pensées*, §410 (413). Pascal said elsewhere that humanity's ability to subdue passions proves the soul's immortality. Ibid., §115 (349).

become attached to creatures is bad, since it prevents us from serving God, if we know him, or seeking if we do not."[64]

Yet, Pascal, in the Augustinian tradition, saw charity as a higher love above lowly passions or cupidity. Charity is of an infinitely high and supernatural nature, typified in the infinite distance between mind and body. Those mastering their passions turn them into virtues, as even avarice, jealousy, and anger are ascribed to God. Pascal said, "We must treat [passions] like slaves, and give them food but prevent the soul feeding on it."[65] Cupidity must be a servant to charity.[66] God most desires humanity's affections; therefore, when individuals attach "sovereign love" to created things they commit the most grievous of sins.[67] Hence Scripture's proofs appeal not to the mind, but to the heart, the seat of charity.[68] The "zeal of charity" can destroy affection for the world.[69]

In England, the "Cambridge Platonist" John Smith (1618–52) held a largely traditional understanding of the soul's powers.[70] Later, Jonathan Edwards found Smith's insight into hypocrites penetrating enough to devote his longest footnote in *Affections* to a citation of Smith's *Discourse* entitled, "A Discovery of the Shortness and Vanity of a Pharisaical Righteousness."[71] Edwards found Smith's observations to be a "remarkable" account of subtle carnal affections rooted in self-love that are

64. Pascal, *Pensées*, §617 (479). Note especially the confusion of human cupidity in §136 (139).

65. Ibid., §603 (502).

66. Ibid., §502 (571). Krailsheimer emphasizes the role of the body in Pascal's thought. Pascal presented "carnality, concupiscence and materialism as the enemies of charity, and shows what happens when the heart looks downwards to the beasts rather than upwards to God; in this sense man is betraying his nature by applying to spiritual truths material values, just as the arrogance of philosophers distorts it by applying only intellectual values." A. J. Krailsheimer, Introduction to Pascal, *Pensées*, 25. Pascal wrote, "All bodies together and all minds together and all their products are not worth the least impulse of charity. This is of an infinitely superior order." Ibid., §308 (793). Charity's importance is self-evident: "It is so obvious that we must love one God alone that there is no need of miracles to prove it." Ibid., §844 (837).

67. Pascal and His Sister Jacqueline to Their Sister, Madame Perier, April 1, 1648, in *Pascal*, trans. M. L. Booth, 325.

68. Pascal, *Pensées*, §298 (283). Compare §926 (582).

69. *Prayer to Ask of God the Proper Use of Sickness*, in *Pascal*, 366. Pascal himself pleaded with God to "take my affections, which the world has stolen; take this treasure thyself, or rather retake it, since it belongs to thee as a tribute that I owe thee, since thy image is imprinted in it." Ibid., 368.

70. See *OCP*, s.v. "Cambridge Platonists." On the influence of John Smith on Jonathan Edwards, see John Smith, "Editor's Introduction," in *WJE* 2:65–66 and Fiering, *Jonathan Edwards's Moral Thought*, 124–25, 124–5n43. Also see *WJE* 26:281–82.

71. John Smith, "A Discovery of the Shortness and Vanity of a Pharisaical Righteousness; or, An Account of the False Grounds upon Which Men are Apt Vainly to Conceit Themselves

false religious affections.[72] According to Smith, some of tenets of Christianity are such that can "seem very delicious to the fleshly appetites of men."[73] This sort of sensual attraction to Christianity Smith set directly against those true saints who "are gently moved by the natural force of true goodness, . . . really informed by the divine Spirit."[74] Smith continued,

> And as the motions of our sense, fancy, and passions, while our souls are in this mortal condition sunk down deeply into the body, are many times more vigorous and make stronger impressions upon us than those of the higher powers of the soul, which are more subtile and remote from these mixt and animal perceptions; that devotion which is there seated may seem to have more energy and life in it than that which gently, and with more a delicate kind of touch, spreads itself upon the understanding, and from thence mildly derives itself through our wills and affections.[75]

Thus Smith maintained the distinction between the higher and lower movements of the soul, adding that lower movements can deceptively appear in some religious hypocrites as movements of the higher, and even as those touched by God's grace. Smith also stressed that, although the fervor of deceptive passions soon fades, the "true celestial warmth" never cools, as it consists of "an immortal nature . . . seated vitally in the souls of men."[76]

The Platonic poet and theologian John Norris (1657–1711) was influential in the early eighteenth century, particularly because of his popular *Miscellanies*.[77]

to Be Righteous," in *Select Discourses*, 3rd ed. (London: Rivingstons and Cochran, 1821), 375–402. See *WJE* 2:217–9n6.

72. *WJE* 2:217–18.

73. Smith, *Select Discourses*, 399. Smith added, "I doubt not but that sometimes the most fleshly and earthly men, that fly their ambition to the pomp of this world, may be so ravished with the conceits of such things as these, that they may seem to be made partakes of 'the powers of the world to come'; I doubt not but that they may be as much exalted with them, as the souls of crazed and distracted persons seem to be sometimes, when their fancies play with those quick and nimble spirits which a distempered frame of body, and unnatural heat in their heads beget within them." Ibid., 400.

74. Ibid., 400.

75. Ibid., 400–01.

76. Ibid., 401. Smith said, "True religion is of no piece of artifice; it is no boiling up of our imaginative powers, nor the glowing heats of passion." Too many people mistake the passions for true religion, which is actually "a new nature informing the souls of men."

77. The full title is *A Collection of Miscellanies: Consisting of Poems, Essays, Discourses, & Letters, Occasionally Written*, 3d ed. (London: S. Manship, 1699). Norris's *Miscellanies* is in Edwards's "Catalogue" (*WJE* 26:124). Notably, Norris, on the debate between voluntarism and intellectualism, takes what he calls a "middle way," wherein God satisfies human beings (the "*Fruition* of God") by "*Vision*" and "*Love*." Norris, *Miscellanies*, 327. This resonates

A disciple of Malebranche, Norris stressed the difference between soul and body. Norris cautioned against finding happiness in the finite world. God has given human beings an appetite for perfect happiness, and he is the "object which alone can satisfie the Appetite of the most capacious soul."[78] God satisfies human happiness through "an Operation of the *Intellectual* Part, and not of the *Sensitive*."[79] Norris also drew a distinction between intellectual and passionate love for God. The intellectual love of God is the movement of the will whereby God is apprehended as "good" and "agreeable." A passionate love for God is "[w]hen the motion of the Will is accompany'd with a sensible Commotion of the Spirits, and estuation of the Blood."[80]

Francis Hutcheson (1694–1746) was an English moral philosopher to whose *Essay on the Nature and Conduct of the Passions and Affections* Edwards responds in *The Nature of True Virtue*.[81] Even though Edwards likely did not read Hutcheson's full *Essay* until the early 1750s, the *Essay* shows how others besides Edwards regarded the affections and passions in the early eighteenth century.[82] In

with Edwards's "sense of the heart" doctrine. For more on Edwards and the "sense of the heart," see the sections "Jonathan Edwards and John Locke" in Chapter 4 and "Spiritual Sense" in Chapter 5.

78. Norris, *Miscellanies*, 326.

79. Ibid., 327. Norris continued, "And this also I take to be very reasonable. First, Because 'tis generally receiv'd, That the Essence of God cannot be the Object of any of our Senses." The intellectual part, as more perfect than the sensitive, is a second reason proving this doctrine.

80. Ibid., 338. Norris insisted that the love of God can be passionate in this life, even though God is not apprehended by the senses. "Whatever some Men pretend, who are Strangers to all the affectionate Heats of Religion, and therefore make their Philosophy a Please for their Indevotion, and extinguish all Holy Ardours with a Syllogism; yet I am fully persuaded, that our Love of God may be not only Passionate, but even *Wonderfully* so, and *exceeding the Love of Women*." Above this division Norris presented *Seraphic* love for God generated by contemplation. Ibid., 338–39.

81. Hutcheson, *An Essay on the Nature and Conduct of the Passions and Affections*, 3rd ed. (Glasgow: Robert & Andrew Foulis, 1769). See Fiering, *Moral Philosophy*, 198–206. The *Essay* is in part a response to Hobbes's psychological egotism. Stephen Darwall, "Egoism and Morality," in *The Oxford Handbook of Philosophy in Early Modern Europe*, eds. Desmond M. Clarke and Catherine Wilson (Oxford: Oxford University Press, 2011), 396. See Alexander Broadie, "Scottish Philosophy in the 18th Century," *The Stanford Encyclopedia of Philosophy*, Fall 2009 ed., ed. Edward N. Zalta, http://plato.stanford.edu/archives/fall2009/entries/scottish-18th/ (accessed December 4, 2017).

82. On the timing of Edwards's exposure to Hutcheson's *Essay*, see Paul Ramsey, "Appendix II: Jonathan Edwards on Moral Sense, and the Sentimentalists," in *Jonathan Edwards, Ethical Writings*, vol. 8 of *The Works of Jonathan Edwards* (New Haven, CT: Yale University Press, 1989), 704.

the *Essay* Hutcheson argued that in addition to the body's senses, humans have a moral sense independent of will whereby they perceive actions to be good or evil.[83]

Hutcheson argued that the mind is modified with either "grateful" or "uneasy" perceptions entirely different from sensation. In sum, affections are either of these two perceptions and "directly incline the mind to action or volition of motion."[84] Moreover, citing Nicholas Malebranche, Hutcheson stated clearly how passions may be distinct from affections:

> When the word passion is imagined to denote anything different from the affections, it includes a strong brutal impulse of the will, sometimes without any distinct notions of good, public or private, attended with "a confused sensation of pleasure or pain, occasioned or attended by some violent bodily motions, which keeps the mind much employed upon the present affair, to the exclusion of every thing else, and prolongs or strengthens the affection sometimes to such a degree, as to prevent all deliberate reasoning about our conduct."[85]

Indeed, Hutcheson specifically references Thomas Aquinas's distinction between the *appetitus rationalis* and *appetitus sensitivus*, contrasting a calm affection for higher good with the passions for sense good.[86] Hutcheson is noticeably more optimistic concerning human nature and the virtue of self-love than any of the predecessors surveyed. Even so, he notably retains traditional Christian distinctions of affections and passions.[87]

Early Enlightenment thinkers began to modify traditional understandings of the affections and passions in important ways. Descartes probably suggested the most radical changes in his scheme of the passions. He interpreted passions as purely physiological movements. Consequently, passions are involuntary, although they are bridled by the soul through the pineal gland. After Descartes, there was a much greater emphasis on the distinction between soul and body. Descartes's thought began to realign the passions, from movements of the lower soul to involuntary bodily responses in the physical realm.

Yet early Enlightenment authors leading up to Edwards, including Descartes, saw the soul's passions generally as inclinations or aversions. Other than a more pronounced Cartesian dualism between soul and body, these figures maintained the distinction between affections and passions, and contrasted the passions with higher movements of the will. These tenets were held by those authors who influenced Edwards like John Smith and John Norris. Even those who tended to

83. Hutcheson, *Essay*, 3–4.

84. Ibid., 25.

85. Ibid., 26–27. Here Hutcheson quoted Nicolas Malebranche's *The Search after Truth*. Chapter 6 contains brief discussion of Malebranche and *The Search*.

86. Ibid., n28. Hutcheson complained that not enough of his contemporaries followed Aquinas's distinction.

87. Dixon, *From Passions to Emotions*, 83–85.

champion forms of Cartesian thought (like John Norris) maintained a largely traditional understanding of human affections and passions.

Affective Psychology in Puritan and Reformed Thought

The Puritans and Reformed schoolmen perpetuated, even in the face of Cartesian thought, the traditional Christian understanding human affectivity. Fundamentally, both affections and passions could be used to speak of the inclinations and aversions of the soul. When a distinction between affections and passions was sustained, often affections represented movements of the higher faculties of the soul, while passions designated movements of the sense appetite toward sense good.

William Ames (1576–1633) The *Marrow of Theology* by William Ames (1576–1633) influenced many generations of New England Puritan pastors. Jonathan Edwards himself knew *Marrow* and other works by Ames.[88] In *Marrow*, Ames said that faith produces the "primary and intimate affection toward God" in saints capable of establishing a relationship between them and God.[89] Ames suggested five properties of this faith:

> 1) a knowledge of what God testifies to; 2) a pious affection toward God which gives his testimony greatest force with us; 3) an assent given to the truth testified to, because of this affection toward God who is the witness of it; 4) a resting upon God for the receiving of what is given; and 5) the choosing or apprehension of what is made available to us in the testimony.[90]

Ames said the affections of faith are seated in the will.[91] Likewise, the love that flows from faith is itself an affection whereby believers submit to God.[92] Ames insisted,

88. On Ames, see John D. Eusden, Introduction to William Ames, *The Marrow of Theology* (1968; repr., Grand Rapids, MI: Baker Books, 1997), 3–11, and Beeke and Pederson, *Meet the Puritans*, 33–51. The Latin title for *Marrow* is *Medulla Theologiae.* On Edwards and Ames, see "Misc. 961," in *WJE* 20:242 n7; *WJE* 2:174–5 n3, 2:362 n9, 2:374 n4; and Smith, "Editor's Introduction," in *WJE* 2:67–68 and 26:429. Edwards used Ames's description of divinity as "*the doctrine of living to God.*" *Sermons and Discourses, 1739–1742*, vol. 22 of *The Works of Jonathan Edwards*, Harry S. Stout and Nathan O. Hatch with Kyle P. Farley, eds. (New Haven, CT: Yale University Press, 2003), 86. See Ames, *Marrow of Theology*, 77.

89. Ames, *Marrow of Theology*, 176. Also see ibid., 241.

90. Ibid., 241. Compare ibid., 258 and William Ames, *The Substance of Christian Religion: Or, A Plain and easie Draught of the Christian Catechisme* (London: T. Mabb for T. Davies, 1659), 50–51.

91. Ibid., 87, 241. Also see ibid., 239 and Fiering, *Moral Philosophy*, 123. Ames argued that the affections attributed to God in Scripture either represent God's will or figuratively apply to God.

92. Ibid., 251.

"We can in no way love God with too much intensity." This "inward affection" is necessary for worship.[93] Ames regarded singing as a way whereby the "pious affections" of saints are stirred up. Christian ministers also have the responsibility to evoke "godly affections."[94]

Ames not only connected affections with the will, but he also distinguished the will and the sensory appetite. Original sin corrupts the whole person, including the affections.[95] Sinful affections are inordinate.[96] The lost, when condemned to eternal death, continue to sin against God with their affections.[97] Ames saw unbelievers as plagued with concupiscence, passions, and inordinate desires, though even saints struggle with such sins.[98] Ministers should not stir up such "carnal affections" with their preaching.[99] Ames distinguished the appetites, both of which are depraved in the wicked.

> For in all men there appears a manifest perversion of our wills, and inward appetite; as much as spiritual and truly good things are of no good relish to all animall and naturall men: but the contrary evils, which of their own nature have no good rellish, seem to them most sweet: Now as the perversion of the sensitive appetite doth denote bodily sicknesse, so the perversion of the inmost & most spiritual appetite, doth point forth unto us sickness that is inward and in the spirit. The same also may be observed of the perversion of the judgement and understanding, from whence come so many and shamefull errours, whereby good is esteemed evill, and evill good.[100]

Ames affirmed the traditional distinction between appetites, but equally upheld the Reformation doctrine that the whole person is depraved. Ames, as a voluntarist, followed Augustine in stressing the role of the heart in salvation, but maintained Scholastic psychological model in differentiating the soul's movements.[101]

93. Ibid., 238. Also see ibid., 239 and 301. Ames calls zeal the "intensity of pure affection." Ibid., 223. See Ames, *Substance*, 215.

94. Ibid., 263, 193. Compare ibid., 195.

95. Ibid., 171, 225, 120. Compare ibid., 313. Also see Ames, *Substance*, 204.

96. Ames, *Marrow of Theology*, 313, 320.

97. Ibid., 126.

98. Ibid., 319, 329. Also see 171.

99. Ibid., 194.

100. Ames, *Substance*, 22. Ames continued, "It is manifest that there is in all men a certain rebellion of the inferiour and animall faculties and appetites against the superiour and most spiritual faculties of the soul; which shews the sickness of the upper part, as not having strength enough to govern the lower; and again, a disorder and confusion of the inferiour faculties, whereby they will not be subject to their Superiour." *Pace* Walton, *Jonathan Edwards*, 79.

101. Fiering explains, "Ames's analysis, we may remark, is an especially clear instance of both the Scholastic and the Augustinian theory of the will combining to break through

John Owen (1616–83) John Owen (1616–83) also said that affections played a crucial role in religion.[102] Owen's thought in many ways anticipates that of Edwards. Owen presented the will and affections as intricately linked faculties.[103] For Owen, the Spirit worked in the regenerate so that affections are no longer drawn to sin but to God.[104] Seated in the heart or rational soul, affections in believers are the result of the Father's own initial love for them.[105] Christ is "a fit object" for the saint's "choicest affections."[106] As Christ's bride, the believing soul has "conjugal affections" with her Savior.[107] Believers reciprocate back to Christ the love their Savior has shown them.[108] Owen described love for Christ as "a πάθος, or earnest affection."[109] Believers should keep their conjugal affections for Christ "chaste and loyal."[110] These affections are the result of the Spirit's grace of regeneration, which

the Thomist Scholastic structure, a process that was going on generally in the seventeenth century." Fiering, *Moral Philosophy*, 122–23. On the inconsistencies and conflicts arising from Ames's voluntarism, see Fiering, *Moral Philosophy*, 122–27.

102. See Peter Toon, *God's Statesman: The Life and Work of John Owen: Pastor, Educator, Theologian* (Grand Rapids: Zondervan, 1971), and Carl R. Trueman, *John Owen: Reformed Catholic, Renaissance Man*, Great Theologians Series (Burlington, VT: Ashgate, 2007). Kelly M. Kapic discusses Owen and affections in *Communion with God: The Divine and the Human in the Theology of John Owen* (Grand Rapids, MI: Baker Academic, 2007), 53–56. He also notes the influence of Aristotle's faculty psychology on Owen. Ibid., 65–66. On Owen and Edwards, see Walton, *Jonathan Edwards*, 104–16.

103. *The Nature, Power, Deceit, and Prevalency of the Remainders of Indwelling Sin in Believers*, in *Works* 6:282. On the connection of will and affections see, for example, ibid., 6:268, 270, 275, 281, 282, 285. At other times Owen clearly distinguished the will and affections. For example, Owen called the will a rational appetite, but departed from a Thomist notion of rational appetite, understanding "rational appetite" to refer to the different influences on the will. So "rational" means the will is "guided by the mind," whereas "appetite" means the will is "excited by the affections." Ibid., 6:254. Also see ibid., 6:195.

104. Kapic, *Communion with God*, in *The Works of John Owen*, ed. William H. Goold (Philadelphia: Leighton Publications, 1857), 2:228. Elsewhere Owen called this work a "habit of grace," which is "*a new, gracious spiritual life, or principle, created, and bestowed on the soul, whereby it is changed in all its faculties and affections, fitted and enabled to go forth in the way of obedience unto every divine object that is proposed unto it, according to the mind of God.*" Ibid., 2:200. See also ibid., 2:240. Also see *The Grace and Duty of Being Spiritually Minded*, in *Works*, 7:270–71.

105. *Πνευματολογια, or a Discourse Concerning the Holy Spirit*, in *Works*, 3:326, 329; Owen, *Communion with God*, in *Works*, 2:28, 34.

106. Ibid., 2:53. On the believer's affections for the excellency of Christ, see ibid., 2:139.

107. Ibid., 2:54–78.

108. Ibid., 2:117–18. Compare Owen, *Spiritual Mindedness*, in *Works*, 7:475.

109. *Communion with God*, in *Works*, 2:126.

110. Ibid., 2:147. Owen said, "[Christ] is married unto us, and we unto him; which spiritual relation is attended with suitable conjugal affections." Owen argued that the

"fills up the affections with spiritual things, fills the soul with spiritual love, joy, and delight, and exerciseth all other affections about their proper objects."[111] Owen understood regeneration to be a physical change in the "whole rational soul" or heart, which includes not only a spiritual change in the mind and will, but also sanctifying the previously depraved affections.[112] More than merely changing depraved affections, in regeneration the Spirit implants "a prevailing *love*" in the soul. This is "circumcision of heart," which Owen emphasizes is the "depravation," not only of the "sensitive part of the soul," but the "*affections*" as well. Thereby the Spirit crucifies the "enmity, carnal prejudices, and depraved inclinations," and gives the saint "*holy spiritual love, joy, fear, and delight*." This work does not alter "the being of our affections," but sanctifies and unites them "unto their proper object in a due manner."[113]

Owen also warned against evil and distorted desires, often designating them "passions."[114] Because, as 1 Thess. 5:23 teaches, sanctification reaches even the body, individuals may not excuse their sins and passions to "their constitutions and inclinations."[115] For Owen, the Spirit's gracious work operated through the souls of believers to "cure morally sinful distempers, as of passion, elation of mind, and intemperances"—states brought about by bodily constitutions.[116] Although the Holy Spirit does not alter the nature of passions in the regenerate, the grace and holiness of the Spirit does "*morally*" influence them "so that the constitution itself shall be no more such a *fomes* and incentive unto disorderly passions as it

reference to "belly" in Song 5:14 speaks of "bowels" or affections. Ibid., 2:77. See the full discussion of the believer's chastity for Christ, ibid., 2:146–52. Compare *Πνευματολογια*, in *Works* 3:187.

111. *Πνευματολογια*, in *Works*, 2:240. Ordinate affections accompany not only regeneration itself, but the preparatory work of the Holy Spirit to regeneration. This preparatory work is moral, and not "physical." See ibid., 2:301–07. The actual or "whole" work of regeneration by the Holy Spirit, however, "is a real physical work, whereby he infuseth a gracious principle of *spiritual life* into all that are effectually converted and really regenerated, and without which there is no deliverance from the state of sin and death which we have described." Ibid., 2:307.

112. Ibid., 3:326, 315, 329–30. A "physical" is a supernatural change of *physis* or nature, as opposed to a moral change produced by mere intellectual persuasion.

113. Ibid., 3:335.

114. See, for example, *Communion with God*, in *Works*, 2:112; *Spiritual Mindedness*, in *Works*, 7:358, 418–19, 468, 470, and especially 494–95; *Πνευματολογια*, in *Works*, 3:217, 360, 422, 554–55, 558, 587, 632, 642, 643, 647. Owen observed, "Vanity, instability, folly, sensual, irrational appetites, inordinate desires, self-quieting and torturing passions, act continually in our depraved natures." Ibid., 3:642.

115. *Πνευματολογια*, in *Works*, 3:422.

116. Ibid. In *Spiritual Mindedness*, Owen carefully warned that "*the wandering and roving of the outward senses*" oppose spiritual affections. *Spiritual Mindedness*, in *Works*, 7:487; see ibid., 7:485–86.

hath been."[117] Owen variously described the affections of unbelievers as corrupt, disordered, rebellious, and drawn to idols.[118] The affections that answer to the sensitive appetite are evil when they control individuals. Those who are enslaved to such "brutish, sensual affections" are "like beasts," debasing themselves and their "more noble faculties."[119] Passions are not intrinsically evil, for Adam was originally created with right affections, and the human nature of Christ in part was characterized by an "*unspeakable zeal* for, and *ardency of affection unto, the glory of God.*"[120] Because of depravity, however, the human will and affections are weakened, impotent, stubborn, and obstinate.[121] All people are naturally disposed to certain passions, and, though not sinful in itself, this disposition "dwells at the next door unto [sin], and as it is excited by the moral pravity of our natures, a continual occasion of it."[122] Moreover, like Calvin and Melanchthon, Owen objected to any notion that the "natural man" in Scripture refers merely to those ruled by corrupt affections. The sensual appetite has its depraved lusts, but so does the mind.[123] Natural affections never receive spiritual things and directly oppose them.[124] The will and affections pursue only evil because they are enslaved to the directives of the deceived and depraved mind.[125]

Similar emphases arise in Owen's *The Grace and Duty of Being Spiritually Minded*, in which he suggested three aspects of having a mind of the Spirit: (1) "[t]he *actual exercise of the mind*, in its thoughts, meditations, and desires, about things of spiritual beauty"; (2) "[t]he *inclination, disposition, and frame of the mind*, in all its affections, whereby it cleaves unto spiritual things"; and (3) "[a]A *complacency of mind*, from that gust, relish, and savour, which it finds in spiritual things, from their suitableness unto its constitution, inclinations, and

117. *Πνευματολογια*, in *Works*, 3:422.

118. *Πνευματολογια*, in *Works* 3:17, 33, 142, 224, 276, 558.

119. *Spiritual Mindedness*, in *Works*, 7:480. Owen added, "Look, how much vile affections, fixed on and furiously pursuing things carnal and sensual, do debase our nature beneath its rational constitution, and make it degenerate into bestiality; so much spiritual affections, fixed on and cleaving unto things spiritual and heavenly, do exalt our nature above its mere natural capacity, making and approach unto the state of angels and of just men made perfect." Ibid., 7:480. For "brutish" affections as sensuality, compare *Πνευματολογια*, in *Works* 3:268, 296.

120. *Πνευματολογια*, in *Works*, 3:101–02, quoting 3:178.

121. Ibid., 3:244.

122. Ibid., 3:167. The incarnate Christ himself took on these passions as part of his human nature, but was free from "the bodily diseases and distempers" that characterize the rest of humanity.

123. *Indwelling Sin*, in *Works* 6:190.

124. Ibid., 6:270.

125. Ibid., 6:281. This passage sounds like the statement of an intellectualist, but Owen is usually considered a voluntarist. See Fiering, *Moral Philosophy*, 140 and Kapic, *Communion with God*, 50–53.

desires."[126] Only the regenerate have spiritual minds in this sense. The basis of spiritual mindedness is in a person's affections, which Owen called "the spring" of one's "thoughts."[127] To be earthly minded, on the other hand, is either to love earthly things in a predominant way or to have "*inordinate* affection" for worldly things.[128] Natural affections for God may arise in a mind not truly spiritual, as they do in hypocrites. Affections, therefore, can be either spiritual or earthly. When Owen stressed the spirituality of the affections, he included three necessary qualities of spiritual affections: (1) a spiritual principle renewing them, (2) a spiritual object, and (3) a spiritual manner of fastening to their object.[129] In sum, God demands more than the moderation of human affections for worldly objects—he also demands to be the object of affections.[130] Even so, Owen seated affections in the higher faculties.[131] Affections are vital for religion, and nothing good is done for God or others without proper affections behind those actions. Affections are to the soul what the "helm" is to a "ship."[132] Therefore, "[t]he chief work of a Christian is to make all his affections, in all their operations, subservient unto the life of God."[133] In addition, Owen observed, "[a]ffections so disposed constantly find *a gust, a pleasant taste, a relish,* in spiritual things"; such affections answer to "a spiritual appetite unto heavenly things."[134]

126. *Spiritual Mindedness*, in *Works*, 7:270. The way that Owen described this complacency especially resonates with the later thought of Edwards: "There is a salt in spiritual things, whereby they are condited and made savoury unto a renewed mind. . . . In this gust and relish lies the sweetness and satisfaction of spiritual life. Speculative notions about spiritual things, when they are alone, are dry, sapless, and barren. In this gust we taste by experience that God is gracious, and that the love of Christ is better than wine, or whatever else hath the most grateful relish unto sensual appetite. This is the proper foundation of that 'joy which is unspeakable and full of glory.'" Ibid., 7:270–71. Note especially Owen's citation of 1 Pet. 1:8, the text behind Edwards's *Religious Affections*. Also see ibid., 7:471–73, 483.

127. Ibid., 7:361, 270–71. Also see ibid., 7:395.

128. Ibid., 7:272–73. Also see ibid., 7:356–57, 361–62, 411–15.

129. Ibid., 7:411. Also see ibid., 7:290–91 and 7:397. Compare ibid., 7:296, 482–83.

130. Ibid., 7:419–23.

131. For example, Owen taught that spiritually minded individuals have better proof of their gracious state by their "*holy complacency*" than "sensible evidence." Ibid., 7:295. Compare ibid., 7:468.

132. Ibid., 7:396–97. Owen wrote, "The great contest of heaven and earth is about the affections of the poor worm which we call men." Ibid., 7:395. Affections are "*the seat of all sincerity.*" Ibid., 7:396.

133. Ibid., 7:419.

134. Ibid., 7:471. Owen said that renewed affections beholding God in Christ, "have *an infinite beauty, goodness, and amiableness in them, which are powerfully attractive of spiritual affections*, and which alone are able to fill them, to satisfy them, to give them rest." Ibid., 7:475. Also see ibid., 7:484.

Other Examples from the Puritan Tradition These themes reverberate through Puritan theology. First, many uphold the distinction between appetites and the soul's movements. Richard Sibbes (1577–1635) said Christ graciously helps saints "subdue in some measure" their "base affections."[135] Although Sibbes exalted the role of affections in religion (see below), he defined passions as movements of the "baser part of the soul."[136] Sibbes understood that passions are natural, but the heart dedicated to God must govern them through judgment.[137] John Preston (1587–1628) said the disposition of an affection differs from the momentary outbursts of passions. Therefore, hatred is an affection, not a passion, because "it is a bent, a disposition and frame of the will," whereas anger, on the other hand, is a passion, as it "dies and flittes away after a time."[138] Similarly, in his influential

135. *The Bruised Reed and Smoking Flax*, in *The Works of Richard Sibbes*, ed. Alexander Balloch Grosart (Edinburgh: James Nichol, 1862), 1:79.

136. *The Bruised Reed*, in *Works* 1:83. Compare *The Soul's Conflict with Itself and Victory over Itself by Faith* in *Works*, 1:130, 147, 149, 160, 173; *The Sword of the Wicked*, in *Works* 1:105; and *The Returning Backslider*, in *Works* 2:416. Clearly, like many others, Sibbes at times considered affections and passions near synonyms. Yet at other times, he distinguished them. So Sibbes warned, "Our affections must not rise to become unruly passions, for then as a river that overfloweth the banks, they carry much slime and soil with them." *The Soul's Conflict*, in *Works* 1:159. Elsewhere Sibbes identified three kinds of love: affection, passion, and grace of love. Affection is natural, and passion is "the excess of the natural affection when it overflows its bound." He continued, "Grace is the rectifying of natural affection, and the elevating and raising it up to a higher object than nature can pitch on. The Spirit of God turns nature into grace, and works corruption and passion out of nature, and elevates and raises that which is naturally good, the affection of love to be a grace of love. He raiseth it up to love God (which nature cannot discover), by spiritualizing of it. He makes it the most excellent grace of all. So that while I speak of the love of God, think not that I speak of mere affection, but of the affection that hath the stamp of grace upon it. For affections are graces when they are sanctified." *A Glance of Heaven*, in *Works* 4:192). Sibbes differently described passions as unruly, sinful, carnal, deformed, and base. *Soul's Conflict*, in *Works*, 1:160, 167, 168; *Bruised Reed*, in *Works*, 1:82; *The Returning Backslider*, in *Works* 2:412. Elsewhere he contrasted the "affection . . . called Love" with the "irregular agitations, and endless motions of the minds of ambitious, voluptuous, and covetous persons." Richard Sibbes and John Davenport, preface to John Preston, *The Breast-Plate of Faith and Love*, 6th ed. (London: George Purflow, 1651), v.

137. *Soul's Conflict*, in *Works*, 1:168. Also see *Bruised Reed*, 78–83. Judgment is vital in Sibbes's understanding of the changed will. Judgment is akin to taste. The Spirit changes believers' "taste of the soul," to "savour" spiritual things "so deeply, that all other things should be out of relish." *Bruised Reed*, 78. Also see *Bowels Opened*, in *Works*, 2:10; Compare Frost, "Bruised Reed," 88–90.

138. *Breast-plate*, 3:97. Later Preston said, "Great sinnes come from great passions, and men are able to see them, and when the passion is gone over, they are easily recalled againe." Ibid., 3:238. Preston not only specialized his divinity studies both in medieval Scholastics

A Treatise of the Passions and Faculties of the Soul of Man, Edwards Reynolds (1599–1676) distinguished mental, sensitive, and rational passions. Mental passions are "high, pure, and abstracted delights" grounded in the understanding and having little contamination by "earthly faculties."[139] Sensitive passions are base affections similar to those found in beasts. The "middle" or "rational" passions are the rational control of the understanding and will over sensitive passions.[140] William Fenner (1600–40) similarly wrote:

> I know *Aristotle* and most of our divines too, doe place the affections in the sensitive part of the Soul, and not in the will, because they are to be seen in the beasts. But this cannot be so, for a man's affections do more stirre at a shame or disgrace; which could not be, if the affections were in the unreasonable sensitive part: the unreasonable sensitive part of a man is not sensible of credit or esteem: call the desires of the appetite greedy and gluttonish; the appetite is sensitive of any disgrace, and therefore the affections must needs be in the heart: the Scripture places the affections in the heart or the will.[141]

Though he did not stress the distinction, Thomas Shepard (1605–49) anticipated that in the age to come all carnal affections will be taken away: "[t]he Lord shall then take away all fleshly appetites or desires; for then our bodies shall be spiritual bodies."[142] Thomas Manton (1620–77), whose sermons proved especially helpful

like Aquinas and Reformers like Calvin, but also declared Richard Sibbes as a mentor. Beeke and Pederson, *Meet the Puritans*, 488–93; John Smith, "Editor's Introduction," in *WJE* 2:63–64. In *Religious Affections*, Edwards cited three different works of Preston's, including *The Golden Sceptre.* Perry Miller said that Preston read Aquinas' *Summa* while receiving haircuts. Peter J. Thuesen, "Editor's Introduction,"in Jonathan Edwards, *Catalogues of Books*, vol. 26 of *The Works of Jonathan Edwards* (New Haven, CT: Yale University Press, 2008), 6 n6. The edition of *Breast-plate* used for this book was composed of three parts or volumes. The page number for the first two parts was continuous, whereas the page numbering for the third part or volume started with 1.

139. Edwards Reynolds, *A Treatise on the Passions and Faculties of the Soul of Man*, vol. 6 of *The Works of Edwards Reynolds*, ed. Alexander Chalmers (Morgan, PA: Soli Deo Gloria Publications, 1996), 31. Reynolds's *Treatise* was often used in undergraduate classes at Oxford until the early eighteenth century. Beeke and Pederson, *Meet the Puritans*, 496–500.

140. Ibid., 32–33.

141. William Fenner, *A Treatise of the Affections; or The Souls Pulse* (London: A.M., 1650), 4. Fiering calls Fenner's *Treatise*, "possibly the most significant work on the passions that emerged English Puritanism." Fiering, *Moral Philosophy*, 159. For Fenner, affections are proper to the will. Indeed, the sensitive soul's appetite is analogical to those affections of the will. "But," Fenner continued, "the Lord doth not call for these sensitive *passions* to be seated upon him." *Affections*, 4; my italics.

142. Thomas Shepard, *The Parable of the Ten Virgins Opened and Applied* (Orlando, FL: Soli Deo Gloria Publications, 1990), 531. Also see Fulcher, "Puritans and the Passions," 132–34.

to a young Jonathan Edwards, also saw the difference between "the sensitive stirring of the affections," that do "strike upon the senses," and the soul's "solid complacency" or "supreme and prevailing delight . . . in spiritual things."[143] For Manton, affection for God was movement of the higher soul. Once again echoing the Scholastic understanding of the human soul, he said:

> In loving, fearing, praising, serving God, the noblest faculties are exercised, in the noblest and most regular way of operation: the soul is in the right temper and constitution; they are the highest actions of the highest faculties, elevated by the highest principles, about the highest objects. The objects are God, Christ, Heaven, the great things of eternity. The principles are the love and fear of God, the faculties, understanding, and will, not sensitive appetite; these exercised in thinking of God, and choosing God.[144]

The Reformed Scholastic Francis Turretin (1623–87) also maintained the distinction between a higher intellectual and lower sensitive soul.[145] The Scottish Presbyterian Thomas Boston (1676–1732) also affirmed this distinction.[146] The

As a pastor, Shepard confronted the nature of true religion, and, given these concerns, Shepard greatly influenced Edwards's own writings. In fact, in *Affections* Edwards cited Shepards's famous *Parable of the Ten Virgins Opened and Applied* more than any other work. For more on Shepard and *Parable*, see Randall C. Gleason, "The Parable of the Ten Virgins by Thomas Shepard (1605–1649)," in Kapic and Gleason, *The Devoted Life*, 123–37; Beeke and Pederson, *Meet the Puritans*, 524–30; and Walton, *Jonathan Edwards*, 91–100.

143. Thomas Manton, *One Hundred and Ninety Sermons on the Hundred and Nineteenth Psalm*, 3 vols. (London: William Brown, 1842), 1:120. Also see ibid., 1:326, 344, 346, 401, 474, and especially 393–94. Manton wrote, "All the affections depend upon pleasure or pain, delight or grief (the one is proper to the body, the other to the soul) which grow from contentment or distaste which we receive from the divers objects which we meet with." Manton concluded, "delight sets all the other affections a-work." Ibid., 1:138. For Manton, the "spiritual appetite" or "gracious appetite" in true believers is drawn toward "the sincere milk of the word." Ibid., 1:174. See ibid., 109. Manton said, "There is a great deal of difference between serious desires, and passionate expressions." Ibid., 145. Compare ibid., 1:262, 342–51, 361–62. For Edwards's references to Manton, see *WJE* 16:758, 774, 776.

144. Ibid., 1:449. Compare ibid., 1:566.

145. Francis Turretin, *Institutes of Elenctic Theology*, trans. George Musgrave Giger, ed. James T. Dennison, Jr. (Phillipsburg, NJ: P&R Publishing, 1994), §13.14.3 (2:353). Turretin was an intellectualist; he said the will followed the dictates of the practical intellect. Turretin, *Elenctic Theology*, §10.2.5 (1:662). Turretin followed Aquinas's psychological model, though he rejected the Scholastic doctrine of propassions. Ibid., §11.21.10 (2:136). All references to Turretin's *Elenctic Theology* will include the topic, question, and section, followed by the volume and page number for the Giger-Dennison edition in parenthesis.

146. Thomas Boston, *Human Nature in Its Fourfold State* (Carlisle, PA: The Banner of Truth Trust, 1964), 43. Boston understood holiness to refer to the "purity and good order

Puritan and Reformed tradition generally maintained a distinction between the appetites of the sensitive and intellectual parts of human beings.

The Reformed tradition, like Calvin and Melanchthon, also drew a close identification between affections or love and the will or heart. For instance, the phrase "the will and affections" often surfaces in their writings.[147] According to John Preston, affections are "the diverse motions and turnings of the will." He continued:

> As the will turnes it selfe this way and that way; so a man is said to be effected, to love or to hate, to grieve or to rejoyce. Now love is this act of the will, whereby it turnes it selfe to a thing, as hatred is that whereby it turnes it selfe from a thing. . . . *Love is nothing else, but a disposition of the will, whereby it cleaves or makes forwards to some good that is agreeable to it selfe.*[148]

Though distinguishing the will and affections, Reynolds nevertheless closely connected the affections to the will, describing them as "the chief subjects to the will."[149] William Fenner taught that the affections were the motions of the will.[150] Manton said that the heart is the seat of the affections.[151] He also identified affections with the will, teaching that the Spirit of God gives Christians a new nature that has an accompanying appetite for holiness. Manton explained, "Desires being the vigorous bent of the soul, discover the temper of it. The carnal nature puts forth itself in lustings, so doth the new nature. The main thing we have by grace is a new

of the affections." In 1747 Jonathan Edwards wrote in a letter to Thomas Gillespie, "I have read [Mr. Boston's] Fourfold State of Man, and liked it exceeding well. I think he therein shows himself to be a truly great divine." *Letters and Personal Writings*, vol. 16 of *The Works of Jonathan Edwards*, ed. George S. Claghorn (New Haven, CT: Yale University Press, 1998), 235.

147. For example, Sibbes, *Bruised Reed*, in *Works* 1:80; John Preston, *The Golden Sceptre Held Forth to the Humble* (London: Religious Tract Society, 1837), 89, 104; Shepard, *The Parable of the Ten Virgins Opened and Applied*, 320; and Boston, *Four-fold State*, 84.

148. *Breast-plate*, 3:6. Preston said: "For what are affections, but divers positions and situations of the will, and the feet it walks upon? They are but the divers motions and inclinations whereby the will shoots itself into the objects of it. Now look, which way thy will is resolved and set, that way are thy affections set also." Preston, *Golden Sceptre*, 104. The heart's train begins with the understanding, followed by the will, followed by the affections, which leads to action. *Breast-plate*, 2:203–04. See ibid., 3:136–37; 3:215.

149. Reynolds, *Treatise*, 39.

150. Fenner formally defined affections as "*forcible and sensible motions of the will, to a thing or from a thing, according as it is apprehended to be evil or to be good.*" Fenner, *Affections*, 7.

151. Manton, *Hundred and Nineteenth Psalm*, 1:153. Also see ibid., 1:329, 565.

heart, that is, new loves, new desires, and new delights."[152] The Puritan emphasis on "will and affections" is significant, for Edwards argued that the affections are merely the stronger movements of the will.

In general, the Puritan Reformed tradition insisted that affections were good and even necessary for true and vital religion. Sibbes advocated a form of Christian piety that made much of the affections:[153]

> God hath made the soul for a communion with himself, which communion is especially placed in the affections, which are the springs of all spiritual worship. Then the affections are well ordered, when we are fit to have communion with God, to love, joy, trust, to delight in him above all things. The affections are the inward movings of the soul, which then move best when they move us to God, not from him. They are the feet of the soul, whereby we walk with, and before God.[154]

Sibbes insisted that first "[o]ur disposition must be changed" through regeneration before individuals can ever love their Maker.[155] "Indeed," Sibbes wrote, "religion is mainly in the affections, whereof there is excellent use. Take away them, and take

152. Ibid., 1:42. Also see ibid., 1:105, 107, 138, 151, 154–55, 343–44. Manton often emphasized the will like a voluntarist (e.g., see ibid., 1:474, 570, 574), but in other places he presented an intellectualist position. For example, he said (in a passage noteworthy for more than intellectualism), "Now man rightly constituted, his actions are thus governed: the understanding and conscience prescribed to the will; the will, according to right reason and conscience, moveth the affections: the affections, according to the command and counsel of the will, move the bodily spirits and members of the body. But by corruption there is a manifest inversion and change; pleasures affect the senses, the senses corrupt the phantasy, phantasy moveth the bodily spirits they the affections; and by their violence the will is carried captive, man blinded, and so man goeth headlong to his own destruction." Ibid., 1:447. Compare ibid., 1:326.

153. Mark Dever and Ronald N. Frost both emphasize Sibbes's "affective theology." See Mark Dever, *Richard Sibbes: Puritanism and Calvinism in Late Elizabethan and Early Stuart England* (Macon, GA: Mercer University Press, 2000), 135–60; Ronald N. Frost, "The Bruised Reed by Richard Sibbes (1577–1635)," in *The Devoted Life: An Invitation to the Puritan Classics*, eds. Kelly M. Kapic and Randall C. Gleason (Downers Grove, IL: InterVarsity Press, 2004), 79–91. On the relationship of Sibbes and Edwards's views of the signs of true piety, see Walton, *Jonathan Edwards*, 81–82.

154. *Soul's Conflict*, in *Works* 1:159. Sibbes continued, "It is the glory of a Christian to be carried with full sail, and as it were with the spring-tide of affections." Ibid., 1:160.

155. *Bruised Reed*, in *Works*, 1:80. Sibbes wrote, "The same Spirit that enlighteneth the mind, inspireth gracious inclinations into the will and affections, and infuseth into the whole man." Ibid., 1:82.

away all religion whatsoever."[156] John Preston seated justifying faith not merely in the understanding, but also in the will and affections. God alone can change a person's will and affections so that saving faith can be exercised.[157] Reynolds taught that love for God should be boundless.[158] Fenner said that God requires the heart's affections to be set upon him. Such affections must be "*forcible.*"[159] In *Parable*, Shepard argued that in conversion, the whole soul, including the "affections and will," come to Christ.[160] Even so, for Shepard, the important point was not whether there are affections for God, but the nature of those affections.[161] Likewise, Thomas Watson (1620–86) insisted that, for people to bring God glory, they direct affection to God. Affections must be "[e]xuberant, not a few drops but a

156. *The Returning Backslider* in *Works*, 2:368. Compare Sibbes's counsel elsewhere: "Labour we, therefore, every day more and more to have larger and larger affections to Christ." *Bowels Opened: Being Expository Sermons on Cant. IV.16, V., VI.*, in *Works* 2:126. Sibbes said, "Our affections shew what we are in religion." *A Glance of Heaven; or, A Precious Taste of a Glorious Feast*, in *Works* 4:182 (to which Grosart, the editor Sibbes's works, affixed a note directing the reading to compare "President Edwards' treatise on 'The Religious Affections'"). On the connection between heart and will and affections in Sibbes's thought, see Dever, *Richard Sibbes*, 142–44.

157. Ibid., 1:86. Preston said, "[W]hen God comes to teach a thing he boweth the will and affections to doe it." Ibid., 1:87. Elsewhere Preston wrote, "[T]he affections are such things as the Lord only can meddle with." Preston, *Golden Sceptre*, 14. Preston also argued that love is "necessary to salvation." *Breast-plate*, 3:18.

158. Reynolds wrote, "And thus we are to love him above all things; first, 'appretiativè,' setting a higher price upon his glory and command, than upon anything besides; all, dung in comparison. Secondly, 'intensivè,' with the greatest force and intention of our spirit, setting no bounds or measure of our love to him. Thirdly, 'adæquatè,' as the complete, perfect, and adequate object of all our love, in whom it must begin, and in whom it must end. And therefore the Wise man, speaking of the love and fear of God, tells us, that it is 'totum hominis,' the whole of man." *Treatise*, 62.

159. *Affections*, 5. Fenner referred to the affections of the will as "*sensible motions*" that carry along the soul's lower faculties and the "humours and parts of the body." *Affections*, 6. For Fenner, "*God is the principle object of our affections.*" Not setting affections on God is a "wofull" sin. For this reason Fenner encouraged ministers to "*stir up the affections of mens hearts,*" by the Word of God, which is itself full of affections. Ibid., 46, 105, 90; compare ibid., 94.

160. Shepard, *The Parable of the Ten Virgins Opened and Applied*, 320. Elsewhere Shepard wrote, "[T]he whole soul by faith comes again to God by Christ. The mind sees, the affections make after him, will fastens on him, and there depends." Ibid., 112. Compare ibid., 323. Also see E. Brooks Holifield, *Theology in America: Christian Thought from the Age of the Puritans to the Civil War* (New Haven, CT: Yale University Press, 2003), 34.

161. Ibid., 193, 326, 331, 35, 364–66, 455, 634. In this sense, Shepard anticipates Edwards.

stream," "superlative," and "intense and ardent."[162] For Manton, every faculty—the understanding, will, and affections—must "express love to God."[163] People should obey God from a spirit "seething hot," with "affections . . . so strong, that they boil over in our lives."[164] Manton said religious acts greatly depend on "the vigour of affections."[165] Turretin likewise insisted that human affections must be God's to love him.[166] Justifying faith includes "the most fervent affection and zeal."[167] Christ in his kingly office reigns over the affections of believers, though saints continue to struggle against them.[168] Yet God's grace must change the understanding, will, and affections before an individual can receive the Word of God by faith.[169] Thomas Boston taught that in regeneration there is a happy change made on the affections: they are both rectified and regulated. "[G]race," Boston said, "raises the affections where they are too low. It gives the chief seat in them to God, and pulls down all other rivals."[170]

Finally, these themes arise in Edwards's favorite theologian, Peter van Mastricht (1630–1706) and his *Theoretico-Practica Theologia*.[171] Like other Protestants,

162. Thomas Watson, *A Body of Practical Divinity, in a Series of Sermons on the Shorter Catechism* (Aberdeen: George King and Robert King, 1838), 19.

163. Manton, *Hundred and Nineteenth Psalm*, 1:21–22. Compare ibid., 1:14, 125–26, 303, 579. Among the other echoes of Manton's thought found in Edwards include the notion that in the study of the Word of God there is "a sweetness" or "delightful taste." Ibid., 1:118.

164. Ibid., 1:38. Also see ibid., 1:39, 175, 178.

165. Ibid., 1:79.

166. Turretin, *Elenctic Theology*, §12.2.27 (2:184).

167. Ibid., §15.15.7 (2:590).

168. Ibid., §14.5.8 (2:393); §15.16.30 (2:608). Compare §15.3.25 (2:517). Elsewhere, Turretin said, "Sanctification necessarily follows saving faith because it purifies the heart (Acts 15:9) and is efficacious through love (Gal. 5:6). So pathetically (*pathetice*) does it represent the incredible love of God towards us and the supreme love of Christ dying that it inflames the believer with a mutual love of his most kind Savior, so that he thinks nothing is preferable to living and dying again for him." Ibid., §15.15.9 (2:591).

169. Ibid., §15.4.33 (2:534). "Cùm ergo apertio ista significet obstaculorum omnium, quæ Verbi ingressum & fructum impediebant, remotionem, quæ tam in mente & voluntate, quàm in affectibus occurrebant, à gratia necessariò fieri debuit distinctè à Verbo." Fransisco Turrettino, *Institutio Theologiæ Elencticæ* (Geneva: Samuelem de Tournes, 1682), 2:582.

170. *Four-fold State*, 219. Also see ibid., 217.

171. Edwards to Reverend Joseph Bellamy, Northampton, January 15, 1746/7, in *WJE* 16:216–18. Edwards wrote his young protégé, "But take Mastricht for divinity in general, doctrine, practice, and controversy; or as an universal system of divinity; and it is much better than Turretin or any other book in the world, excepting the Bible, in my opinion" (*WJE* 16:217). For Cotton Mather's assessment of Mastricht, see Brandon Withrow, Introduction to Peter van Mastricht, *A Treatise on Regeneration* (1769; repr., Morgan, PA: Soli Deo Gloria Publications, 2002), xxix. On the life of Peter van Mastricht, see Adriaan Cornelis Neele, *The Art of Living to God: A Study of Method and Piety in the*

Mastricht saw faith as "always joined with a certain pious affection towards God," and this affection of faith, conquering the world, is "transcendental to God and spiritual things."[172] Faith is the "first act of life, in which the whole man lives spiritually," and involves all the faculties: intellect, will, and affections.[173] Faith quickens human affections through the will to love God and goodness, to rejoice and to hate. Affections are considered an act (*actus*), not a passion.[174] This faith was possible after regeneration, which in turn brings spiritual life to "the whole man," including "understanding, will, affections, sensitive faculties, and so forth, that all may be quickened and renewed thereby."[175]

Mastricht taught that, while regeneration illumines the understanding so that it may apprehend the truth and goodness of spiritual objects, the regenerative work is seated in the will or heart, through which the Spirit of God "implants" a "new inclination or propensity towards spiritual good."[176] Regeneration also begins to restore the mind's rule over the passions, which are connected to the "inferior faculties common to brutes," thereby influencing even "members of the body."[177] In his discussion of faith, Mastricht described the affections as acts, and he regards affections as passions of the sensitive appetite. The will of the regenerate has "a new propensity towards spiritual objects." As a result, their affections and passions

Theoretico-Practica Theologia *of Peter van Mastricht (1630–1706),* Perspectives on Christianity, 8th series, vol. 1 (Pretoria: University of Pretoria, 2005), 35–63, and Withrow, introduction to *Regeneration,* viii–xv.

172. "Semper conjuncta est cum pio quodam *affectu* versus Deum (Rom. 4:20). Insuper 3. vincit mundum & mundana (1 Jo 5:4). quatenus affectum ciet *transcendentalem,* versus Deum & spiritualia." Peter van Mastricht, *Theoretico-Practica Theologia, qua Per singula capita Theologia, pars exegetica, dogmatica, elenchtica & practica, perpetua successione conjugantur* (Utrecht: W. Van de Water, J. v. Poolsum, J. Wagens, G. v. Paddenburg, 1724), *Moralis* §2.2.3 (1221). References to Mastricht's *Theologia* will give the book, chapter, and section, followed by the page number. The subsequent *Idea Theologia Moralis* part restarts its book numbering with one, but is not cited.

173. *Theoretica-Practica Theologia*, §2.1.8 (52). Also see Neele, *Art*, 115–19.

174. See *Theoretica-Practica Theologia*, §2.1.10 (52). Also see Neele, *Art*, 127. Neele argues that Mastricht "broadens the [Amesian] definition [of faith] with respect to the intellect and affections," whereas Mastricht's contemporaries saw intellect and affections to be central but separate acts in faith. Ibid., 127–28.

175. Mastricht, *Regeneration*, 13. Mastricht defined regeneration as "that physical operation of the Holy Ghost whereby he begets in men who are elected, redeemed, and externally called, the first act or principle of spiritual life, by which they are enables to receive the offered Redeemer, and comply with the conditions of salvation." Ibid., 13. On the practical understanding and the will, which were very close to Edwards's own view, see ibid., 39–42. The *Treatise on Regeneration* is a portion of the *Theoretico-Practica Theologia* translated into English. Compare Morimoto, *Catholic Vision*, 18–22, 52–53.

176. Ibid., 23.

177. Ibid., 25–26.

are more spiritually orientated. A similar distinction is found in Mastricht's explanation of God's will and affections. Echoing traditional theology, he taught divine impassibility, as God is both incorporeal and active.[178] Nevertheless the impassible God does will, and as the affections of God may describe the effects of the eternal and immutable divine will, Mastricht called on believers to conform their own affections—the acts of their will or "rational appetite"—with the "affections of God." Believers should not only change their affections, but they should also subject their passions under the divine will.[179]

Conclusion

Most contemporary understandings of emotions have little in common with the portrait of affections and passions presented here. Emotions are not considered inclinations or aversions of the soul and are never distinguished between higher and lower movements. They are most often understood as bodily feelings largely outside a person's control, contrary to a traditional Christian understanding of human affectivity.

From the earliest days of post-apostolic Christianity until the time of Jonathan Edwards, Christian teachers of widely varying theological traditions approached affections and passions as movements of the soul. At the most basic level, the affections and passions were understood as inclinations or aversions. With widespread and near agreement, the various doctors distinguished between the higher and lower appetites of the soul and the movements that corresponded to them. This distinction is clearly seen in the constant affirmation of divine impassibility and the reality of divine love. Moreover, throughout the pre-modern church, a host of theologians distinguished explicitly between rational and sensitive appetite. Sometimes Christian teachers also distinguished them nominally, in which the movements of the rational appetite were called *affections* and the movements of the sensitive appetite *passions*. Affections were seen as acts or movements of the will toward and away from rational or spiritual good and evil. The passions occur when the subject is affected by an external object, at which point the passions themselves act upon the will to entice it toward earthly or sensory good.

Although different accounts were given for the problem of the will and its freedom, the affections and passions were not considered to be outside one's volition *per se*. Christian theologians believed passions to be unruly, requiring the control of the rational faculties. When passions rule in an individual, that person was controlled by passions *willingly*. Seated in the soul, passions were often believed to have accompanying effects on the body, but these effects were considered distinct from the passion itself.

178. Mastricht, *Theorectica-Practica Theologia*, §2.15.32 (166–67).

179. Ibid., §2.15.40 (168–69). Also see §2.15.19 (161).

By the time of the Puritans and the Reformed Scholastics, the affections were seen as the positive movements of the soul, often in connection with the will. By definition a genuine believer has a will and affections bent toward God. Because humanity is utterly depraved, changed affections could only come through God's grace and the regenerating work of the Spirit of God. People are unable in themselves to change their will toward God. Following the teaching of Calvin and Melancthon, faith included changed affections or inclinations toward the Triune God and away from sin. As time went on, more and more attention was given to the problem of counterfeit affections. Professing believers would show signs of having such changed affections, but they would eventually reveal themselves to be mere hypocrites.

Chapter 4

YOUNG JONATHAN EDWARDS'S EDUCATION IN AFFECTIONS

Jesus lives, and by His grace,
Victory o'er my passions giving,
I will cleanse my heart and ways,
Ever to His glory living.
Me He raises from the dust;
Jesus is my Hope and Trust.

— Christian F. Gellert, tr. John Dunmore Lang

From his early days, Jonathan Edwards's understanding of reality was closely tied to his idea of the affections. His notion of the affections developed from his reading of Reformed and Puritan theology. Reformed thought included both an emphasis on Spirit-wrought affection for God and a distinction between the affections (the inclinations of the will) and passions (the movements of the sensory appetite). Nevertheless, some scholars say that Edwards, influenced by John Locke, reworked Puritan psychology to justify and defend the affections.

This chapter will show how Edwards's education and reading connected to traditionally Christian affective psychology as discussed in the previous chapter. This connection will provide the foundation for a response to the theory that Edwards's ideas came from the empiricist psychology of John Locke. The writings of Edwards himself will show how he understood affections and passions.

Edwards's defense of religious affections against the challenges of Charles Chauncy during the Great Awakening and its aftermath is well known. Edwards's early affective psychology shows that the basic ideas that he used to defend the Great Awakening were already present in his writings and preaching from the early 1740s. Edwards reiterated the traditional Christian understanding of human affectivity and changed his positions little throughout his life. Both in his private writings and in his regular pulpit ministry, Edwards affirmed the necessity of true affections for God and their distinction from other movements of the soul.

Edwards's Educational Background

In 1716, shortly before his thirteenth birthday, Jonathan Edwards left Windsor, Connecticut, for Connecticut's Collegiate School. The Collegiate School (later Yale) had been formed in 1701 in part to respond to suspicious trends at Harvard. Students learned the Westminster Catechism (in Latin) and Ames's *Medulla Theologiae*.[1] The "Dummer Collection," donated to New Haven in 1714, introduced young Jonathan to early Enlightenment thought and the fashionable books of moderate Latitudinarianism. At thirteen, Edwards was a few years younger than the average scholar.[2]

William S. Morris's excellent study on Jonathan Edwards in his youth documented the theological influences on the budding minister, both at Yale and in his reading.[3] Edwards would have been trained principally in Protestant Scholasticism via John Wollebius and William Ames in particular. Yale's curriculum was eclectic by design. Edwards learned logic by reading Ramus and modified Aristotelianism by reading Burgersdicius, corrected at points by the Cartesian-influenced logic of Brattle, Legrand, Arnauld, and John Locke. Edwards was also exposed to the warm piety of English and American Puritanism, including that of Richard Baxter and John Flavel. Morris argued that Edwards gave his attention to books from several fields, while studying most carefully Puritan and theological literature.[4]

Edwards likely had at least some interaction with patristic and medieval theology. Although Edwards may not have read Augustine, William Morris believed that he was exposed to Augustinian thought. Edwards showed interest

1. For more on the affective psychology in Ames's *Medulla Theologiae*, see the previous section.

2. See Marsden, *Jonathan Edwards*, 25–43; Murray, *Jonathan Edwards*, 25–37; Franklin Bowditch Dexter, ed., *Documentary History of Yale University: Under the Original Charter of the Collegiate School of Connecticut 1701–1745* (New Haven, CT: Yale University Press, 1916), 1–7, 27–34, 163–64, 226–29; Franklin Bowditch Dexter, *Sketch of the History of Yale University* (New York: Henry Holt and Co., 1887), 7–12; Edwin Oviatt, *The Beginnings of Yale (1701–1726)* (New Haven: Yale University Press, 1916), 136–37; and Thuesen, "Editor's Introduction," in *WJE*, 8–13. On Edwards's earliest writings, see Egbert C. Smyth, "Some Early Writings of Jonathan Edwards. A. D. 1714–1726." Proceedings of the American Antiquarian Society 10 (October 1895): 212–36. On his "intellectual context," see McClymond and McDermott, *Theology of Jonathan Edwards*, 40–59 and Peter J. Thuesen, "Edwards' Intellectual Background," in *The Princeton Companion to Jonathan Edwards*, ed. Sang Hyun Lee (Princeton, NJ: Princeton University Press, 2005), 16–33 (hereafter *PCJE*). American Puritans were not as hostile to science as is sometimes imagined. Sarah Rivett, *The Science of the Soul in Colonial New England* (Chapel Hill: University of North Carolina Press, 2011).

3. William Sparkes Morris, *The Young Jonathan Edwards: A Reconstruction*, *JECSS* 1 (1991; repr., Eugene, Oreg.: Wipf & Stock Publishers, 2005).

4. Morris, *Young Jonathan Edwards*, 61, 72–77, 101, 103–28, 270–86.

in the *Confessions* and Yale likely held a copy; if Edwards did not read Augustine first hand, he read summaries of his thought in John Owen, the Cambridge Platonists, or Melanchthon.[5] Norman Fiering also highlights the influence of Augustinian voluntarism on Edwards's thought.[6] Indeed, the Dummer collection included a ten-volume set of Augustine's works in Latin.[7] Edwards likely reviewed condensations of patristic thought such as those by John Sharp and Louis Ellies Du Pin.[8] As for medieval figures, Edwards cited Bernard of Clairvaux a few times.[9] Solomon Stoddard owned many volumes by Thomas Aquinas, but Edwards had little regard for his thought.[10] Although he did not emphasize the sayings of patristic and medieval theologians in his writings, Edwards likely read some of them directly. Little evidence indicates that pre-Reformation theologians directly influenced Edwards's ideas of the affections and passions, yet Edwards was indirectly influenced by their thought through the Reformed Scholastic and Puritan tradition.[11]

By the time Edwards read *The Marrow of the Theology* at Yale, Ames's theology had long been a staple for New England Puritanism.[12] Ames distinguished affections and passions, and stressed the role of affections in saving faith.[13] Norman Fiering's interest in the connection between Ames and Edwards springs from their mutual voluntarism, but he also notes that Edwards's identification of the will with the affections came from Ames and other Reformed authors.[14] Fiering's observations are significant, especially given the close connection between the will and affections in Ames.

5. Morris, *Young Jonathan Edwards*, 497–98. Also see Thuesen, "Editor's Introduction," in *WJE* 26:64.

6. Norman Fiering, "Will and Intellect in the New England Mind," *WMQ* 29 (1972): 515–58.

7. *WJE* 26:123.

8. *WJE* 26:127, 165; also see Thuesen, "Editor's Introduction," in *WJE* 26:64.

9. See *WJE* 2:322–23n1 and "44. Sermon on Ps. 139:7-10," in *Sermons, Series II, 1723–1727*, vol. 42, *The Works of Jonathan Edwards Online*, ed. Jonathan Edwards Center (New Haven, CT: Yale University Press, 2008), http://edwards.yale.edu/archive?path=aHR0cDovL2Vkd2FyZHMueWFsZS5lZHUvY2dpLWJpbi9uZXdwaGlsby9nZXRvYmplY3QucGw/Yy40MDoxOS53amVv (accessed December 4, 2017).

10. Thuesen, "Editor's Introduction," in *WJE* 26:6, 63–64.

11. See Miller, *The New England Mind*, 89–108; Fiering, *Moral Philosophy*; Amy Plantinga Pauw, *The Supreme Harmony of All: The Trinitarian Theology of Jonathan Edwards* (Grand Rapids, MI: Eerdmans, 2002), 44–46; George Marsden, *Jonathan Edwards*, 460; and McClymond and McDermott, *Theology of Jonathan Edwards*, 695–97, 727.

12. Thuesen, "Editor's Introduction," *WJE* 26:8; Fiering, *Moral Philosophy*, 28 n51.

13. See Chapter 3.

14. Fiering explains that for Augustine, Ames, and Edwards, the actions of the will, particularly in love and hate, came not from intellectual deliberation, but divine grace. "Will and Intellect," 522.

Edwards's study of John Wollebius's *Abridgement of Christian Divinity* at Yale would have taught him similar themes.[15] Wollebius argued that humans, made in the image of God, were originally created with "the clearness of the understanding, the liberty and rectitude of the will, the conformitie of the appetites and affections, the immortality of the whole man, and dominion over the inferior creatures."[16] The Fall resulted in a darkened understanding, a depraved will, and a vitiated inferior appetite.[17] Wollebius also taught that the First Commandment implied that there should be "[r]eligious affection towards God," consisting in "Faith, Hope, Charity, Confidence in God, Fear, Repentance, Patience, and Thankfulness of minde."[18] The Law demands that people sanctify God's name "in affection," by having a zeal for God's glory and sorrow for sin.[19] Finally, Wollebius understood the law to regulate the right use of all "concupiscence." Using the distinction between the sensitive and spiritual aspects of humanity, Wollebius said that the Tenth Commandment addresses the desires of the sensitive appetites and the higher affections, both of which can be used for good or evil.[20] Therefore, both Ames and Wollebius, two of the foremost theologians Edwards studied at Yale, stressed the importance of affection for God and perpetuated the traditional Christian distinction between higher and lower movements of the soul.

Another important early influence was Richard Baxter.[21] In his *The Reasons of the Christian Religion*, Baxter stressed the distinction between soul and body. The will in particular was disposed to what the mind understood to be good. What the "*sensitive pleasure*" apprehends to be good may not comply with what reason discerns as good.[22] Baxter considered it self-evident that the "*sense and bodily faculties*" should be subservient to reason and the will, the "*superior faculties*."[23] In Baxter, Edwards would have further read that God's will must have good for its

15. John Wolleb, *The Abridgement of Christian Divinitie*, 3rd ed., trans. Alexander Ross (London: T. Mabb, 1660). Morris, *Young Jonathan Edwards*, 72–79; Oviatt, *The Beginnings of Yale*, 418–24; and David Hall, "The New England Background," in *Cambridge Companion to JE*, 69.

16. Wolleb, *The Abridgement of Christian Divinitie*, 69.

17. Ibid., 79.

18. Ibid., 323.

19. Ibid., 355–56.

20. Ibid., 424–26.

21. See Morris, *Young Jonathan Edwards*, 270–80; Thuesen, "Editor's Introduction," 52–53; and Walton, *Jonathan Edwards*, 116–18.

22. Richard Baxter, *The Reasons of the Christian Religion. The First Part, of Godliness: Proving by Natural Evidence the Being of God, the Necessity of Holiness, and a future Life of Retribution; the Sinfulness of the World; the Desert of Hell; and what hope of Recovery Mercies intimate. The Second Part, of Christianity: Proving by Evidence Supernatural and Natural, the certain Truth of the Christian Belief: and answering the Objections of Unbelievers* (London: R. White for Fran. Titon, 1667), 1–3.

23. Baxter, *The Reasons of the Christian Religion*, 4.

object. God's will is then love or complacency toward the good. Furthermore, the good which God loves must be in "*In his BEING HIMSELF*," "*In his KNOWING HIMSELF*," and "*In his LOVING AND ENJOYING HIMSELF*."[24] Baxter also identified the will closely with love.[25]

Furthermore, if the affective psychology of Ames, Wollebius, and Baxter alone had insufficiently influenced Edwards, Edwards would have assuredly been exposed to similar thought in other Reformed works that he read and studied.[26] Richard Sibbes, Thomas Shepard, John Owen, Thomas Watson, Thomas Manton, Francis Turretin, Peter van Mastricht, and Thomas Boston all perpetuated, to some degree, the Reformed teachings on the heart, affections, will, and sense appetites, and it is evident that Edwards knew their writings well, especially their writings concerning the affections. The young Edwards was immersed in a world of Christian theology in which affections and passions at their most basic level referred to inclinations and aversions of the soul.[27]

Throughout his ministry, Edwards held that truly gracious affections came only from the Spirit. His approval of the affections echoed leading Puritan authors, including John Owen, Thomas Manton, and Thomas Shepard. It also characterized the preaching and writing of Edwards's own maternal grandfather, Solomon Stoddard. Granted, in *The Safety of Appearing*, Stoddard did caution that natural affections could actually hinder someone from coming to Christ.[28]

24. Ibid., 24.

25. Ibid., 25. The close relationship of the will and love is also found in Peter Sterry. Baxter would later read Sterry and express his appreciation for the strength of Sterry's statement. See Vivian de Sola Pinto, *Peter Sterry: Platonist and Puritan 1613–1672: A Biographical and Critical Study with Passages from his Writings* (Cambridge: Cambridge University Press, 1934), 136–37. Richard Baxter, *The Practical Works of The Rev. Richard Baxter with a Life of the Author, and a Critical Examination of his Writings*, 23 vols., ed. William Orme (London: James Duncan, 1830), 1:86nq.

26. See Thuesen, "Editor's Introduction," 52–58; Walton, *Jonathan Edwards*. For Sibbes, see *WJE* 2:433; Shepard is cited multiple times in *Affections*; for Owen, see *WJE* 2:251, 372–73, et al.; for Watson, see *WJE* 26:136, 224; for Turretin, see *WJE* 2:289; for Mastricht, see *WJE* 2:337; for Boston, see *WJE* 2:489 and *WJE* 26:224.

27. Norman Fiering, despite his conflation of the terms with modern emotions, correctly observed, "Passions, affections—or, to use the modern word, emotions—were responses to apprehended good or evil, or to present or anticipated pleasure or pain." Fiering, *Moral Philosophy*, 199.

28. Solomon Stoddard, *The Safety of Appearing at the Day of Judgment in the Righteousness of Christ, Opened and Applied* (Northampton: Thomas M. Pomroy, 1804), 307. Stoddard noted that the Bible contained many examples of those who experienced religious affections of a counterfeit nature. It is dangerous for such to be "much affected with their affections." Ibid., 137; compare 215. The Devil can work on human affections. Ibid., 129. See Stoddard, *A Guide to Christ, or The Way of Directing Souls That Are under the Work of Conversion. Compiled for the Help of Young Ministers, and May Be Serviceable*

He wrote, "Many carnal men have had very *strong pangs of affection*; their hearts may overflow in a religious way. Many that have no principle of grace, have had great impressions on their hearts from the word of God."[29] Nevertheless, Stoddard also offered a more positive assessment of the affections. Although he affirmed divine impassibility, he also ascribed affections to God. God's regenerating grace included a work on the affections of hope, love, and fear.[30]

The foregoing shows that Reformed and traditional Christian thought powerfully shaped Edwards's ideas on human affectivity. Traditional perspectives on the affections and passions would have entered Edwards's thought through the writings of Ames and Wollebius. Their ideas may have been reinforced through study of patristic and medieval theology. These categories would have further been confirmed by the Reformed authors (including Edwards's grandfather) whose works filled his bookshelves.

Though schooled in the Reformed tradition, Edwards read widely. The Dummer collection included a selection of non-theological literature, including works by John Locke.[31] Here the question of Locke's influence must be considered.

Jonathan Edwards and John Locke

Scholars are still responding to Perry Miller's argument that John Locke strongly influenced Jonathan Edwards.[32] According to Miller, Edwards embedded his Reformed rhetoric with the "radical and foreign psychology" of Locke's

to Private Christians, Who are Enquiring the Way to Zion (Northampton: Andrew Wright, 1816), 26, 48.

29. Stoddard, *Safety*, 187.

30. Stoddard, *Safety*, 237–38. For Stoddard's reference to God's affections, see Stoddard, *Safety*, 183, 334. Concerning divine impassibility, see Stoddard, *Safety*, 304. Eugene White says, "[I]n effect Stoddard accepted the primacy of Affections in spiritual persuasion. In addition, Stoddard appears to have sponsored the role of the emotions in initiating and in determining the ideational conviction of the Understanding." White, *Puritan Rhetoric*, 45.

31. See Thuesen's summary of the Dummer collection in his introduction to *WJE* 26:8–13. See Thuesen's "Edwards' References to Printed Works in His Manuscripts and the Yale Edition," in 26:428–72.

32. Miller, *Jonathan Edwards*. The pages that ignited the controversy can be found in Hopkins, *The Life and Character of Jonathan Edwards*, 3–4. For examples of ante-Miller attempts to deal with the problem of Edwards and Locke, see Edwards Beecher, "The Works of Samuel Hopkins," *BSac* 10 (1853): 68–82; Adam Leroy Jones, *Early American Philosophers* 2 (June 1898): 394–403; Frederick J. E. Woodbridge, "The Philosophy of Jonathan Edwards," in *Exercises Commemorating the Two-Hundredth Anniversary of the Birth of Jonathan Edwards, Held at Andover Theological Seminary, October 4 and 5, 1903*, ed. John Winthrop Platner (Andover, MA: Andover Press, 1904), 47–72; and Jay Wharton Fay, *American Psychology before William James* (New Brunswick, NJ: Rutgers University Press, 1939).

philosophy.[33] Miller's argument touches directly on Edwards's understanding of affections. For Miller, Edwards's debate with Charles Chauncy showed how radical Edwards had become.

Perry Miller's Long Shadow

Miller said that Chauncy espoused the old faculty psychology of Reformed Scholasticism, which affirmed affections as a distinct power of the soul alongside the separate faculties of reason, imagination, and will. Chauncy frowned on the "passions," forcing Edwards to invent a new psychology (via Locke) to defend the Great Awakening.[34] As Miller saw it, "Locke started one of the great revolutionary movements of modern times when he rejected the scholastic psychology, with its theory that each 'faculty' is a separate province or power capable of acting like a distinct being, as 'a confused notion of so many distinct agents in us.'"[35] Edwards, seizing this new psychology, portrayed the human being as a living organism, whereby he altogether dispensed with the idea of faculties (though retaining the word *faculty* because "[n]o other term was available").[36] Miller explained,

> By the understanding he [Edwards] conceived the soul as it perceives, and by the will he meant the soul perceiving as a sentient, passionate being, with hopes and fears, and therefore perceiving according to its vital inclination. The coherence of a person is not a mathematical sum of his faculties, but his abiding disposition, of which his reason and will are expressions—are, as he called them in his notebooks, a person's "image." There is, in fact, only one faculty: "it is our inclination that governs us in our actions."[37]

For Miller, Edwards's rejection of the faculties resulted in "the supremacy of passion." By dividing understanding and the "sense of the heart" Edwards intentionally placed affections over understanding. Given this new doctrine, Edwards had to find a way "to distinguish, scientifically, between emotions which are mechanical reflexes, one in kind with collision among stones, and those which signify something other than the juices of the glands."[38] In sum, "Edwards rejected

33. Miller, *Jonathan Edwards*, 52.

34. The debate between Edwards and Chauncy is discussed in Chapter 6.

35. Ibid., 181. Miller cited John Locke, *An Essay Concerning Human Understanding*, ed. Alexander Campbell Fraser, Great Books of the Western World 35 (Chicago, IL: Encyclopædia Britannica, Inc., 1952), §2.21.6 (180). All subsequent citations of Locke's *Essay Concerning Human Understanding* will cite the book, chapter, and section, followed by the page number in parenthesis of the Great Books edition.

36. Miller, *Jonathan Edwards*, 182.

37. Ibid., 182. Compare Ramsey, "Editor's Introduction," in *WJE* 1:47–52.

38. Ibid., 184.

the metaphysics and psychology of original Puritanism, and substituted [Isaac] Newton and Locke."[39]

Many scholars have responded to various points of Miller's thesis. In order to understand Edwards's affective psychology, the most important question is the extent to which Edwards depended upon Locke in that specific area. Conrad Cherry agreed with Miller that Edwards could respond to Chauncy's rationalistic attack on the Great Awakening because of Edwards's acceptance of Lockean psychology.[40] Roland Delattre also echoes Miller's exposition.[41] John E. Smith sums up his own research by saying: "Edwards' philosophical stance can best be defined as a subtle interweaving of the Augustinian tradition and its later outcropping in the Cambridge Platonists, with one fundamental idea derived from Locke which he made the basis of his theological empiricism."[42] According to Smith, Edwards used Locke's "simple idea" to account for the mark of true religion, the "new sense of the heart." Although Locke believed human minds received simple ideas passively, Edwards saw a partially active and inclined mind receiving such ideas in religious experience.[43] For J. Rodney Fulcher, Edwards's innovations freed the affections previously encumbered by Puritan faculty psychology.[44] Patricia Tracy says that Edwards, borrowing from Lockean psychology, fused Calvinism with the "new language of sensibility."[45] D. G. Hart echoes Miller's commentary, noting that Edwards invented a psychology that merged the understanding and will into an "organic one."[46] Stephen J. Nichols also says that Edwards found Locke's "faculty psychology" "detrimental," and "countered by enlisting the idea of affections." Nevertheless, he believes that Edwards borrowed "from Locke the idea that the soul consists of both the understanding and what he refers to as *inclination*."[47]

39. Ibid., 194.

40. Cherry, *Theology*, 164–68.

41. Roland A. Delattre, *Beauty and Sensibility in the Thought of Jonathan Edwards: An Essay in Aesthetics and Theological Ethics*, *JECSS* 4 (1968; repr., Eugene, OR: Wipf and Stock Publishers, 2006), 41–42.

42. John E. Smith, "Jonathan Edwards as Philosophical Theologian," *Review of Metaphysics* 30 (1976): 311.

43. Smith, "Jonathan Edwards as Philosophical Theologian."

44. Fulcher, "Puritans and the Passions," 123–39.

45. Patricia J. Tracy, *Jonathan Edwards, Pastor: Religion and Society in Eighteenth-Century Northampton* (New York: Hill and Wang, 1980), 5, 75–76. Yet Tracy critiques Miller's emphasis, observing that Edwards was a pastor more than a "thinker by profession." Ibid., 5–9.

46. Hart, "Jonathan Edwards and the Origin of Experimental Calvinism," 168. Compare Oliphint, "Jonathan Edwards on Apologetics," 132.

47. Stephen J. Nichols, *Jonathan Edwards: A Guided Tour of His Life and Thought* (Phillipsburg, NJ: P&R Publishing, 2001), 112.

Edwards's notion of affections, according to Nichols, unify the self.[48] Although Leon Chai finds differences between Edwards and Locke, Chai believes Edwards agreed with Locke to such an extent that he is post-Lockean (and post-Enlightenment).[49] Finally, William Danaher traces Edwards's emphasis on "the whole soul" to Locke and Malebranche, and argues that Edwards's innovation was in making affections the "locus of virtue."[50]

Correctives to Miller's Thesis

Many scholars accept Perry Miller's reading of Edwards, and his interpretation has seen wide acceptance among Edwardseans. Several scholars, however, have suggested that Miller's emphasis on Edwards's appropriation of Locke's psychology is overstated. The findings of scholars such as William Morris, Norman Fiering, Brad Walton, and others are especially helpful for rightly interpreting the influence of Locke on Edwards's affective psychology. This study will briefly review their work here.

William Morris's study is significant in that it downplays the relationship of Edwards and Locke. He noted that Edwards's explanation of his own conversion was not Lockean, but Puritan in its vocabulary.[51] Edwards read Locke in the context of an academic setting steeped in Reformed Scholasticism.[52] Locke himself, Morris said, did not think his most important contribution in the *Essay* to be "a new way of ideas of sensation and reflection," but epistemological certainty, put forth in a

48. Ibid., 113. Without referencing Locke's influence, Strobel notes Edwards's departure from "faculty psychology," as his faculties "do not have their own being." *Theology*, 213.

49. Chai, *Jonathan Edwards and the Limits of Enlightenment Philosophy*, v–xi, 9–35. Compare Amy Plantinga Pauw, Review of *Jonathan Edwards and the Limits of Enlightenment Philosophy*, by Leon Chai, *CTJ* 35 (2000):167–68; Douglas A. Sweeney, Review of *Jonathan Edwards and the Limits of Enlightenment Philosophy*, by Leon Chai, *ThTo* 56 (1999):438–41; John F. Wilson, Review of *Jonathan Edwards and the Limits of Enlightenment Philosophy*, by Leon Chai, *CH* 67 (1998):811–12; and Christopher J. Vascardi, Review of *Jonathan Edwards and the Limits of Enlightenment Philosophy*, by Leon Chai, *TS* 60 (1999):193–94.

50. Danaher, *Trinitarian Ethics*, 122.

51. Morris, *Young Jonathan Edwards*, 210.

52. Ibid., 134–35. Locke was viewed with some suspicion at Yale as early as 1710. Ibid., 61. Morris stated, "*It cannot be too strongly stressed that before, during, and after his reading of John Locke, the main element in Jonathan Edwards' training, apart from the Bible and the Scholastic analysis of the Bible, was . . . Scholastic disputation.*" Ibid., 107. Morris also noted, "It cannot be too much stressed that during those two years of theological training at Yale, 1720–22, and during the subsequent two years, most of which, apart from the eight months spent in pastoral work in New York, were spent in study in his father's homestead, Edwards was being nourished spiritually and theologically upon the great stream of Puritan writers." Ibid., 267.

conservative tone.[53] Although Edwards lauded Locke (according to his friend and biographer Samuel Hopkins), he was likely unimpressed with Locke's theological and moral remarks, and, as Hopkins observed, Edwards considered no one his master.[54] Furthermore, Edwards read the Dummer books with an intention of using his intellectual gifts to defend orthodoxy against the trends of Deism, Arminianism, and Latitudinarianism.[55]

Morris also addressed the relationship of Edwards to Lockean psychology. First, Edwards worked at solving the soul-body problem to a much greater extent than Locke.[56] Second, Edwards clearly disagreed with Locke's definition of the will as uneasiness, and this disagreement arose from Edwards's category of consent (and, by implication, inclination) which he believed fundamental to existence itself.[57] Third, while Edwards echoed Locke's maxim that human knowledge comes from the senses, he understood better the deceptiveness of the senses and accepted the necessity for abstraction by reason.[58] In spite of these observations, Morris concluded that Edwards both read Locke and was deeply influenced by him. Edwards accepted and dismissed varying elements of Locke's psychology. Specifically, he seemed more skeptical than Locke on the usefulness of sensory apprehension over reason.

Morris noted that Edwards had one more "radical and profound difference" with Locke in the distinction between "sense of the heart" and "speculative understanding." The "sense of the heart" was the way God had contact with the regenerate. God gave heart knowledge when he influenced his affections.[59] Edwards settled early his ideas on the divinely affected mind, influenced by the writings of John Owen and other Reformed theologians. These notions were

53. Ibid., 158–60, 164–65. See Ernst Cassirer, *The Philosophy of the Enlightenment*, trans. Fritz C. A. Koelln and James P. Pettegrove (Princeton, NJ: Princeton University Press, 2009), 93–133.

54. Ibid., 165–70.

55. Ibid., 101–02. On Edwards and Deism, see Gerald R. McDermott, *Jonathan Edwards Confronts the Gods: Christian Theology, Enlightenment Religion, and Non-Christian Faiths* (New York: Oxford University Press, 2000); and William M. Schweitzer, *God is a Communicative Being: Divine Communicativeness and Harmony in the Theology of Jonathan Edwards* (London: T&T Clark, 2012), 11–30 and 53–80.

56. Morris, *Young Jonathan Edwards*, 407.

57. Morris wrote: "An inclination is, of course, an inclination toward something. . . . To have placed inclination and feeling outside the biblical realm of 'the heart' (i.e., the will), in a new and third category of 'feeling' that was surely affective and passive, rather than active, would have cut right across that fundamental structure of experience as passive reception in understanding through sensation, and active response in heart and mind through both will and understanding, the one as efficient cause, the other as active reflection on the ideas of sense." Ibid., 415–16.

58. Ibid., 424.

59. Ibid., 434.

in a different category from Edwards's reflections on the *natural* mind seen in his notebook on "The Mind." Although Edwards gleaned some insight from Locke on the nature of the natural mind, such reflections were in a separate domain from the mind's supernatural operations, for which Locke gave him no real aid.[60]

Harold P. Simonson also notes that Edwards rejected Locke's supposition that the will is moved by uneasiness. For Edwards, humanity rose above animals in their ability to contemplate and enjoy spiritual realities. In this, "he [Edwards] pushed beyond Lockean psychology and into religion."[61] Diverting from Locke's emphasis on sensory perception, Edwards taught that human knowledge of spiritual things determined a person's actions. Therefore, the will is determined by the strength of the sense of the good in the mind. Simonson believes that the influence of Locke over Edwards ends at terms Edwards used: "[W]hat Edwards tried to describe through the language of sensation is a dimension of existence that transcends the sensation itself."[62]

For Simonson, Edwards pilfered for Christian theology Locke's emphasis on experience in epistemology while rejecting Locke's idea of mental passivity in knowing.[63] Edwards, however, was no empiricist (a philosophy which could never function well in a Christian epistemology). Empiricism's inherent skepticism and neutrality conflict with Edwards's doctrines. *Religious Affections* is not a scientific treatise.[64]

Terrence Erdt demonstrates that Edwards's "sense of the heart" is actually an old Calvinist concept used to describe religious experience.[65] As Locke believed that judgment could overcome uneasiness in the soul, Erdt argues that Locke's position on the will was quite close to the classical position.[66] Because Locke left his theory of the passions incomplete, Edwards identified will and affections in his idea of the "sense of the heart."[67] Erdt notices that Edwards also departed from Locke when he distinguished sensation and reflection.[68] By moving sensation from the realm of understanding to the realm of the will, Edwards gave the will much more significance than Locke did. Yet Erdt adds, "The traditional distinction

60. Ibid.

61. Harold P. Simonson, *Jonathan Edwards: Theologian of the Heart* (1974; repr., Macon, GA: Mercer University Press, 1982), 26.

62. Ibid., 27.

63. Ibid., 29.

64. Ibid., 29–30.

65. Erdt, *Jonathan Edwards*, 20.

66. Ibid., 24.

67. Ibid., 25.

68. Ibid., 26. "Misc. 782" is Edwards's fullest early treatment of "sense of the heart" and its relationship to conversion. Erdt defines Edwards's notion of sensation as a "repetition of the sensation that furnishes the idea," rather than a fundamental inclination to or aversion from the object apprehended.

between speculative knowledge, and the sense of the heart, the new learning could explain, in part, as the difference between apprehension through reflection of an idea of pleasure or pain by means of a sign or through the repetition of the actual feeling."[69]

Erdt concludes that Edwards used Locke's psychology to clarify the traditional notion of the "sense of the heart." The original doctrine had problems with the line between will and understanding, often attributing to the will too much apprehension. Edwards solved this difficulty by saying that the will presented the understanding with a reflective idea. Some reflective ideas were mere signs of the original movement in the soul, and others were actual repetitions of original movement. The "sense of the heart," as a reflective idea, was the repeated perception of the original feeling.[70]

Norman Fiering pushes the critique of Miller still further. Fiering argues that Miller's "dramatic picture of the relationship between Edwards and Locke must be rejected."[71] Fiering notes that Miller attributed too many of Locke's revolutionary ideas as originating with Locke himself, including the distinction between primary and secondary qualities, and the idea that the soul's faculties are not distinct entities. Concerning moral philosophy, Fiering says Edwards borrowed "hardly any" point from Locke.[72] Edwards looked to Locke as a logician and was undoubtedly "enormously excited" by the *Essay*, but the book was not decisive intellectually.[73] Malebranche was a greater influence on Edwards. As far as Edwards's dependence on Locke for psychology, Fiering believes that Edwards had most of his core positions set before he read Locke.[74] In *Moral Philosophy at Seventeenth Century Harvard*, Fiering argues that Perry Miller misread the issue between Chauncy and Edwards as being about faculty versus Lockean psychology. Instead, Fiering casts the controversy as another iteration in the centuries' old debate between intellectualism and voluntarism. Edwards's voluntarism was only modern and Lockean "in the sense that Augustinian voluntarism fed into the rising tide of romanticism, which was yet to reach full height." Fiering continues, "The issue in the Great Awakening was not old versus new, but rather the perennial opposition of head and heart, both sides of which have found able supporters in every age."[75]

James Hoopes argues against Miller's theses even more forcefully than Fiering. Using Fiering's research, Hoopes says Edwards saw Locke as a "threat to orthodoxy," and therefore Edwards used Locke's empiricist terminology to

69. Ibid., 27.
70. Ibid., 41–42.
71. Fiering, *Jonathan Edwards's Moral Thought*, 36.
72. Ibid., 37.
73. Ibid., 38.
74. "Fiering, "Rationalist Foundations," 77.
75. Fiering, *Moral Philosophy*, 144.

uproot empiricism.[76] "Edwards's metaphysical idealism permitted him to subvert the premises of sensational psychology while employing Locke's fashionable terminology."[77] Because Edwards rejected Locke's idea of substance, he also rejected Locke's dogma that ideas came through the senses.

Hoopes says Edwards also affirmed innate ideas against Locke.[78] For Hoopes, scholars have missed Edwards's critical distinction between "sense of the heart" and "new spiritual sense"; the former can be found in believers and unbelievers alike, while the latter is reserved for believers alone.[79] Edwards used *sense* to speak of "the mind's willful relation to a reflexive *idea* such as holiness . . . . The new spiritual sense thus resembles the natural external senses in every possible way."[80] The new spiritual sense is a new sense altogether. Yet Hoopes believes that Edwards altered the Calvinist and Puritan tradition in subtle ways.[81] In sum, Hoopes says, "Only his idealist metaphysics made it possible for him to use the word 'sense' in strictest accuracy as he spoke of the 'new spiritual sense.'"[82] Hoopes finds Edwards in opposition to Locke's metaphysics.

Janice Knight also pushes back against Miller, but from a different perspective. Her critique is that Miller found the Puritans monolithic because he overemphasized divines she calls "Intellectual Fathers"—men like Perkins, Ames, William Bradshaw, and Thomas Hooker who emphasized works as the evidence of salvation and the preparation of hearts for conversion. Another vital tradition, one Knight calls the "Spiritual Brethren," consisted of authors such as John Cotton, Sibbes, Preston, and Thomas Goodwin. They focused on inner spiritual vitality for assurance and God's transforming love in conversion. Although she only hints at conclusions regarding Edwards, Knight suggests he echoed the Spiritual Brethren on "almost every important issue."[83] She says studying Edwards's connections with the Spiritual Brethren and his use of "Sibbesian rhetoric" might show that his "seemingly radical definition of grace as a new sense" had a source other than Locke.[84]

76. James Hoopes, "Jonathan Edwards's Religious Psychology," *The Journal of American History* 69 (1983): 851–52.

77. Hoopes, "Jonathan Edwards's Religious Psychology," 854.

78. Ibid., 854–55.

79. Ibid., 857.

80. Ibid., 860. Hoopes has the courage to observe, "Many modern scholars have no idea of what it feels like to perceive holiness, and those who do can no more describe the sensation to the rest of us than one can tell a man blind since birth what it feels like to see." Ibid., 861.

81. Ibid., 862–63.

82. Ibid., 865.

83. Janice Knight, *Orthodoxies in Massachusetts: Rereading American Puritanism* (Cambridge, MA: Cambridge University Press, 1994), 199.

84. Knight, *Orthodoxies in Massachusetts*, 211.

Sean Michael Lucas, building upon Janice Knight's research, says that Edwards's *Religious Affections* should be understood in a Puritan rather than Lockean context.[85] After outlining Knight's two opposing Puritan parties, Lucas asserts that Edwards was trying to hold the two understandings of sanctification (assurance vs. works) "in tension." Although Edwards repeatedly cites Shepard in *Affections*, the book shows the influence of Sibbes and Cotton, especially in the doctrine of the spiritual sense.[86]

Brad Walton finds much of Edwards's thought anticipated in Puritan theology of the affections.[87] The "spiritual sense" concept is found in the writings of William Perkins and the term itself is used and developed by Richard Sibbes, Thomas Goodwin, Thomas Brooks, and John Owen. Cambridge Platonist John Smith also spoke of a "spiritual sensation" whereby human beings were able truly to know the things of God.[88] The presentation of a spiritual sense in "sensual and aesthetic terms" is found not only in Edwards but in his predecessors as well.[89] Edwards's Puritan heritage also seated the affections and inclinations in the heart. Walton says too many scholars have failed to note the continuity between Edwards and the Puritan tradition.[90] Even Reformed Scholastics like Turretin and Mastricht emphasized the spiritual perception or sensation of the heart.[91]

Walton highlights the points of discontinuity between Edwards and Locke. For instance, Locke deliberately rejected the view that the will included affectivity.[92] Walton grants that Edwards used the Lockean term "complex idea" to refer to his "notion of God," but he asserts that Edwards did not use the term in a "strict, Lockean sense, but in a loose, analogous fashion."[93] Edwards departed from Locke's system in "Misc. 782" by advocating speculative knowledge, heart-language, and perception as affective.[94]

Walton concludes that Edwards "reinterpreted" some Lockean concepts to articulate an epistemology that was essentially Puritan.[95] Edwards did not describe Calvinist conversion in the language of Lockean empiricism; his terminology

85. Sean Michael Lucas, "'What Is the Nature of True Religion?': *Religious Affections* and Its American Puritan Context," in *All for Jesus: A Celebration of the 50th Anniversary of Covenant Theological Seminary*, eds. Robert A. Peterson and Sean Michael Lucas (Ross-shire, Great Britain: Mentor, 2006), 118.

86. Lucas, "What Is the Nature of True Religion?", 119.

87. Walton, *Jonathan Edwards*.

88. Compare Smith, "Editor's Introduction," in *WJE* 2:65–6.

89. Walton, *Jonathan Edwards*, 137.

90. Ibid., 43–138.

91. Ibid., 200–01.

92. Ibid., 208.

93. Ibid., 212.

94. Ibid., 216.

95. Ibid., 217.

and his concept of conversion remained Reformed. Locke's terms are used only "metaphorically, in an un-Lockean sense."[96] Walton adds, "So far from adapting puritanism to Lockean empiricism, Edwards reinterprets Lockean empiricism, where he refers to it at all, to fit traditional puritan ideas about knowledge and feeling."[97] Locke said that ideas came from sensation; Edwards said that a Christian's idea of God came from the Spirit.

Josh Moody voices agreement with Morris's conclusions: "It is important to grasp that this 'spiritual sense' is not a nod and a wink toward Lockean empiricism, but rather an appeal to the language of that philosophy to explain the experience of what might be termed 'spiritual appreciation.'"[98] Moody rejects Perry Miller's conclusions and argues that, with respect to "sense of the heart," Edwards borrowed the language of Lockean empiricism to express an idea that had Puritan and biblical roots.[99] Yet Moody asserts that Edwards's notion of "idea" in his Trinitarian doctrine is an instance of his dependence on Locke.[100] Therefore, one should not see Edwards as either Enlightenment-touting with vestiges of Puritanism, or as a Puritan rejecting the Enlightenment. Instead Edwards "reformed the Enlightenment by re-defining the language and presuppositions of the age and interpreting them on Reformed grounds."[101]

Peter Thuesen interprets Edwards as an eclectic thinker who "resisted unambiguous identification" with both Puritanism and Enlightenment rationalism.[102] For Thuesen, Miller's thesis is credible because Edwards rejected the traditional psychological distinctions between faculties and because of the "Lockean overtones" of Edwards's "new spiritual sense" in *Affections*. He concludes, "The complex of ideas in Edwards on virtually any question of philosophy or theology defies a clear-cut genealogy."[103] Yet Thuesen helpfully acknowledges that Edwards read the unorthodox (like Locke) to refute them. He also agrees with Fiering that on most points Edwards was opposed to Locke's thought. Edwards held to "an un-Lockean immaterialism," and was more speculative in his thought than Locke would have permitted.[104]

96. Ibid., 218.

97. Ibid. Compare Strobel, *Theology*, 151 n3.

98. Josh Moody, *Jonathan Edwards and the Enlightenment: Knowing the Presence of God* (Lanham, MD: University Press of America, 2005), 63.

99. Moody, *Jonathan Edwards and the Enlightenment*, 80–1 n46.

100. Ibid., 101–03.

101. Ibid., 156. A similar conclusion is reached by Daniel, "Edwards as Philosopher," 165.

102. Thuesen, "Editor's Introduction," in *WJE* 26:17. Thuesen warns that how one interprets the extent of Edwards's dependence on Enlightenment thought "may say as much about" the interpreter "as about Edwards himself" (*WJE* 26:16).

103. Ibid., 23. Thuesen does not cite Walton.

104. Ibid., 22, 27.

Toward an Understanding of Locke, Edwards, and Affective Psychology

The foregoing survey shows that, although the question of how much Edwards depended on Locke is not settled, scholars give good reason to view the connection with caution. Moreover, a few important conclusions concerning the relationship of Edwards and Locke can be reached. First, most scholars today believe that Edwards first read Locke's *Essay* while a graduate student or tutor at Yale.[105] Although Edwards recalled his unusual delight in reading Locke, he never explained clearly the source of that delight.[106] Second, Edwards was an idealist, not an empiricist, and his philosophy greatly influenced his psychology.[107] Third, Edwards clearly cited Locke's "simple idea" and "complex idea," but modifies them in important ways.[108] Fourth, Edwards diverged from Lockean empiricism on important points, including innate ideas and the legitimacy of metaphysical speculation.[109] Fifth, many ideas that originally sounded most Lockean to Perry Miller have since been shown to have earlier precedent in the Reformed thought Edwards defended.

105. See Leon Howard, *"The Mind" of Jonathan Edwards: A Reconstructed Text* (Berkeley: University of California Press, 1963), 6–7; Fiering, *Jonathan Edwards's Moral Thought*, 33–40; Norman Fiering, "The Rationalist Foundations of Jonathan Edwards's Metaphysics," in *JEAE*, eds. Hatch and Stout, 76; Anderson, "Editor's Introduction," in *WJE* 6:26; and Thuesen, "Editor's Introduction," in *WJE* 26:90. *Pace* Hopkins, *Jonathan Edwards*, 3. According to Thuesen, there are eighteen references to Locke's *Essay* in Edwards's printed works and manuscripts (*WJE* 26:450).

106. Hopkins said it thus: "In his second Year of College, and thirteenth of his Age, he read *Locke* on the human Understanding, with great delight and profit. His uncommon Genius, by which he was, as it were by Nature, form'd for closeness of Thought and deep Penetration, now began to exercise and discover it self. Taking that Book into his Hand, upon some Occasion, not long before his Death, he said to some of his select Friends, who were then with him, That he was beyond Expression extertain'd and pleas'd with it, when he read it in his Youth at College; that he was as much engaged, and had more Satisfaction and Pleasure in studying it, than the most greed Miser in gathering up handfuls of Silver and Gold from some new discovered Treasure." Hopkins, *Life and Character of Jonathan Edwards*, 3–4. Compare *WJE* 2:299.

107. See James Hoopes, *Consciousness in New England: From Puritanism and Ideas to Psychoanalysis and Semiotic* (Baltimore, MD: The John Hopkins University Press, 1989), 75–81.

108. For example, *WJE* 2:205; "Misc. 782," *WJE* 18:452–66. See Anderson, "Editor's Introduction," in *WJE* 6:101–02. McClymond and McDermott cite Edwards's use of these concepts as the place where Edwards's borrows Locke's psychology. *Theology*, 26. Also see Hoopes, *Consciousness*, 83–84.

109. Anderson notes that Locke's *tabula rasa* and Edwards's human depravity are opposed. He continues: "In his lifelong study of the *Essay*, Edwards used Locke's views more as a foil for developing his own conception of the spiritual world than as a source or authority for it." "Editor's Introduction," in *WJE* 6:120. Compare *WJE* 6:392. Also see McClymond and McDermott, *Theology*, 110–11.

Striking parallels can also be found in other early sources, such as the Cambridge Platonist John Smith.[110] Sixth, Edwards's study was "eclectic," using varied sources to inform himself and to defend the Reformed faith from her foes.

Furthermore, Miller's suggestion—echoed by others—that Edwards reinvented Reformed psychology in response to the Great Awakening can be discarded altogether. First, Locke and Edwards had very different ideas both of the will and of the affections. Locke (as Walton notes) denied an overlap of the will and affections. The will's one "simple act" was that of choosing. The will was distinct from other mental acts. Locke lamented, "I find the will often confounded with several of the affections, especially desire, and one put for the other."[111] Unlike Edwards, Locke separated the will and affections.[112]

For Locke, the will pertained only to human actions, and "terminates there." Locke continued, "[V]olition is nothing but that particular determination of the mind, whereby, barely by a thought, the mind endeavours to give rise, continuation, or stop, to any action which it takes to be in its power."[113] Will and desire may contradict each other. "Desire is uneasiness," Locke said, and uneasiness determines the will, so that the will acts in order to rectify the absence of good.[114] According to Locke, sensation has nothing to do with the will. It is the way ideas move from the senses to the understanding.[115] Likewise, the "internal sense"

110. Wilson H. Kimnach argues Smith significantly influenced Edwards. "Editor's Introduction," in Jonathan Edwards, *Sermons and Discourses, 1720–1723*, vol. 10 of *The Works of Jonathan Edwards* (New Haven, CT: Yale University Press, 1992), 3–10. Smith studied under the Cambridge Platonist Benjamin Whichcote. His father likely had Puritan leanings and Smith received his training in Protestant theology. John Tulloch, *The Cambridge Platonists*, vol. 2 of *Rational Theology and Christian Philosophy in England in the Seventeenth Century* (Edinburgh: William Blackwood and Sons, 1874), 117–92. Smith said, "Were I to define divinity, I should rather call it a *divine life*, than a *divine science*; it being something rather to be understood by a spiritual sensation, than by any verbal description, as all things of sense and life are best known by sentient and vital faculties." Smith, *Select Discourses*, 3. By "sense," Smith meant: "The soul itself hath its sense, as well as the body: and therefore David, when he would teach us how to know what the divine goodness is, calls not for speculation but sensation, 'Taste and see how good the Lord is.' That is not the best and truest knowledge of God which is wrought out by the labour and sweat of the brain, but that which is kindled within us by a heavenly warmth in our hearts." Ibid., 4. See Chapter 3.

111. Locke, *Essay Concerning Human Understanding*, §2.21.30 (185).

112. Edwards's own understanding of the will and affections will be explained more fully below.

113. Ibid.

114. Ibid., §2.21.31–2 (185). Edwards stated only qualified agreement with this (*WJE* 1:139).

115. Ibid., §2.1.3 (104). Perry Miller recognized Edwards's departure from Locke on this particular point. See Miller, "Jonathan Edwards on the Sense of the Heart" *HTR* 41 (1948):125–26.

is the mind's perception of the ideas of its own operations, and is unrelated to the will or heart.[116] As the understanding receives ideas, it attaches to them, through the senses, notions of their goodness or evil. Perceived good or evil greatly influences the will's choices through uneasiness, yet judgment is able to determine the will's acts more powerfully than the sense of uneasiness.[117]

The difference between Locke and Edwards on the affections and passions is striking. Locke devoted little space and attention to the passions, and he argued that the passions themselves are derived from "sensation and reflection" and the "simple ideas" of "pain and pleasure."[118] Locke, in seating the ideas of pleasure and pain in the understanding and not the will, was arguing that passions arose, not from the will, but from the understanding. Locke even went so far to argue that a person's love for spiritual beings was "founded" on previous apprehension of sense pleasure and pain.[119]

Although many scholars trace Edwards's supposed emphasis on the disintegration of the soul's faculties to Locke, Edwards did not learn the unity of the human soul from him. On the contrary, Edwards's own Reformed heritage often taught that the soul's faculties were not distinct entities. On this point, Miller and his heirs have overstated the legacy and ingenuity of Locke. Francis Turretin, a magisterial divine of Reformed Scholasticism, explicitly rejected the strict bifurcation of intellect and will. He wrote,

> [T]he Scholastics are divided on this point [concerning which faculty of the soul receives the operation of blessedness in the life to come]. Some with Thomas Aquinas hold that it is the intellect and maintain that the blessedness consists in the vision of God. However, others with Scotus hold that it is the will, who on this account place happiness in the love of him. But both are at fault in this—they divide things that ought to be joined together and hold that happiness is placed separately, either in vision or in love, since it consists conjointly in the vision and the love of God. Thus neither sight without love, nor love without sight constitutes its form. This the Scripture teaches, describing it now by "sight" (1 Cor. 13:12; 2 Cor. 5:7; 1 Jn 3:2), then by "love" and perfect holiness (1 Jn 4:16; 1 Cor. 13:13).[120]

116. Ibid., §2.1.4 (104–05).

117. Ibid., §2.21.48 (190).

118. Ibid., §2.20.1 (176).

119. Ibid., §2.20.5 (176). In "Misc. 782," Edwards would express his disagreement with this as well. Locke and Edwards's view of morality also differed. Locke said that virtue and vice could be promoted or curbed through education. Locke contended, "Change but a man's view of these things; let him see that virtue and religion are necessary to his happiness." Ibid., §2.21.62 (194).

120. Turretin, *Institutes* §20.8.5 (3:609). Compare Turretin's definition of faith: "It ought not to seem strange that faith is assigned to two faculties of the soul. For besides the fact that not a few unrenowned or mean philosophers acknowledge no real distinction

Turretin, who resisted "dividing" the faculties "that ought to be joined together," was not alone. Others Reformed authors before Edwards collapsed traditional faculty psychology to stress the unity of the soul.[121] Cotton Mather, who also influenced Edwards, reminded his students not to stress the distinction between the soul's faculties.[122] Solomon Stoddard also occasionally lifted the distinctions between the faculties to make a greater point, once arguing that the understanding and the will are "faculties of the same soul, and really one and the same thing."[123]

Miller also charged that, as Edwards discarded faculty psychology, he looked at the soul as a basic unity, and thereby placed affections over the understanding. Against this idea Norman Fiering's insights concerning the Western tradition of Augustinian voluntarism are instructive. Fiering notes that in the West two traditions emerged that emphasized either the understanding or the will. Intellectualism, the tradition Fiering traces from Aquinas, held that the last dictate of the practical intellect determined the will. Voluntarism, which can be traced back to Augustine, viewed the will, not as rational appetite, but as the "heart" or inner essence of the whole man. According to Fiering, William Ames accepted voluntarism.[124] Fiering's account significantly shows that many Christian theologians emphasized the will in the same way Edwards did.[125] Edwards's close identification of the will and affections should be considered neither novel nor derived from Locke, as similar ideas are found in Augustine, Ames, Owen, and Baxter.

In conclusion, Locke apparently influenced Edwards, and sometimes in important ways. Indeed, it seems that Edwards occasionally recast Locke's empiricist terminology to express the well-worn axioms of the Reformed faith. Yet, with respect to his psychology, the analysis of Perry Miller (and others, after him) that Edwards reworked faculty psychology to defend the Great Awakening cannot be sustained. Although Jonathan Edwards may have learned much from

between the intellect and the will, but wish the soul (as understanding and knowing) to be called intellect, but as willing and seeking will; it is no more repugnant for faith to belong to two faculties than either free will or the image of God (which have their seat partly in the intellect, partly in the will). Faith is not a unique and simple habit, but composed and aggregate. Therefore it cannot be comprehended by a single conception, but includes various conceptions subordinate to itself (which are well referred to both faculties)." *Institutes* §15.9.13 (2:564). For more on Edwards rejection of Locke's understanding of the mind's operations, see Anderson, "Editor's Introduction," in *WJE* 6:124–29.

121. See Fiering's citation of similar remarks by Aquinas and Ames in *Moral Philosophy*, 107–09.

122. White, *Puritan Rhetoric*, 29–33. For Cotton Mather's influence on Edwards, see *WJE* 26:26–27, 452.

123. Stoddard, *Safety*, 6–7. See Cherry, *Theology*, 14–15 and White, *Puritan Rhetoric*, 33–40.

124. Fiering, *Moral Philosophy*, 104–27.

125. See Chapters 2 and 3.

John Locke, he did not accept the philosopher's psychology. Quite to the contrary, on almost every point Edwards diverged from Locke's psychology. Through his education, Edwards was instructed in the traditional Puritan understanding of human affections. Reformed authors taught the distinction between the movements of the immaterial soul and those connected with the sensitive appetite of the body's senses. From Ames, Turretin, Stoddard, and others, Edwards learned that the faculties of the soul are not distinct entities in a strict sense. Edwards also learned that the will and love or affections were closely related.

overplays JL-JE distinctions.

Chapter 5

JONATHAN EDWARDS'S EARLY PSYCHOLOGY

Jesu, Thy boundless love to me
No thought can reach, no tongue declare;
O knit my thankful heart to Thee,
And reign without a rival there!
Thine wholly, Thine alone I am;
Be Thou alone my constant flame!
O grant that nothing in my soul
May dwell, but Thy pure love alone!
O may Thy love possess me whole!
My joy, my treasure, and my crown;
Strange flames far from my heart remove;
My every act, word, thought, be love.

— Paul Gerhardt, tr. John Wesley

From his early years, into those leading up to the Great Awakening, Edwards maintained an interest in the soul. As his metaphysical conclusions developed, affection for God became increasingly important to his philosophy and theology. Like his predecessors, Edwards viewed affections as lively inclinations and aversions of the soul. In his private writings, Edwards returned to several topics related to human love and affections. From the earliest days of his public ministry, Edwards taught Christians the necessity of true affection for God. When the first waves of Awakening washed over his Northampton parish and subsequently ebbed into interchurch rancor, he applied his insight into the soul's affections.

Edwards's discussions of other matters also illumine his affective psychology. His idea of being touches on human affections because it included consent, excellency, and beauty. Excellency and beauty in turn arise in Edwards's discussions of the will. Edwards's discussion of appetite is important to test the extent to which he avowed the distinction between the affections and sense appetite. For similar reasons, the distinctions Edwards drew between the soul and body bear scrutiny. His doctrine of the Trinity, as it mirrors the human soul, helpfully clarifies the nature of the affections as well. Finally, any study of Edwards's affective psychology should look at the ways he used and explained the terms *affections*, *passions*, and *emotions.*

"The Mind"

In September 1723, Edwards began "The Mind," a private notebook dedicated to articulating the operations of the mind. He probably originally created the notebook to prepare logic lessons during his tutorship. Edwards composed it while working alongside several sources, including Locke's *Essay Concerning Human Understanding.*[1] "The Mind" illustrates Edwards's early thought on affective psychology, although, like with any of Edwards's private notebooks, one can render only a qualified significance to Edwards's thoughts.[2] Although Edwards started the notebook as a young man, he continued to work on it for much of his life.[3] Edwards's writings in "The Mind" especially show the extent to which he viewed the will and love as central to human existence.

Excellency and its relation to being are essential to Edwards's affective psychology, as Edwards's metaphysics are grounded in a theory of consent that includes the will and affections. Edwards opens "The Mind" with a discussion of excellency, which is found in proportion, the "equality, or likeness of ratios" (6:332). Beauty is found in proportionate relationships (6:334). This is true for all the "pleasures of the senses," whether music, colors, tastes, or smells (6:335). Yet, physical beauty could not be the essence of beauty; this secondary beauty typifies primary, spiritual beauty. Just as physical beauty is found in the physical consent of proportion, so spiritual beauty is found in the proportion found in spiritual consent, which can only occur between intelligent beings. This is the excellency of beings. Lack of proportion is contrary to being (6:336). Being is in the consent or proportion of beings; therefore, being is directly related to beauty or excellency.[4]

1. Anderson, "Editor's Introduction," in *WJE* 6:27–34. Anderson presents evidence that Edwards worked on the notebook while reading Brattle's *Compendium of Logic* and Locke's *Essay.* Ibid., 6:33. Leon Howard also highlights the presence of the work of Port Royal logic, Antoine Arnauld and Pierre Nicolet's *The Art of Thinking. "The Mind,"* 7. As William Morris said, Edwards read Locke as a logician rather than an empiricist. Morris, *Young Jonathan Edwards,* 133–38.

2. Howard cautions, "Edwards' grasp of the system he accepted and followed (at least in the early stages of acceptance) was neither complete nor firm." *"The Mind,"* x. Howard and Anderson both have excellent introductions to "The Mind."

3. Anderson argues that Edwards is still writing in "The Mind" notebook in 1728. "Editor's Introduction," in *WJE* 6:328. Edwards likely set the manuscript aside in 1731 as his workload in Northampton increased, and then added nos. 61–69 to the notebook sometime around 1747 or 1748. Ibid., 6:328. The last three notes were probably added thereafter.

4. Morris observes: "If we ask how Edwards arrived this early at this highly complex, and yet nobly simple, theory of being, we must at least reply that it is extremely unlikely that he did so unaided by any previous thinkers. He most certainly did not derive it or its main elements from Richard Cumberland, John Locke, Anthony Ashley Cooper (the third Lord Shaftesbury), or Bishop Berkeley. It is essentially a Scholastic theory in its tight a priori mode of argumentation, and one must look in the direction of the Scholastics for probable

Spiritual beauty comes up often in Edwards's thought, and it is worth making explicit now how beauty connects to the affections. Edwards uses two groups of nearly interchangeable words throughout his writings. The first group is the "affections group" and includes the similar concepts of affections, consent, love, will, pleasure, inclination, and disposition. The second group is the "beauty group" and includes the relating ideas of beauty, glory, holiness, proportion, and excellency. These two groups of concepts describe the way rational souls relate to other beings. The ideas of the "affections group" describe the *action* of an intelligent being toward other intelligent beings and (ultimately) the Triune God who is infinite being. The ideas of "beauty group" describe both the *object* of consent and the *result* of mutual consent. Beings are inclined to beauty and, as they are, the result is a beautiful union. How important are these ideas to Edwards? Edwards opened "The Mind" with a discussion of excellency and (as pointed out below) his "Miscellanies" with holiness. The affections were a central idea in his theology.

This explains why *spiritual* beauty (as opposed to physical beauty) was vital to Edwards. Christian theology had always emphasized spirituality over physicality. The physical world, though not evil in the Platonic sense, is nonetheless changing, cursed, and marred by sin. God, on the other hand, is an unchanging spirit. Nevertheless, Edwards believed that physical beauty was highly significant. For him, the beauty of the physical world consisted in proportion, which itself was something like consent. The consent of physical proportions typifies the consent or will or affections toward spiritual beauty in God's infinite being that is the ground of all reality. For this purpose God made human beings. Since the Fall, however, humans have been driven toward physical rather than spiritual pleasure. Those appetites for physical pleasure are the passions.

The importance of consent is why Edwards did not wholly dismiss self-love. Sinful self-love cannot consist merely in inclination to pleasure and aversion to pain. To be is to consent, and so inclination to good is essential to being itself. An inclination to good involves "no affection" or self-love. A being is acting according to its nature.[5]

For Edwards, the essence of all intelligent beings was in love. They were made to love. The beauty of spiritual beings is in their consent to being. Consent to being is a mental and volitional act. Love is the will's consent toward other wills. This

sources of Edwards's thought." Morris, *Young Jonathan Edwards*, 391. Morris posits Suárez, who considered being as being. Ibid., 392. Also see Delattre, *Beauty and Sensibility*, 15–57.

5. *WJE* 6:337. Even conscience, according to Edwards, comes out of a "sense" of excellency or beauty (6:356). Richard A. S. Hall says George Berkeley (1685–1753) influenced Edwards's moral thought. See "Did Berkeley Influence Edwards? Their Common Critique of the Moral Sense Theory," in *Jonathan Edwards's Writings: Text, Context, and Interpretation*, ed. Stephen J. Stein (Bloomington: Indiana University Press, 1996), 100–21. Also see Danaher, *Trinitarian Ethics*, 69–71.

love changes in the proportion of its consent to greater and lesser spirits (6:362). Because God has created other intelligent minds, the beauty of those minds comes from their resemblance to his mind. "His infinite beauty is his infinite mutual love of himself." Therefore God, whose perfection is love, is the pattern and perfection of all excellent spirits (6:363).

If spiritual beauty is in consent to being, then spiritual deformity is in the dissent of being from being. This dissent aggravates as the dissension is directed to a being of greater excellency. Dissent is especially odious if someone refuses to consent to an excellent being who actually consents to the one dissenting. Edwards explained, "[A]ll virtue, which is the excellency of minds, is resolved into love to being. And nothing is virtuous or beautiful in spirits any otherwise than as it is an exercise, or fruit, or manifestation of this love; and nothing is sinful or deformed in spirits but as it is the defect of, or contrary to, these." God himself is "being in general," for all other beings are "as nothing" compared to his infinite being (6:363).

For Edwards, God was quintessentially excellent. Although humans ought to love God, they cannot initiate their own love for God. Consequently, God must communicate to his creatures the love they have for him. God's love for himself is what makes him excellent, and this divine self-love is the very love that God communicates to humankind so that they love him. As humans partake more of the love for God that God communicates to them, they increase in spiritual beauty by consenting to his infinite being. For Edwards, this spiritual beauty, or love, is holiness (6:364). Love, which is the excellency of intelligent creatures, is what the Scriptures often extol as fulfilling the entire law. For Edwards, to exist was to love.[6]

Edwards observed that perceiving beings naturally desire to consent to being. This is the ground behind the human desire for truth:

> The exercise of this disposition of the soul to a high degree is the passion of admiration. When the mind beholds a very uncommon object, there is the pleasure of a new perception, with the excitation of the appetite of knowing more of it, as the causes and manner of production and the like, and the uneasiness arising from its being so hidden. These compose that emotion called admiration. (6:637)

Granted, this use of *emotion* may at first glance appear to approximate the modern notion. Edwards made this remark while reading Jean-Pierre de Crousaz's *A New Treatise of the Art of Thinking*. Where Crousaz noted that managing "Admiration" was necessary to control the passions, Edwards emphasized from Crousaz's

6. Danaher says that for Edwards, "to be is to be in love." Danaher, *Trinitarian Ethics*, 33. See Edwards H. Davidson, *Jonathan Edwards: The Narrative of a Puritan Mind*, Riverside Studies in Literature (Boston: Houghton Mifflin, 1966), 16–19; Gerald R. McDermott, *One Holy and Happy Society: The Public Theology of Jonathan Edwards* (University Park: Pennsylvania State University Press, 1992), 97–101.

remarks the natural human bent toward admiration. Thereby Edwards used the proclivity for admiration as another argument that being is in consent.[7] In so doing, Edwards borrowed the language of Crousaz, who used "emotion" to refer to the motions of the heart (figuratively speaking), which Edwards understood to be spiritual.[8]

Essential to Edwards's understanding of the affections and passions was the distinction between soul and body. For Edwards, the physical world, including human bodies, typified the spiritual world.[9] In fact, Edwards describes bodies as a "shadow of being." Consequently, the physical consent of bodies is but a shadow of the excellency in spiritual consent (6:337). Because the typological connection between the world of physical objects and the immaterial world of spiritual realities was tightly knit, the language of the physical world could, with terms like "imagination" and "conception," make the greater truths of the spiritual world more intelligible (6:649). Here Edwards's distinction between affections and passions is implicit. He recognized that love or consent stemming from a physical, lower love (passions), can cloud the importance of spiritual consent between beings (affections) (6:338). Again, true beauty is in the love between intelligent spirits, just as deformity is in hatred between spirits.[10]

7. According to de Crousaz, a perennial problem for philosophers is overcoming "Admiration," which is the "Passion" which is "the Original of all the others." For de Crousaz, a perceived object "affects" people "agreeably or disagreeably," and thus "engaged or disengaged the heart." Therefore admiration must be carefully governed. As a state of admiration gradually wears off, a wise man remains unchanged in his happiness with his object. Inclination may surrender to indifference, "as the object has ceas'd to be new, it has ceas'd to surprise; and because we are no longer affected but very weakly, we behold it without Emotion; and a State of Indolence being a State we are soon tired of, we seek others to move the Heart afresh." Jean-Pierre de Crousaz, *A New Treatise of the Art of Thinking; or, A Compleat System of Reflections, Concerning the Conduct and Improvement of the Mind*, 2 vols. (London: Tho. Woodward, 1724), 153–54. For evidence that Edwards had access to this work, see *WJE* 26:251.

8. Compare Edwards's expression "angry emotions of mind," where he simply referred to movements of the soul (*WJE* 16:782).

9. In *Types*, Edwards said, "I expect by very ridicule and contempt to be called a man of a very fruitful brain and copious fancy, but they are welcome to it. I am not ashamed to own that I believe that the whole universe, heaven and earth, air and seas, and the divine constitution and history of the holy Scriptures, be full of images of divine things." Jonathan Edwards, *Typological Writings*, vol. 11 of *The Works of Jonathan Edwards*, eds. Wallace E. Anderson, Mason I Lowance, Jr., with David H. Watters (New Haven, CT: Yale University Press, 1993), 152.

10. For Edwards, materialism was impossible. Matter consists of solidity, extension, motion, and gravity, and all these ideas are mutually dependent upon the others. Perception, on the other hand, has no dependence on solidity or the others. Matter has no property that would allow for thought (*WJE* 6:347–48).

In his early thought, Edwards closely identified the heart with the will and affections together. This was something confirmed, not only by Reformed teaching, but by the Scriptures. Therefore, Edwards could say that the soul was seated both in the brain, as well as (in another sense) in the "heart or the affections."[11]

The essential differences between humans and animals, another topic addressed in "The Mind," also informed Edwards's notion of the affections and passions. Humanity has a divine-like aspect and an animal aspect. The reasonable soul is the aspect people share with spirit beings, like God and the angels. They also have a body like the animals. Affections are inclinations stemming from their spiritual aspect, and passions are inclinations from their corporeal aspect. "Men are capable," Edwards said, "of viewing what is in themselves contemplatively. Man was made for spiritual exercises and enjoyments, and therefore is made capable by reflection to behold and contemplate spiritual things. Hence it arises that man is capable of religion" (6:374).

Beasts cannot control their thoughts; their "minds" are entirely passive, whereas the human minds are both passive and "abundantly active" (6:374). All appetites, like ideas, are in the mind. A material appetite is as inconceivable as a material thought. Not all appetites, however, are "natural to the soul." The "natural appetite" to "meat and drink," for instance, comes from experiencing the pain of hunger or thirst, as a person learns that meat or drink satisfies that appetite (6:372). Experience builds innate, nonrational habits. Hence beasts perform habitual actions to satisfy their appetites. The minds of beasts have no capacity for contemplation, but only "direct consciousness" (6:374). Animal appetites move toward or away from different sensations, where the will is "active" over its own thoughts.[12] Beasts, as purely passive beings, are entirely controlled by appetites and habits. Human beings, on the other hand, have a rational will that is influenced by both sensitive appetites and spiritual, intellectual desires.

With later entries in "The Mind," Edwards not only echoed and clarified earlier ideas, but he also addressed the will much more specifically.[13] Edwards

11. *WJE* 6:352. Edwards clearly identifies the will and the affections in his early theology. As I argue above, this was not uncommon in Puritan theology. *Pace* Stout and Hatch with Farley, who call Edwards's identification of the will and the affections "a bold psychological innovation," in response to the Great Awakening. See Stout and Hatch with Farley, "Preface to the Period," in *WJE* 22:45.

12. *WJE* 6:374. Many of Edwards's remarks on the will in "The Mind" were used in *Freedom of Will*. See Anderson, "Note on 'The Mind,'" in *WJE* 6:328. Compare Danaher, who emphasizes the role of "self-consciousness" in Edwards's psychology. Danaher, *Trinitarian Ethics*, 19–26.

13. As a new pastorate's responsibilities burgeoned upon Edwards, he set aside "The Mind," adding nine or ten entries right after the Awakening. Anderson, "Notes on 'The Mind,'" in *WJE* 6:328–29.

rejected the Lockean theory that pleasure and pain were "ideas."[14] He believed the "faculties" were necessary for understanding the soul, explaining the functions of the understanding and will to be entirely different acts. When it receives ideas, the mind is passive. Pleasure and pain are not ideas, despite the element of perception that causes them.[15] He explains, "The will, choice, etc. is nothing else but the mind's being pleased with an idea, or having a superior pleasedness in something thought of, or a desire of a future thing" (6:384). Just as love, choice, and understanding are acts, so pleasure and pain are acts as well, for in pleasure or pain the mind acts upon the object, attributing to it good or evil through the will. These clarifications illustrate how Edwards's understanding of being as consent to being permeated his thought.[16] As he wrestled with his sources on the nature of the mind, Edwards eventually rejected Locke's theory of the will for one that better accounted for the centrality of the will, and, more significantly, a will inclined toward the Triune God. As Morris aptly observed, Edwards's own conversion and new affections for God was no small factor contributing to these emphases.[17] Other personal writings during this time reflect this development.

14. *WJE* 6:384. See Locke, *Essay Concerning Human Understanding*, §2.20.1. Howard comments, "Edwards seems to have been constitutionally incapable of following for long in Locke's footsteps. Locke had treated Pleasure, Pain, and Love as ideas (II, xx, I, 4), but Edwards denied them that classification and, in doing so, apparently denied Locke's concept of ideas of reflection or of any sort other than those simple ideas which were received passively by the Understanding (II, I, 24–25). Whether he realized he was going to such an extreme is doubtful, for he seems to have accepted Locke's classification of the Understanding and the Will as powers or faculties of the mind (II, vi; II, xxi, 5–6)." Howard, *The Mind*, 57.

15. Morris wrote, "Despite his stress on feeling and affection, the 'inner sense' and 'the sense of the heart,' Edwards refused to adopt a third category for the affective elements in experience. Hence in these articles we see him struggling with the questions of how to include these affective elements in the category of the will." Morris, *Young Jonathan Edwards*, 361–62.

16. See Morris, *Young Jonathan Edwards*, 382.

17. Morris said, "[T]he difference between Edwards and Locke lies not only in the training of the former in the philosophies of being of Burgersdicius and Heereboord, but also, and more significantly, in the fact that Edwards had experienced, and Locke had not experienced, such a metaphysical conversion, and had found his whole piety grounded authentically in that experience." Morris, *Young Jonathan Edwards*, 183. Edwards's thoughts on excellency (which Morris closely connected to Edwards's conversion) are not influenced by Locke at all. "After his reading of Locke, and before setting pen to paper to write on the mind, Edwards had undergone the experience that was to determine his thinking more than the reading of any author, be he Locke or Shaftesbury or Berkeley." Ibid., 183.

Personal Writings

Edwards's understanding of the affections and passions is not only seen in philosophical notebooks like "The Mind," but in other personal writings as well. Edwards began his "Resolutions," a collection of guidelines for life, sometime before 1722. Edwards recorded his successes and failures during these years in his diary. In showing the central place God had in Edwards's inner life, these personal documents also illumine Edwards's affective psychology.[18] In these writings, Edwards was concerned with the genuineness of his own religious affections. As a young man, he resolved not to allow any affection that undermined religion (16:756). He regarded his whole person, including his understanding, will, and affections, as belonging to God.[19]

Edwards's diary illustrates how his ideas on human affectivity remained fairly consistent throughout his entire ministry. Perennial themes like the perils of false affections and the importance of affections for holy beauty are present. For instance, Edwards knew the spiritual danger of natural affections. Edwards worried that his affections may be "hypocritical outside affections" (16:759). One day he expressed his relief that he had been "[a]ffected with the sense of the excellency of holiness." Elsewhere Edwards gratefully noted that he "[f]elt more exercise of love to Christ than usual," and that he "felt sensible repentance of sin."[20] Upon leaving New York City, Edwards used the experience to evaluate his own spiritual state and pray to God that his "thoughts, affections, desires, and expectations" be set on "the heavenly state," where saints never break fellowship. In aesthetic rapture, Edwards wrote, "How sweetly will the mutual lovers join together to sing the praises of God and the Lamb! How full will it fill us with joy to think, this enjoyment, these sweet exercises, will never cease or come to an end, but will last to all eternity" (16:768).

Edwards's diary also demonstrates how Edwards applied his understanding of the passions of the sensitive appetite to his struggle to maintain Christian temperance. Edwards understood himself to be fighting intense and irrational

18. On the "Resolutions" and Edwards's diary, see Murray, *Jonathan Edwards*, 42–44; George S. Claghorn, "Introduction," in *WJE* 16:741–45; and Marsden, *Jonathan Edwards*, 50–52. Douglas Sweeney helpfully highlights Edwards's later wisdom concerning his earnest resolutions. See Sweeney, *Edwards and the Ministry of the Word*, 44–46.

19. *WJE* 16:762. Edwards believed that he could actively submit the operations of the soul toward God. In a November 1725 diary entry Edwards observed, "When one suppresses thoughts that tend to divert the run of the mind's operations from religion, whether they are melancholy, or anxious, or passionate, or any others; there is this good effect of it, that it keeps the mind in its freedom. Those thoughts are stopped in the beginning, that would have set the mind a-going in that stream." Edwards continues, "There are a great many exercises, that from the present, seem not to help, but rather impede, religious meditation and affections, the fruit of which is reaped afterwards, and is of far greater worth than what is lost" (*WJE* 16:788).

20. *WJE* 16:759. Compare Edwards's use of "sense" in *WJE* 16:789.

appetites of the flesh. He lamented the way natural affection or appetite "blinds the mind": "How doth appetite stretch the reason to bring both ends together" (16:778). Even the distinction between soul and body related to Edwards's personal devotion. "The very thing I now want, to give me a clearer and more immediate view of the perfections and glory of God," he wrote in 1725, "is as clear a knowledge of the manner of God's exerting himself, with respect to spirits and mind, as I have, of his operations concerning matter and bodies" (16:787).

Edwards's early personal writings show that as a young man he believed gracious affections to be an important indicator of spiritual health. Human affection for God was more than the subject of theory, but the fabric of Edwards's Reformed piety and tantamount to his salvation. The important foundational elements of his understanding of human affectivity were in place early on in his life.

The Early "Miscellanies"

Jonathan Edwards's "Miscellanies" is a collection of over 1,400 theological observations comprising nine volumes recorded by Edwards throughout his entire ministry. He began the notebooks in 1722 during his interim pulpit ministry in New York City. The notebooks illustrate both Edwards's intellectual development and commitment to biblical interpretation, intellectual rigor, and theological clarity.[21] The early entries reveal that Edwards was concerned with such theological issues as the decrees of God, the regulative principle of worship, the will, Hades, the Sabbath, and original sin. Sometimes, the "Miscellanies" include a quotation of some author Edwards found to be either helpful or damning. At other times, Edwards filled these notebooks with commentaries on Scripture, theological observations, or Scripture types. Throughout his early "Miscellanies," Edwards developed the idea of human affections from several different perspectives.

The initial "Miscellany" entry is itself striking and illustrates how vital Edwards believed the soul's inclination toward God to be. "Holiness," Edwards wrote, "is a most beautiful and lovely thing." Edwards refused to see it as "melancholy, morose, sour and unpleasant." On the contrary, holiness is "sweet and ravishingly lovely." Edwards piled the adjectives to characterize the spiritual beauty of holiness: "sweet, pleasant, charming, lovely, amiable, delightful, serene, calm and still." Similarly, he described the soul's delight in God as both a "sweet calmness" and "calm ecstasy."[22]

21. Marsden believes the "Miscellanies" were driven Edwards's ambition to be a widely read writer. Marsden, *Jonathan Edwards*, 59. On the "Miscellanies," see the excellent introduction of Thomas A. Schafer, "Editor's Introduction," in Jonathan Edwards, *The "Miscellanies," a–500*, vol. 13 of *The Works of Jonathan Edwards* (New Haven, CT: Yale University Press, 1994), 1–160. Also see Murray, *Jonathan Edwards*, 137–51. The name "Miscellanies" come from Edwards himself.

22. "Misc. a," *WJE* 13:163. The theme of calm affections reverberates through Edwards's early writings. It has already been seen in *WJE* 16:768 above, and will come up again in *Charity and Its Fruits* below. Edwards's notebook entries present an emphasis on the

A Will against a Will Edwards struggled to articulate the relationship and nature of the soul and body in human beings, always accentuating the spiritual nature of the person. Because spirits are "more substantial" than bodies, the most "solid and substantial" happiness is "spiritual happiness" ("Misc. f," 13:166).[23] Because spiritual realities are superior to earthly, the corporeal beauty of earthly objects is a shadow of the beauty of Christ.[24] Furthermore, one can approximate the pleasure of heaven's beauty when one multiplies the pleasure of earthly beauty. If it is true that Christ's beauty can be dimly seen in physical beauty, "how sweet will it be to behold the proper images and communications of Christ's excellencies in intelligent beings" ("Misc. 108," 13:280).

Despite this emphasis on the spirituality of humanity, Edwards jointly affirmed God created human beings as a unified whole in soul and body. For example, in "Misc. 101," Edwards explained that God takes no delight in the motions and gestures of bodily worship *per se*. God delights in the worship of the soul of rational creatures. Even so, humans naturally connect "things spiritual and things bodily."[25] Because of this, restricting or changing the "manner of expression" in worship hinders the spiritual affection. Therefore, "some bodily worship is necessary to

placidness of affections. For instance, Edwards said that he disliked a "whining tone" in public prayer or preaching, as it seemed to him "very ridiculous." Yet Edwards believed such a tone helpful in his private prayer, Scripture reading, and meditation, for he found it "stills the animal spirits and calms the mind and fits it for the most sedate thought, the clearest ideas, brightest apprehensions and strongest reasonings." The mind must be calmed before it can enjoy the high contemplations of religious matters ("Misc. w," in *WJE* 13:175). Similarly, Edwards did not believe it inconsistent that true religion brought pleasure and discouraged laughter. Human beings never laugh at great things, and laughter is often fleeting. "The pleasure of religion raises one clear above laughter, and rather tends to make the face shine than screw it into a grimace; though when it is at its height it begets a sweet, inexpressibly joyful smile, as we know only a smile is begotten by the great pleasure of dear friends' society" ("Misc. x," in *WJE* 13:176). Yet, such a smile is not always on the faces of true saints, for they know the severity of their sins and the displeasure they have brought God.

23. In *The Great Divorce,* C. S. Lewis memorably described heaven, "It was the light, the grass, the trees that were different; made of some different substance, so much solider than things in our country that men were ghosts by comparison" (New York: Macmillan, 1946), 28.

24. "Misc. 108," in *WJE* 13:279 and 6:390. Wallace Anderson observes, "[Edwards's] distinction of beauty into primary and secondary was characteristic of his theology: Being-in-general was primary, spiritual, and, ultimately, divine; being-as-manifest was secondary, corporeal, and only a reflection of God" ("Editor's Introduction," in *WJE* 11:19).

25. "Misc. 101," 13:269. Edwards illustrated the connection of soul and body: "Thus when we are joyful and express our joy, 'tis natural to do it with a lively voice; and when we express sorrow, to do it with what we call a mournful voice."

give liberty to our devotion" ("Misc. 101," 13:269). Even so, the more rational a person is, the less his state of mind depends on his body ("Misc. 101," 13:270).

When the body is redeemed in the New Jerusalem, it will have an important role in the aesthetics of that golden age marked by both physical and spiritual beauty. There the glorified bodies of saints will be beautiful in their various proportions, including in the relationship between body and soul. The bodily effects of the affections will be far more fitting than in the present age.[26] Yet, future beauty will be defined as it is now, in the excellency of proportion. Among the acts of individual minds, among the various minds, and among the Trinity itself—which is "the supreme harmony of all"—there will be an "exquisite spiritual proportion" ("Misc. 182," 13:328–29). In the present age, the human mind is "much obscured" and its sense "flattened" when beholding spiritual beauty; whereas, in heaven, the capacities of human minds will be "exceedingly enlarged," perceiving all the various relations. Heavenly minds will immediately apprehend the beauty of these spiritual proportions ("Misc. 182," 13:329). For Edwards, if the wicked will endure endless bodily torment, it followed that saints will enjoy bodily pleasures "of the exquisite kind" suited to "refined" bodies. Such pleasures are not those that "clog the mind, and divert from mental and spiritual pleasure and the pure joys of holiness." Bodily pleasures will only augment the soul's joy in God.[27]

Edwards also used the "Miscellanies" to articulate the concepts of the sensitive appetites and passions. For Edwards, God sustained every power of the soul. He originally created Adam and Eve with both an inclination for holiness and natural inclinations (or appetites) for the physical provisions that sustain the body.[28] Before the Fall, the inclinations of the intellect were not encumbered by "the inferior inclination." The inferior inclinations are the passions. Because Adam and Eve were not ruled by the passions, they enjoyed greater "freedom of will" ("Misc. 291," 13:383).

Since the Fall, the inclinations of reason and judgment often conflict with the lower, natural inclinations, and, because self-love reigns in human beings, the lower inclinations or passions often control the unregenerate. Therefore, humans

26. Edwards wrote, "'Twill consist very much in the air of their actions and speech, and cast of their countenance, denoting the greatest wisdom and prudence and purity of mind; and such as will naturally result from an inexpressible sweetness, the greatest benevolence and complacence, and the highest joy" ("Misc. 149," in *WJE* 13:301). On how benevolence and complacence differ, see *WJE* 8:212–13, 375.

27. Edwards explained eschatological sensual pleasure thus, "The sweetness and pleasure that shall be in the mind, shall put the spirits of the body into such a motion as shall cause a sweet sensation throughout the body, infinitely excelling any sensual pleasure here" ("Misc. 233," in *WJE* 13:351).

28. "Misc. 301," in *WJE* 13:387–88. Solomon Stoddard's own view of original sin greatly influenced Edwards's. See *WJE* 13:387n4. Also see *JEE*, s.v. "Appetite (Natural and Spiritual)."

now have "a will against a will."[29] This other "will" is a natural inclination that conflicts with "reason and judgment" ("Misc. 291," 13:383). This latter "will" rules over the rational will in an unregenerate person.[30] The influence of the lower will or "appetite" comes from the powerful way sensual good presents itself to the mind ("Misc. 436," 13:485).

Edwards asserted that, after the Fall, humanity has been governed by self-love alone, without holiness, resulting in "all manner of exorbitancies." Self-love has become "in innumerable cases a vile and odious disposition," causing "thousands of unlovely and hateful actions."[31] All sin is the result of self-love unregulated by love for God.[32] After Eden's sin, God withdrew the soul's capacity to be inclined toward holiness, yet upheld the soul's natural inclinations, resulting in "all those exorbitances."[33] With only self-love remaining, pride, envy, malice, and their ilk consequentially arose. Unbridled self-love also impairs the body's temperament or balance. This impairment aggravates the "sensual appetites," and hinders the

29. "Misc. 291," in *WJE* 13:383. Elsewhere Edwards referred to "the will against a will" as "two wills" ("Misc. 436," in *WJE* 13:485).

30. "Misc. 436," in *WJE* 13:484. Edwards did not always use "appetite" to refer to lust or concupiscence. In fact, he sometimes spoke of a spiritual appetite. So, for example, the "appetite" wherein Christ is "embraced" as the Savior to forgive sin, to the same extent the believer ought to abhor his own sin ("Misc. 669," in *WJE* 18:216).

31. "Misc. 291," in *WJE* 13:383. Adam, Edwards argued, fell because his rational judgment was deceived. Edwards drew a distinction between a gracious and an inferior appetite. Adam and Eve could only have escaped the Fall if they would have had a "sense of spiritual excellencies and beauties" that overcame "the inferior kind of appetites" or lusts to the extent that the rational judgment was rendered unnecessary. The "gracious appetite" must be stronger than all the other appetites and desires. Edwards was careful not to overstate the virtue of the rational will without the grace of God. Even if the rational will rules the appetites, unless the inclination toward spiritual good prevails, the rational will can only prevail with a struggle, "so that the will is not entirely free." Edwards added, "To have a sinful inclination is sin, but the inclination of the man is to be found by composition of inclinations; the excess of one above the other is the inclination of the man: if the excess of inclination be to inferior objects in many cases, the prevailing inclination will be [away] from God" ("Misc. 437," in *WJE* 13:486). Angels were similarly overcome by "an appetite to their own honor" ("Misc. 488," in *WJE* 13:487).

32. Elsewhere Edwards wrote, "A man's love to sensual pleasure, if love to God be gone, will very often be contrary to love to God, or excite to those things that love to God, if it were present, would restrain from." The soul's love for eternal life properly knows no limit ("Misc. 457," in *WJE* 13:501).

33. The natural affections have the power to deceive people into thinking that they have been regenerated by the Spirit. When the soul is fearful or under other "natural affections," the strength of such an "emotion of the soul" may imitate the "work of grace" for a few minutes. This dangerous tendency toward hypocrisy, Edwards believed, was a reason why the Scriptures offered so many tests to try believers ("Misc. 394," in *WJE* 24:460).

mind's ability to function properly. The more this self-love cycle gains control, the more it spirals into further degeneracy ("Misc. 301," 13:387–88).

Edwards did not regard passions to be sinful in themselves. Not every "natural inclination" is a "lust." Some natural inclinations, such as a love for "happiness in general," a love for eternal blessedness, or a fear of hell, cannot, by definition, ever have any excess. On the other hand, "[a]s to many of the particular appetites and inclinations, they brake [*sic*] bounds as soon as a spirit of love to God, that was wont to restrain and govern them, left the soul; as, a love to his outward pleasure and profit and honor" ("Misc. 457," 13:500). When true love for God is absent in a soul, the soul's appetites quickly become "unlawful."[34]

If passions were sinful, then Jesus Christ was not sinless, for he experienced the temptations of the carnal appetite, but overcame them. Like all human beings, Christ knew "the importunate desires and inclinations of the animal nature."[35] His temptations reached their climax with his approaching death, the prospect of which Christ dreaded.

Voluntariness . . . to an Infinitely Greater Height During his early years, Edwards also concluded that, given God's purpose in creation, human affections are central in that purpose. For Edwards, God created the world in order to communicate his glory to his creatures. Only rational creatures can perceive a spiritual reality like the glory of God. [36] Therefore, God created the world for intelligent and immortal beings ("Misc. gg," 13:185). Intelligent, volitional beings glorify God the best. A world created for the glory of God is a world created for religion; and as such, devotion to God is the chief end of humanity.[37]

Although God created human beings to love him, they have turned away from him and have become enslaved to lower inclinations toward the sensual world. In

34. "Misc. 457," in *WJE* 13:501. Elsewhere Edwards said: "Wicked men are sensual" ("Misc. 471," in *WJE* 13:512).

35. "Misc. 791," in *WJE* 18:494. On the influences of the carnal appetite, see *WJE* 18:324.

36. Gerald McDermott puts it memorably and accurately: "For Jonathan Edwards . . ., all thinking about the affections must begin with the inner-trinitarian life of God." "Affections and the Spirit," in *The Spirit, the Affections*, 279.

37. "Misc. kk," in *WJE* 13:186. The way Edwards reconciled God's love for his own glory and God's genuine love for his saints also informs his theology of Christian affections. For Edwards, God's delight in saints was a delight in his own image, and thus a delight in himself. He delights in his loveliness; therefore, he loves putting that love on display. And because his loveliness when on display is enjoyed by true saints, this too brings God delight. Neither should the love God has for the happiness of his creatures be distinguished from his own happiness, for their happiness is found in him, and he delights to meet that happiness by exercising his own goodness toward them thus making them happy. God, who is infinitely happy and not dependent on his creatures for any fulfillment, is in this way the exclusive source of their love and happiness. "But yet in one sense it can be truly said that God has the more delight for the loveliness and happiness of the creature, viz. as God would

other words, though created to have affections for God, humans more often are enslaved to worldly passions. When this happens, humans act like unintelligent beasts rather than intelligent, volitional beings. Sin has "brought them down nearer to the beasts, a sort of animals incapable of religion at all" ("Misc. ll," 13:187). God created the world in order that people would be happy. This happiness is found in the joy humans have beholding and enjoying the glory of God in creation ("Misc. 3," 13:200). For Edwards, God designed human nature such that its "rectitude" is in having greater affections for "high excellencies" and lower affections for those lower. Human beings, as intellectual creatures, were created to love and to delight in God's excellence ("Misc. 99," 13:265). Tragically, the opposite has happened ("Misc. 34," 13:218).

Given his immensity and infinity as an object of love, love for God should eclipse humanity's love for any created thing. The whole soul ought to love God "ardently" and "vehemently," so enjoying communion with God that any abatement or discontinuation of this love is abhorred ("Misc. 99," 13:266). To this end, God created humans with an appetite "proportioned" for the happiness God alone could give.[38] God designed people in his image so that they may, as intelligent and volitional, find happiness in him.[39]

be less happy if he were less good, or if it were possible for him to be hindered in exercising his own goodness, or to be hindered from glorifying himself." In this God's happiness does not increase, yet as God delights in exercising holiness, and would be "less happy" if this "act of holiness" was in some way prevented ("Misc. 679," in *WJE* 18:238).

38. "Misc. 99," in *WJE* 13:268. Edwards believed that God created humans for communion with him. As intelligent creatures commune via conversation, God communes with saints by the Word of God and the Holy Spirit who brings "influences and teachings" of various Scriptures to saints' "thoughts, affections, and our case" ("Misc. 204," in *WJE* 13:340).

39. For Edwards, human happiness was found exclusively in God. As such, self-love was essential to every human being. Edwards said that self-love—the mere "capacity for enjoyment or suffering"—and love for God are not opposed. In fact, one cannot even say that love for God ought to exceed human delight, for one cannot delight in God any more than the capacity of his delight—"our delight in God's good can't be superior to our love to delight in general" ("Misc. 530," in *WJE*18:73). If a human being loves another, that person desires that other person's good, which in turn brings delight to that person. Delight is essentially what self-love is. Human beings may love good that pertains to them or to another strongly enough that it becomes their own good. Edwards believed that when people condemn self-love, at issue is a certain *kind* of self-love. Sinful self-love consists in persons' delighting in something that is their own good "directly and immediately." Sinful self-love should always be less than love to God ("Misc. 530," in *WJE* 18:74). A person may surrender his own distinct good and embrace something like misery for God, but even then a superior delight and self-love is satisfied. Edwards explained: "He has greater delight in what is obtained for God, than he had in what he has lost of his own; so that he has only exchanged a lesser joy for a greater." Consequently, if a person makes love for God superior

For Edwards, humans have affections because they were created in the image of a loving God. This means that the soul's affections are higher and divine like. If human affections are patterned after God's affections, then a distinction should be drawn between affections and the passions, or the movements answering the sensitive appetite. More important, this doctrine also means that affections are crucial to true religion.

Edwards deduced that the created world reveals itself to have been caused by a being with understanding and will. The world showed itself to have been designed for a future purpose or "end." If so, "an intelligent voluntary agent" necessarily created the world ("Misc. 749," 18:392–98). Furthermore, if the agent that first caused the world be intelligent and voluntary, then this agent is "infinitely the most intelligent and sensible being of all."[40] His perception must infinitely surpass his creatures' perception. As sensible or voluntary, he is more so than his creatures:

> He acts more of himself, infinitely more purely active, and in no respect passive, as all created minds are in a great measure passive in their acts of will. And the acts of will are more voluntary. Though there be no proper passions as in created minds, yet voluntariness is exercised to an infinitely greater height. The divine love, which is the sum of all the exercises of the divine will, is infinitely

to such an extent that he has no true self-love when love for God is preeminent, then that person is unwilling and very far from true love for God ("Misc. 530," in *WJE* 18:75).

40. "Misc. 749," in *WJE* 18:396. This use of word "sensible" with respect to the will of God shows, *pace* Hoopes, that Edwards did not have literal "sense" in mind when he speaks of the sensibility or sense of the heart (or mind or will). Hoopes writes: "[Edwards] called such emotion a 'sense of the heart' for physiological reasons; God has so joined soul and body that as the soul experiences pleasure or displeasure in its ideas it stirs the blood and causes 'some bodily sensation, especially about the heart.' Edwards's purpose in ['Misc.'] '782' was not so much to locate the uniqueness of religious experience in the sense of the heart as to establish that genuine spiritual perceptions, *in common* with ordinary external sensations, involve the will or emotions." Edwards meant the term *sense* analogically, corresponding to the physical senses in strength, but wholly spiritual and immaterial. The citation of *Affections* in Hoopes's remarks do not show that Edwards had a physiological notion of the "sense of the heart," but that there is "sometimes" a corresponding effect of the soul's immaterial movements on the body in general and the heart in particular. The "sense of the heart" is not literally, but analogically, called a "sense." As Norman Fiering explains: "Edwards meant by spiritual sense not only a new capacity for being affected by the things of God, but also a new inclination or a new will directed toward those things. The new sense of the heart brought about by the workings of grace is also a new disposition or an infused habit that is identical to holy love or holiness." Fiering, *Jonathan Edwards's Moral Thought*, 126. See ibid., 123–29; Danaher, *Trinitarian Ethics*, 126; and Mark Valeri, "Preface to the Period," in Jonathan Edwards, *Sermons and Discourses, 1730–1733*, vol. 17 of *The Works of Jonathan Edwards* (New Haven, CT: Yale University Press, 1999), 42.

stronger, more lively and intense, as not only the light of the sun, but his heat, is immensely greater than that of the planets whose light and heat is derived from him. ("Misc. 749," 18:396–97)

This remark by Edwards is instructive, not only for the contrast between the wills of God and created beings, but in the observation that "proper passions" do not belong to the mind of God as to creatures. Further, divine "voluntariness" infinitely surpasses human wills. While Edwards said that "passions" and passivity "in a great measure" marks human wills, he adds that, because God is an intelligent and voluntary Creator, he should be worshiped "by voluntary acts, as expressions of our thoughts and volitions and motions of our hearts" ("Misc. 749," 18:397).

The nature of God, as a voluntary being, informed Edwards's notion of human affections.[41] Affections resemble the love and volition of the immaterial God. In his Trinitarian theology, Edwards saw the Son to be the Father's idea of his own essence.[42] The Spirit is the infinite love between the Father and perfect image of God in the Son. The act of infinite delight between the Father and the Son is distinct from the Father or the Son, just as "the delight and energy that is begotten in us by an idea is distinct from the idea."[43] Edwards continued, "[The love] is distinct from each of the other two, and yet it is God; for the pure and perfect act of God is God, because God is a pure act. It appears that this is God, because that which acts perfectly is all act, and nothing but act."[44]

Edwards derived from Scripture (and not speculative theology) the doctrine that the Holy Spirit was the divine love between the Father and the Son in the

41. Sang Hyun Lee observed: "What is striking about Jonathan Edwards's writings on the Trinity is that there is none of this bifurcation between the doctrine of the Trinity and the Christian life of faith and practice. Everything Edwards wrote about the Trinity expresses the intertwining connectedness of the Trinity and the Christian's experience of God as the Creator, Savior, and Sanctifier, and thus between the immanent and the economic Trinity." "Editor's Introduction," in Jonathan Edwards, *Writings on the Trinity, Grace, and Faith*, vol. 21 of *The Works of Jonathan Edwards* (New Haven, CT: Yale University Press, 2003), 3. Also see Pauw, *Supreme Harmony*, 151–59 and Chapter 1 of Kyle C. Strobel, *Jonathan Edwards's Theology: A Reinterpretation* (London: Bloomsbury T&T Clark, 2013).

42. For Edwards, the Son, as the light of the Father, represented the thought or understanding of God ("Misc. 134," in *WJE* 13:299). In the *Discourse on the Trinity*, Edwards said: "Though we cannot conceive of the manner of the divine understanding, yet if it be understanding or anything that can be anyway signified by that word of ours, it is by idea. Though the divine nature be vastly different from that of created spirits, yet our souls are made in the image of God: we have understanding and will, idea and love, as God hath, and the difference is only in the perfection of degree and manner" (*WJE* 21:113).

43. "Misc. 94," in *WJE* 13:260. Compare "Misc. 151," in *WJE* 13:301–02.

44. "Misc. 94," in *WJE* 13:260. Edwards found further proof that the Holy Spirit represents the infinite love of God because the Spirit is represented by the dove, the mates of which show "remarkable and wonderful love" to each other ("Misc. 98," in *WJE* 13:265).

Trinity. Edwards noted, "The word 'spirit,' most commonly in Scripture, is put for affections of the mind; but there is no other affection in God essentially, properly and primarily, but love and delight—and that in himself, for into this is his love and delight in his creatures resolvable" ("Misc. 146," 13:299). From this premise, Edwards began to explore the possible biblical connection between "spirit" and "affections" ("Misc. 143," 13:298–99). He found it significant that only *logos* and *agape*—reason and love—were said to "be God" in Scripture. So when the Apostle John said in 1 John that God dwells in believers by his Spirit, his love abides in them, "which is God" ("Misc. 146," 13:300). The Bible's description of the Holy Spirit as God's breath also shows his relationship to affections, for "what are so properly said to be the breathings of the soul, as its affections?" ("Misc. 157," 13:307).

Eventually, Edwards found several passages that represented the Spirit as love, including 2 Cor. 6:6 and Rom. 15:30.[45] The manifold Scripture metaphors of the Spirit (e.g., fire, breath, water, oil, wine) represented him as "the perfectly active flowing affection, holy love and pleasure of God" ("Misc. 336," 13:412). Therefore, when the Bible used the word "spirit" concerning God (and did not refer to the divine essence), it spoke of God's affection, disposition, or "holy temper," all of which referred to the Holy Spirit. When the Spirit of God, the Trinity's affection, dwells in believers, then the "divine temper" or "affection" of "infinite love" resides there, as taught in 2 Pet. 1:4.[46]

The Holy Spirit, as the divine love between the Father and the Son, indwells saints, and so becomes the source of holy affections. "Partakers of the divine nature" in 2 Pet. 1:4 was an important Scripture for Edwards. He understood it to teach that the Spirit itself was the love indwelling believers. The passage further taught the opposition between the divine nature and lust. Saints alone partake

45. Also Phil. 1:1-2; Rom. 5:5; Gal. 5:22-23; Eph. 5:9; Col. 1:8; 1 Thess. 1:6; and Rom. 14:17; see "Misc. 305," in *WJE* 13:390–91; compare "Misc. 341," in *WJE* 13:415; "Misc. 355," in *WJE* 13:429; and "Misc. 364," in *WJE* 13:364.

46. "Misc. 396," in *WJE* 13:462. Compare the "Discourse on the Trinity," where Edwards writes: "The name of the third person in the Trinity, viz. The Holy Spirit, confirms [that divine love is the Holy Spirit]. It naturally expresses the divine nature as subsisting in pure act and perfect energy, and as flowing out and breathing forth in infinitely sweet and vigorous affection" (*WJE* 21:122). On Edwards's theology of the Holy Spirit as divine love, see Robert W. Caldwell III, *Communion in the Spirit: The Holy Spirit as the Bond of Union in the Theology of Jonathan Edwards*, Studies in Evangelical History and Thought (Eugene, OR: Wipf and Stock Publishers, 2006), 42–49. Stephen A. Wilson is largely right in saying, "[F]or Edwards the locus of God's regenerative activity increasingly became the communication of God's own loving nature to the actual ethico-religious make-up of the person," though this was an Edwardsean theme for a long time. *Virtue*, 44. Also see Danaher, *Trinitarian Ethics*, 39–44.

of the divine nature. The unregenerate only have lust in them.[47] By nature people lack that "relish and sense of spiritual things," for they, not partaking of the divine nature, have never experienced them. "They are words without a meaning to him; he knows nothing of the matter any more than a blind man of colors" ("Misc. 683," 18:245). Because unbelievers do not have the Spirit or the affections he gives, they have no communion with Christ.

To believers the Holy Spirit communicates the very affections and loves of Christ ("Misc. 683," 18:247). The soul must be prepared for such enjoyments of God; therefore, God opens and extends the "appetite of the soul" to receive even greater satisfaction ("Misc. 822," 18:533). In heaven, Edwards said, every craving shall be satisfied in such a way that there is a simultaneous desire for greater enjoyment of God.[48]

Sometime in early 1727, Edwards's contemplation of the Trinity yielded another development of his theology of the human mind. For Edwards, the mind's operations (understanding, will, love, and the like) "are not properly ideas." On the contrary, mental operations are actually repetitions of the acts themselves. In other words, the idea of love is actually love; the idea of an affection is an affection. To have an idea of an affection is to experience that affection. When applied to the Trinity, this means God's idea of himself is "absolutely himself again" ("Misc. 238," 13:353–54).

Although Edwards would caution against pressing any metaphor for the Trinity too far, he saw an image of the Trinity in the soul of man. The mind corresponds to the Father, "its understanding or idea" to the Son, and "the will or affection or love" to the Spirit ("Misc. 370," 13:442). Edwards expanded on this theme in his *Discourse on the Trinity*, another theological notebook he began in the early 1730s. There he observed that the understanding of God cannot be further distinguished (e.g., between perception or idea), because his understanding is perfect and complete. Similarly, "with respect to the other faculty, as it is in God, there are no distinctions to be admitted of faculty, habit and act, between will, inclination and love: but that it is all one simple act" (21:113). If Edwards did not borrow the close identity of will, love, and affections from Ames or Baxter, his own Trinitarian theology would have supplied it.[49]

47. Elsewhere Edwards observes that the reason unregenerate persons have no interest in holiness is that they do not know what it is ("Misc. 123," in *WJE* 13:286–87). Compare Edwards, *Discourse on the Trinity*, in *WJE* 21:114–15.

48. "Misc. 822," in *WJE* 18:533. Edwards continued, "Now the views we have cause uneasy desires. We find obstructions and opposition in the way of our obtaining those things that our spiritual views excite an appetite after, and great failing of such a satisfaction as we stand in great need of for the present, and many and great frustrations in our desires. Hence we read of groanings that cannot be uttered" ("Misc. 822," in *WJE* 18:534).

49. Edwards's Trinitarian theology illustrates his emphasis in *Affections* that holy affections are not "heat without light" (*WJE* 2:266). Edwards explained: "The Father understands because the Son, who is the divine understanding, is in him. The Father loves

Spiritual Sense From his doctrine of the Trinity, Edwards turned to the human heart. That the Holy Spirit, the loving bond of the Trinity, indwells the hearts of saints means that he actually gives them a love for God they could never produce themselves. The foundation of the spiritual change in a person was an altered "temper" or "disposition." As the Spirit indwells saints, "divine light" shines in the soul where it did not before, making spiritual things "appear excellent, beautiful, glorious."[50] This doctrine informs Edwards's notion of the "spiritual sense" and the "sense of the heart."

As Edwards penned observations on the work of the Spirit in conversion, a subtle migration on the concept of "sense" can be seen. His earliest ideas of conversion, dating from spring 1729, held that the Spirit's first act was the "sense of the mind," whereby the human *understanding* sees the glory of Christ.[51] The will is exercised "as immediately" as the intellect, but it follows the Spirit's work on the understanding.[52] Edwards clearly moved from this position. Although he said

because the Holy Ghost is in him. So the Son loves because the Holy Spirit is in him and proceeds from him. So the Holy Ghost, or the divine essence subsisting in divine love, understands because the Son, the divine idea, is in him. Understanding may be predicated of this love, because it is the love of the understanding both objectively and subjectively. God loves the understanding and the understanding also flows out in love, so that the divine understanding is in the Deity subsisting in love. It is not a blind love. Even in creatures there is consciousness included in the very nature of the will or act of the soul; and though perhaps not so that it can be so properly be said that it is a seeing or understanding will, yet it may truly and properly [be] said so in God by reason of God's infinitely more perfect manner of acting, so that the whole divine essence flows out and subsists in this act" (*WJE* 21:133–34). Compare Danaher, *Trinitarian Ethics*, 65–66; 117–19; and Strobel, *Theology*, 59–65.

50. Strobel also asserts that Edwards's Trinitarian theology informed his idea of spiritual knowledge. *Theology*, 149–52, 176. Edwards earlier said faith apprehends such a powerful idea of God that it recognizes the idea to be divine ("Misc. aa.," in *WJE* 13:177–78). Faith consists of both understanding and will. The understanding knows the truth of the gospel together "with a clear and sensible idea of the excellence of it, that is true faith" ("Misc. 212," in *WJE* 13:342). See "Misc. 507," in *WJE* 13:53.

51. Edwards used "sense of the mind" synonymously with his famous phrase, "sense of the heart." Though he clearly identified "sense of the mind" in "Misc. 397" with the understanding, in *On the Nature of True Virtue* he connected "sense of the mind" with "disposition" and the will, which is nearly synonymous with his notion of "sense of the heart" (*WJE* 8:573). The difference is not in the terms "sense of the mind" and "sense of the heart," as much as it is between the faculty wherein the *sense* lies. Compare "Misc. 123," in *WJE* 13:286. *Pace* Sang Hyun Lee, *The Philosophical Theology of Jonathan Edwards* (Princeton, NJ: Princeton University Press, 1988), 149–50.

52. "Misc. 397," in *WJE* 13:463. According to "Misc. 397," the Spirit's "first act" in a Christian is in giving a "spiritual understanding" or "sense of the mind," whereby the mind perceives divine beauty. This precedes any act of will. "By this sense or taste of the mind, especially if it be lively, the mind in many things distinguishes truth from falsehood." As

in "Misc. 397" that the "sense" given by the Spirit affects the understanding and immediately includes the will, he would finally conclude that the "sense" is a "sense of the heart," or *will*, whereby an individual is inclined toward what is already held in the understanding.

By 1733, Edwards believed that the soul is "sensible" toward good in two different ways corresponding to the two faculties. First, a mind may conclude rationally that something is good or a mind may be "sensible" of good when it senses the beauty of something. "This kind of sensibleness of good," Edwards added, "carries in it an act of the will, or inclination, or spirit of the mind, as well as the understanding."[53] The "sense of the heart" is distinct from the speculative understanding, but arises from it, which is a reason for the necessity of the means of grace.[54]

Edwards used the phrase "sense of the heart" in many places, including "A Divine and Supernatural Light" and *Religious Affections*, both of which are treated below. He also discussed it in his "Miscellanies," of which "Misc. 782" is one of the fullest treatments.[55] Edwards closely linked the "the sense of the heart" to his understanding of the affections. Once again, some scholars see Locke's influence behind Edwards's emphasis on the "sense of the heart."[56] Yet, many authors

Edwards struggled to describe conversion with respect to human understanding, he first argued the light given by the Spirit in the mind affected the understanding. Yet, he quickly added that the will "is as immediately exercised in that sense of the mind which is called spiritual understanding, as the intellect." Schafer said Edwards wrote "Misc. 397" and its related entries while working on a series of sermons on Jn 16:8 ("Editor's Introduction," in *WJE* 13:28–29). In a similar entry, Edwards said that the will is directed by the varying degrees of good sensed in the soul. Conversion occurs when God changes "the mind's ideas of spiritual good" ("Misc. 284," in *WJE* 13:381).

53. "Misc. 489," in *WJE* 13:533. Compare "Misc. 507," in *WJE* 18:53; "Misc. 540," in *WJE* 18:88–89. See Strobel, *Theology*, 171–73.

54. "Misc. 540," in *WJE* 18:88–89. Also see "Misc. 539," in *WJE* 18:88.

55. John Smith dates "Misc. 782" to 1745. "Religious Affections and the 'Sense of the Heart,'" in *PCJE*, 106. Other evidence, however, points to 1738 or early 1739. See Chamberlain, "Editor's Introduction," in Jonathan Edwards, *The "Miscellanies" (Entry Nos. 501–832)*, vol. 18 of *The Works of Jonathan Edwards* (New Haven, CT: Yale University Press, 2000), 42–48. Compare Kenneth P. Minkema, "Chronology of Edwards's Life and Times," Jonathan Edwards Center at Yale University, http://edwards.yale.edu/research/chronology (accessed December 4, 2017). An abridged version of Minkema's chronology can also be found in "Chronology of Edwards' Life and Writings," *PCJE*, xxiii–xxviii.

56. Scholars have exhaustively debated what the "sense of the heart" means in Edwards's thought. For a helpful survey of scholarship up to the close of the twentieth century, see Michael J. McClymond, "Spiritual Perception in Jonathan Edwards," *The Journal of Religion* 77 (1997): 195–216. Perry Miller and his article "Jonathan Edwards on the 'Sense of the Heart'" began the controversy. Miller interpreted the phrase as a literal sense: "In Edwards' 'sense of the heart' there is nothing transcendental; it is rather a sensuous apprehension of the total situation"; again: "the Spirit of God works through the mechanism of sense impression." Ibid., 127. For Miller, Edwards naturalized the supernatural. Edwards linked

connected the will and the spiritual sense, from the Cambridge Platonist John Smith and Protestant Scholastic Francis Turretin to the Puritans Thomas Goodwin

the "sense of the heart" to the "passions," and consequently used naked words to evoke the "sense of the heart" in his hearers. *Errand into the Wilderness*, 167–83. Davidson largely agrees with Miller. *Jonathan Edwards*, 16–19. William J. Wainwright espouses the same position as well. *Reason and the Heart: A Prolegomenon to a Critique of Passional Reason*, Cornell Studies in the Philosophy of Religion (Ithaca, NY: Cornell University Press, 1995), 7–54. Cherry critiqued Miller, stressing that the *heart* of the sense is an intellectual volition that collapses the traditional faculties. *Theology*, 12–24. Helm, though himself reading "sense of the heart" akin to a literal sense, argues against Miller and Davidson that Edwards was not dependent on Locke, but "used Lockean empiricism as a *model* for religious experience and nothing more." "John Locke and Jonathan Edwards: A Reconsideration," *Journal of the History of Philosophy* 7 (1969): 54. Helm says the "sense of the heart" is different from the five senses, yet a "sixth sense." Ibid., 57. Hoopes largely follows Helm, but suggests an important distinction between "sense of the heart," something enjoyed by all humankind, and "spiritual sense," which is only for the regenerate. "Edwards's Religious Psychology," 857–59. Hoopes also says that Edwards emphasized the "sense" because the "sense of the heart" is always a bodily sensation. Ibid., 857–58. Stephen R. Yarbrough and John C. Adams disagree, arguing "sense of the heart" is a "new perspective." *Delightful Conviction: Jonathan Edwards and the Rhetoric of Conversion*, Great American Orators 20 (Westport, CT: Greenwood Press, 1993), 18. McClymond uses Hoopes's crucial distinction and argues that "sense of the heart" is Edwards's complex and heavily qualified attempt both to vindicate the unique spiritual experience of the regenerate as well as to demonstrate the employment of normal faculties within that experience. "Spiritual Perception," 213–14; compare "Jonathan Edwards," in *OHRE*, 408–10. Miklos Vetö argues that the "sense of the heart" is a volitional apprehension of ideas as they are and perceived as good or evil. See Miklos Vetö, "La Connaissance Spirituelle Selon Jonathan Edwards," *Revue de Theologie et de Philosophie* 111 (1979): 233–51, trans. in Michael J. McClymond, "Spiritual Knowledge according to Jonathan Edwards," *CTJ* 31 (1996): 161–81. Compare Norman Pettit, *The Heart Prepared: Grace and Conversion in Puritan Spiritual Life* (New Haven, CT: Yale University Press, 1966), 210 and Paul Lewis, "Springs of Motion," 281–82. John E. Smith notes the contrast between speculation and "sense of the heart," identifying it "with all the ideal apprehensions of dignity, greatness, awesome majesty, meekness, value, and importance which, for him, constitute a *sensible* knowledge that goes far beyond any notional understanding." "Religious Affections and the 'Sense of the Heart,'" 110. In a 2016 article, Gerald McDermott adds his own take: "My position is that Edwards's new sense involved an interplay of natural and gracious experience. Pace Miller, the experience of conversion is foundational to Edwards's religious epistemology. . . . Edwards made this vision dependent on a prior operation of divine grace. Pace Helm, however, the mental breakthrough of grace, or 'divine and supernatural light,' operates in and through the natural sense faculties, and so grace does not destroy or bypass nature but perfects it." "Affections and the Spirit," in *The Spirit, the Affections*, 289. Also see Michael J. McClymond, *Encounters with God: An Approach to the Theology of Jonathan Edwards* (New York: Oxford University Press, 1998), 9–26.

and John Owen. John Norris's theory of vision and love is also strikingly similar to Edwards's doctrine.[57]

In "Misc. 782," Edwards explained that people can think of spiritual realities in two ways. First, some conceive of spiritual realities indirectly, akin to using words as signs in speech. Others have an apprehension of spiritual realities, where the mind has an "*ideal view* or *contemplation*" of the object of thought.[58] Signs are

57. On John Smith, see the section "Affective Psychology in the Early Enlightenment" in Chapter 3. Smith said, "The soul itself hath its sense, as well as the body: and therefore David, when he would teach us how to know what the divine goodness is, calls not for speculation but sensation, 'Taste and see how good the Lord is.' That is not the best and truest knowledge of God which is wrought out by the labour and sweat of the brain, but that which is kindled within us by a heavenly warmth in our hearts." Smith, *Select Discourses*, 4. Significantly, Smith's long quote in *Affections* is found in Edwards's first discussion of the "spiritual sense" (*WJE* 2:217–19 n6). Terrence Erdt notes that the language of "sense" filled the Reformed tradition since the time of Calvin. *Jonathan Edwards*, 1–20. On the Puritan use of "sense," see Geoffrey F. Nuttall, *The Holy Spirit in Puritan Faith and Experience* (Chicago: University of Chicago Press, 1992), 33–47. Francis Turretin used the very phrase "*sensu . . . cordis.*" *Elenctic Theology* §15.16.31 (2:629). On Norris, *Miscellanies*, 327–29. Mason I. Lowance, Jr. also argues that Norris and Nicolas Malebranche influenced Edwards's notion of the spiritual sense. See "Jonathan Edwards and the Platonists: Edwardsean Epistemology and the Influence of Malebranche and Norris," *Studies in Puritan American Spirituality* 2 (1992): 129–52. Also see Paul Copan, "Jonathan Edwards's Philosophical Influences: Lockean or Malebrachean?" *JETS* 44 (2001): 107–24; and Danaher, *Trinitarian Ethics*, 26, 47–49.

58. "Misc. 782," in *WJE* 18:458. Edwards explained the indirect sign-knowledge thus: "So when he read the word 'man,' let him inquire whether he had any actual idea of that which was signified by this word. In order to this he must have an actual idea of man. I don't mean only a confused idea of an outward appearance, like that of man, for if that was all, that was not an idea of man properly, but only a sign made use of instead of an idea; but he must have an actual idea of those things wherein manhood most essentially consists: as an idea of reason, which contains many other actual ideas—as an actual idea of consciousness, an actual idea of a disposal of ideas in the mind, an actual idea of a consequent perception of relations and connections between them, etc.; and so he must have an actual idea of will, which contains an actual idea of pleasure or pain, agreeableness or disagreeableness, and a consequent command, or imperate act of the soul, etc" ("Misc. 782," in *WJE* 18:453). Edwards's point is that people often substitute signs for real ideas of things. Sometimes these signs are images in the imagination. In speech, the signs are words or names. God, Edwards was careful to point out, never has a sign in his mind, but only the ideas themselves. Edwards continued: "From what has been said, we see that there are two ways of thinking and understanding, especially of spiritual or mental things, that we receive a notion of by reflection or consciousness; viz. (1) that wherein we don't directly view the things themselves by the actual presence of their ideas, or (which is the same thing in mental matters) sensation of their resemblances, but apprehend them only indirectly in their signs, which is a kind of mental reading, wherein we don't look on the

often used in speech and in thought for convenience. Incidentally, that Edwards noted the abstract nature of the "sense," shows that his use of "sense" in "sense of the heart" is analogical, not literal. He was not referring to a corporeal sense, but of a sense of the mind or a sense of the heart.[59]

Not only are there two ways of thinking (indirectly or ideally), but there are two ways the mind ideally views ideas. For Edwards, the mind may view things either by apprehending the objects ideally with the understanding or "head," or by having an ideal "sense" (note, this is *not* a "sense of the heart") of the object with the will or "heart" ("Misc. 782," 18:458). When an object is viewed with the understanding, it merely beholds it. To have an ideal apprehension of an object, the heart must have a "sensation of agreeableness or disagreeableness, or a sense or feeling of the heart of pleasedness or displeasedness; therefore everyone that has an ideal view of those things has therein some measure of that inward feeling or sense" ("Misc. 782," 18:459). The heart or will's view of an object sees its good or evil. The soul draws toward or recoils away from the object in view. Consequently, all ideal apprehension includes both intellect and volition.

Edwards not only distinguished indirect and ideal thinking, and two aspects of ideal apprehension, but he also found differences between speculation and the "sense of the heart." Mere speculation consists of all understanding that is not ideal apprehension (whereby only signs are used) or ideal apprehension where the understanding alone (and not the will) is active. Sensible knowledge, by contrast, joins the will and understanding and includes beauty, pleasure, pain, and other "affections." Sensible knowledge is of the heart, the realm of the will and affections. All human knowledge ought to move the will and affections in some way, and so sensible knowledge is vital, for this is the very end of knowledge ("Misc. 782," 18:460). The "sense of the heart" is the soul's affectionate knowledge, uniting together the inclination or will with ideal apprehension.

things themselves, but only on those signs of them before our eyes. This is a mere cogitation without any proper apprehension of the things thought of. (2) There is that which is more properly called apprehension, wherein the mind has the direct *ideal view* or *contemplation* of the thing thought about" ("Misc. 782," in *WJE* 18:458).

59. Note Edwards's belief that the "faculty of the will" is "*figuratively* called the heart." Edwards also said ideal apprehension in the will "is *vulgarly* called having A SENSE" and "(to speak *figuratively*) some feeling of the heart." The "sense" is a "*kind* of *inward* tasting or feeling, of sweetness or pleasure, bitterness or pains." Again: "An ideal apprehension or view of these things is in *vulgar* speech called an having a *sense* of them; and in proportion to the intensive degree of this *ideal apprehension*, or the clearness and liveliness or the *idea* of them, so persons are said to have a greater or lesser sense of them, and according to the easiness or difficulty of persons receiving such a sense of things." Edwards also explicitly distinguished the pleasure and pain of the literal bodily senses and that of the mind ("Misc. 782," in *WJE* 18:458–61, emphasis mine). Compare Lee, *Philosophical*, 148–65. In tying sense of the heart to imagination, Lee downplays Edwards's emphasis on the *externality* of the imagination. See *WJE* 2:210–11.

For Edwards, one obtained the "sense of the heart" in one of two ways: through nature and through the Spirit of God. Humans attach pleasure and displeasure to ideas as the literal senses perceive excellency or various displeasure in objects. Sensible knowledge is also aroused with "some immediate influence of the Spirit" ("Misc. 782," 18:461). Just as people find it difficult to recollect a physical object, so for a person to have any sensible knowledge of spiritual things requires the grace of the Holy Spirit.[60] Yet this sensible knowledge through the Spirit is "ORDINARY," which means that is *not* saving knowledge ("Misc. 782," 18:462). Such sensible knowledge is not revelation. In this the Spirit does not give new content, but takes the things the soul already knows about God and eternal matters and gives the individual a sensible knowledge of them.[61]

Edwards also differentiated natural sensible knowledge from moral. The natural good or evil that human beings sensibly know are those things "agreeable or disagreeable to their human nature as such." Here human beings do not sense "the real *moral* beauty and excellency" of spiritual realities.[62] Some people can have a sensible knowledge about spiritual realities, but only because it pertains to their natural welfare. Any possible natural sensible knowledge of spiritual realities is not strong or "lively." On the other hand, moral or spiritual sensible knowledge is saving. Edwards said,

> But as to the other, viz. a sense of divine things with respect to spiritual good and evil, because these don't consist in any agreeableness or disagreeableness to human nature as such, or the mere human faculties or principles, therefore man, merely with the exercise of these faculties and his own natural strength can do nothing towards getting such a sense of divine things; but it must be wholly and entirely a work of the Spirit of God, not merely as assisting and co-working with natural principles, but infusing something above nature. ("Misc. 782," 18:463)

This distinction explains the difference between natural and gracious affections in a revival.[63] The Spirit may give a natural knowledge of the things of God. Such

60. Edwards explained: "But the exciting a sense of things pertaining to our eternal interest, is a thing that we are so far from, and so unable to attain of ourselves, by reason of the alienation of the inclinations and natural dispositions of the soul from those things as they are, and the sinking of our intellectual powers, and the great subjection of the soul in its fallen state to the external senses, that a due sense of those things is never attained without immediate divine assistance" ("Misc. 782," in *WJE* 18:461–62).

61. Edwards called it "inspiration," when the Spirit gives a speculative knowledge of divine things. Enthusiasm is when one falsely maintains that the Spirit has revealed to them new speculative knowledge ("Misc. 782," in *WJE* 18:462). Compare *WJE* 22:87.

62. "Misc. 782," in *WJE* 18:462, emphasis mine.

63. Because "Misc. 782" was written in the late 1730s, a few years after the mid-1730s revival (see the section "Spiritual Sense"), the genesis of the entry may have been an attempt by Edwards to explain his understanding of the successes and failures of that Awakening

people are "awakened" and experience "convictions" in only a common way ("Misc. 782," 18:463). Yet, a sensible knowledge of spiritual good differs from such natural sensible knowledge.

The Spirit of God gives persons a sensible knowledge of the natural good of religious things, but this is not a gracious work *per se*. A gracious work happens when the Spirit gives sensible knowledge concerning religious matters such that their spiritual good or evil is tasted. Spiritual sensible knowledge consists "in a sense of the spiritual excellency, beauty, or sweetness of divine things, which is not by assisting natural principles, but by infusing something supernatural" ("Misc. 782," 18:464). That "something supernatural" is the Holy Spirit. Such sensible knowledge results in a conviction of the truth of Christianity.

Passionate Love of Christ The contours of Edwards's affective psychology are also displayed in his thought concerning the theanthropic person of Christ. Anchored to a traditional Reformed understanding of the Godhead, young Edwards did not believe that God experienced passions. Thus God's love for humanity is not properly "a passion" such as human beings "feel."[64] Yet the incarnation of the Son means that now God loves human beings in the same way humans love. Because of the incarnation, the love of God should not be abstracted such that it is unrecognizable from human love. "Now this passionate love of Christ, by virtue of the union with the divine nature, is in a sort infinite" ("Misc. z," 13:176–77). Nevertheless, Edwards believed that the love of the glorified Christ is different from ordinary human love.

The human faculties of the glorified Christ are "so enlarged" that he can consider all the saints at once, and exercise "a passionate love (such as we experience) to all of

(see the section "*Charity and Its Fruits*"), although Edwards was concerned about these issues throughout his ministry.

64. Compare *WJE* 10:432 and Danaher, *Trinitarian Ethics*, 78–84. For an example of a discussion of divine impassibility that Edwards would have likely been familiar with, see Richard Fiddes, *Theologia Speculativa: or, The First Part of a Body of Divinity Under that Title. Wherein are explain'd the Principles of Natural and Reveal'd Religion* (London: W. Bowyer, 1718), 73–77. Fiddes said, "That passion, as it denotes, according to the proper import of the word, a state of suffering, and any painful or uneasy sensation, cannot be attributed to God, is indeed universally acknowledged." Yet, Fiddes explained, it is improper to say that passions, when referring to acts of the will "without any real perturbation of mind," can be said to be true of God. Some attribute passions to God when they distinguish "passion" as a movement of the soul from their accompanying "commotion of the animal spirits" in humanity. "If it were derogatory to the honour of God," Fiddes asked, "to ascribe passions to him in this sense, why do we express the motions of his will by the same names whereby we are agreed to express human passions?" Ibid., 73. Fiddes suspected that medieval Scholasticism rejected divine impassibility because they believed erroneously from Aristotle that passions were seated in the body. Only a soul can suffer. "And if it be impossible that any being, but what thinks, should suffer, then 'tis absurd to attribute passions in a proper

them in particular" ("Misc. 81," 13:247). Jesus does not merely love the church, but individual believers, in this way.[65] As God created human beings with natural love for the other sex, so Christ himself, in taking a human nature, is inclined to love human beings and especially his own spouse, the church. Yet differences remain: "He is as much of a purer and better and more benevolent nature than we, whereby he is inclined to a higher degree of love, as he is of a greater capacity, whereby he is capable of a more exalted, ardent and sweet love" ("Misc. 189," 13:332).[66]

Summary of the "Miscellanies" In addition to the themes already discussed, Edwards's personal notebooks in general show that, even from his youth, the young student and minister was keenly interested in nature and role of the affections and passions. This fact will be important later when Edwards's response to the spiritual conundrums the Great Awakening is more carefully considered. The "Miscellanies" repeatedly show that Edwards did not invent a psychology in order to defend the Awakening. His affective psychology was tightly bound to his theology. Throughout his private writings, he recognized the importance of the affections in religion and their distinction from the passions.

Edwards used his private theological writings to reflect on the unique nature of holy affections. He supposed that Canticles (Song of Solomon) was inspired so that the church would have a song "particularly adapted to the dispositions and holy affections of a true Christian's soul towards Christ."[67] Scripture likens the union enjoyed between Christ and believers to a marriage. For Edwards, the marital analogy represented the essence of saving faith, for it is by faith that the soul receives her Christ. Faith has "affections and motions of heart" proper to it. Edwards found, in the husband and wife, characteristic affections that represent the fitting affections between Christ and the church.[68]

sense to the body, under any modification whatever; tho' by accident the body may be an occasion of exciting or fortifying certain sensations, to which we give the name of passions, in the soul." Fiddes preferred to call such movements of the will or soul "affections." Ibid., 73. He affirmed that there are "reasonable affections." "Is it below the character of a rational being to have any motion of love towards itself, to take complacency in its own happiness, or to *exercise loving kindness*, towards promoting the happiness of other beings[?]" Ibid., 74. The Scripture speaks of God's love, delight, and hatred. His will is not indifferent. Fiddes did not understand the existence of affections in God to deny divine simplicity, any more than the several other attributes do. As for "those passions which seem to be attended with the greatest imperfection," divine anger (for example) is but the "external appearance of some like commotion" in God as in men. Edwards likely read Fiddes before 1724 (*WJE* 26:139).

65. "Misc. 96," in *WJE* 13:264. Compare "Misc. 180," in *WJE* 13:327.

66. Compare "Misc. 213," in *WJE* 13:343.

67. "Misc. 359," in *WJE* 13:433. See Edwards, *A History of the Work of Redemption*, vol. 9 of *The Works of Jonathan Edwards*, ed. John F. Wilson (New Haven, CT: Yale University Press, 1989), 289.

68. "Misc. 37," in *WJE* 13:219–21. Compare "Images," no. 33, in *WJE* 11:59.

Basic point: affections, dispositions integral

The love of glorified saints grows throughout eternity in heaven ("Misc. 105," 275–76). The heavenly saints will be "full of happiness," having "as much happiness as they can contain" ("Misc. 106," 13:277). The affection between believers in this life, when "virtuous, . . . duly subordinated to divine love," continues for eternity ("Misc. 639," 18:172–73).

The early "Miscellanies" of Edwards prove that affections were central in his thought. He was aware, even as a young man, of those who said that too much devotion to God was a bad thing.[69] Edwards strongly disagreed, noting that the Bible taught that love was essential for true Christianity.[70] These notebooks also show Edwards subtly developing on affections. Specifically, he came to reject the Lockean notion of the will. The more Edwards considered God himself, Christ's love, and the Holy Spirit, the more the necessity of affections cemented in his thought. The more he considered the Trinity, the more he was convinced of the connection between will and affections.[71] Indeed, the "Miscellanies" show that love to God was central to Edwards's rational apologetic of Calvinistic Christianity. He used love to argue for the Trinity, the afterlife, and the immaterial soul.

Early Sermons and Revival Writings

From the beginning of his public ministry, Edwards urged his hearers to have greater affection for God. He also commonly contrasted affections for God with lower passions and earthly desires. Although Edwards inherited his idea of the affections from Reformed theology, the early sermons show that he confirmed that concept through his own study of the Scriptures.[72]

69. See "Misc. tt," in *WJE* 13:189–90.

70. Edwards sees 1 Corinthians 13 teaching, "[t]hose that go furthest in religion that are in a natural condition," lack love. Thus affections are necessary for true Christianity ("Misc. 673," in *WJE* 18:232).

71. See, for example, "Misc. 362," in *WJE* 13:435.

72. The same could be said for Edwards's "Miscellany" entries. Stephen J. Stein observes, "[Edwards's] commentary is a clear product of eighteenth-century evangelical religious culture." "Editor's Introduction," in Jonathan Edwards, *The "Blank Bible,"* vol. 24, part 1 of *The Works of Jonathan Edwards* (New Haven, CT: Yale University Press, 2006), 4. For more on Edwards and the Bible, also see Robert E. Brown, *Jonathan Edwards and the Bible* (Bloomington: Indiana University Press, 2002); Robert E. Brown, "The Bible," in *PCJE*, 87–102; Stephen J. Stein, "Editor's Introduction," in Jonathan Edwards, *Notes on Scripture*, vol. 15 of *The Works of Jonathan Edwards* (New Haven, CT: Yale University Press, 1998), 1–34; Stephen J. Stein, "Edwards as Biblical Exegete," in *Cambridge Companion to JE*, 181–95; and Douglas A. Sweeney, "Edwards, Jonathan (1703–1758)," in *Dictionary of Major Biblical Interpreters*, ed. Donald K. McKim (Downers Grove, IL: IVP Academic, 2007).

About a month before his nineteenth birthday, Edwards moved to New York City in order to serve as a supply pastor in a small Presbyterian church.[73] Edwards left New York City in spring 1723, received his MA from Yale later that year, and was elected tutor of Yale the following year. He resigned that position in 1726 in order to assist his grandfather Stoddard in Northampton, Massachusetts.

In his first sermon, *Christian Happiness*, preached in late 1720 from Isa. 3:10, Edwards's doctrine was, "A good man is a happy man, whatever his outward circumstances are."[74] The godly are happy because of "the spiritual advantages, joys and satisfactions" they have as reconciled to God. "How great a pleasure and satisfaction," the young Edwards preached, "must it be to him to think of it." Jesus evokes "joyful and gladsome" thoughts in the believer (10:299). Evoking aesthetic overtones, Edwards pointed to "the excellent and desirable nature of true godliness" (10:302). The Christian's higher pleasures and delights far surpass those of unbelievers.

In his exhortation to unbelievers, Edwards reminded them that they were unacquainted with godly pleasures. The pleasure they sought was sensory and beastly. "[Y]ou have taken up, contented hitherto, with such a sort of pleasure as the beasts enjoy as well as you." Only divine happiness can "satisfy your desires" (10:305):

> You perhaps think yourselves mighty happy in enjoying your hateful and abominable lusts, and so are the beasts ten times as happy as you are in the same things; those be not the pleasures of a man. The pleasures of loving and obeying, loving and adoring, blessing and praising the Infinite Being, the Best of Beings, the Eternal Jehovah; the pleasures of trusting in Jesus Christ, in contemplating

73. On Edwards in New York City, see Marsden, *Jonathan Edwards*, 45–58; Murray, *Jonathan Edwards*, 41–54; Kimnach, "Preface to the New York Period," in *WJE* 10:261–93.

74. Jonathan Edwards, *Christian Happiness*, in *WJE* 10:297. For this sermon's history, see Kimnach's note, *WJE* 10:294–95. On Edwards the preacher, see Kimnach's magisterial introduction to *WJE* 10:3–258. Elsewhere Kimnach observes: "The sermon of Edwards's youth was essentially the seventeenth-century Puritan sermon, as busy in its formal structure as the music of Johann Sebastian Bach." "Edwards as preacher," in *Cambridge Companion to JE*, 104. Also see, Hopkins, *Life and Character of Jonathan Edwards*, 46–49; Turnbull, *Jonathan Edwards the Preacher*; Kenneth P. Minkema, "Preface to the Period," in Jonathan Edwards, *Sermons and Discourses, 1723–1729*, vol. 14 of *The Works of Jonathan Edwards* (New Haven, CT: Yale University Press, 1997), 3–46; Valeri, "Preface to the Period," in *WJE* 17:3–44; M. X. Lesser, "Preface to the Period," in Jonathan Edwards, *Sermons and Discourses, 1734–1738*, vol. 19 of *The Works of Jonathan Edwards* (New Haven, CT: Yale University Press, 2001), 3–36; Kimnach, "The Sermons: Concept and Execution," in *PCJE*, 243–57; Michael D. McMullen, "Introduction to Jonathan Edwards the Preacher," in Jonathan Edwards, *The Blessing of God: Previously Unpublished Sermons of Jonathan Edwards* (Nashville, TN: Broadman and Holman, 2003), 1–11; and Sweeney, *Jonathan Edwards and the Ministry of the Word*.

> his beauties, excellencies, and glories, in contemplating his love to mankind and to us, in contemplating his infinite goodness and astonishing loving-kindness; the pleasures of [the] communion of the Holy Ghost in conversing with God, the maker and governor of the world; the pleasure that results from the doing of our duty, in acting worthily and excellently: these, these are the pleasures that are worthy of so noble a creature as a man is. (10:305–06)

All those who listened to young Edwards preach heard an emphasis on the soul's affection for God. In *The Value of Salvation*, Edwards explained that the immortal soul is more valuable than the entire world. The saved soul has such "inestimable worth" because its future happiness will be "inestimable."[75] Heaven's light and joy will satisfy both the understanding and will. "The affections also will be satisfied; their love will [be] very much enlarged and yet satisfied."[76] In *Wicked Men's Slavery to Sin*, enslavement to sin abandons the greater life God intends for creatures with a rational soul. Sin is far below human nature as created by God. "When you serve sin," Edwards continued,

> You admit him not only into your house, and the best room of it, but into your very hearts, into the inward closet of your soul; and there place him in the throne of your affections where reason, your most excellent [faculty], and religion, which vastly exalts reason, ought to sit, and subject your reason and all those excellent faculties which your Master has given you to him.[77]

Another theme in Edwards's early sermons is that, when humans follow their sensual appetites, they jettison their higher faculties and empty themselves of their humanity.[78] Sinners are fools who set aside reason, acting "more filthily than the

75. *WJE* 10:322. In the sermon on the *Importance of a Future State*, Edwards says the soul and the body are "quite distinct." The soul is immaterial and the body material. Of the two, only the soul "can think and understand" (*WJE* 10:359). Edwards noted that for some people, even their body is dying, the soul is as alert as ever (*WJE* 10:359–60).

76. *WJE* 10:324. Compare *God's Excellencies*, in *WJE* 10:415–35.

77. *WJE* 10:347. Also see Edwards, *A Glorious Foundation for Peace*, in *The Glory and Honor of God: Volume 2 of the Previously Unpublished Sermons of Jonathan Edwards*, ed. Michael D. McMullen (Nashville, TN: Broadman & Holman, 2004), 179–80.

78. This theme, that the person enslaved to lower appetites is like a beast, is a favourite of Edwards. It was touched on in the discussion of the "Miscellanies" above. In *The Duty of Self-Examination*, Edwards, drawing from Hag. 1:5, began, "It is the property of a beast to do things without any reflection or consideration, but to go just as their animal appetites lead them." Animals do not reflect on the past or plan for the future. Sense and instinct are the only guides beasts have. Human beings, on the other hand, have been given much more from God: the "higher faculty, even reason and understanding." Because of these faculties, they ought to plan for eternity. Edwards continued his contrast between humans and animals throughout the sermon. "We ought not to eat and drink like beasts, never

brute beasts" (10:348). Edwards likened enslavement to lust to a pig's wallowing in the mud. No person with an exalted, reasonable, and immortal soul should ever be so depraved (10:348). As he argued in *The Nakedness of Job*, even the ancient philosophers were able to determine that human beings were not made for earthly happiness.[79]

Christianity was, for Edwards, a reasonable religion, and so beastly passions were unfit for it.[80] In *True Nobleness of Mind*, Edwards showed that the Bereans, in receiving the gospel, "act like reasonable, ingenuous and good-spirited men."[81]

considering whence these good things come" (*WJE* 10:485). Edwards urged his hearers to consider how they use their minds. "How are the faculties of our souls chiefly employed; are our thoughts and our affections chiefly exercised upon earthly things, about what we shall eat, what we shall drink, and wherewithal we shall be clothed? . . . Do we give our thoughts the reins to go where they incline, sometimes upon the pleasing objects of concupiscence and the lusts of the flesh?" (*WJE* 10:486). Moreover, due consideration ought to be given to actions, "whether we live soberly and humbly, chastely and temperately; whether we are patient in afflictions and deny and mortify evil desires and curb unruly passions or no, and keep under our bodies and bring them into subjection" (*WJE* 10:488). While applying the doctrine, Edwards lamented that most people would justly conclude, upon observing the lives of men and women, that God had not given them intellectual capacities at all. The reason for this is their "reprobate minds" (*WJE* 10:489). Also see *A Spiritual Understanding*, where Edwards said, "Sin has made their souls in this respect of a beastly nature, and you may as soon infuse the learning of schools into the beasts, as infuse into a natural man this spiritual understanding" (*WJE* 14:83). Also see *WJE* 14:235 and 17:288.

79. "[W]e were not made for an earthly happiness," Edwards said, and therefore the more happiness a person imputes to earthly goods results in only greater frustration. "This," Edwards added, "the wise heathen plainly saw, and for that reason taught it as a great part of the wisdom of man, to abstract his thoughts and affections from all earthly things. Though they had no other knowledge of a future happiness than what naked reason taught them, even they discovered so much unsatisfaction and vexation of these enjoyments, that many of them, of their own choice, sequestered themselves from these things, and denied themselves even the common comforts of life" (*WJE* 10:409). Compare Edwards, *That It is the Temper of the Truly Godly to Delight to Exalt God and Lay Themselves Low*, in *The Blessing of God*, 71–87.

80. Edwards said, "'Tis a most rational thing thus to entertain Christianity" (*WJE* 14:231). His desire to defend Christianity against the Enlightened assaults of his age can be seen in 1729 or 1730 simple outline of what he hoped would be "A Rational Account of the Main Doctrines of the Christian Religion." Such an account would have included a treatment "of created minds, free will, etc" (*WJE* 6:396–97).

81. Commenting on this sermon, Minkema explains, "Medieval faculty psychology, which posited a hierarchy of human faculties, still largely prevailed in the eighteenth century. The highest and most noble faculty was reason or understanding, while the lowest was the will or emotion. To be ruled by passion was to be a 'brute creature'; the proper order within the human psyche was thereby overturned." "Preface to the Period," in *WJE* 14:24.

Throughout the entire sermon, Edwards had as his silent interlocutors those carried away with the polite philosophy of the early Enlightenment.[82] The most rational person believes the gospel (14:231). Christian doctrines, like the nature of God, the immortality of the soul, and divine revelation, are "exceeding congruous to human reason" (14:232).

What a carnal person pursues is far below the dignity of human nature, "not at all suitable to be chosen for the happiness of those beings that have a spiritual substance within." Instead, they revel in beastly pleasures, rather than "those that have the image of God upon them and an immortal nature."[83] The "heart" of the true Christian "is lifted" above such trivialities (14:234). Christians, as rational, abhor "filthiness," or that which is "impure and beastly" (14:235). The wicked love filthy things: "They make themselves like beasts by delighting in sensual lusts, by worldlymindedness, intemperance, lasciviousness" (14:235). Christians have a "noble mind" because Christ has freed them from "slavery to their passions." Edwards explained: "They are inferior servile minds that are most under the government of their passions, that are slaves to those worst of masters. Our passions were given us to be our servants, and not our masters" (14:236).

For Edwards, the Christian mind was calm, free from the violent control of passions.[84] The saint "has the dominion over other passions and appetites. He governs himself by reason and true wisdom, and is able to deny himself and cross his carnal appetites for the sake of his own real interest, and for the good of others, and for the sake of what is truly decent and excellent" (14:236). Christians therefore ought "not to be slaves to their passions, but to be of calm and serene minds."[85]

82. Marsden puts well the context of Arminianism, Arianism, Deism, and latitudinarianism: "In the face of the onslaught of modern fashion, New England orthodoxy could look hopelessly quaint." *Jonathan Edwards*, 139.

83. *WJE* 14:234. Compare *Warnings of Future Punishment Don't Seem Real to the Wicked*, where Edwards said of the wicked, "Their business of their life has been about things that they can see and hear and feel and taste. . . . They have tied down their mind to such objects of their senses, and therefore nothing seems real to them but only what they can see or hear or feel, etc. . . . Hell is another world, and it is invisible. And therefore it don't enter into them that there is any such place; and if there be, the pains of it ben't so much sensitive as mental and spiritual, and therefore it don't enter into them that they are very great. God's wrath don't seem very terrible to them because they never see God, and because they can't see with their bodily eyes what sort of being he is" (*WJE* 14:206). On Edwards and hell, see Bruce W. Davidson, "Glorious Damnation: Hell as an Essential Element in the Theology of Jonathan Edwards," *JETS* 54 (2011): 809–22 and Chris Morgan, *Jonathan Edwards & Hell* (Ross-shire, Scotland: Christian Focus, 2004).

84. Calm affections was an early emphasis of Edwards. See *A Faithful Narrative*, in *The Great Awakening*, vol. 4 of *The Works of Jonathan Edwards*, ed. C. C. Goen (New Haven, CT: Yale University Press, 1972), 178–79 and "Misc. a," in *WJE* 13:163.

85. *WJE* 14:240. In a May 1731 sermon entitled, *Christians a Chosen Generation*, Edwards urged his congregants, "Let Christians take heed so to walk that they mayn't

Edwards did not exclusively call the motions of the soul toward sensual appetites *passions*. People act passionately when they act hastily in anger, or in jealousy speaking against others.[86] The passion of envy stunts the progress of religion in men, for envy is "an Uncomfortable sort of Passion," accompanied by "grief and uneasiness."[87] At other times, he used the term *affections* rather than *passions*.[88] Edwards said of Christians, "How much a glorious Lord have they over them than wicked men, who are under the prince of the power of the air, whose hearts are under the dominion of Satan, who have their reason and all their other faculties lorded over by impure lusts and vile affections" (14:466). Hence Edwards spoke, in another sermon, of human beings, "as long as we are flesh and blood," having "animal properties and affections" (17:440).

One sermon, in particular, shows the importance in Edwards's early thought both of the soul's great love for holiness, as well as his use of the ancient Christian contrast between higher and lower affections.[89] Edwards's sermon text was Isa.

dishonor their pedigree." For Edwards, this meant that Christians should not be ruled by passions. "There are many things that are very base and too mean for such [Christians], as a giving way to earthly-mindedness, a groveling like swine or moles in the earth, a suffering your soul to cleave to those earthly things, to be fastened to them which ought to be neglected and despised by those who are of heavenly descent. A giving way to the lusts of the flesh, suffering the soul to be immersed in filth, a being taken up with mean and unworthy delights common to the beasts, a being intemperate in the gratification of any carnal appetites whatsoever, a being overmuch concerned about earthly honor: 'tis surely a disgrace to them that are accounted to God for a seed or a generation much to care whether or no they are accounted great upon this dunghill. So 'tis unworthy of your noble descent for you to governed by your passions. Such as you shall be guided by higher principles of reason and virtue and an unbiased respect to the glory and honor of God" (*WJE* 17:288).

86. See Jonathan Edwards, "God Will Not Be Slack in Punishing Wicked Men" (Deut. 7:10), in *Sermons Series II, 1729*, vol. 44 of *The Works of Jonathan Edwards Online*, Jonathan Edwards Center, http://edwards.yale.edu/archive?path=aHR0cDovL2Vkd2FyZHMueWFsZS5lZHUvY2dpLWJpbi9uZXdwaGlsby9nZXRvYmplY3QucGw/Yy40Mjo2LndqZW8= (accessed December 4, 2017). Jonathan Edwards, "The Nearness of Death" (Mt. 24:43), in *WJEO* 44, http://edwards.yale.edu/archive?path=aHR0cDovL2Vkd2FyZHMueWFsZS5lZHUvY2dpLWJpbi9uZXdwaGlsby9nZXRvYmplY3QucGw/Yy40MjoyNi53amVv (accessed December 4, 2017).

87. Jonathan Edwards, "Envious Men" (Jas 3:16), in *Sermons, Series II, 1729–1731*, vol. 45 of *The Works of Jonathan Edwards Online*, http://edwards.yale.edu/archive?path=aHR0cDovL2Vkd2FyZHMueWFsZS5lZHUvY2dpLWJpbi9uZXdwaGlsby9nZXRvYmplY3QucGw/Yy40MzoxMC53amVv (accessed December 4, 2017).

88. In *Affections*, Edwards said, "The *affections* and *passions* are frequently spoken of as the same, and yet, in the more common use of speech, there is in some respect a difference" (*WJE* 2:98).

89. It is important to remember that during Edwards's New York days he had important personal "encounter" with holiness. Kimnach explains the importance of this sermon: "As

35:8, which says that "the unclean shall not pass over" the "way of holiness." The following verse speaks of the absence of lion or ravenous beast. For Edwards, this symbolized the wicked who are more like animals than humans "in their eager raging and lustful appetites and evil affections." Such people "violently" desire the world, and pursue it by whatever means necessary.[90] Edwards's doctrine from the text was, "Those only that are holy are in the way to heaven" (10:470). Holiness is the conformity of the heart to God, Jesus, and God's commands (10:472–73). The unholy cannot be in the way to heaven, for it would violate God's justice and holiness. The profanity of unholiness would "defile heaven and interrupt the happiness of the saints and angels" (10:475). Sin is misery, which is also contrary to heaven. "Sin is a woeful confusion and dreadful disorder in the soul, whereby everything is put out of place, reason trampled underfoot and passion advanced in the room of it, conscience dethroned and abominable lusts reigning. As long as it is so, there will unavoidably be a dreadful confusion and perturbation in the mind" (10:476). Edwards exhorted the New York believers to pursue holiness. They ought, like the saints and angels, to love God above all else and delight themselves with "the beauties of Jesus Christ." The reason is self-evident, for "holiness is a most beautiful, lovely thing" (10:478). Clearly borrowing from his words in his "Misc. a" entry, Edwards concluded the sermon by extolling the glories of holiness.[91]

Despite his strong emphasis that the passions associated with the carnal appetite ought to be controlled by reason, Edwards taught that no such limits were to be set on holy affections. Affections are essential for genuine religion. "The Word of God," he said in a 1728 sermon, "makes those that understand it to be of holy dispositions and affections, to have holy desires and motions of heart that are acceptable unto God." Such "motions of the heart" include "the exercises of love to God and longing desires after him, the exercise of delight in Jesus Christ," and "that inward worship and devotion that a pious soul often exercises."[92] For holy affections toward spiritual good to even exist, that spiritual good must be seen (14:264). Per Edwards, this was why human beings were created with affections to begin with (17:190). But he was also aware that many claims of affections were counterfeit.[93] Even the affections of true Christians may have "natural principles" as their source (14:341). Only the Holy Spirit can give spiritual nourishment to the soul.[94] It is through his "operation and indwelling" that "the knowledge of God

the first and only public statement correlating directly with it, the sermon clearly presents matter of deep and lasting significance for an understanding of Edwards himself, not least of all in its imagery and tonality" (*WJE* 10:466).

90. *WJE* 10:470. In *Affections*, Edwards noted that the passions are "violent" (*WJE* 2:98).

91. Compare *WJE* 10:478–79 to *WJE* 13:163–64. On "Misc. a," see the section "The Early 'Miscellanies.'"

92. *WJE* 14:258. Compare "Images," no. 113, in *WJE* 11:93–94.

93. See *WJE* 14:255, 341, 349, 389, 540; *WJE* 17:157, 169, 412.

94. See *WJE* 14:284, 435.

and divine things, and a holy disposition, and all grace is conferred and upheld."[95] In heaven, "[t]he glorious excellencies and beauty of God will be what will forever entertain the mind of the saints, and the love of God will be their everlasting feast" (17:208).

The sermon *A Divine and Supernatural Light* was an important milestone for the early preaching and affective thought of Edwards. Mark Valeri observes, "In *A Divine and Supernatural Light*, Edwards condensed much of a decade of preaching, rumination, and private writing on the nature of spiritual knowledge into a single, remarkable effort."[96] Edwards preached the sermon in Northampton in 1733 and the following year it was published with a brief preface. Even then, Edwards was aware that his subject was "unfashionable" (17:425). Edwards used Jesus's words to Peter in Mt. 16:17 to propose, "*There is such a thing, as a spiritual and divine light, immediately imparted to the soul by God, of a different nature from any that is obtained by natural means*" (17:410).

The gracious work of the Spirit is quite different from natural operations. The Spirit may give common grace to assist the soul's faculties in performing natural operations "more fully," but such a work is not saving.[97] The spiritual light given to the soul by the Spirit, Edwards was careful to emphasize, is not new revelation or information. Nor is the spiritual light just any "affective view" of the truth of Christianity. People can be naturally affected with Christian matters just as they can by nonreligious matters (17:412). In other words, someone may have natural affections by an account of heaven, a story about Jesus, or even his suffering, or yet not really believe or receive it.[98]

The Spirit's light is not new content, and it is not a common affection experienced by natural men. On the contrary, Edwards defined this light as a supernaturally changed will or inclination. The divine and supernatural light is "a true sense of the divine excellency of the things revealed in the Word of God, and a conviction of the truth and reality of them" (17:413). This divine light reveals the beauty of

95. *WJE* 17:203. This comes from Edwards's first published sermon, *God Glorified in Man's Dependence*.

96. *WJE* 17:405.

97. WJE 17:410–11. Edwards said that in the saving work of the Spirit, "those things are wrought in the soul that are above nature, and of which there is nothing of the like kind in the soul by nature; and they are caused to exist in the soul habitually, and according to such a stated constitution or law, that lays such a foundation for exercises in a continued course, as is called a principle of nature" (*WJE* 17:411). Compare *Treatise on Grace* in *WJE* 21:153–60.

98. Edwards explained: "We read in Scripture of many that were greatly affected with things of a religious nature, who yet are there represented as wholly graceless, and many of them very will men" (*WJE* 17:413). For more on Scripture and the divine sense, see Brown, *Edwards and the Bible*, 45–55. In his *Personal Narrative*, Edwards relates his own "affecting sense" of the Bible's "excellency" (*WJE* 16:801).

the Christian religion revealed in Scripture and, consequently, an assurance of its truthfulness.

Throughout this sermon, Edwards liberally used the word "sense" to refer to the will's inclination. The spiritual light is interchangeably a "true sense," a "real sense," or simply a "sense." What is sensed is the *spiritual* "excellency," the "sublime nature," the "gloriousness," the "loveliness," and the "beauty" of God, Jesus Christ, redemption, and holiness. The mind can know the goodness of something in two different ways: through the "speculative" knowledge of the understanding and the "sense of the heart." The latter knowledge, which pertains to the will, is the divine light to which Edwards referred. The "sense of the heart" is "a sense of the beauty, amiableness, or sweetness of a thing; so that the heart is sensible of pleasure and delight in the presence of the idea of it" (17:413).

For Edwards, the "sense of the heart" was not reason, for reason was incapable of perceiving excellency. This crucial distinction is the difference between heaven and hell. The mind may understand Christianity, but remain disinclined toward it. Edwards illustrated: "There is a difference between having a rational judgment that honey is sweet, and having a sense of its sweetness."[99] Natural persons are uninterested in God, but, with the Spirit's work, their hostility toward God is removed, their reason is sanctified, and their mind receives the gospel. So the Spirit negatively eliminates enmity toward God and positively awakens the "powers of the soul" to find the things of God good (17:415).

Although the Spirit works on the natural faculties, the light itself is not given by nature, Edwards preached. The faculties are active when God lets in his light, but the light is still from God. The faculties are the subjects of God's work, not its cause. God deals humans as "rational" beings (17:416). Therefore, although the Spirit gives spiritual light, the Word is essential.[100] The wicked cannot see divine light because their "minds are full of spiritual pollution, and under the powerful

99. *WJE* 17:414. The honey metaphor was a common one for Edwards, and one used by Stoddard and others before him. See Minkema, "Editor's Introduction," in *WJE* 14:67–68. Edwards further explained the relationship of the "sense of the heart" to reason. The "sense of the heart" requires more than rational powers, "for 'tis not a thing that belongs to reason, to see the beauty and loveliness of spiritual things." One does not use speculative faculties to behold beauty. Yet, Edwards added: "Reason indeed is necessary in order to it, as 'tis by reason only that we are become the subjects of the means of it." Beauty cannot be deduced from arguments: "the perceiving of spiritual beauty and excellency no more belongs to reason, than it belongs to the sense of feeling to perceive colors, or to the power of seeing to perceive the sweetness of food. It is out of reason's province to perceive the beauty or loveliness of anything: such a perception don't belong to that faculty. Reason's work is to perceive truth, and not excellency" (*WJE* 17:422).

100. Edwards said: "Indeed a person can't have spiritual light without the Word. . . . The mind can't see the excellency of any doctrine, unless that doctrine be first in the mind; but the seeing the excellency of the doctrine may be immediately from the Spirit of God; though the conveying of the doctrine or proposition itself may be by the Word" (*WJE* 17:416–17).

filthy lusts" (17:421). Divine light changes the soul's nature by directing its will toward spiritual beauty. "[I]t causes the heart to embrace the joyful tidings, and entirely to adhere to, and acquiesce in the revelation of Christ as our Savior; it causes the whole soul to accord and symphonize with it, admitting it with entire credit and respect, cleaving to it with inclination and affection" (17:424).

The "divine and supernatural light" is a work of the Holy Spirit whereby the nature of the will is changed to consent to the Triune God. Although the soul must first understand divine revelation, this spiritual change alters not the understanding, but the will. Where before the soul was naturally opposed to God, in this supernatural work, the Spirit gives himself to the soul so the beauty of divine things is perceived and desired.

A Faithful Narrative

When Solomon Stoddard died in 1729, Jonathan Edwards became Northampton's third senior minister. Approximately four years into this ministry, Edwards believed the town to be in "a far more degenerate time . . . than ever before," mostly because of the town's loose youth culture.[101] What followed was "a surprizing work of God," largely due to the unexpected deaths of prominent young people and Edwards's preaching on justification by faith. Thus the first ripple of awakenings began under Edwards's ministry in 1734, the account of which was later published under the title *A Faithful Narrative*.[102]

As Edwards's first public account of an awakening, *A Faithful Narrative* is instructive to show his early understanding of affections in revivals. Edwards was well acquainted with his own father's and grandfather's encounters with periods of religious renewal.[103] In *A Faithful Narrative* Edwards is evidently optimistic concerning the work of God among his parishioners, believing that "more than 300 souls" experienced the regenerating grace of the Spirit.[104] The newly changed wills and affections were evidence of God's activity. "God's work," Edwards explained, "has also appeared very extraordinary in the degrees of the influences of his

101. Edwards, *A Faithful Narrative*, in *WJE* 4:146.

102. For more on the awakening of the mid-1730s and *A Faithful Narrative*, see Goen, "Editor's Introduction," in *WJE* 4:32–46; Marsden, *Jonathan Edwards*, 150–98; Murray, *Jonathan Edwards*, 115–33; Edwin Scott Gaustad, *The Great Awakening in New England* (New York: Harper & Brothers, 1957), 16–24; Tracy, *Jonathan Edwards, Pastor*, 109–22; and Thomas S. Kidd, *The Great Awakening: The Roots of Evangelical Christianity in Colonial America* (New Haven, CT: Yale University Pres, 2007), 13–23.

103. See *WJE* 4:145–46 and 16:790–91.

104. *WJE* 4:158. See *WJE* 4:149–58. Among the evidence Edwards put forth is a concern for eternal things, joy over conversions, tears during the sermons, lively singing ("unusual elevation of heart and voice"), and frequent conversations about Christ and spiritual things ("even at weddings").

Spirit, both in the degree of awakening and conviction, and also in the degree of saving light, and love, and joy, that many have experienced" (4:159). Yet, not every apparent affection was gracious.[105]

The true converts seemed to have a new appreciation of spiritual things. Edwards used a handful of phrases to describe their new love for God through divine grace: the saints have "earnest longings of the soul after God and Christ," or "a sweet sense," "a holy repose of soul in God through Christ," a "secret disposition to fear and love him," or a "delightful contemplation of the glory and wonderful grace of God."[106] God powerfully "moved and wrought upon" them that at times they laughed, cried, wept, or shouted (4:174–75). Although he acknowledged that some of the townspeople had false affections, Edwards affirmed that affections of the soul could have great effects on the body.

Much in *A Faithful Narrative* echoed the themes Edwards had been working on in his "Miscellanies" and sermons. As Edwards observed his congregation, he saw the Spirit's work. Those awakened in the revival had a new inclination of the will and a new conviction of spiritual truth (4:179–81). Repeatedly, Edwards spoke of the "sense" the new believers had of spiritual things, describing this sense as "longing desires" for spiritual things. Although the affections for God were at times overwhelming, the state of some of the awakened were "perfectly sober, and very remote from anything like enthusiastic wildness."[107] The delight these people experienced in divine things far surpassed the delight of "earthly pleasures" and "the vanity of earthly enjoyments" (4:183). The power of their new pleasure in the things of God made their "bodily appetite" fade away. Among the newly converted Northamptonites, the revival resulted in praise to God, love for the Bible, and even "a good effect to unite the people's affections much to their minister" (4:184).

On a different note, in *A Faithful Narrative* Edwards was forced to address the interplay between different aspects of the soul, particularly between the affections and the imagination. To minimize the legitimacy of the work, rumors were spreading in New England that the imaginations of some of the awakened had been unduly active. New Englanders viewed the imagination with suspicion. Edwards admitted that some irregularities had taken place in the awakening, but

105. For some people, the affections they experienced were not truly gracious. Edwards explained: "And oftentimes, at first setting out, their affections are moved, and they are full of tears, in their confessions and prayers, which they are ready to make very much of, as though they were some atonement, and had power to move correspondent affections in God too; and hence they are for a while big with expectation of what God will do for them, and conceive that they grow better apace, and shall soon be thoroughly converted. But these affections are but short-lived; they quickly find that they fail, and then they think themselves to be grown worse again" (*WJE* 4:164).

106. *WJE* 4:172, 173, 173, 181.

107. *WJE* 4:182. Edwards said that some had such a "sense" of God's "awful greatness and majesty" that they feared that "they should instantly have died" had they not have been assured they were loved by him (*WJE* 4:184).

added "they have been easily corrected." An increase in such phenomena should be expected, given the way minds and hearts were being stirred in the revival. If this is the way the human affections naturally work with respect to "temporal things," then it should be expected when someone's affections are strongly moved with spiritual realities, it has some influence on the imagination. Nevertheless, the extent to which the imagination accompanies such affections varies across individual human beings. Ultimately, Edwards reassured his readers, he had always used caution and stressed to his flock that strong impressions on the imagination could not be trusted (4:188–89). Not only the imagination, but the body may also be overcome by the affections (4:198–99).

What would later be published *A Faithful Narrative* in 1735 was originally a letter Edwards wrote to Benjamin Coleman, the highly regarded minister of Boston's Brattle Street Church.[108] To the final publication of the *Narrative* Edwards added a postscript, including an admission that the work of God was dying out. Yet Edwards remained confident. He believed that those who had been converted had "a new sense of things, new apprehensions and views of God, of the divine attributes, and Jesus Christ, and the great things of the Gospel." The hearts of the converts had been changed and been given "new sweetnesses and delights" that still remained. "[T]here seems to be an inward ardor and burning of heart that they express, the like to which they have never experienced before." The Spirit had given a spiritual appetite where there was none before: "there are new appetites, and a new kind of breathings and pantings of heart, and groanings that cannot be uttered. There is a new kind of inward labor and struggle of soul towards heaven and holiness" (4:208).

Charity and Its Fruits

After the revival of 1734–35, a period of spiritual lethargy settled over the Northampton congregation.[109] Edwards was dismayed at the sin; old town disputes

108. See *WJE* 4:99–110.

109. On the period between the revival of the mid-1730s and the Great Awakening and how that brought out an emphasis on the difference between true and false Christians, see Bryan McCarthy, "Introduction: Historical Context," in *True and False Christians (On the Parable of the Wise and Foolish Virgins)*, vol. 1 of *Sermons by Jonathan Edwards on the Matthean Parables*, eds. Kenneth P. Minkema, Adriaan C. Neele, and Bryan McCarthy (Eugene, OR: Cascade Books, 2012), 14–27. Also see Winslow, *Jonathan Edwards*, 160–64; Tracy, *Jonathan Edwards, Pastor*, 123–31; Paul Ramsey, "Editor's Introduction," in *WJE* 8:1–7; and Marsden, *Jonathan Edwards*, 184–200. Murray understates the problems in Northampton in the late 1730s. *Jonathan Edwards*, 149–51. Edwards's pointed remarks on the interchurch squabbles can be seen in several sermons. For example, the seventh concludes: "Considering the profession which we make of Christianity, we are too selfish. Everyone is ready to take care of himself, and of himself only. . . . We in this land are

reemerged, and even fresh disagreements over the seating arrangement of the new meetinghouse created discord in the town. In 1737, a discouraged pastor Edwards wrote to Benjamin Coleman: "We are sensibly by little and little, more and more declining," evidenced by "contention and a party spirit" (16:67). The news that his glowing account of the Northampton awakening in *A Faithful Narrative* was being warmly received in England only added to the conflict. In this context of parish upheaval, Edwards brought fifteen sermons from the thirteenth chapter of 1 Corinthians on the nature of true Christian love that would become one of his most loved posthumous publications, *Charity and Its Fruits*.[110]

Charity and Its Fruits reveals the Edwardsean theme that love, which is given by the Spirit, is the essential mark of a true saint.[111] For this reason, the fifteen sermons anticipate ideas Edwards later returned to in *Religious Affections*, especially in his emphasis on divinely given affections as necessary for genuine Christianity. Indeed, Edwards said authentic Christian love is "altogether a sweet disposition and affection of the soul" (8:136). Without it, all outward acts are hypocrisy. Saving faith is not merely speculative, but is quickened by love.[112] Edwards applied this doctrine directly at the Northampton strife: "religion and contention do not consist together" (8:146). If love is "the very sum of all Christian virtue," then the Northamptonites should have abounded in love (8:147). Love necessarily displays itself in external actions.[113] The affections of a true believer are not blind, but are

trained up from generation to generation in a too niggardly, selfish spirit and practice; and notwithstanding all our professions of religion, and though there are many good things done which are worthy to be commended, yet without doubt we do in general come vastly short of what is required of Christians in the New Testament" (*WJE* 8:271).

110. Ramsey summarizes the sermons in his "Editor's Introduction," in *WJE* 8:59–104. Marsden observes the sermons to be "more positive than negative, and always preached in an appropriately gentle tone." *Jonathan Edwards*, 191.

111. Compare Tryon Edwards, introduction to *Charity and Its Fruits; or, Christian Love as Manifested in the Heart and Life*, by Jonathan Edwards (New York: Robert Carter & Brothers, 1852), iii–vi. Edwards did not bifurcate love between love for God and love for humanity. "All truly Christian love is one and the same in its principle. It may be various in its exercises and objects, it may be exercised towards God or towards men; but it is the same principle in the heart which is the foundation of the exercises of a truly Christian love, whether to God or men." The Holy Spirit, the "Spirit of love," does not separately give love to God and love for men. "Christian love to both God and men is wrought in the heart by the same work of the Spirit" (*WJE* 8:132–33). See *WJE* 8:328, 333–34 and Ramsey, "Editor's Introduction," in *WJE* 8:59.

112. *WJE* 8:139–41. Also see *WJE* 8:329. Edwards said Christians "should try their faith by their love. If there faith seems to have light in it, but no heat or warmth, it is not the true light" (*WJE* 8:336). The opposite of this is also true.

113. Edwards continued, "If your heart is full of love, it will find vent; you will find or make ways enough to express your love in deeds" (*WJE* 8:148). Compare the tenth sermon of *Charity*, "Grace Tends to Holy Practice," *WJE* 8:293–312.

built upon a believing conviction of the truthfulness of Christian dogma (8:336). This love, without which even a martyr's death is regarded godless, is necessary to render a person's deeds the *acts* of "an intelligent, voluntary being" (8:178).

Throughout the sermons, Edwards showed that all the Christian virtues hinge on love. For instance, humility is a product of love. It prevents unloving acts and attitudes (8:238–43). Christian love has humility embedded in it. "True divine love is an humble love." Love is humble because love has "a sense of the loveliness of God," whereby human beings perceive how much more excellent God is than they.[114] Genuine Christian love also causes humility as it loves God "as an infinite superior" (8:245). True saints love Christ for his infinite humility.[115] Love is at the core of Edwards's ethics.

Edwards said that true Christian charity comes from the indwelling Spirit. The Holy Spirit gives three different kinds of gifts to human beings.[116] The Spirit's common gifts, including "common convictions of sin, common illuminations, common religious affections," can be bestowed on the unregenerate.[117] The Spirit also gives extraordinary or miraculous gifts. These are powers outside the normal laws of God's providence.[118] The third and greatest gift of the Spirit is saving grace or holiness, in which the indwelling Spirit produces true affections in the believer's soul.

The communion between the saint and the indwelling Holy Spirit produces holy love in the soul. Alluding to 2 Pet. 1:4, Edwards said, "By producing this effect the Spirit becomes an indwelling vital principle in the soul, and the subject becomes a spiritual being, denominated so from the Spirit of God which dwells in him and of whose nature he is a partaker."[119] The nature of true love in a Christian,

114. *WJE* 8:243. Edwards added: "Love is a disposition of the heart, or it is respect towards God as lovely. If the knowledge of God as lovely causes humility, than a respect to God as lovely implies humility. And from this love to God arises a Christian love to men" (*WJE* 8:245).

115. *WJE* 8:247. Compare *WJE* 2:311–40.

116. Haykin, *Jonathan Edwards*, 59–73.

117. *WJE* 8:355. Compare *WJE* 8:152, 8:152–3 n5.

118. In the second sermon, Edwards foreshadowed an argument in *Affections*, "if anything appears to persons as though they had a vision of some visible appearance, and heard some voice, such things are not to be taken as signs of grace; for if they are real, and from God, they are not grace, but extraordinary gifts of the Spirit, which we have shown are not saving. All the fruit of the Spirit, upon which we are to lay weight as evidential of grace, is summed up in Christian charity or Christian love, because this is the sum of all grace" (*WJE* 8:169). Compare *WJE* 2:234–37.

119. *WJE* 8:158. In the twelfth sermon, Edwards returned to this theme. From 1 Cor. 13:7, Edwards argued the various Christian graces are all "concatenated together," for they all from the same Spirit. "The graces of Christianity are all from the Spirit of Christ sent forth into the heart, and dwelling there as an holy principle and divine nature" (*WJE* 8:332). Humanity's original parents were given the Spirit, but they lost him through original sin

which has direct bearing on a true Christian's will and affections, comes from the creature's intimate union with the Spirit. Christ himself purchased the Spirit from the Father to give to his bride (8:353–54).

The distinction between sensitive and rational aspects of humankind informed Edwards's notions of happiness in *Charity*. Spirit-wrought holiness unites rational beings to God and is therefore human beings' "highest happiness." In other words, for rational beings, the best happiness is the soul's happiness: "[h]appiness does so essentially consist in knowing and loving and serving God, and having a holy and divine temper of soul, and the lively exercises of it, that those things will make a man happy without anything else" (8:161). This spiritual love will be the eternal happiness of saints, who will forever exercise and enjoy the divine love given by the Spirit (8:358–59).

Edwards drew a similar distinction between natural affection and divine love. Examples of natural love include real friendship and the love of parents for their children. Such love is often rooted in natural loves. Christian love, since it is supernatural, goes beyond natural love. Divine love is not a kind of natural love rooted ultimately in self-love, for it is nobler (8:262–64). "This divine love," Edwards explains, "is no plant which grows naturally in such a soil as the heart of man" (8:264). The Holy Spirit himself plants such love in the soul. Therefore, like no other kind of love, divine charity rises above selfishness. Both God and fellow humans are loved for God's sake.

In *Charity*, Edwards once again employed the traditional distinction between the affections and passions. The passions are the antithesis of Christian love. A Christian's love bears injuries from others "without those inward motions and passions which tend to interrupt and destroy it."[120] In saying that believers must maintain a loving "inward calmness" in the face of interpersonal conflict, Edwards stressed once again the peace of Christian affections (8:190). In *Charity*, Edwards

(*WJE* 8:354). For Edwards, the indwelling Spirit was also a reason why all true Christians maintain private prayer: "The true spirit of prayer is no other than God's own spirit dwelling in the hearts of saints. And as this spirit comes from God, so doth it naturally tend to God in holy breathings and pantings. It naturally leads to God to converse with him by prayer. Therefore the Spirit is said to make intercession for the saints with groaning which cannot be uttered (Rom. 8:26)." *The Works of Jonathan Edwards*, ed. Edwards Hickman (Edinburgh: Banner of Truth Trust, 1974), 2:72. Again: "The spirit of a true convert is a spirit of true love to God, and that naturally inclines the soul to those duties wherein it is conversant with God, and makes it to delight in approaching him" (*WH* 2:73).

120. *WJE* 8:190. Tryon Edwards (1809–94), who first edited and published *Charity and Its Fruits*, altered his great, great grandfather's manuscript on occasion. One such instance is here, where he altered this passage to read, "*without those inward emotions and passions which tend to interrupt and destroy it*." In the same paragraph, when Jonathan Edwards wrote, "We should not only lay violence on ourselves," he softened the language to read, "We should not only control our passions" (*WJE* 8:190). *Charity*, 106. Also see Ramsey, "Editor's Introduction," in *WJE* 8:104–13 and 8:190 n5.

also returned to the doctrine of original sin. As a result of the Fall, human beings forfeited their "nobler and more extensive principles," leaving them under the power of self-love alone.[121]

Edwards's definition of anger in *Charity* revealed most clearly his distinction between sensitive passions and spiritual affections. For Edwards, anger was "an affectionate and earnest opposition of spirit against any real or supposed evil or fault of anyone." Other mental opposition (e.g., in the judgment or will) may not be anger. For example, people may experience "grief" when natural evil (evil not done by moral agents) happens to them. Anger is neither mere dislike nor even opposition in the will, for it is a heightened or passionate opposition. "There is earnestness of spirit in opposition. The spirit is moved and stirred in men when they are angry. Anger is one of the passions or affections" (8:272–73).

Edwards did not regard all anger to be evil. Anger in general may be good or evil. Inordinate or "unsuitable" anger is always evil. Anger is unsuitable when it has a "desire of revenge" (8:273). Anger may have good will, as in a father who rightly disciplines his sinning child. The Bible, Edwards added, condemns a spirit of ill will. Anger is unsuitable when it is unjustified.[122]

Moreover, a person's anger can be unsuitable "with respect to the end of it" (8:277). On this point, Edwards employed the distinction between rational affections and beastly passions. At first glance, when Edwards said above that anger "is one of the passions or affections," a cursory interpretation may conclude that Edwards was not distinguishing between affections and passions as technical terms for distinct movements. This is not so. Purposeless anger—anger that has no respect to a given end—is irrational.

> Reason has no hand in the business. Their passions go before their reason. They suffer anger to arise before they so much as turn inward their thoughts to what advantage or benefit will it be for me to be angry in this case. And so they go on in their anger without any such inquiry. Such anger is not the anger of men but of beasts. It is a kind of beastly fury, rather than any affection of a rational creature.

121. *WJE* 8:252. See the discussion of "Misc. 301" above. In *Charity*, Edwards said that, though Adam was created with "that noble principle of divine love," his sin surrendered nobler principles, and he thereby his soul "shrunk into a little point, circumscribed and closely shut up within itself to the exclusion of others. God was forsaken and fellow creatures forsaken. Individuals retired within themselves and became wholly governed by narrow, selfish principles" (*WJE* 8:253). Nevertheless, as Edwards said in the "Miscellanies," self-love is natural and good. Human beings naturally love happiness. The problem is with the self-love condemned in 1 Cor. 13:5 and other Scriptures is its "inordinate" nature (*WJE* 8:254–55). Also see "Misc. 530," in *WJE* 18:73.

122. Unjustified anger is (1) when anger is directed toward people who have done nothing wrong, (2) when anger is aroused "upon small and trivial occasions," and (3) when the anger is aroused because others' faults affect the person angry rather than God (*WJE* 8:274–77).

> All things in the soul of man should be under the government of reason, which is the highest faculty; and every other faculty or principle in the soul should be governed and directed by that to their proper ends. Therefore when men's anger works after this manner, it is a sinful and unchristian anger. (8:277)

The last way anger is sinful is when it is immoderate in measure. Human beings get too angry and lose self-control. This too is passionate and irrational anger.[123]

For Edwards, the biggest problem with passionate anger was its opposition to true charity. When people love God, they oppose the excesses of anger. In addition, love for God "will tend to keep men's irascible passions down in subjection, so that reason and love may have the regulation of them, and will prevent their being in an ordinate degree, or of long continuance" (8:278). Edwards, like Aquinas (and others), described anger as an irascible passion, a movement of the soul opposing an object. He also embraced the classic Christian distinction between lower, sensitive movements of the soul, and higher, rational movements. Love, the will, and affections are associated with the latter.

The most famous sermon in *Charity* is the last. *Heaven is a World of Love*, from 1 Cor. 13:8-10, reiterates the primacy of love one final time. Of all the gifts of the Spirit, charity alone will endure into that age of "manhood and perfection" (8:367). The vision of the sermon is that heaven is a place where love reigns, from and between the Triune God, down to the lowest saint.[124] Edwards's affirmation of the traditional doctrine of divine impassibility was seen above, but in *Heaven* Edward underlined the unbridled spiritual love flowing from God. Because of his distinction between passions and affections, Edwards held these two ideas without contradiction. Indeed, "the God of love dwells in heaven," and there "the Supreme Being . . . is both the cause and source of all holy love" (8:369). The Father and the Son are "united in infinitely dear and incomprehensible mutual love."[125] The

123. Edwards asserted: "Men's passions sometimes rise so high that they are, as it were, drunk with passion. Their passion deprives them very much of the use of reason" (*WJE* 8:277).

124. Stephen J. Stein observes: "Edwards spent an inordinate amount of time and thought throughout his career on the subject of heaven." Stephen J. Stein "Eschatology," in *PCJE*, 237.

125. Only a full quotation of this passage does it justice: "There [in heaven] dwells God the Father, who is the Father of mercies, and so the Father of love, who so loved the world that he gave his only begotten Son, that whosoever believeth in him should not perish, but have everlasting life. There dwells Jesus Christ, the Lamb of God, the Prince of peace and love, who so loved the world that he shed his blood, and poured out his soul unto death for it. There dwells the Mediator, by whom all God's love is expressed to the saints, by whom the fruits of it have been purchased, and through whom they are communicated, and through whom love is imparted to the hearts of all the church. There Christ dwells in both his natures, the human and divine, sitting with the Father in the same throne. There is the Holy Spirit, the spirit of divine love, in whom the very essence of God, as it were, all

Spirit itself is "breathed forth in love" (8:370). God himself is the "original seat" of heaven's love.[126] God's love is "as it were" an infinite and unchangeable "energy" or "act of love" (8:373).

Edwards described saintly love as holy affections distinct from the passions. The love saints reflect back to God is the very love they receive from God.[127] The only things in heaven are "lovely objects"—there is no offensive object or cause "for any passion or motion of hatred" (8:370). In heaven, saints will find all those objects that brought their souls delight, above all the pleasures of this world (8:371–72). The saints love God and the other saints sincerely, delighting in the real loveliness of others.

The love of saints is not like the love of this world, which is generated by carnality and selfishness. In heaven the love of saints is "a pure flame" of holiness (8:374). Edwards explained, "There shall be no remaining enmity, distaste, coldness and deadness of heart towards God and Christ; not the least remainder of any principle of envy to be exercised towards any angels or saints who are superior in glory, no contempt or slight towards any who are inferior" (8:375). Edwards described the love of saints in heaven as "without control" (8:376). Heaven's love will be mutual and uninterrupted by jealousy.[128]

From his understanding of the relationship of the soul and body, Edwards contrasted heaven's love with the dullness of saints' love in the present age. He said,

> In this world [the saints] find much to hinder them. . . . They carry about with them a heavy moulded body, a lump of flesh and blood which is not fitted to be an organ for a soul inflamed with high exercises of divine love, but is found a great clog to the soul, so that they cannot express their love to God as they would. They cannot be so active and lively in it as they desire. (8:378–79)

In this world, the body does not cooperate with the soul and her affections; it slows the soul and fails to express adequately the high love therein. In heaven,

flows out or is breathed forth in love, and by whose immediate influence all holy love is shed abroad in the hearts of all the church. There in heaven this fountain of love, this eternal three in one, is set open without any obstacle to hinder access to it. There this glorious God is manifested and shines forth in full glory, in beams of love; there the fountain overflows in streams of rivers of love and delight, enough for all to drink at, and to swim in, yea, so as to overflow the world as it were with a deluge of love" (*WJE* 8:369–70). Edwards referred again the infinite mutual love of the Father and Son later in the sermon (*WJE* 8:373).

126. Edwards said, "Divine love is in him not as a subject which receives from another, but as its original seat, where it is of itself" (*WJE* 8:373). He compared God's love to the unreflected light of the sun.

127. *WJE* 8:373–74. For Edwards, saints receive divine love at regeneration (*WJE* 8:387).

128. *WJE* 8:377–78. When Edwards defined heavenly love as mutual, he echoed his earliest writings on being, for heavenly love is always "in due proportion" (*WJE* 8:377). Compare *WJE* 6:332–38.

no such hindrances exist. Saints will have all the strength and energy they need to praise and see God in accordance with their love.[129] The "affections" will not clog or overpower the reason.[130] Those fleshly inclinations are "downward" (8:395). Saints who enjoy the divine gift of holy love struggle after holiness, for divine love struggles to increase and grow. The affection of divine love ought never be controlled or dampened in a human being, for by its very nature it ever increases throughout eternity.

Echoing earlier themes, *Heaven* depicts the love of heavenly saints as a love of perfect peace.[131] "Holy, humble and divine love is a principle of wonderful power to give ineffable quietness and tranquility to the soul." Love brings peace and rest, and "makes all things appear calm and sweet" (8:384). No storms are raised in the soul enjoying heavenly love.[132] Heaven's love is pure and holy without any carnality. "O!" Edwards exclaimed, "what tranquility may we conclude there is in such a world as this! . . . What a calm is this, what a heaven of rest is here to arrive at after persons have gone through a world of storms and tempests, a world of pride, and selfishness, and envy, and malice, and scorn, and contempt, and contention and war?" (8:385). This heaven is a "Canaan of rest," where divine love reigns in peaceful harmony.[133]

Great Awakening Sermons

Edwards's sermons during the Great Awakening resembled his earlier sermons—although, given the revival's perplexities, they emphasized the difference between true and false affections. Edwards maintained the distinction between the spiritual and sensitive aspects of humanity. The rational faculties are what distinguish humans from beasts, and those higher faculties are to be employed in the very thing for which they were created: the glory of God.[134] The higher faculties are

129. Edwards said, "Love naturally desires to express itself; and in heaven the love of the saints shall be at liberty to express itself as it desires, either towards God or one another" (*WJE* 8:379). See *WJE* 8:389.

130. This may be an occasion where Edwards used the term *affections* as synonymous with passions.

131. See *WJE* 14:236, 240; 16:768; "Misc. a," in *WJE* 13:163; "Misc. w," in *WJE* 13:175.

132. Edwards explained, "Those are principles contrary to love which make this world so much like a tempestuous sea. It is selfishness, and revenge, and envy, and such things which keep this world in a constant tumult, and make it a scene of confusion and uproar, where no quiet rest is to be enjoyed, unless it be in renouncing the world, and looking to another world" (*WJE* 8:384).

133. *WJE* 8:385. Later Edwards added that saints who live in contention with their families "do not enjoy much of that spiritual calm and sweetness which others do who live in love and peace" (*WJE* 8:386).

134. Edwards explained, "The reason why we have faculties superior to those of the brutes given us, is, that we are indeed designed for a superior employment. That which the

not only to be used, but "improved," which is done through increasing in the knowledge of God. Edwards continued:

> So that those who make not this very much their business; but instead of improving their understanding to acquire knowledge, are chiefly devoted to their inferior powers, to provide wherewithal to please the senses, and gratify their animal appetites, and so rather make their understanding a servant to their inferior powers, than their inferior powers servants to their understanding; not only behave themselves in a manner not becoming Christians, but also act as if they had forgotten that they are men, and that God hath set them above the brutes, by giving them understanding.[135]

That which human beings share with the animals include the "outward senses," sensual appetites, corporeal pleasure, and pain.[136] Because God, however, gave them the faculty of understanding, humans differs profoundly from animals.

Edwards urged his congregants not only to know the Scriptures and its doctrines in their speculative knowledge, but to be inclined toward them in their will. "Thus there is a difference between having a right speculative notion of the doctrines contained in the Word of God, and having a due sense of them in the heart" (22:87). Yet, the sense of the heart was useless without a real knowledge or understanding of the content of God's Word. Similarly, "there can be no love without knowledge. . . . The heart cannot be set upon an object of which there

Creator intended should be our main employment. That which the Creator intended should be our main employment, is something above what he intended the beasts for, and therefore hath given us superior powers" (*WJE* 22:90). Elsewhere he noted that Christians renounce all lusts: "[W]hen a person thus wholly gives up his whole life to the business of religion, all hopes of ever indulging his slothful ease or any of his sinful appetites any more are cut off" (*WJE* 22:316). Edwards believed that carnal appetites are strongest in young people (*WJE* 22:325; compare *WJE* 22:333). Also see *WJE* 22:396.

135. *WJE* 22:90. For a similar emphasis, see "Zeal an Essential Virtue of a Christian" (*WJE* 22:139–55). Edwards defines zeal as "a fervent disposition, an affection of mind in prosecuting that which is for God's glory and in opposing those things that are against it" (*WJE* 22:140). For Edwards, love was the fuel of zeal. "Love to God and Christ, divine love, is the foundation of all those other affections that are exercised in Christian zeal." This divine love is active. Yet, Edwards cautions, true Christian zeal is "according to knowledge" (*WJE* 22:149). The zeal of Roman Catholic and Muslims lead headlong to hell (*WJE* 22:150). Zeal always acts consistently with love and charity. "The weapons of its warfare are not carnal but spiritual. They are not reproachful reflections and angry speeches but fervent prayers and earnest, but yet meek endeavors to suppress iniquity and to promote holiness" (*WJE* 22:152).

136. *WJE* 22:90. Edwards noted that even the pagan philosophers understood that the improvement of the rational faculties was more important than submission to bodily appetites (*WJE* 22:91).

is no idea in the understanding" (22:88). For Edwards, external worship (church attendance, singing, praying, etc.) and moral duties toward others were essential to Christian piety, but "internal worship," the "worship of the heart," was foremost (22:117–18). Some people are cold, without interest in religion. The lukewarm have "some show of religion," but remain indifferent to Christ. "True Christians" are "hot," having "that holy ardor and engagedness of mind in religion" (22:143). Holy affections are necessary for a happy life, Edwards said (22:178–79).

As the Awakening progressed, Edwards used his pulpit ministry to shape the movement toward greater good.[137] Looking over his congregation, many of whom believed they were experiencing the Spirit's work, Edwards compelled them to test their faith: "Have you tasted that in Christ that has turned the stream of your affections that way and filled you with longings after more of him?" (22:315). In an April 1742 sermon preached during the Awakening's apex, Edwards exhorted some congregants to continue seeking the Lord and rebuked others for their mixed affections. The Northampton pastor pleaded with his hearers not to allow the Awakening to slip away. "Take heed of a gradual degenerating of experiences from spiritual to carnal," he said. All gracious experiences come mixed with carnal experiences. Edwards explained,

> There is often a mixture of three things with great discoveries: natural passion, a degree of secret spiritual pride, and imagination. The devil works with these. And the person, being insensible of his danger and through ignorance not distinguishing, by and by their great discoveries come to little else but strong impulses, beats of animal spirits, great imaginations. And the person, because he is violently moved, still imagines he has great discoveries, and spiritual pride then is risen to a great height. (22:532–33)

Even so, Edwards hesitated to dampen any degree of God's work. "Be as filled as you will," he encouraged the people (22:533). As the Awakening fires became embers, Edwards preached that true affections persevere. In a November 1742 sermon from Mt. 24:12, Edwards urged, "'Tis necessary for those that have religious affections and seem to have a love to Christ that they should endure to the end in order to their being saved."[138]

Among Edwards's most important discourses during the Great Awakening was the address he delivered at Yale's 1741 commencement. Edwards arrived while Yale was embroiled with the Awakening extremist James Davenport

137. See, for example, *Sinners in Zion*, in *WJE* 22:265–84; *Seeking after Christ*, in *WJE* 22:285–97; and *Like Rain upon Mown Grass*, in *WJE* 22:298–321.

138. Jonathan Edwards, sermon on Mt. 24:12, L. 1r., folder 501, box 7, Beinecke Rare Book and Manuscript Library, Yale University. Edwards spoke directly to the young people in the congregation who were tempted to abandon Christ: "Consider what you said to God. . . . Consider what you said to others. Consider what you said to me." Ibid., L. 14r.

(1716–57).[139] Davenport's meetings lacked decorum, and he made matters worse when he declared New Haven's First Church minister unconverted. Meanwhile Yale's administration struggled to control the frenetic tendencies Davenport had spawned among the Yale students. In this difficult context, Edwards preached his defense of the revival, *Distinguishing Marks*.[140]

The stated purpose of *Distinguishing Marks* was "to show what are the true, certain, and distinguishing evidences of a work of the Spirit of God" (4:227). Like in *Some Thoughts*, Edwards addressed the revival generally. The primary question is the evidences that the Spirit has been at work in an alleged revival. Edwards began with nine negative signs—those which neither proved nor disproved the Spirit's work in a revival. One cannot prove or disprove a revival, he said, because (1) the work is "very unusual," (2) the work has great effects on people's bodies, (3) the work "occasions a great ado," (4) the work results in great impressions on peoples' imaginations, (5) the work flourishes because people influence each other, (6) the work has "great imprudences and irregularities," (7) the work is tinged by Satan's influence, (8) the work affects some people who eventually fall away, or (9) the work increases while ministers preach about "the terrors of God's holy law, and that with a great deal of pathos and earnestness."[141]

Having systematically removed the objections some people had to the Awakening, Edwards suggested five proofs from 1 Jn 4 that a genuine work of God's Spirit had taken place. A genuine work of God (1) raises the esteem believers have of Jesus, (2) operates against "Satan's kingdom," (3) increases peoples' love

139. See Marsden, *Jonathan Edwards*, 227–38. The great-grandson of New Haven's first minister John Davenport, James Davenport was also the top of his 1732 Yale class. He became the pastor of the Southold, Long Island Congregational church in 1738. George Whitefield's preaching motivated Davenport in 1740 to become an itinerant preacher. Marsden says, "Davenport carried every tendency of the awakening to an extreme and his critics believed him mad. As he marched to his services he sang all the way, 'head thrown back, and his eyes staring up to heaven.'" *Jonathan Edwards*, 232. Davenport aroused significant controversy in New Haven with his commencement week revival meetings, whereupon he called the minister of the First Church in New Haven a "Wolf in sheep's clothing." He was arrested several times during the Awakening, and was once released on the grounds that he was out of his mind. For many, his revival career hit a new low with his 1743 New London bonfire incident. After the Awakening Davenport changed his ways, however, and served quietly as a Presbyterian minister from 1747 to his death. See Kidd, *Great Awakening*, 138–55; Donald M. Lewis, *Dictionary of Evangelical Biography 1730–1860* (1995; repr., Peabody, MA: Hendrickson, 2004), s.v. "Davenport, James"; and Robert E. Clay, "James Davenport's Post-Bonfire Ministry, 1743–1757," *Historian* 59 (1996): 59–73. Robert W. Brockway credits Davenport with influencing some Baptists in the southern Awakening. "Significance of James Davenport in the Great Awakening," *JRT* 24 (1967–68): 93.

140. Kidd, *Great Awakening*, 117–20.

141. *WJE* 4:228, 230, 234, 235, 238, 241, 243, 244, 246.

for the Bible, (4) leads them to have a sensible knowledge of the truth, and (5) produces in people love for God and humanity.[142]

Given the evidence, Edwards concluded that God was at work. "I will venture to draw this inference, viz. that that extraordinary influence that has lately appeared on the minds of the people abroad in this land . . . is undoubtedly, in the general, from the Spirit of God" (4:260). Edwards granted that there were problems scattered throughout the Awakening, but the positive evidence of God's work was overwhelming. Because the revival was God's work, people should show great pause before opposing it. Those who opposed the revival pitted themselves precariously against God.

Edwards closed *Distinguishing Marks* with an admonition to the "friends of this work," that they might "avoid all errors and misconduct" (4:276). Despite his arguments against and cautions toward those sympathetic to the revival, Edwards did not win over New Haven. Yale never invited him back.

Conclusion

Edwards's early notebooks and personal writings show that Edwards embraced and built upon his theological training. For Edwards, reality was grounded in consent and beauty. As such, the affections were key to Edwards's metaphysics. God is a God of volition, and the Holy Spirit is the love uniting the Father and the Son in Trinitarian communion. The Holy Spirit, as divine love, is given to true Christians, and he produces in them a genuine and holy affection or inclination toward the true moral beauty of divine things ideally apprehended by the understanding. This "sense of the heart," when spiritually alive toward divine good, amounts to holy affections.

Edwards acknowledged that there were lower, natural desires, that were learned from sense pleasure and displeasure connected with the body. Like his predecessors, Edwards did not always use technical terms to differentiate between these movements, but he recognized the distinction and employed it often in his pulpit ministry. He saw affections to be actions of the will; passions are violent movements connected with sensitive pleasure and desires in the natural world. Affections, when gracious and directed toward God, should know no limit. The higher, rational faculties of the soul should control passions.

This distinction between affections and passions also illustrates an important distinction between human beings and animals. Animals were capable of passions, but were incapable of rational affections and acts of the will. Human beings are to rule over fleshly passions with their higher faculties. Those who did not were acting on the level of beasts.

Edwards's notions of affections and passions are at odds with contemporary ideas concerning emotions. Emotions are a "class of feelings, differentiated from

142. *WJE* 4:248–59.

sensation or proprioceptions by their experienced quality."[143] Edwards drew a distinction between affections of the will and the passions that arise because of sensitive good and evil where contemporary understandings make no such distinctions. Both affections and passions are properly related to the soul in a way that emotions are not.

Edwards only understood affections and passions to be feelings *figuratively*. Given the union of soul and body, it is quite natural for the affections and passions of the soul to affect the body. But, properly speaking, the affections and passions are the movements of the immaterial soul of human beings. In both instances, he conceived of the affections and passions to be simple inclinations and aversions, distinct from those bodily movements that often accompany them.

This understanding of affections and passions was an important theme of Edwards's early ministry and theology. When George Whitefield and the Great Awakening came to New England in the early 1740s, this understanding aided Edwards as he provided counsel to those sympathetic to the Awakening. Edwards also used this affective psychology rooted in the Christian tradition to argue against the criticisms of those so-called Old Light opponents of the Great Awakening, including the Boston minister Charles Chauncy.

143. A proprioception is a sense beyond the five typical senses of knowing the state of body parts and organs and your location in space.

Chapter 6

ENTHUSIASM, PASSIONS, AND THE GREAT AWAKENING DISPUTES OVER THE ROLE OF AFFECTIONS IN RELIGION

Love divine, all loves excelling,
Joy of heaven to earth come down,
Fix in us Thy humble dwelling;
All Thy faithful mercies crown.
Jesus, Thou art all compassion;
Pure, unbounded love Thou art;
Visit us with Thy salvation;
Enter every trembling heart.

— Charles Wesley

The Great Awakening was like a great earthquake in New England, turning subterranean political and social fault lines into great chasms of division. Before the Awakening, Jonathan Edwards and Charles Chauncy were allies. Afterward, Edwards stood as a fountainhead of evangelical thought, while Chauncy emerged as a quasi-Arian, Arminian universalist. The Awakening also brought to the fore Edwards's articulation of Christian affectivity in the now classic work, *A Treatise Concerning Religious Affections.*

To highlight the contrast between Edwards and Chauncy, which especially clarifies Edwards's thought, this chapter does not present materials in a strictly chronological fashion. It opens with the history of the Awakening, followed by a summary of Chauncy's theory of passions and religion. An analysis of Edwards's thought against Chauncy follows, beginning with his sermons and *Some Thoughts*. Edwards's notion of affections is then explained in relation to the will, passions, body, and religion. A summary of *Affections* concludes the chapter. Edwards's revival writings are crucial to interpret his affective psychology, because amidst Chauncy's rationalism and the extremists' antics Edwards articulated most clearly the character of gracious affections.

Historical Background

From Edwards's standpoint in 1739, Reformed Christianity was languishing.[1] Nevertheless, Edwards resisted despondency. In Edwards view, the Bible prophesied that the future glories awaiting the church would be fulfilled through a worldwide revival.[2] This fulfillment would happen soon, he believed. Consequently, Edwards welcomed the news that a successful young itinerant preacher named George Whitefield was visiting New England. In February 1740, Edwards invited the Reformed Anglican to speak at Northampton. Whitefield's tour of New England beginning September 1740 was a great success. Soon, another itinerant minister, the Presbyterian Gilbert Tennent, began preaching around New England. The Great Awakening had begun.[3]

1. See Marsden, *Jonathan Edwards*, 196–200.

2. Stephen J. Stein argues that the term *post-millennial* is anachronistic when used of Edwards. "Editor's Introduction," in Jonathan Edwards, *Apocalyptic Writings*, vol. 5 of *The Works of Jonathan Edwards* (New Haven, CT: Yale University Press, 1977), 7 n6. Also see Wilson, "Editor's Introduction," *WJE* 9:90–94. Edwards's eschatology was closely tied to his defense of the Awakening. Other shared this view, including Watts (see *WJE* 4:137; compare 140–44). This may be the reason Edwards wept while listening to Whitefield. George Whitefield, *George Whitefield's Journals* (London: Banner of Truth Trust, 1960), 467–77, cited in Edwin S. Gaustad and Mark A. Noll, *A Documentary History of Religion in America to 1877*, 3rd ed. (Grand Rapids, MI: William B. Eerdmans, 2003), 162. Also see *WJE* 4:140–44; Stephen J. Stein, "Editor's Introduction," in *WJE* 5:1–54; Stein, "Eschatology," in *PCJE*, 226–42; Stout, "Edwards as Revivalist," in *Cambridge Companion to JE*, 125–43. Smart, *Jonathan Edwards's Apologetic*, 97–99; and McClymond and McDermott, *Theology*, 572–77. See *WJE* 22:339–77.

3. See C. C. Goen, "Editor's Introduction" in *WJE* 4:32–89; Winslow, *Jonathan Edwards*, 165–81; Gaustad, *Great Awakening*; Murray, *Jonathan Edwards*, 153–76; Miller, *Jonathan Edwards*, 133–63; Richard L. Bushman, ed., *The Great Awakening: Documents on the Revival of Religion, 1740–1745*, Documentary Problems in Early American History (New York: Atheneum, 1970); Murray, *Jonathan Edwards*, 155–76; Gaustad and Noll, *A Documentary History of Religion in America to 1877*, 160–76; Frank Lambert, *Inventing the "Great Awakening"* (Princeton, NJ: Princeton University Press, 1999); Holifield, *Theology in America*, 92–101; Marsden, *Jonathan Edwards*, 201–67; Kidd, *Great Awakening*, 40–54, 83–93, 117–37; See David C. McCollum, "A Study of Evangelicals and Revival Exercises from 1730–1805: Tracing the Development of Exercise Traditions through the First Great Awakening to the Southern Great Revival," (PhD diss., Southeastern Baptist Theological Seminary, 2009), 57–71; and Smart, *Jonathan Edwards's Apologetic*, 13–35. On the Great Awakening and its relationship to the rise of evangelicalism, see Mark A. Noll, *The Rise of Evangelicalism: The Age of Edwards, Whitefield, and the Wesleys*, A History of Evangelicalism: People, Movements and Ideas in the English-Speaking World 1 (Downers Grove, IL: InterVarsity Press, 2003), 100–35.

In May 1741, Edwards saw the young adults of Northampton respond remarkably to the preaching of the gospel. He later described August and September of that year as "most remarkable . . . for appearances of conviction and conversion of sinners, and great revivings, quickenings, and comforts of professors, and for extraordinary external effects of these things" (16:118). During the summer of 1741, throughout New England, men and women experienced incredible raptures. So great was their sense of spiritual things that they would cry out, faint, or experience convulsions, sometimes out of anxiety, sometimes out of joy. This response became normal in the revivals. That July, as Edwards preached from Deut. 32:35 in Enfield, the great shrieks and moans forced him to cut his sermon short. The title of the sermon, still well-known today, was *Sinners in the Hands of an Angry God.*[4]

All was not well, however. Yale College invited Edwards give an address for their September 1741 commencement. Yale was embroiled in controversies concerning the Awakening. Despite his gentle critiques of the Awakening's problems, Edwards's strong defense of the Awakening, later published as *The Distinguishing Marks of a Work of the Spirit of God*, received an icy response from Yale's leadership.[5]

The revival had been amassing a large group of opponents, led most notably by the Boston minister Charles Chauncy (1705–87). By 1742, Chauncy published two tracts against the work. Later, Edwards observed that the summer of 1742 saw "some abatement of the liveliness of people's affections in religion" (16:125). At the end of that year, Edwards sent the printers *Some Thoughts*, a lengthy "sequel" to *Distinguishing Marks*. It addressed both the Awakening's extremists and opponents.[6] *Some Thoughts* was published in March 1743. Two months later, the soft divisions between revival friends and opponents hardened when the Massachusetts clergy met to denounce the extreme practices of the Awakening.[7]

4. *WJE* 22:400–35. For more on this episode, see Miller, *Jonathan Edwards*, 145–47; Miller, *Errand*, 163–83; Marsden, *Jonathan Edwards*, 219–24; Wilson H. Kimnach, Caleb J. D. Maskell, and Kenneth P. Minkema, eds., *Jonathan Edwards's* Sinners in the Hands of an Angry God: *A Casebook including the Authoritative Edition of the Famous Sermon* (New Haven, CT: Yale University Press, 2010); and Douglas L. Winiarski, "Jonathan Edwards, Enthusiast? Radical Revivalism and the Great Awakening in the Connecticut Valley" *CH* 74:4 (2005): 683–739.

5. *WJE* 4:213–88.

6. *WJE* 4:289–530. The full title is *Some Thoughts concerning the Present Revival of Religion in New England.* See Marsden, *Jonathan Edwards*, 263.

7. Parts of the May 1743 *Testimony of the Pastors of the Churches of the Province of Massachusetts* (the published denouncement) can be found in Bushman, *The Great Awakening*, 127–28. The "Old Light" clergy agreed: "Though we deny not, that the human Mind, under the Operation of the Divine SPIRIT, may be overborn with *Terrors* or *Joys*; yet, the many Confusions that have appeared in some Places, from the Vanity of the Mind, and ungoverned Passions of People, either in the Excess of *Sorrow* or *Joy*, with the *disorderly Tumults* and *indecent Behaviors* of Persons, we judge to be so far from an Indication of

Charles Chauncy's *Seasonable Thoughts on State of Religion in New England* (1743), published just six months after and directly in response to Edwards's *Some Thoughts*, was a setback to New Light pastors. Its subscription list, at eighteen pages long (on page 14 the publisher shifts to two columns), was a "social register for New England in 1743."[8] By spring 1744, Edwards conceded to a friend that the revival was over. The final blow did not come until 1750, when the Northampton church, Edwards's early model of revival, asked Edwards to vacate his office.

Jonathan Edwards was convinced that the Awakening had come from the Holy Spirit. He saw the high affections experienced by his wife and others and believed them to be genuine.[9] He also believed that the New England revival was the first faint lights before the "great and glorious times of the church."

As *Some Thoughts* neared publication in the winter of 1742–43, Edwards preached what later became *A Treatise Concerning Religious Affections*. When *Affections* was finally published in 1746, it never mentioned Chauncy or *Seasonable Thoughts*. Although it countered Old Light positions, Edwards likely did not view *Affections* as a direct response to Chauncy's *Seasonable Thoughts* or a further argument in the debate.

Affections explains how one knows a person's affections are gracious. In it Edwards navigated Christian piety through both unruly enthusiasm and the Old Light marginalization of affections in religion. As such, the book was Edwards's attempt to define the true version of Christianity that avoided both extremes. There was little intellectual "development" in Edwards's thought on these matters between the publication of *Some Thoughts* and *Affections*. Although Edwards's views matured between his early thought on affections and the sobriety of *Religious Affections*, they did not substantially change.[10]

Charles Chauncy on the Place of Affections in Religion

"Old Brick" was Charles Chauncy's nickname, likely referring to both his appearance and temperament. He would later epitomize New England "Arminianism," denying

the *special Presence of* GOD with those Preachers that have industriously excited and countenanced them, or in the Asssemblies where they prevail, that they are a plain Evidence of the Weakness of human Nature; as the History of the *Enthusiasms* that have appear'd in the World, in several Ages, manifests.... At the same Time, we bear our Testimony against the *impious Spirit* of those, that, from hence, take Occasion to reproach the *Work of the Divine* SPIRIT, in the Hearts of the Children of GOD." Ibid., 128.

8. Charles Chauncy, *Seasonable Thoughts on the State of Religion in New England, A Treatise in Five Parts* (Boston: Rogers and Fowle, 1743). Miller, *Jonathan Edwards*, 175.

9. Marsden, *Jonathan Edwards*, 239–52. C. C. Goen, "Editor's Introduction," in *WJE* 4:68–70. For a full exposition of Edwards's defense of the Great Awakening, see Smart, *Jonathan Edwards*.

10. Compare Wilson, *Virtue*, 167–79.

the substitutionary atonement and affirming universalism and "high Arianism."[11] Yet, Edwin Gaustad made the noteworthy suggestion, established by Edward Griffin's study, that in 1741 Edwards and Chauncy held similar perspectives. The upheaval of the Great Awakening set them toward their destinies.[12]

Chauncy's fullest response to Edwards was *Seasonable Thoughts on the State of Religion in New England* in 1743. When Edwards wrote *Some Thoughts* and began to prepare *Affections*, he was responding primarily to ideas in Chauncy's 1742 sermon *Enthusiasm, described and caution'd against*. Chauncy's *Seasonable Thoughts*, published in the autumn of 1743, responded directly to Edwards's *Some Thoughts*, and Edwards had begun working on *Affections* before *Seasonable Thoughts* was published.[13] Yet, *Seasonable Thoughts* is a fuller expansion of the same ideas in *Enthusiasm*. In both works, Chauncy declared the revival's biggest issue: the passions were ruling reason.

Enthusiasm

In 1742, Chauncy's sermon *Enthusiasm* served as the Old Light's first punch, landed by the man who was their champion. He identified the revivalists with enthusiasts, known by their wild-eyed look and violent "convulsions and distortions."[14]

Chauncy said reason should rule the affections, and, even more significantly, that reason was primary in religion. "Next to the Scriptures, there is no greater enemy to *enthusiasm*, than *reason*." He continued: "'Tis indeed impossible a man

11. Marsden, *Jonathan Edwards*, 268–69. On Chauncy, see Walker, *Ten New England Leaders*, 267–310; Edward M. Griffin, *Old Brick: Charles Chauncy of Boston, 1705–1787*, Minnesota Monographs in the Humanities (Minneapolis: University of Minnesota Press, 1980); and Charles H. Lippy, *Seasonable Revolutionary: The Mind of Charles Chauncy* (Chicago, IL: Nelson-Hall, 1981). On Chauncy and the progressive religious movement, see G. Adolf Koch, *Religion of the American Enlightenment* (New York: Thomas Y. Crowell, 1968), 3–27 and Gary Dorrien, *The Making of American Liberal Theology: Imagining Progressive Religion, 1805–1900* (Louisville: Westminster John Knox Press, 2001), 1–5.

12. Gaustad, *Great Awakening*, 101. See Griffin, *Old Brick*, 32–33, 38–39.

13. Marsden says, "Edwards explicitly attacked this low view of the affections in *Seasonable Thoughts* as based on 'philosophy' rather than Scripture." Edwards, however, made the "philosophy" criticism in *Some Thoughts*, and not in *Religious Affections* (the Edwards remark Marsden cites is from *Some Thoughts*). *Some Thoughts* preceded *Seasonable Thoughts*. See *Jonathan Edwards*, 281–82.

14. Charles Chauncy, *Enthusiasm, described and caution'd against* (Boston: J. Draper, 1742), 4. The text is also in Alan Heimert and Perry Miller, *The Great Awakening: Documents Illustrating the Crisis and its Consequences* (Indianapolis, IN: Bobbs-Merrill, 1967), 228–56. See C. C. Goen, "Editor's Introduction," in *WJE* 4:62. Chauncy was not the only New Light spokesperson. For instance, John Caldwell's *An Impartial Trial of the Spirit Operating in this Part of the World* was preached against Edwards's *Distinguishing Marks*. See Kidd, *Great Awakening*, 121–23.

shou'd be an *enthusiast*, who is in the just exercise of his understanding; and 'tis because men don't pay a due regard to the sober dictates of a well inform'd mind that they are led aside by the delusions of a vain imagination."[15] To avoid enthusiasm, not only should reason be followed, but the workings of the "*passions* and *affections*" should have their proper role. They could properly awaken the "*reasonable powers*," but should be controlled:

> We shall mistake the right use of the passions, if we place our religion *only* or *chiefly*, in the heat and fervour of them. The *soul* is the *man*: And unless the *reasonable nature* is suitably wrought upon, the *understanding* enlightened, the *judgment* convinc'd, the *will* perswaded, and the *mind* entirely chang'd, it will avail but little purpose; tho' the passions be set in a blaze.[16]

Chauncy jettisoned the affections to the periphery in religion. Edwards felt compelled to correct that; he regarded Chauncy's psychology to be too "philosophical." For Chauncy, passions must be governed by the understanding; when the passions "are uppermost," people are in an unsafe state.[17]

Seasonable Thoughts

Although Edwards conceded that there were many undesirable excesses in the revival, he believed them to be the exception. In *Seasonable Thoughts*, Chauncy argued that the revival was *defined* by such frenzied external shows. Chauncy intended the book to be a direct response to Edwards, whose views he reckoned dangerous. The disturbances were not simply on the fringe, but at the heart of the revival. Itinerant preaching (36–76), abnormal and enthusiastic behavior that could "scarce be described in Words" (76–140), the judgment being leveled against clergy (140–76), the "divine" impressions many claimed to have had (176–226), lay preachers (226–39), confusion in public worship (239–42), and many other "errors" (242–333) were all painstakingly cataloged and condemned.

The "terrors" Chauncy described paint a revival of frenzy and excess: fainting, screams, and convulsions; such were "common all over the land."[18] Both the "*religious Fears*" and their resulting effects on the body were questionable. "It ought to be carefully remembered, the Passion of *Fear* may be excited, not only from a just Representation of Truth to the Mind by the SPIRIT of GOD, but from the *natural Influence* of *awful Words* and *frightful Gestures*."[19] Chauncy suspected the "fear" was not graciously given by the Spirit, but naturally caused by a "*mechanical Impression* on *animal Nature*," a "mere *sensitive Commotion*," or "a sudden and

15. Chauncy, *Enthusiasm*, 18.
16. Ibid., 20.
17. Ibid.
18. Chauncy, *Seasonable Thoughts*, 77.
19. Ibid., 79–80.

strong Impression on the *animal Oeconomy*."[20] He brushed off the historical instances that one "noted *Writer* of the Times" (Edwards) had cited of Christian piety accompanied by such demonstrations.[21]

Chauncy admitted that in religion, "there will be love to God; the *Reality* of it in the *Heart*, and the genuine *Appearance* of it in the *Life*." He continued:

> It may discover itself in the *Passions*; and this in a *lower* or *higher* Degree, according to the Temper, Education and other Circumstances of the Persons who are the Subjects of it: And where the *passionate Appearance* may be greatest, many may be ready to think, there is the truest and highest Love: But this is a Mistake. The *passionate* Discovery of Love is not the best Evidence, either of its *Being* or *Strength*: The surest and most substantial Proof is, *Obedience to the Commandments of GOD*; and the *stronger* the Love, the more uniform, steady and pleasant will be this *Obedience*.[22]

Edwards agreed that great external demonstrations of affections could never prove spiritual reality. Chauncy stressed that the marks of the revival did not conform to the fruit of the Spirit. The Spirit's fruit includes peace, which only happens when "Men's Passions" are "under a divine Government."[23] By contrast, those influenced by the revival were schismatic and "Disturbers of Society," proving that the Spirit was *not* at work.

Disturbances during preaching did not prove to be Spirit's work either. Chauncy lamented: "Such *bodily Effects* as have prevailed in the Land, have always been *rare* among *sober* Christians." Moreover, the ways these demonstrations were provoked needed further scrutiny. It is "as though the Preacher rather aimed at putting their Passions into a Ferment, than filling them with such a *reasonable* Solicitude."[24] Such terrors often arise in the youth and women, for their passions are most easily upset.[25]

Natural, not gracious, means had caused the revival. "And can it be suppos'd, the *GOD of Order*, would, by the Exertment of his Power, raise this Concern to such a Height, as that his *own Worship* should be broke up upon the Account of it? 'Tis Impossible."[26] The New Light preaching was "more fit for the *Stage* than the *sacred Desk*."[27]

20. Ibid., 80.
21. Ibid., 81.
22. Ibid., 26. The parallels with Hoadly on this point are striking. See note 43 of this chapter.
23. Ibid., 28.
24. Ibid., 93.
25. Ibid., 105.
26. Ibid., 108.
27. Ibid., 109.

Chauncy repeated themes found in his sermon *Enthusiasm* concerning the place of affections in the Christian life. "I am not against the *Preaching of Terror*," he wrote. "But whenever this is done, it ought to be done in a Way that may enlighten the Mind, as well as alarm the Passions."[28] People ought to experience conviction for sin, but only in a way that affects the passions through the understanding, not *vice versa*.

Chauncy cited authorities in his defense. He noted Stephen Charnock's (1628–80) observation that, in a natural work, the affections are influenced instead of judgment. The Spirit's convictions rest on the judgment, but the Devil affects the mind through the passions. For Chauncy (and Charnock), when the affections were prevalent in conversion, they impeded the role of reason, a crucial faculty in the Spirit's work of conviction.[29] External effects do not indicate that people have the Spirit. Chauncy also quoted Baxter's warning against "placing your Humiliation, either *only*, or *principally*, in the *passionate* Part, or in the *outward Expressions* of the Passions."[30] Great outward sorrow and tears are not essential for conversion; a proper will toward God is what matters.

Chauncy defined the affections on display as sensitive passions. He warned that manifestations of joy may be hypocritical and arise "in *animal Nature*." The Awakening's converts lived in a way that showed that "their Joy was only a *sudden Flash*, a *Spark of their own kindling*: Nay, some have been made sensible, their Joy was nothing more than a meer *sensitive Passion*, and have own'd they were under a Delusion, while they imagin'd it was of a divine *Origin*."[31] On this point Chauncy marshaled Robert Bolton (1572–1631) and Richard Baxter to his defense. The frothy joy of the Awakening, Chauncy said, had all the marks of counterfeit.[32]

28. Ibid.

29. Ibid., 110–11. Stephen Charnock, *A Discourse of Conviction of Sin*, in *The Works of Stephen Charnock*, ed. Thomas Smith (Edinburgh: James Nichol, 1865), 4:197. Chauncy also quoted John Owen to make a point about the danger of imitating the work of grace perceived in others.

30. Ibid., 116. Richard Baxter, *Directions and Persuasions to a Sound Conversion*, in *Works* 8:78.

31. Ibid., 121.

32. Chauncy asked, "Is it not just Matter of Complaint, that *its Praises of GOD* have been too *ostentatious*, too much favouring of a Desire to be *seen of Men?* Has it been content with silent Admirations of the Loving-Kindness of GOD in JESUS CHRIST; venting it self in secret Breathings of Love, and Returns of Gratitude to the Father of Mercies? No, but the *Houses of Worship*, the *Places of Concourse*, are those in which it has been generally broke forth, in Acknowledgements to GOD: Nay, han't been common in some Parts of the Land, and among some Sorts of People, to express their *religious Joy* by *singing through the Streets*, and in *Ferry-Boats*? And has not this Joy almost universally shown it self in *Raptures* and *Transports?* Nay, in *Swoonings*, and *Out-cries*, and *Screamings*, so like to these same Effects under *Terror*, that it han't been known, whether Persons were in *Joy* or *Sorrow*, but by asking them the Reason of the Commotion their Passions have been in? Yea, has it not been a usual

Chauncy, near the end of the first section, addressed Edwards again, particularly his defense of earnest preaching in *Some Thoughts*. Chauncy conceded that the "passions" are useful, and it is "*reasonable* they should be excited." Yet, the New Light ministers had made it the "*main Thing*" to stir the "*Passions*," denying reason's priority.[33] Instead of addressing their hearers' "*Understanding*," revival preachers had adapted "a *wild Manner* . . . to *affrighten* People out of their *Wits*."[34]

According to Chauncy, the best proof of God's work is when people govern their passions through reason. The uncontrolled nature of the passions proved that they were not from God. Such behavior is expected when "Men's *Passions* are in *great Commotion*, and they *generally* act under the *Guidance* of them in this *tumultuous* State."[35] Chauncy systematically addressed Edwards's excuses for the revival improprieties, hoping to prove that the revival could not justifiably be called the Lord's work. "A mere *passionate* Religion," he said, always results in the lapses in judgment seen in the revival.[36]

In *Some Thoughts* Edwards attributed some of the missteps of those highly affected to the great power of God, but Chauncy countered that the power of God should result in just the opposite. "These don't look like the Fruit of *extraordinary* Discoveries of GOD; but they are the very Things which may be expected, where Men's *Passions* are rais'd to an *extraordinary* Height, without a proportionable Degree of Light in their Understandings."[37] Chauncy directly addressed his remarks to Edwards:

> Such *high Affections*, I know, are freely spoken of as owing to the SPIRIT OF GOD; and this, when there is not given "*Strength of Understanding* in *Proportion*"; and by Means hereof, the *Subjects* of these Affections may be driven, "through ERROR, into an *irregular* and *sinful* Conduct." But it may justly be question'd, whether *extraordinary Warmth* in the *Passions*, when there is not *answerable Light* in the *Mind*, is so much owing to the SPIRIT of GOD, as some may be ready to imagine.[38]

Thing to shew this Joy by *clapping of Hands*, by *jumping up and down*, by *Congratulations in the Way of Kissing*, by breaking out into *hearty loud Laughter*?" Ibid., 126.

33. Ibid., 302.

34. Ibid., 303. Chauncy added, "And under the Notion of speaking to the *Affections*, were the Things of GOD and another World, ever preached with more Confusion of Thought; with greater Incoherence; with the undue Mixture of more rash, crude, unguarded Expressions; or with Conceit to a higher Degree, appearing in fulsome Self-Applauses, as well as unheard of Contempt of others?"

35. Ibid., 311.

36. Ibid., 320.

37. Ibid., 323.

38. Ibid., 323–24.

According to Chauncy, only reason's control of the passions can curb the problem of enthusiasm. The Spirit's work never results in passions controlling Christians. Such a situation would upset the ordained order, and "invert their Frame." A mark of regeneration is "the Reduction of their *Passions* to a proper Regimen." People should not be "guided by *Passion* or *Affection*, though the Object of it should be God, and the Things of another World."[39] An informed discernment should rule Christians; only enthusiasts and Roman Catholics are ruled by the affections.

Why did Chauncy minimize religious affectivity? Norman Fiering traces the Edwards-Chauncy conflict to a centuries-long debate between intellectualism and voluntarism.[40] Michael McClymond suggests that Chauncy was influenced by Locke's comments on enthusiasm. Locke also said that reason should control enthusiasm.[41] Yet, Locke omits an explanation of the role of passions in enthusiasm. With the increasing influence of early Enlightenment thought, a prevailing spirit of cool and detached religious devotion was becoming increasingly fashionable in New England.[42] Edwards had long known the trend to diminish the role of affections in religion ("Misc. tt," 13:189–90). An issue of *The Spectator* cautioned, "DEVOTION, when it does not lie under the Check of Reason, is very apt to degenerate into Enthusiasm," and the influential Latitudinarian Benjamin Hoadly (1676–1761) minimized love for God.[43] The traditional distinction between

39. Ibid., 324.

40. Fiering, *Moral Philosophy*, 104–46.

41. McClymond, "Spiritual Perception," 204–05. In his passage on enthusiasm, Locke argued against those who believed they had received divine inspiration (enthusiasts): "This seeing, is it the perception of the truth of the proposition, or of this, that it is a revelation from God? This feeling, is it a perception of an inclination or fancy to do something, or of the Spirit of God moving that inclination? . . . How do I know that God is the revealer of this to me; that this impression is made upon my mind by his Holy Spirit; and that therefore I ought to obey it? If I know not this, how great soever the assurance is that I am possessed with, it is groundless; whatever light I pretend to, it is but *enthusiasm*." Locke, *Essay concerning Human Understanding*, § 4.19.10 (386). Perhaps Edwards turned Locke's argument on its head when formulating his own thought on spiritual sense, concluding that having a sense of the heart of the truth of God's Word was given by the Spirit of God, though it was not enthusiastic inspiration as Locke defined it.

42. See Dorrien, *Making of American Liberal Theology*, 2–3. Compare *WJE* 2:121. Also see n91 in this chapter.

43. Joseph Addison, *The Spectator*, No. 201, October 20, 1711, in *The Spectator, Vol. III*, 12th ed. (London, 1739), 129. Hoadly wrote, "Prayer, in all our Lord's Directions about it, and particularly in that *Form*, which He himself taught his Followers, was a calm, undisturbed, *Address* to *God*, under the Notion of a *Father*, expressing those Sentiments and Wishes before Him, which every sincere Mind ought to have. But the same *Word*, by the help of Men, and voluminous Rules of Art, is come to signify *Heat* and *Flame*. . . . Once more; the *Love of God*, and of *our Saviour*, was at first, in his own Words, and those of St. *John*, many Times repeated, the *keeping his Commandments, or doing his Will*. . . . But the

affections and passions may also have begun to lose influence in the early eighteenth century.

Although Edwards and Chauncy had nearly equal disdain for the wildest elements of the revival, and even agreed on points, Chauncy believed the revival was wholly corrupt, and rejected all of Edwards's claims that the work was God's. Chauncy said that the chief faculty in religion was reason, which ruled over the affections. The mind's rule over passion was essential to true Christianity. He did not distinguish affections and passions (nearly every affection is a "passion"), and failed to wrestle in a productive way with the biblical mandate for affections that Edwards found utterly compelling.

Jonathan Edwards on the Affectionate Part of Man

Many of Chauncy's critiques attempted to counter the affective psychology of Jonathan Edwards. On the other end of the spectrum were the Awakening's extremists, who besmirched the revival's good through wild escapades and claims of inspiration.[44] Edwards placed himself in the center. Against Chauncy, Edwards argued that Spirit-wrought affections were essential to true religion and believed the Spirit of God to be genuinely at work in the Awakening. Against the

Notion of it [love] was, it seems, left very jejune; and so hath been improved by his *later Followers*, till the same *Name*, still kept up in the Language of *Christians*, is far removed from the *Thing* principally and first intended; and is come by degrees to signify a violent *Passion*, *Commotion*, and *Ecstasy*, venting it self in such sort of Expressions and Disorders, as other *Passions* do." "The Nature of the Kingdom, or Church of Christ," in *Sixteen Sermons Formerly Printed, Now Collected into One Volume. To which are added, Six Sermons upon Public Occasions, Never before Printed* (London: John and Paul Knapton, 1754), 288–89. See especially Andrew Starkie, *The Church of England and the Bangorian Controversy, 1716–1721*, Studies in Modern British Religious History 14 (Woodbridge, Suffolk, UK: Boydell Press, 2007), 155–87.

44. In a late 1741 sermon, Edwards conceded that "imprudences and errors" always accompany a work of God, but asked, "But must we therefore always harp upon them?" (*WJE* 22:507). See Stout and Hatch with Haley, "Preface to the Period," in *WJE* 22:37–39. Michael McClymond observes, "In defending religious affections, and suggesting that even intense emotions and bodily manifestations could play a role in true religion, Edwards confronted and challenged a contemporary prejudice against enthusiasm. In effect he narrowed the definition of the term, and spurned only a part of what others rejected." "Jonathan Edwards," in *OHRE*, 413. Edwards did narrow the term from *contemporary* definitions, but Edwards's concept of enthusiasm was largely in line with Reformed thought. See Ryan J. Martin, "'Violent Motions of Carnal Affections': Jonathan Edwards, John Owen, and Distinguishing the Work of the Spirit from Enthusiasm" *Detroit Baptist Seminary Journal* 15 (2010): 99–116. Also see *JEE*, s.v. "Enthusiasm."

extremists, Edwards cautioned that the affections must be carefully judged—not every affection came from the Spirit of God.

Some Thoughts Concerning the Revival

Edwards expanded upon some of his core ideas from *Distinguishing Marks* in *Some Thoughts concerning the Revival.* The work had five heads: (1) the New England revival was a "glorious work of God"; (2) as the Spirit's work, all were obligated to rejoice in and promote the Awakening; (3) several friends of the Awakening have been unjustly maligned; (4) those sympathetic to the revival should correct and avoid their behavior on several points; and (5) what should be done to promote the revival.[45]

For Edwards, the "vain, carnal, worldly spirit" in some ministers was worse before God than "all the imprudence and intemperate heats, wildness and distraction (as some call it)" of the young revival preachers (4:296). Edwards was especially troubled by the tendency of the opposition to reject the entire Awakening because of its improprieties: "The weakness of human nature has always appeared in times of great revival of religion, by a disposition to run to extremes and get into confusion; and especially in these three things—enthusiasm, superstition, and intemperate zeal" (4:319). This is common throughout church history, even under the Apostles' ministry. Edwards noted that before the Awakening, churches had been in "a strange stupor"; the Spirit's work had been "but little felt." The newly awakened had never known a "supernatural influence" before, and so they "run into enthusiasm, taking every strong impulse or impression to be divine" (4:321). Such circumstances beg for patience. Edwards conceded that "errors and irregularities" accompanied the present work, but they arose from the peoples' "infirmity and weakness and common corruption" (4:323). Nevertheless, the Awakening had many genuine conversions evidenced in holy living. Even if the work had "imprudences, darkness and sin" with it, every minister should thank God for it (4:331).

A Synthesis of Edwards's Affective Psychology

Jonathan Edwards had a keen interest in how the soul worked. He was aware of the rival theories and had read widely on the subject. Everything Edwards embraced when it came to the affections found its roots in the Christian tradition generally, and the Reformed tradition specifically. He was not an innovator with respect to his notions of the soul's workings, yet, from an early age, he struggled in his personal

45. *WJE* 4:293, 348, 384, 409, 496. *Some Thoughts* is probably best remembered for two passages: the masked description of Sarah Edwards's religious experiences and Edwards's interpretation of a biblical prophecy to be possibly about America. See Marsden, *Jonathan Edwards*, 239–52; 263–67.

theological notebooks and papers to articulate his psychology in a thorough and persuasive way.

Edwards's psychology was rooted in the primacy of a will inclined toward the Triune God. Indeed, humans were created so that their will might consent to that Being without which they could not exist. The Bible revealed that human love must be directed toward God, and, through him, to other rational beings. Even Edwards's understanding of the Trinity confirmed the importance of the will.[46] For Edwards, affections were, at their simplest level, strong inclinations of the soul. The sensitive appetites, however, moved the passions to desire violently what was connected with needs of the body. Human beings have an understanding and will like God, and a body and sensuality like beasts.[47]

When the Great Awakening controversies fell on New England, Edwards applied this psychology to the issues that surfaced. To understand Edwards's thought on the affections, the affections will be explained in connection to his thought on the will, the body, passions, and religion.

Affections and the Will Scripture convinced Edwards that holy affection for God was essential to true Christian piety. On this point, Edwards parted ways with Chauncy. Edwards said, "Some make philosophy instead of Holy Scriptures their rule of judging of this work: particularly the philosophical notions they entertain of the nature of the soul, its faculties and affections."[48] He continued,

> In their philosophy, the affections of the soul are something diverse from the will, and not appertaining to the noblest part of the soul, but the meanest principles that it has, that belong to men as partaking of animal nature, and what he has in common with the brute creation, rather than anything whereby he is conformed to angels and pure spirits. (4:296–97)

A philosophical system was behind the Old Light's suspicion of the affections. Edwards's opponents relegated all movements of the soul to sensitive appetite or body. Both Edwards and opponents agreed that the affections were in some

46. Danaher argues that Edwards's originality in *Affections* is his Trinitarian interpretation of affections. *Trinitarian Ethics*, 118–19.

47. See Chapter 5. Compare Malebranche's preface in *Search after Truth*, xxxiii.

48. *WJE* 4:296. Compare his *Affections Notebook*, "No. 7," where Edwards said, "[E]veryone has had a philosophy of his own about the nature and faculties of the soul and their dependence one on another, and have drawn a multitude of consequences from their schemes, and have made as many rules and signs of grace as has been agreeable to their philosophy." *Documents on the Trinity, Grace and Faith*, vol. 37, *The Works of Jonathan Edwards Online*, ed. Jonathan Edwards Center (New Haven, CT: Yale University Press, 2008), http://edwards.yale.edu/archive?path=aHR0cDovL2Vkd2FyZHMueWFsZS5lZHUvY2dpLWJpbi9uZXdwaGlsby9nZXRvYmplY3QucGw/Yy4zNTozLndqZW8 (accessed December 4, 2017).

way necessary for Christianity, but they disagreed concerning their importance. Edwards viewed affections as substantial; his opponents, accidental. Here was the fundamental rift. By undermining affections, the opponents of the revival were surrendering something crucial to the Christian faith. "True religion, in great part, consists in holy affections."[49]

Edwards's idea of the affections differed severely from Chauncy's. Leaning upon the thought of his Reformed forebears, Edwards had thought deeply about the will since his early days at Yale. Now, in the midst of the Great Awakening, confronted with Chauncy's assault against affections, Edwards countered that the affections were higher movements of the soul connected with the will. This point shows up in both *Some Thoughts* and *Affections*. In the latter he wrote, "The affections are no other, than the more vigorous and sensible exercises of the inclination and will of the soul" (2:96). Affections and will are not "two faculties in the soul."[50] Understanding and will are the soul's two faculties, although even there a clear distinction cannot always be made.[51] The will is synonymous with the "inclination" and "heart." Sometimes people are little inclined or disinclined toward things, and

49. *WJE* 2:95. Compare *Some Thoughts*: "It seems to me that the very life and soul of all true religion consists in them [affections]" (*WJE* 4:297).

50. *WJE* 4:297. In *Some Thoughts*, Edwards presented this assertion guardedly: "I *humbly conceive* that the affections of the soul are not properly distinguished from the will, as though they were two faculties in the soul" (*WJE* 4:297, emphasis mine).

51. *WJE* 2:272. As has been seen, this loose view of the faculties was not uncommon among Edwards's teachers. Despite some remarks that seem to be to the contrary, Edwards believed the distinctions between faculties were vital. Edwards's understanding of the faculties was complex. Around 1747, Edwards, in his reorganization of his notebook "The Mind," wrote, "the Scriptures are ignorant of the philosophic distinction of the understanding and the will, and how the sense of the heart is there called knowledge and understanding" (*WJE* 6:389). This comment comes from an outline, so it answers few questions. It should probably not be read as a repudiation of that "philosophic distinction," as much as an affirmation of the "sense of the heart" as Edwards understood it. Elsewhere he said there was a "vast difference between the understanding and the will" (*WJE* 6:387). Indeed, even though the "sense of the heart" includes both ideal apprehension and a "sense" of the will, Edwards's distinction between the speculative understanding and the sense of the heart makes no sense without some real distinction between the faculties. Edwards repeatedly referred to the soul's faculties in his writings without qualification. Given that Edwards understood the *one God* himself to have perfect understanding and will, which was the *logos*, or Son, and *agape*, or Spirit, is it any wonder that Edwards insisted that man is indivisible while having faculties of understanding and will? Compare Holmes, *God of Grace*, 180–84. In *Freedom of Will*, he even chides his opponent Chubb for conflating the understanding and the will (*WJE* 1:223). Compare *WJE* 1:133, 172, 370. For these reasons, commentaries like that of Stephen J. Nichols, that say Edwards "*repudiates* the separation of the will or heart from the intellect," ought to be tempered. See Stephen J. Nichols, *An Absolute Sort of Certainty: The Holy Spirit and the Apologetics of Jonathan Edwards*

at other times more so. The will and affections are not substantially different, but the affections are the will's more intense actions.[52]

By connecting the affections with the will, Edwards argued for the legitimacy of heightened love and desire for God in religion.[53] Edwards believed this was the Bible's teaching.[54] This was hardly an innovation, however. Because holiness cannot be too great in a person, "holiness of the heart or will," which Edwards identified with religious affections, cannot be too high. Affections are extremely high in heaven, and not blameworthy there. "Therefore these things in the saints and angels in heaven, are not to be despised and cashiered by the name of great heats and transports of the passions" (4:298). The Scriptures describe the Spirit as powerful, so one should expect some religious affections to be powerful. Nevertheless, high affections must be the right kind. Edwards wrote to Thomas Prince in late 1743 that "it is not the degree of religious affections, but the nature of them that is chiefly to be looked at" (16:126).

Edwards's observations on the role of preaching in moving the affections illustrate how high affections and the will converge with the understanding. Holy affections cannot be raised too high. For this reason God prescribed ordinances for the church (2:114–16). Those who said that Awakening preaching had raised inordinate affections did not understand how affections worked. The mind must

(Phillipsburg, NJ: P&R Publishing, 2003), 56. Compare Scott Oliphint, "Jonathan Edwards: Reformed Apologist," *WTJ* 57 (1995): 165–86.

52. Compare *In True Conversion Men's Bodies Are in Some Respect Changed as Well as Their Souls* (hereafter *True Conversion*), where Edwards connected "spirit" in 1 Thess. 5:23 to "the will, including the tongue, the disposition and affections of the mind, as in Ephesians 4:23." Edwards, *The Blessing of God*, 300.

53. Susan James, who tends to lump all seventeenth-century language under "passion," writes, "For early-modern writers, desire—and feeling such as love, anger, or sadness—are all states of a single kind, and all answer to the rough definition of passion outlined above. In holding this view, seventeenth-century theorists differ sharply from contemporary philosophers, who tend to distinguish desires and emotions. . . . Consequently, their category of passions does not coincide with modern interpretations of the category of emotion, from which desire is excluded." Susan James, *Passion and Action: The Emotions in Seventeenth-Century Philosophy* (Oxford: Clarendon Press, 1997), 7.

54. In *Some Thoughts*, Edwards succinctly laid out the biblical defense that consumes several pages in *Affections*, "*If we take the Scriptures for our rule*, then the greater and higher are the exercises of love to God, delight and complacence in God, desires and longings after God, delight in the children of God, love to mankind, brokenness of heart, abhorrence of sin, and self-abhorrence for sin; and the 'peace of God which passeth all understanding' [Phil. 4:7], and 'joy in the Holy Ghost' [Rom. 14:17], 'joy unspeakable and full of glory' [1 Pet. 1:8]; admiring thoughts of God, exulting and glorying in God; so much the higher is Christ's religion, or that virtue which he and his apostles taught, raised in the soul" (*WJE* 4:299, emphasis mine). See "The Nature of Affections" and especially note 78 in this chapter.

apprehend an object for the will to be inclined appropriately toward it. Edwards continued: "All affections do certainly arise from some apprehension in the understanding; and that apprehension must either be agreeable to truth, or else be some mistake or delusion; if it be an apprehension or notion that is agreeable to truth, then it is light in the understanding."[55]

As Edwards said in *Religious Affections*, "Holy affections are not heat without light" (2:266). By increasing doctrinal understanding, preachers can increase the affections of their hearers.[56] An "affectionate way of preaching" better ornaments the truthfulness of the matter preached "than a moderate, dull, indifferent way of speaking of 'em" (4:386–87). Yet this manner of preaching must be "agreeable to the nature of the subject, and ben't beyond a proportion to its importance and worthiness of affection." Neither should it be forced nor should it be strained.[57] The content of preaching demands high affections, and therefore sermons should be given with high affections. Although revival opponents disparaged affectionate preaching, they misunderstood human nature. People do not need theological light alone, but heat with that light. "Our people don't so much need to have their heads stored, as to have their hearts touched" (4:388). Affections are crucial to religion.

55. *WJE* 4:386. Compare the role of 1 Tim. 1:17 in Edwards's conversion (*WJE* 16:792–93). Sereno E. Dwight wrote, "[Edwards] regarded [the revival] caused—not by appeals to the feelings or the passions, but—by the truth of God brought home to the mind, in a subordinate sense by the preaching of the gospel, but in a far higher sense by the immediate agency of the Holy Spirit." *Memoirs of Jonathan Edwards*, in *HW*, 1:lxxi. Strobel asserts, "Importantly, Edwards does not allow for affections to exist outside the understanding, even though they are a kind of willing." *Theology*, 214. Compare Danaher, *Trinitarian Ethics*, 123. Even so, Edwards's category "sense of the heart" merges understanding and will better than the category "affections" by itself.

56. C. C. Goen says, "Edwards was far from denying the noetic dimension of religious address and response, but he held firmly that the dynamic center of a willing, acting, personal being lies not in the intellect but in the disposition." "Editor's Introduction" in *WJE*, 4:66. Clyde A. Holbrook, when stressing that affections were of the will *and* mind (or reason), seemed to miss Edwards's point that the will is seated in the soul. *The Ethics of Jonathan Edwards: Morality and Aesthetics* (Ann Arbor: The University of Michigan Press, 1973), 28.

57. *WJE* 4:387. Later Edwards continued: "I don't think ministers are to be blamed for raising the affections of their hearers too high, if that which they are affected with be only that which is worthy of affection, and their affections are not raised beyond a proportion to their importance, or worthiness of affection. I should think myself in the way of my duty to raise the affections of my hearers as high as possibly I can, provided that they are affected with nothing but truth, and with affections that are not disagreeable to the nature of what they are affected with" (*WJE* 4:387).

Affections and the Passions Edwards did not fully reject the "philosophical" model. Although connecting affections with the will and "the noblest part of the soul," he differentiated "affections" from "passions." Both *Some Thoughts* and *Religious Affections* repeat this distinction. "'Tis true," he conceded, "distinction must be made in the affections or passions. There's a great deal of difference in high and raised affections, which must be distinguished by the skill of the observer" (4:297). He continued,

> There are many exercises of the affections that are very flashy, and little to be depended on; and oftentimes there is a great deal that appertains to them, or rather that is the effect of them, that *has its seat in animal nature, and is very much owing to the constitution and frame of the body; and that which is sometimes more especially obtains the name of passion*, is nothing solid or substantial. But it is false philosophy to suppose this to be the case with all exercises of affection in the soul, or with all great and high affections; and false divinity to suppose that religious affections don't appertain to the substance and essence of Christianity: on the contrary, it seems to me that the very life and soul of all true religion consists in them. (4:297, emphasis mine)

Edwards observed that many use these two terms interchangeably, although "common speech" allows for some differentiation.

> Affection is a word, that in its ordinary signification, seems to be something more extensive than passion; being used for all vigorous lively actings of the will or inclination; but passion for those that are more sudden, and whose effects on the animal spirits are more violent, and the mind more overpowered, and less in its own command.[58]

Edwards's distinction between affections and passions was not new. As previous chapters made clear, Christian theologians for many centuries had articulated it in varying ways. Edwards's genius notwithstanding, given the reiteration of the distinction in the writings of Reformed Scholastics, Puritans, and early Enlightenment thinkers, it would have been extraordinary for Edwards to have concluded this independently.[59] For Edwards, affections were in the nobler soul, and passions were associated with the body and animal spirits. Affections are the stronger inclinations of the mind *via* the will; passions are violent, overpowering the mind.

58. *WJE* 2:98. Edwards referred to violent passions again later in *Affections*. "I have known of several persons, that have had a fond desire of something of a temporal nature, through a violent passion that has possessed them, and they have been earnestly pursuing the thing they have desired" (*WJE* 2:174).

59. See Dixon, *From Passions to Emotions*, 75. See Chapters 2 and 3.

Edwards's description of passions as "violent" echoes a reoccurring theme, from John Calvin to Thomas Manton and Solomon Stoddard. This specific point of distinction even could have come from the French philosopher Nicolas Malebranche (1638–1715).[60] In *The Search after Truth*, Malebranche not only saw a love for good in the will, but also the "*natural inclinations.*" These latter inclinations are the passions, the motions affecting the soul "upon the occasion of extraordinary motion in the animal spirits."[61] Before the Fall, Adam mastered his passions, but since the Fall "the body acts too forcefully on the mind."[62] The "union of the soul and body" is such that the soul's inclinations and passions are "sensible" by "motions in the spirits." Passions, however, especially result in the violent descent of the "animal spirits . . . into the heart."[63]

Edwards believed that passions, contrary to affections, should be controlled by the mind. For example, revival promoters attacked the clergy and authorities under the banner of "Christian fortitude." Edwards countered that true Christian fortitude strengthens the mind "through grace" to govern "the evil, and unruly passions and affections of the mind," and to follow "good affections and dispositions" (2:350). The revival's excesses were the very exercise of the passions true fortitude should

60. Nicolas Malebranche was a French priest and philosopher. Descartes had a tremendous influence on him, but Malebranche disagreed with on the nature of ideas. Malebranche believed that the object of human perception is an idea in the mind of God. He is also known for occasionalism, which holds that natural causes are occasional and really caused by God, the one true cause. See Thomas M. Lennon, introduction to Nicolas Malebranche, *The Search after Truth: with Elucidations of The Search after Truth*, eds. Thomas M. Lennon and Paul J. Olscamp, Cambridge Texts in the History of Philosophy (Cambridge: Cambridge University Press, 1997), vii–xxiii. Jason Skirry argues that Malebranche's psychology comes more from Augustinianism than Cartesian influences. See "Malebranche's Augustinianism and the Mind's Perfection," *Publically accessible Penn Dissertations*, Paper 179 (PhD diss., University of Pennsylvania, 2010), 7–55. http://repository.upenn.edu/edissertations/179 (accessed December 4, 2017). Also see Elmar J. Kremer, "Malebranche on Human Freedom," in *The Cambridge Companion to Malebranche*, ed. Steven Nadler (Cambridge: Cambridge University Press, 2000), 190–219. Francis Hutcheson also cited Malebranche's definition of passions when distinguishing affections and passions. *Essay*, 26–27.

61. Malebranche, *The Search after Truth* §5.1 (337). Malebranche defined the passions of the soul as "impressions from the Author of nature that incline us toward loving our body and all that might be of use in its preservation." Ibid., §5.1 (338). All references to *The Search after Truth* will provide the book, chapter, and section (if applicable), followed by the page number in parenthesis.

62. Ibid., §5.1 (339). Humanity's first sin reordered the union of soul and body. Ibid., §5.1 (340).

63. Ibid., §5.3 (349). Compare the "violent passions" mentioned in §5.2 (345). Malebranche's comments on the difference between "intellectual joy" and "sensible joy" are also instructive. Ibid., §5.3 (356). Also see ibid., §5.7 (377) and §5.8 (389).

suppress. Holy inclinations are to be set free; sinful passions were to be controlled by the mind.

Thomas Dixon argues that Edwards's view of the affections and passions is "substantially in tune" with older Christian views.[64] Edwards did consider affections motions of the soul, not of the body. Yet Dixon notes two possible signs of Descartes's influence on Edwards: Edwards's strong dualism and his belief that sometimes people could be affected by bodily change. Dixon charts this as part of a larger movement toward Cartesian thought.[65] He further argues that Edwards's emphasis on the "new inward perception" shows the extent to which he was a person of his times.[66]

Although Edwards disagreed with his opponents' reduction of the importance of high affections in religion, his answer to the problem contained both a revision of and agreement with their view. Edwards at times critiqued the Awakening's radicals by maligning their "affections" as passionate movements rather than gracious affections. He agreed with Chauncy that the passions are to be controlled in religion; "passions" were "more sudden . . . and more violent," with great effect on the "animal spirits." Against his opponents, he said affections are not distinct from the higher movements of the soul, and do not come from the "animal nature." They are the vigorous inclinations of the soul.

Affections and the Body Early modern thinkers did not place the locus of human affectivity in the body *per se*. The passions were passions of the body; the body was not acting upon the soul, but vice versa. In this classic understanding, the sensitive appetites (lower soul) act upon the rational soul.[67] Jonathan Edwards largely agreed with this perspective.

The strength of inclination in the will varies. The affections are the more vigorous motions of the will. As the soul's attraction toward or aversion from an object grows, "the soul comes to act vigorously and sensibly, and the actings of the soul are with that strength that . . . the motion of the blood and animal spirits

64. *From Passions to Affections*, 77.

65. Ibid., 78. Dixon cites Isaac Watts to have embraced Cartesian dualism to a much greater extent than Edwards.

66. Dixon writes, "That even gracious affections were treated by Edwards as a species of inner 'perception' analogous to bodily sensations is a telling sign of the extent to which thought about the mind in terms of sensation and (external and internal) perceptions, through the influence of Descartes and Locke, had come to displace models of acts of the will and movements of the soul." Ibid., 80.

67. Dixon, *From Passions to Emotions*, 58–59. He writes, "Vicious passions were primarily disorders of the will, which would imply that they were strictly passions of the body (that the disordered will acted upon the body to make it suffer passion)." Ibid., 59. See Chapters 2, 3. Steven Edwards summarizes Edwards in this way: "As forces stir within the heart, 'gracious' affections bridge the rational and material and promote an active, visceral engagement with the supernatural and spiritual." *JEE*, s.v. "Affections."

begins to be sensibly altered" (2:96). Human affections always produce "by the laws of the union of soul and body" some bodily effect.[68] Still, for Edwards, bodily sensations that accompany affections were not necessary, or else spirit beings would have no affections (which is impossible). "It is not the body, but the mind only, that is the proper seat of the affections. The body of man is no more capable of being really the subject of love or hatred . . . than the body of a tree, or than the same body of man is capable of thinking and understanding."[69]

Yet, Edwards conceded, although the affections are not seated in the body, the body may affect "the present emotion of the mind" (2:118). Edwards rarely used the word *emotion*, and, when he did, he spoke in a figurative sense of the movements of the mind or as a synonym for *movement*. For instance, in *Affections* Edwards described this way the disembodied affections of heaven: "Now it would be very foolish to pretend, that because the saints in heaven be not united to flesh and blood, and have no animal fluids to be moved (through the laws of union of soul and body), with those great emotions of their soul, that therefore their exceeding love and joy are no affections."[70] Therefore, when Edwards said that the body may affect an emotion of the mind, he meant that the body can influence higher movements of the soul.

Ideally, bodily effects from the affections do not get out of hand, something Edwards had seen happen too often. Those guilty of excess did not rightly view together the perfections of God that evoke "awe and reverence" with those that "win and draw and encourage us." Some of the awakened overemphasized God as a righteous Judge, others as loving Father. This "defect" resulted in "odious"

68. Later in *Affections*, Edwards said, "All affections whatsoever, have in some respect or degree, an effect on the body" (*WJE* 2:132). Compare *WJE* 2:269. Compare Malebranche, *Search after Truth*, §5.2 (345–46).

69. *WJE* 2:98. In the 1740 sermon *True Conversion*, Edwards argued against "a false notion" that the body is itself depraved. He explains this view to hold that "Adam, when he sinned, had the nature of his body poisoned by the forbidden fruit that he ate and thereby his bodily appetites that before were mediate became extreme, and so the body infected the soul and made that corrupted." Edwards countered that corruption "begins in the soul and from thence infects the body." When God sanctifies a person, he sanctifies the soul and the results are shown in the body. Sanctification's effect on the body is not "on the flesh or blood or constitution," but in "the natural and necessary senses of the influence and gracious act which the soul has over the body." *True Conversion*, in *The Blessing of God*, 303. In conversion, the saint denies the "appetites of the body" and "those appetites are lessened and brought lower by his appetites' being infused into the soul." Ibid., 304. In other words, spiritual desires overwhelm those of the body.

70. *WJE* 2:113. Compare *WJE* 2:120, where Edwards referred to the "emotions of the mind." Edwards clearly contrasted the "emotion of the mind" from the "constitution of the body" (*WJE* 2:118).

revival expressions, such as "laughter or a light behaviour" while speaking of religious things.[71]

Instead, the two visions of God (as righteous Judge and loving Father) should together control the "motion of animal spirits" from improprieties. Edwards knew of instances in which those "greatly affected" by Christ's "dying love" and the happiness of heaven had seen the "great emotion" of "their animal spirits" from the joys of the Christian faith "quieted" by "a deep sense of the awful, holy majesty of God." The beautiful symmetry of "the majesty and grace of God" together "caused a more happy sedateness and composure of body and mind" (4:465).

For Edwards, the passions influenced the best religious experiences very little. Saints should avoid "the violent affections and most vehement motions of the animal spirits" and other bodily effects. Christianity thrives when gracious affections are (1) little affected by natural affections, (2) proportioned by both the terror of and love for God, and (3) raised most highly. The highest affections, reserved for the eschaton, are ordered by God and "shall not have so great an effect in proportion on the body" (4:466).

Finally, Edwards said that the bodily effect of affections can generate still more affections. According to Edwards, the soul alone is the source of affections, although the body and "animal spirits" move in such a way as to cause the mind's affections to be heightened (2:269). Sometimes the body can be the first cause of affections. By the Devil or some other cause, the animal spirits move in some people, "causing persons to feel pleasantly in their bodies," and in a way that is similar to "the exhilaration of the mind."[72] Such motions, of course, do not come from the mind at all, even though the subject may interpret it as the Spirit's work. "And then," Edwards continued, "the mind begins to be affected and raised: there is first great joy; and then many other affections, in a very tumultuous manner, putting all nature, both body and mind, into a mighty ruffle" (2:269).

These concerns also surface in Edwards's letters toward the end of the revival, where he blamed the bodily effects in individuals outside Northampton for his own congregation's problems. The Northampton believers concluded that they had received less of God's grace when they saw believers in other towns with greater "raptures and violent emotions of the affections, and a vehement zeal, and what they called boldness for Christ." This gave the awakened in Northampton "a deep and unhappy tincture." For Edwards, this "plainly" showed that the "degree of grace" does not depend on the "degree of joy" or "zeal," but the nature of the affections. Those who experienced great bodily effects often had lacked "the temper

71. *WJE* 4:465. Comparing the mid-1730s and early 1740s revivals, Edwards said the latter was better at the beginning, since the affections were "attended with greater solemnity, and greater humility and self-distrust" (*WJE* 16:125).

72. The view that the Devil could function as a supernatural agent on the passions was held by both Edwards and Chauncy. See Dixon, *From Passions to Emotions*, 92ff.

of Christians, in their conduct since."[73] Edwards saw other instances of those who experienced such "extraordinary joys and emotions of mind, with frequent great effects on their bodies," who had since acted like exemplary Christians. Counterfeit affections can show the same bodily characteristics as gracious ones. Therefore, "the goodness of [a] person's state is not chiefly to be judged of by any exactness of steps, and methods of experiences, . . . but . . . we must judge more by the spirit that breathes, the effect wrought on the temper of the soul, in the time of the work, and remaining afterwards" (16:126).

Affections and Religion Edwards wrote an entire treatise (or more) on the affections and religion, an effort Perry Miller called "the most profound exploration of the religious psychology in all American literature."[74] This discussion will examine how Edwards understood the function and relationship of affections and passions in religion, most closely attending to his ideas in *Some Thoughts*. General remarks on the argument of *Religious Affections* will follow.

Edwards said that Christian experiences are almost always mixtures of nature and grace. Believers never experience anything "wholly pure, entirely spiritual." Edwards observed, "There is very often with that which is spiritual a great mixture of that affection or passion which arises from natural principles: so that nature has a very great hand in those vehement motions and flights of the passions that appear." Consequently, people with different "tempers" saw different outward effects from the same cause. "I know remarkable instances of this," Edwards added (4:459).

To clarify this point, Edwards introduced an additional observation. Religious experience can not only be a mixture of gracious affections and natural affections, but can also be a mixture of gracious affections and passions: "sometimes there is not only a mixture of that which is common and natural with gracious experience, but even that which is animal, that which is in a great measure from the body, and is properly the result of the animal frame" (4:459–60). The affections Christians "feel" for God do not always arise out "spiritual principles." Love for God may arise out of self-love; love for other saints may be mixed with natural love for others. Zeal is most susceptible to such a "corrupt mixture" of grace and nature. Zeal can be good and virtuous, but in new believers, "'tis very apt to be mixed with human passion, yea, with corrupt hateful affections, pride and uncharitable bitterness, and other things that are not from heaven but from hell" (4:460).

When mixed experiences are raised high, the passions strengthen from unchecked spiritual pride that can arise from those experiences. This may eclipse the work of grace. When those awakened have the "great external effects and vehemence of the passions, and violent agitations of the animal spirits," it is most often caused by a dangerous mixture of nature and grace (4:461). When people have affection for God, they talk about him; when they do not, they talk about

73. By temper, I read Edwards to mean the mental state or condition. Compare *OED*, s.v. "Temper."

74. *Jonathan Edwards*, 177.

themselves. "In others their earnestness seems to arise from a great mixture of human passion, and an undue and intemperate agitation of the spirits, which appears by their earnestness and vehemence not being proportioned to the nature of the subject they insist on, but they are violent in everything they say, as when speaking of things of greater weight" (4:462). Edwards especially cautioned against those persons who only speak of some pleasurable "bodily pressure," without having a clear idea of anything in their minds.

Spiritual experiences often degenerate when natural and gracious affections are mixed, Edwards warned. Natural affections aggravate when they are indulged by those with mixed affections. The gracious affections, in turn, decrease. Therefore, the Devil stirs up natural affections, hoping that "the experiences of some persons who began well, come to but little else but violent motions of carnal affections, with great heats of the imagination, and a great degree of enthusiasm, and swelling of spiritual pride" (4:467). This explains the origin of many heresies and enthusiasts.[75]

Edwards knew that religious truth can easily produce natural affections. The glories of heaven and love of God can stir up the natural affection of self-love. Natural, social principles can easily manufacture the mutual fellowship saints enjoy (4:467–68). The mixture of grace and nature is inevitable, and Edwards even cautioned against avoiding it altogether (4:469–71). Yet, Christians should be aware that the Devil will exploit the natural element in this mixture to produce harmful passions and ill effects.

Another problem Edwards identified is that the imagination can both legitimately attend religious affections and illegitimately stir up natural affections. The Devil often excites the imagination and stirs up the affections. Gracious affections never immediately suggest something to the imagination; instead, they supply a spiritual sense of the moral excellency of divine things (2:216–18). Strong gracious affections often excite the imagination because of "men's infirmity in the present state" (2:217). On this point Edwards in *Affections* cites the Cambridge Platonist John Smith. Smith's "remarkable" comments compared the experience of those drawn to the natural goodness of religion to the "faster" growth of the seed on the stony ground in Jesus's parable:

75. For Edwards, as for many in the Reformed tradition (and beyond), enthusiasts were those who claimed to have received inspired revelation from the Spirit outside the Scripture. Chauncy expanded the definition to dismiss the emphasis on high affections in the Awakening. See Martin, "'Violent Motions.'" The charge of enthusiasm against Edwards continues today. For example, see Maurice W. Armstrong, "Religious Enthusiasm and Separatism in Colonial New England," *HTR* 38 (1945): 111–40; Douglas L. Winiarski, "Jonathan Edwards, Enthusiast? Radical Revivalism and the Great Awakening in the Connecticut Valley," *CH* 74:4 (2005): 683–739; Michael McClymond, *Encounters with God* (New York: Oxford University Press, 1998), 107–12; and (to a somewhat lesser extent) Lambert, *Inventing the "Great Awakening."* Compare Conrad Cherry, *Theology*, 164–76; John D. Hannah, "Jonathan Edwards, the Toronto Blessing, and the Spiritual Gifts: Are the Extraordinary Ones Actually Ordinary Ones?" *TrinJ* (1996): 167–89.

> And as the motions of our sense and fancy and passions, while our souls are in this mortal condition, sunk down deeply into the body, are many times more vigorous, and make stronger impressions upon us, than those of the higher powers of the soul, which are more subtle, and remote from these mixed animal perceptions: that devotion which is there seated, may seem to have more energy and life in it, than that which gently, and with a more delicate kind of touch, spreads itself upon the understanding, and from thence mildly derives itself through our wills and affections. But however, the former may be more boisterous for a time, yet this is of a more consistent, spermatical and thriving nature.[76]

Edwards appreciated Smith's view that the attraction to the natural goodness of religion is not a mark of true piety, as well as Smith's explanation for how desire for natural goodness stirs up false affections and passions.

Edwards further recognized that the bodily effects of the affections were largely shaped by custom, and that individuals influence the outward expressions of affections in others. "These things," he observed, "have a vast influence in the manner of persons manifesting their joys, whether with smiles and an air of lightness, or whether with more solemnity and reverence" (4:472). Disapproving of all outward demonstrations of the affections is therefore "very unreasonable and prejudicial to the interest of religion," because some of them benefit Christianity. Edwards, however, disagreed with those who wanted such expressions "wholly unlimited." People should not be encouraged to let external expressions go "to the utmost length that they feel themselves inclined to." Such actions should be wisely restrained, or else the affections will be more and more natural. When this happens, individuals grow "louder and louder," until their "behavior becomes indeed very absurd." "These things," Edwards added, "experience proves" (4:473).

Religious Affections

Edwards's *Religious Affections*, published in 1746, is the Northampton minister's fullest treatment of the nature of true religion. Where *Distinguishing Marks* and *Some Thoughts* considered the evidence of the Spirit's work in a revival, Edwards narrowed the scope of *Affections* to a discussion of the saving work of the Spirit.[77] *Affections* has three parts. The first part discusses the nature of affections; the

76. *WJE* 2:218–9 n6. See Chapter 3. For the citation, see Smith, *Select Discourses*, 400–01.

77. *WJE* 2:89. On *Affections*, see Smith, "Editor's Introduction," in *WJE* 2:1–89; McDermott, *Seeing God*; Murray, *Jonathan Edwards*, 251–67; Smith, "Religious Affections and the 'Sense of the Heart,'" in *PCJE*, 103–15; Nichols, *Jonathan Edwards*, 107–24; Marsden, *Jonathan Edwards*, 284–90; Walton, *Jonathan Edwards*; Danaher, *Trinitarian Ethics*, 117–56; Haykin, *Jonathan Edwards*, 121–35; Storms, *Signs of the Spirit*; Smart, *Jonathan Edwards's Apologetic*; Craig Biehl, *Reading* Religious Affections: *A Study Guide to Jonathan Edwards' Classic on the Nature of True Christianity* (Birmingham, AL: Solid Ground Christian Books, 2012);

second part offers twelve "no signs" of the Spirit's work (those signs that are neither positive nor negative); and the third part suggests twelve signs that the Spirit has graciously worked in an individual. Edwards explained that holy affections come only through the Holy Spirit supernaturally changing the heart. As such, *Affections* serves as a defense and explanation of the centrality of affections in saints. It carries a more somber and mature tone, still insisting that Spirit had been at work in the Awakening, but recognizing its mixed results.

The Nature of Affections The first part of *Affections* defines affections as heightened movements of the will distinct from passions, and affirms their necessity in true Christianity. Edwards's defense of gracious affections shows the extent to which Scripture shaped his convictions concerning the role of affections against Chauncy. "[W]ho will deny" Edwards asked, "that true religion consists, in a great measure, in vigorous and lively actings of the inclination and will of the soul, or the fervent exercises of the heart" (2:99). To argue this, Edwards inundated his readers with Scripture summarized under ten proofs.[78]

Not every affection, Edwards stressed, is truly spiritual in character, but that does not make them any less central to true religion.[79] Therefore, those who

and Strobel, *Theology*, 209–24. Also see Gregory Clapper, *John Wesley on Religious Affections*, and *JEE*, s.v. "*Treatise Concerning Religious Affections* (1746)."

78. Besides 1 Pet. 1:8, the main text for *Affections*, Edwards cited the following Scriptures in this section: Rom. 12:11; Deut. 10:12; 6:4-5; 30:6; 2 Tim. 3:5; 2 Tim. 1:7; Lk. 24:32; 1 Cor. 13:13; Ps. 146:5; Jer. 17:7; Ps. 31:24; 33:18; 147:11; Rom. 8:24; 1 Thess. 5:8; Heb. 6:19; 1 Pet. 1:3; Prov. 8:13; Pss. 97:10; 101:2-3; 119:104, 128; 139:21; Isa. 26:8; Pss. 27:4; 42:1-2; 63:1-2; 84:1-2; 119:20; 73:25; 143:6-7; 130:6; Song 3:1-2; 6:8; Mt. 5:6; Rev. 21:6; Pss. 37:4; 97:12; 33:1; Mt. 5:12; Phil. 3:1; 4:4; 1 Thess. 5:16; Ps. 149:2; Gal. 5:22; Ps. 119:14; Mt. 5:4; Ps. 34:18; Isa. 61:1-2; Ps. 51:17; Isa. 57:15; 66:2; 57:1; Ps. 37:21, 26; Mt. 5:7; 23:23; Mic. 6:8; Hos. 6:6; Mt. 9:13; 12:7; Tit. 2:14; Rev. 3:15-16, 19; Mt. 22:37-40; Rom. 13:8; Gal. 5:14; 1 Tim. 1:5; 1 Cor. 13; 2 Cor. 5:14-15; 12:19; Phil. 4:1; 2 Tim. 1:2; 2 Cor. 2:4; 1 Thess. 2:7-8; Phil. 1:8; Phlm. 12, 20; 2 Cor. 8:16; Phil. 2:1; 2 Cor. 2:4; Col. 2:1; Rom. 9:2; 2 Cor. 6:11; 1 Thess. 2:8; Rom. 1:11; Phil. 1:8; 4:1; 2 Tim. 1:4; 2 Cor. 1:12; 7:7, 9, 16; Phil. 1:4; 2:1-2; 3:3; Col. 1:24; 1 Thess. 3:9; Phil. 4:10; Phlm. 1:7; Phil. 2:1, 7; 2 Cor. 7:13; 7:4; 6:10; 2:14; 2 Thess. 1:4; Rom. 5:3; Phil. 1:20; 2 Cor. 11:2-3; 2:4; Acts 20:19, 31; Ps. 69:9; Jn 2:17; Mk 3:5; Lk. 19:41-42; 13:34; 22:15; Mt. 15:32; 18:34; Lk. 7:13; Mt. 9:36; 14:14; Mk 6:34; Jn 11; 13-17; Prov. 4:18; Jn 4:14; 6:40, 47, 50-51, 54, 58; 1 Jn 3:15; 1 Cor. 13:8-12; 2 Pet. 1:12-13; Eph. 4:11-12, 16; 1 Tim. 1:3-5; 2 Cor. 1:24; Ps. 95:7-10; 2 Chron. 36:13; Isa. 63:17; Acts 19:9; Rom. 9:18; Jn 12:40; Heb. 3:8, 12, 13; Ezek. 11:19; 36:26; 2 Kgs 22:19; Job 39:16; and Prov. 28:14.

79. Edwards wrote, "[T]he degree of religion is rather to be judged of by the fixedness and strength of the habit that is exercised in affection, whereby holy affection is habitual, than by the degree of the present exercise: and the strength of that habit is not always in proportion to outward effects and manifestations, or inward effects, in the hurry and vehemence, and sudden changes of the course of the thoughts of the mind" (*WJE* 2:118–19).

oppose affections are in "great . . . error," and would likely damage others spiritually (2:119). In words directly aimed at Chauncy and his ilk, Edwards was clear:

> The prevailing prejudice against religious affections at this day, in the land, is apparently of awful effect, to harden the hearts of sinners, and damp the graces of many of the saints, and stunt the life and power of religion, and prelude the effect of ordinances, and hold us down in a state of dullness and apathy, and undoubtedly causes many persons greatly to offend God, in entertaining mean and low thoughts of the extraordinary work he has lately wrought in this land. (2:121)

More serious yet, Edwards warned, they were hazarding their own eternal destiny.

Because true religion consists in holy affections, ministers should use religious exercises and ordinances to move hearts.[80] God created human beings so that they might fulfill their chief end through true religion (2:122). Nothing is more worthy of high affections than the Triune God. "How great cause have we therefore to be humbled to the dust, that we are no more affected!" (2:123). Human beings ought to repent of their hardness of heart and cold affections toward God.

"No Signs" In part two of *Affections*, Edwards suggested twelve "no signs" of gracious affections. Like *Distinguishing Marks*, the "no signs" are those experiences or evidences that neither prove nor disprove religious affections. These signs often cut both ways, denying the opposition that which they believed definitively disproved the Spirit's work, as well as discouraging those revival sympathizers and their own evidence. Consequently, the second part shows Edwards's intent to strike a mediating position on the Awakening.

The "no signs" that neither prove or disprove affections are: very highly raised affections, affections with great bodily effects,[81] much talk of religious matters, affections apparently coming from some source external to the person experiencing them, affections with sudden Bible passages coming into the mind, affections with an "appearance of love" (2:146), diverse kinds of affections running

80. In a statement that shows Edwards's concern that the downplaying of affections was a new and dangerous development, Edwards noted that stirring up true affections "formerly" had been "highly approved of and applauded" (*WJE* 2:121–22).

81. Affections always affect the body: "So subject is the body to the mind, and so much do its fluids, especially the animals spirits, attend the motions and exercises of the mind, that there can't be so much as an intense thought, without an effect upon them. Yea, 'tis questionable, whether an embodied soul ever so much as thinks one thought, or has any exercise at all, but that this is some corresponding motion or alteration of motion, in some degree, of the fluids, in some part of the body" (*WJE* 2:132).

after each other,[82] affections with convictions and comforts in a certain order,[83] affections that move people to perform religious acts or attend "the external duties of worship" (2:163), affections that result in expressions of praise and glory to God, affections which the subject believes are divine, and affections that impress other true saints or even "win their hearts" (2:181). Indeed, false religious affections may have many of the external characteristics of true religious affections.[84] But equally, many complaints of the Old Light opposition were groundless.

Signs of Gracious Affections What, then, are the signs that the affections someone has experienced are truly saving? Before answering this, Edwards cautioned that the evidences do not give anyone certain knowledge of the nature of the affections in others or even in themselves when they are living in a carnal and unchristian way.[85] God's intent is that assurance of salvation comes from in the growth of inward grace demonstrated in good works.

The first sign of gracious affections is that they come from the "*spiritual, supernatural* and *divine*" work of the Spirit in a person's heart.[86] Here Edwards reiterated the "new sense" doctrine. The "new sense" is a gracious work wherein the Holy Spirit communicates himself to the saints and, as no unbeliever so enjoys the Spirit's graces, produces affections completely new from any natural affections (2:203–05). As a result of the Spirit's grace, the saint perceives within him new

82. Edwards said, "Let us suppose a person who has been for some time in great exercise and terror through fear of hell . . . being made to believe, through some delusion of Satan, that God has pardoned him, and accepts him as the object of his dear love, and promises him eternal life. . . . [W]hat various passions would naturally crowd at once, or one after another, into such a person's mind? It is easy to be accounted for, from mere principles of nature, that a person's heart, on such an occasion, should be raised up to the skies with transports of joy, and be filled with fervent affection" (*WJE* 2:149).

83. On this point, Edwards warned against affections mixed with the imagination. Some people's bodily constitution lends itself to greater terrors. Such have impressionable imaginations, which influences the affections, "so affection and imagination act reciprocally, one on another, till their affection is raised to a vast height, and the person is swallowed up, and loses all possession of himself" (*WJE* 2:156–57).

84. Compare Edwards's *Personal Narrative*, where he explained away his early affections: "many are deceived with such affections" (*WJE* 16:791).

85. *WJE* 2:193. Edwards explained, "'Tis not God's design that men should obtain assurance in any other way, than by mortifying corruption, and increasing in grace, and obtaining the lively exercises of it. And although self-examination be a duty of great use and importance, and by no means to be neglected; yet it is not the principle means, by which the saints do get satisfaction of their good estate. Assurance is not be obtained so much by self-examination, as by action" (*WJE* 2:195).

86. *WJE* 2:197. Edwards believed that the Spirit gives *common* (non-saving) religious affections to unbelievers and *special* (saving) religious affections to believers. See, for example, *WJE* 2:183, 199–200, 206–07. Also see Chapter 5.

affections unlike any experienced before, making the Spirit's work "a new spiritual sense."[87] This new spiritual sense is not, Edwards stressed, a new faculty, but "new principles of nature." The Spirit does not give a new understanding or will, but he exercises those natural faculties in a new way.[88] Furthermore, the spiritual sense is not an idea in the imagination, because this would be tantamount to an idea from natural sensation.[89] On the contrary, spiritual sense is wholly unlike the "external senses," those "inferior powers" that "the beasts have in as great perfection as we." Such would amount to "turning Christ, or the divine nature in the soul, into a mere animal" (2:213).

The second sign of gracious affections is that they are objectively grounded in the "transcendently excellent and amiable nature of divine things" as they are in themselves, and not in their relation to the saint.[90] In other words, holy affections are directed toward divine realities, not because of the natural benefits they bring, but because divine things are spiritually glorious in and of themselves. Here Edwards explained the difference between self-love and love for God. Self-love may have a *role* in gracious affections, but it never serves as the *foundation* of true affections. Love for God may arise out of self-love, but this love is natural without a spiritual principle undergirding it. Because of self-love, the affections of hypocrites "are often renewedly set agoing" (2:246).

The foundation of the saint's love for God is the beautiful glory of God himself, not the benefits received from God. Saints are grateful for receiving these benefits, but this is the overflow, the "secondary joy" of seeing God as desirable in himself (2:250). Note the contrast: "that which is the true saint's superstructure, is the hypocrite's foundation" (2:251). Meanwhile, the high affections of the hypocrite, built upon self-love, spin out of control: "their affections rise higher and higher, till they sometimes are perfectly swallowed up: and self-conceit, and a fierce zeal rises withal; and all is built like a castle in the air, on no other foundation but imagination, self-love and pride" (2:252).

The objective ground of affections leads into Edwards's third sign. If the "first objective ground" of affections is the excellency of divine things, then the kind of excellency in divine things (upon which gracious affections are grounded) is the

87. *WJE* 2:205. Sarah Rivett puts the locus of Locke's influence on the human perception of the Spirit's work: "Thoughts, purified through the Lockean empirical model, transform the sensory impressions of spiritual things into real knowledge of the unseen" (*Science*, 299).

88. *WJE* 2:206. Compare "Images," no. 166, in *WJE* 11:112.

89. Edwards said the imagination can raise passions "to an exceeding great height" (*WJE* 2:217).

90. *WJE* 2:240. In his *Personal Narrative*, Edwards related that after his conversion, upon reading 1 Tim. 1:17, he "began to have a new kind of apprehensions and ideas of Christ, and the work of redemption, and the glorious way of salvation by him. I had an inward, sweet sense of these things, that at times came into my heart; and my soul was led away in pleasant views and contemplations of them" (*WJE* 16:793).

moral excellency or holiness of God. Thus, "[t]hose affections that are truly holy, are primarily founded on the loveliness of the moral excellency of divine things" (2:253). Saints love the things of God primarily because those things are holy.

Christians have a "new supernatural sense," a "certain divine spiritual taste," different from any of the body's senses. Thus, spiritual experience is completely different from the experiences of the unregenerate, "as the sweet taste of honey is diverse from the ideas men get of honey by looking on it or feeling of it." Edwards was clear: "the beauty of holiness is that thing in spiritual and divine things, which is perceived by this spiritual sense: this is the sweetness that is the proper object of this spiritual taste" (2:259–60).

This principle is tremendously important, as it suggests a way of testing whether one's affections are gracious or not, especially with love and joy. The chasm that separates saints from the unregenerate is split by self-love. Natural humans love God because it betters their situation, but saints find God beautiful in himself, the "*bonum formosum*" (2:262). The mark of true saints is that they have affections that find God beautiful for his moral excellency.[91]

The fourth sign explains the role of understanding in the affections. "Gracious affections do arise from the mind's being enlightened, rightly and spiritually to understand or apprehend divine things." Thus, "Holy affections are not heat without light" (2:266). The mind's affections must be grounded in the mind.

Although the affections should be grounded in the mind, there are, nevertheless, many examples of affections arising from elsewhere, including from the body. On this point, Edwards reiterated the distinction between the soul and body. Natural "affections" can be driven into something like hysteria, when natural affections, coming from bodily sensations, are driven higher by more sensations.[92] By contrast, the mere improvement of the understanding resulting in higher affections is not a

91. Edwards explained, "Various kinds of creatures show the difference of their natures, very much, in the different things they relish as their proper good, one delighting in that which another abhors. Such a difference is there between true saints, and natural men: natural men have no sense of the goodness and excellency of holy things; at least for their holiness; they have no taste of that kind of good; and so may be said not to know that divine good, or not to see it; it is wholly hid from them: but the saints, by the mighty power of God, have it discovered to them: they have that supernatural, most noble and divine sense given them, by which they perceive it: and it is this that captivates their hearts, and delights them above all things; 'tis the most amiable and sweet thing to the heart of a true saint, that is to be found in heaven or earth; that which above all others attracts and engages his soul; and that wherein, above all things, he places his happiness, and which he lots upon for solace and entertainment to his mind, in this world, and full satisfaction and blessedness in another. . . . There are many high affections, great seeming love and rapturous joys, which have nothing of this holy relish belonging to 'em" (*WJE* 2:262).

92. *WJE* 2:269. Edwards emphasized the calm of true affections. In his *Personal Narrative*, he said heaven is a place "where reigns heavenly, sweet, calm and delightful love, without alloy" (*WJE* 16:798).

mark of gracious affections either. Only a "spiritual, supernatural understanding," enjoyed by saints alone, is the proper ground of gracious affections. This spiritual understanding "consists in a sense of the heart of the supreme beauty and sweetness of the holiness or moral perfection of divine things, together with all that discerning and knowledge of things of religion, that depends upon, and flows from such sense." This is not mere speculative knowledge, but a knowledge where the mind "relishes and feels" (2:272). Gracious affections impart a divine "sense of the heart," a "spiritual taste" of the moral excellency and spiritual beauty of divine things.[93] For Edwards, the heart's knowledge of divine things may be compared to "the sweet taste of honey": only the one who has tasted truly knows it (2:272).

The sense of the beauty of holy things is a crucial sign of gracious affections. No fallen, natural person has this sense, and when God puts it in the soul, that person is profoundly changed, more so than one born blind would be changed at receiving sight. Therefore, "those affections that arise wholly from any other kind of knowledge, or do result from any other apprehensions of the mind, are vain" (2:275). Doctrinal knowledge, conviction of sin, appreciation of Christ's death ("which all men love, as they love themselves"), and an understanding of Scripture are therefore not properly marks of gracious affections (2:276–80).

Edwards aimed the "sense of the heart" doctrine directly against the Awakening's enthusiasts who claimed to have received new revelation from the Holy Spirit. Spiritual understanding differs strongly from "all kinds and forms of enthusiasm, all imaginary sights of God and Christ and heaven, all supposed witnessing of the Spirit; . . . all enthusiastical impressions and applications of the words of Scripture; . . . and all interpretations of the mystical meaning of the Scripture" (2:286). These were not "the divine sense and relish of the heart," but mere "impressions in the head," the common fare of the enthusiasts from the Pythagoreans to the "French Prophets."[94]

93. *WJE* 2:272, *passim*. For more on the "sense of the heart," see chapter 5. Cochran suggests that *Affections* may have "an underlying Hutchesonian framework in Edwards's conception of moral formation." Elizabeth Agnew Cochran, *Receptive Human Virtues: A New Reading of Jonathan Edwards's Ethics* (University Park: Pennsylvania State University Press, 2010), 111. She says that Edwards's developed his idea of the "spiritual sense" from "Hutcheson's ideas of apprehension and approbation." Ibid., 112. To prove this, Cochran not only observes points of similarity on Hutcheson and Edwards's emphasis on approbation, but also observes that, in the midst of his discussion on the spiritual sense, Edwards cites the entry on "taste" from Ephraim Chamber's *Encyclopedia* (which was influenced by Hutcheson). Ibid., 114–15; compare *WJE* 2:282–83 and *Cyclopedia: or an Universal Dictionary of Arts and Sciences* (London: n.p., 1728), s.v. "Taste." Although Cochran notes plausible similarities, Chapter 4 of this book showed that Edwards's emphasis on "sense" was likely from other sources and interests.

94. Chauncy penned under the name "Antienthusiasticus" a tract on the "French Prophets," whom Gaustad aptly described as the "epitome of enthusiasm." The publication linked the Awakening to this notorious group. Gaustad, *The Great Awakening*, 89. In the

Edwards's fifth sign is that "[t]ruly gracious affections are attended with a reasonable and spiritual conviction of the judgment, of the reality and certainty of divine things." Christian doctrines are indisputably true to a saint. Christian truth is "of great weight" to believers, having "a mighty power upon their hearts, and influence over them, and in some measure answerable to infinite importance" (2:291–92). A true conviction of Christianity arises, not merely from reason (although it is at least a reasonable conviction), but from "a spiritual belief or conviction." In defining "spiritual conviction," Edwards returned to the idea "spiritual understanding": "a spiritual conviction of the truth of the great things of the gospel, is such a conviction, as arises from having a spiritual view of apprehension of those things in the mind."[95]

The sixth sign of gracious affections is that they come with "evangelical humiliation." Evangelical humiliation is "an answerable frame of heart, consisting in a disposition to abase themselves, and exalt God alone" (2:312). "This is," Edwards insisted, "a great and most essential thing in true religion."[96] Such humility is the primary part of the Christian's self-denial. This kind of humility is void of hypocritical shows and pretense. The more grace a person has, the more they apprehend how holy and righteous God is, and the more they consider their own state, even if gracious, to be "less worthy of notice" (2:327). This matter was again for Edwards "of great importance."[97]

Edwards proposed a seventh sign of gracious affections: "they are attended with a change of nature" (2:340). Edwards said: "Conversion . . . is a great and universal

preface to *French Prophets*, Chauncy said that in Christian history "the *sober* and *judicious* among Christians, those who place Religion in that which is the Life and Essence of it" were not susceptible to the visions and ecstatic behaviour seen in the revivals. Ibid., vi. Chauncy did not deny that true religion was mixed with the recent enthusiasm, but added that the displays of enthusiasm was not the reason to think so. Ibid., viii, ix. Chauncy wrote, "And, if, when their Passions are subsided, and their Imaginations cooled, they now continue to discover a truly Christian *Temper* and *Conduct*, there is Reason to hope well concerning them." Ibid., x. The book's name is a tongue-in-cheek response to Edwards's *Faithful Narrative*. Charles Chauncy, *The Wonderful Narrative: Or a Faithful Account of the French Prophets, their Agitations, Extasies, and Inspirations* (Glasgow: Robert Foulis, 1742).

95. *WJE* 2:296. Compare Edwards's *Personal Narrative*, where pre-conversion doubts were proof of his unregenerate state (*WJE* 16:792). Compare "Misc. 782," in *WJE* 18:465–66.

96. *WJE* 2:312. This emphasis also arises in Edwards's *Personal Narrative*, where he wrote, "My wickedness, as I am in myself, has long appeared to me perfectly ineffable, and infinitely swallowing up all thought and imagination; like an infinite deluge, or infinite mountains over my head" (*WJE* 16:802).

97. *WJE* 2:336. Edwards explained, "[O]ut of such a [humble] heart as this, that all truly holy affections do flow. . . . All gracious affections, that are a sweet odor to Christ, and that fill the soul of a Christian with an heavenly sweetness and fragrancy, are brokenhearted affections. All truly Christian love, either to God or men, is a humble broken hearted love" (*WJE* 2:339).

change of the man, turning him from sin to God" (2:340–41). This change is permanent, though regeneration does not inviolably change the "natural temper" (2:341). The Spirit is united to the faculties of man, to live there. Therefore holy affections last.

The eighth sign of gracious affections is that they are characterized by a Christ-like meek and "lamblike . . . spirit and temper" (2:344–45). Since Christians are being renewed into the image of Jesus Christ, they should be like him, especially in meekness. For this reason, Christ taught that believers should become like children. Although some people downplay Christian meekness because of the biblical emphasis on Christian fortitude, Edwards turned this argument on its head. The *extremists* had nullified Christian fortitude in their bad behavior. Christian fortitude is "an exceeding diverse thing from a brutal fierceness, or the boldness of beasts of prey." Edwards explained: "True Christian fortitude consists in strength of mind, through grace, exerted in two things; in ruling and suppressing the evil, and unruly passions and affections of the mind; and in steadfastly and freely exerting, and following good affections and dispositions, without being hindered by sinful fear, or the opposition of enemies" (2:350). Christ Jesus himself did battle this way (2:351). False fortitude arises out of pride. Those confused about Christian boldness are also confused about its zeal: "'Tis indeed a flame, but a sweet one: or rather it is the heat and fervor of a sweet flame" (2:352).

Ninthly, gracious affections "soften the heart, and are attended and followed with a Christian tenderness of spirit" (2:357). Counterfeit affections "harden the heart" and instill in hypocrites "some kind of passions" flowing out of self-love. Consequently, false affections "stupefy the mind" against true affections. To such people, the Christian life in all its difficulties becomes repulsive. Therefore, "[s]uch persons as these, instead of embracing Christ as their Saviour from sin, they trust in him as the Saviour of their sins" (2:358). True saints, however, become like children before God. Anticipating that some people may object to a tender spirit because a Christian can boldly approach God, Edwards replied that those who have the Spirit "speak trembling"; they are clothed "with a kind of holy fear in all their behavior towards God and man" (2:361).

The tenth sign of true religious affections is their "beautiful symmetry of proportion" (2:365). Although believers never have perfectly proportioned affections in this life, their affections are never characterized by the "monstrous disproportion" one observes in hypocrites. True saints both hope and fear; their joy is joined to sorrow for sin; their love for God is complemented by a love for others.[98] Saints not only fellowship with other believers socially, but also with God himself secretly.

98. In his *Personal Narrative*, Edwards said that, after conversion, his mind had "a sweet sense of the glorious majesty and grace of God, that I know not how to express. I seemed to see them both in a sweet conjunction: majesty and meekness joined together: it was a sweet and gentle, and holy majesty; and also a majestic sweetness; an awful sweetness; a high and great, and holy gentleness" (*WJE* 16:793).

The eleventh sign of gracious affections is that "the higher they are raised, the more is a spiritual appetite and longing of soul after spiritual attainments, increased" (2:376). By contrast, hypocrites rest satisfied in their present state. Saints desire ever-increasing holiness and affection for God. Although hypocrites may have some such longings, they quickly die out. God designed religious affections to satisfy humanity's great appetites. The satisfaction of this appetite is permanent, not like natural appetites which are sated, only to arise again. Spiritual things satisfy the soul adequately if people will but apply themselves to taking them in. "Spiritual good is of a satisfying nature; and for that very reason, the soul that tastes, and knows its nature, will thirst after it, and a fullness of it, that it may be satisfied" (2:379). Therefore, in saints, there remains "a holy breathing and panting after the Spirit of God, to increase holiness, as natural to a holy nature, as breathing is to a living body" (2:382–83).

The most significant sign of holy affections is the twelfth, that they "have their exercise and fruit in Christian practice" (2:392). For Edwards, such obedience and holiness were universal, not only to avoid wickedness, but to obey universally God's positive commands. Such obedience is the "main business" of Christians. "All Christ's peculiar people, not only do good works, but are zealous of good works" (2:387). This twelfth sign also implies that universal obedience continues "to the end of life" (2:388). Edwards argued that since gracious affections are spiritual, they have a profound effect on the individual in holiness and resisting temptation. He then tied this principle, that holy affections result in Christian practice, to all the preceding signs.

As Edwards saw it, the supernatural work of the indwelling Spirit necessarily results in a changed life.[99] "Regeneration," he explained, "which is that work of God in which grace is infused, has a direct relation to practice; for 'tis the very end of it, with a view to which the whole work is wrought" (2:398). Holy practice is the "*principle sign*" whereby one's sincerity may be judged (2:407). The biblical mandate for good works does not respect mere external acts; true external obedience is "the obedience of the soul" (2:422). God's view of obedience depends upon a human being's "superior part" (2:424). The soul, or internal part of human persons, cannot be severed from his external acts.

The Scriptures emphasized good works. Works are the proper evidence of Christian faith. Humans cannot discern the secret state of other people's hearts, for the affections are endlessly complex:

> The ways are so many whereby persons' affections may be moved without any supernatural influence, the natural springs of the affections are so various and so secret, so many things have oftentimes a joint influence on the affections, the imagination (and that in ways innumerable and unsearchable), natural temper, education, the common influences of the Spirit of God, a surprising concourse of affecting circumstances, an extraordinary coincidence of things in the course

99. Wilson, *Virtue*, 95–96.

> of men's thoughts, together with the subtle management of invisible malicious spirits; that no philosophy or experience will ever be sufficient to guide us safely through this labyrinth and maze, without our closely following the clue which God has given us in his Word. (2:460)

The solution to the confusion, Edwards insisted, is to return to what Christ and the apostles emphasized: judging professors on their Christian practice.

Conclusion

Psychology was central to the controversy that led Jonathan Edwards and Charles Chauncy to offer different responses to the Great Awakening. Drawn from his Puritan heritage, his theological reflections on the nature of God and humanity, and, even more, his interpretation of Scripture, Edwards argued that affections were indispensable for true religion. Affections are different from passions. He conceded that the Awakening had its share of natural affections (affections where the Spirit of God was entirely absent), but argued that this did not discount the work as a whole—the challenge was in distinguishing what was true from what was false. Chauncy disagreed on all these points. Religious affections were to be reined in and subject to reason. Given the widespread abuses, the Awakening as a whole, Chauncy argued, was not of God.

Throughout his discussion of affections, Edwards maintained a threefold distinction between bodily passions, natural affections, and gracious affections.[100] Passions were connected with humanity's body or animal part. Affections were spiritual with a small *s*, connected with the soul and will. Passions, properly defined, are *never* gracious. They are the result of sense appetites and violent movements of the body. Animals experience passions, but they never have affections. Affections are the stronger movements of the will. They can be natural or gracious. By natural, Edwards meant that such affections were not the result of the saving grace of the Holy Spirit. The love between family members or friends is often natural. Even affection for God can be natural. Holy affections, on the other hand, come from the Holy Spirit. They cannot be manufactured, although God has given his Word whereby an object for holy affections can be supplied to the will through the understanding. As the proper object of affections, the Word ought to be preached with an appropriate external demonstration of affections.

Note again that Edwards's notion of both affections and passions differs strongly from contemporary notions of emotions. First, affections and passions both refer to inclinations toward good and aversions from evil. For Edwards, affections referred to the inclinations and aversions of spiritual realities, and passions to those of sense objects. Edwards recognized the role of the bodily effects of affections and passions, but he consistently distinguished those effects from the affections and

100. *Pace* Danaher, *Trinitarian Ethics*, 123.

passions themselves. It is misleading to say that Edwards emphasized emotions in the Great Awakening against Charles Chauncy, for Edwards conceived of affections in a way entirely different from the way most people speak of emotions today. Like many Christian theologians before him, Edwards distinguished the higher desires of the will from the brutish sensitive appetites. Affections were not about feeling something physically, but in themselves entirely distinct from such bodily movements, although such physical effects may occur with them. Affections were the soul's inclinations toward spiritual realities.

Finally, Edwards—although recognizing the necessary effect on bodies from the affections of embodied souls—was pessimistic concerning the value of such bodily effects for religious affections. Granted, Edwards was unconcerned by what ministers should condone as legitimate bodily effects of affections. In Edwards's view, ministers should not even concern themselves with the bodily effects. "Ministers are made the watchmen of men's souls, and not their bodies," he said (4:300).

Bodily effects, however, which occur because of human weakness, are not the focal point of affections. The effects are deceptive and tend to pernicious spiritual results. When Edwards wanted to characterize the enthusiasts, he often disparaged the extravagance of the bodily effects of their natural affections. Well-proportioned affections prevented the bodily effects from getting "out of hand." In the age to come, Edwards posited, affections will not so trouble the body. Not only did Edwards find the body's movements to be purely natural, he cautioned against making too much of them. For Edwards, to focus on the bodily effect of affections was to miss the entire point of holy affections.

Chapter 7

AFFECTIONS AND CHRISTIAN APOLOGY: THE LATER PSYCHOLOGY OF JONATHAN EDWARDS

I am a little world made cunningly
Of elements and an angelic sprite,
But black sin hath betrayed to endless night
My world's both parts, and, oh, both parts must die.
You which beyond that heaven which was most high
Have found new spheres, and of new lands can write,
Pour new seas in mine eyes, that so I might
Drown my world with my weeping earnestly,
Or wash it if it must be drowned no more
But oh it must be burnt! Alas the fire
Of lust and envy have burnt it heretofore,
And made it fouler; let their flames retire,
And burn me, O Lord, with a fiery zeal
Of Thee and Thy house, which doth in eating heal.[1]

— John Donne

In his later years—leading up to his dismissal from Northampton and to the end of his life—Edwards reiterated and elaborated his understanding of affections. He repeatedly used this affective psychology as a weapon against moralist philosophy and Arminian theology. This chapter explores Edwards's thought in these later years. During this time, Edwards used his understanding of affective psychology to bolster his apologetic for Reformation theology in his monumental treatises, such as *The Life of David Brainerd*, *Freedom of Will*, *Original Sin*, and *Two Dissertations*. Edwards's sermons and "Miscellanies" will also be considered.

1. *John Donne's Poetry*, 2nd ed., ed. Arthur L. Clements, Norton critical edition (New York: Norton, 1992), 117.

Historical Survey

With the passing of the Awakening and its controversies, Edwards's personal life descended into greater difficulties. In 1750, after Edwards famously rejected the Half-Way Covenant of his grandfather and predecessor Solomon Stoddard, the Northampton congregation removed him as their pastor. In 1751, Edwards became the minister in Stockbridge, Massachusetts, but this pastorate quickly degenerated into vitriol between him and the other townspeople working with Stockbridge's school for Indians. Edwards left Stockbridge in February 1758 to become president at Princeton's College of New Jersey. He died just over a month later, due to complications from a small pox inoculation.

The Dismissal at Northampton

In the years following the Great Awakening, Edwards saw its conquests abate. He tried to consolidate the Awakening's gains by leading the Northampton church in a covenant renewal. By 1743 (just a couple of years after the Awakening's heights in 1741), Edwards wrote to a friend, "There is a great decay of the work of God amongst us, especially as to the Awakening and converting influence of the Spirit of God" (16:108). Amidst increasingly desperate circumstances, Edwards published in 1747 *An Humble Attempt*, a proposal to ignite international prayer for revival.[2] In 1749, he published the "epilogue to his revival writings," *The Life of David Brainerd*.[3] Soon, however, another doctrinal controversy would undo his ministry in Northampton.

The original New England Congregationalists believed that a local church was a covenanted community of visible saints. If a person desired access to the church's benefits, including the Lord's Supper, that individual needed first to profess to be a genuine Christian. This profession was called "owning the covenant." Baptism was insufficient; all had to embrace the promises of God through Christ symbolized in their baptism. This standard quickly became problematic. Parents who had not owned the covenant—who had made no verbal profession of experiencing God's saving grace—nevertheless brought their children for baptism, a church benefit they hoped to claim despite their standing apart from the church.

In 1657, the Massachusetts clergy decided to permit all baptized parents (even if they were not church members) the privilege of having their own children baptized. The clergy, however, did not permit the uncovenanted to partake of the Lord's Supper. This compromise became known as the Half-Way Covenant.

2. Stein, "Editor's Introduction," in *WJE* 5:29–48; the text is in *WJE* 5:308–436. The full title is *An Humble Attempt to Promote Explicit Agreement and Visible Union of God's People in Extraordinary Prayer.*

3. Norman Pettit, "Editor's Introduction," in Jonathan Edwards, *The Life of David Brainerd*, vol. 7 of *The Works of Jonathan Edwards* (New Haven, CT: Yale University Press, 1985), 10.

Solomon Stoddard made use of the Half-Way Covenant in his early ministry, but saw few people own the covenant and become full church members. In 1679, he proposed two ideas somewhat radical to New England Congregationalists. First, there was no more half-way membership—if one was baptized and mentally agreed to the church's confession, that person was a full church member. Second, everyone baptized could enjoy the Lord's Table, whether one professed to be a Christian, or not. Stoddard reasoned that the Lord's Table was a converting ordinance and that regeneration could not be absolutely proven.[4] Therefore, in Stoddard's view, ministers should not ban from the Table those who had doubts about their standing in divine grace.

When joining his grandfather Stoddard in Northampton, Edwards accepted Stoddard's modifications of the Half-Way Covenant.[5] Yet, over the course of many years, Edwards developed reservations. According to Edwards's remarks in his "Narrative of the Communion Controversy," when he finally studied what the Scriptures said concerning church membership, he concluded that only those who made a profession of godliness could be admitted to church sacraments (12:507–08).

In part, Edwards had seen too many people insincerely agree to the church's confession to gain admittance to the Lord's Supper.[6] In Edwards's view, the Scriptures condemned hypocrisy and the apostolic church itself only admitted saints to its membership. This was a position with which the Northampton church did not agree (complications arising from Edwards's pastoral ministry may have exacerbated the situation).[7] In 1749, Edwards published his views on church

4. Perry Miller, "Solomon Stoddard, 1643–1729," *HTR* 34 (1941): 277–320. On this controversy see Increase Mather and Solomon Stoddard, *Increase Mather vs. Solomon Stoddard: Two Puritan Tracts*, Research Library of Colonial America (New York: Arno Press, 1972); Robert G. Pope, *The Half-Way Covenant: Church Membership in Puritan New England* (Princeton, NJ: Princeton University Press, 1969); and E. Brooks Holifield, *The Covenant Sealed: The Development of Puritan Sacramental Theology in Old and New England, 1570–1720* (New Haven, CT: Yale University Press, 1974); David D. Hall, "Editor's Introduction," in *Ecclesiastical Writings*, vol. 12 of *The Works of Jonathan Edwards*, ed. David D. Hall (New Haven, CT: Yale University Press, 1994), 17–62; Marsden, *Jonathan Edwards*, 29–33.

5. *WJE* 16:271. See Hall, "Editor's Introduction," in *WJE* 12:44–46; Tracy, *Jonathan Edwards*, 73–74; Marsden, *Jonathan Edwards*, 129. *Pace* William J. Danaher, Jr., "By Sensible Signs Represented: Jonathan Edwards' Sermons on the Lord's Supper," *Pro Ecclesia* 7 (1998): 261–87.

6. See *WJE* 16:344–45; Also see Jonathan Edwards, *Sermons and Discourses, 1743–1758*, vol. 25 of *The Works of Jonathan Edwards*, ed. Wilson H. Kimnach (New Haven, CT: Yale University Press, 2006), 489–91; and Wilson, *Virtue*, 303. Compare *WJE* 2:417.

7. The pastoral difficulties between the Great Awakening of the early 1740s and the Communion Controversy of the late 1740s included disagreements over salary, the infamous "Bad Book" episode, and instances of church discipline gone awry. For more, see Winslow,

communion in *An Humble Inquiry*. Nevertheless, his church removed him from his office on June 22, 1750.[8] After Solomon Williams responded to *An Humble Inquiry*, Edwards printed a 1752 rejoinder in *Misrepresentations Corrected, and Truth Vindicated*.[9]

Stockbridge and Princeton

Even before the dismissal from Northampton was official, Edwards was anxious about his future. He wrote to his friend William McCullough, "I am now separated from the people, between whom and me there was once the greatest union. Remarkable is the providence of God in this matter. In this event, we have a great instance of the instability and uncertainty of all things here below."[10] After a visit to Stockbridge, Massachusetts, during the winter of 1750, Edwards accepted a call from the church in 1751. The town was on Massachusetts's western "frontier," established some twenty years earlier to evangelize and civilize the Mahican Indians.

Edwards found the Indian school floundering. The Williamses, Stockbridge's most influential family, were allowing financial and political concerns to undermine their care for the Indians. This led to conflict between Edwards and the Williams family. In 1753, Edwards hit one of his lowest points. He still owned the Northampton home and suffered embarrassing financial duress with Stockbridge's lower salary. Meanwhile, the Williamses were working behind Edwards's back to remove him from Stockbridge. Edwards wrote to a friend in October, "I am still meeting with trouble, and expect no other as long as I live in this world."[11] Despite the Stockbridge troubles, in those years Edwards finished three great theological treatises: *Freedom of Will* (1754), *Two Dissertations* (finished in 1755, published in 1765), and *Original Sin* (1758).[12]

Jonathan Edwards, 200–22; Tracy, *Jonathan Edwards*, 147–70; Murray, *Jonathan Edwards*, 271–87; Gura, *Jonathan Edwards*, 135–67; Marsden, *Jonathan Edwards*, 291–305, 341–56.

8. The full title is *An Humble Inquiry into the Rules of the Word of God, Concerning the Qualifications Requisite to a Compleat Standing and full Communion in the Visible Christian Church*. See *WJE* 12:166–348.

9. Solomon Williams's answer to Edwards is *The True State of the Question Concerning the Qualifications Necessary to Lawful Communion in the Christian Sacraments* (Boston: S. Kneeland, 1751).

10. *WJE* 16:358. Also see *WJE* 16:284; 347–54. Also see Marsden, *Jonathan Edwards*, 357–74; Winslow, *Jonathan Edwards*, 247–69; and Murray, *Jonathan Edwards*, 353–70; Arthur Cushman McGiffert, Jr., *Jonathan Edwards*, Philosophy in America (1932, repr., New York: Harper & Row, 1980), 139–64.

11. *WJE* 16:610. See Murray, *Jonathan Edwards*, 381.

12. Douglas A. Sweeney observes: "Edwards did manage to produce a tremendous amount of writing [in Stockbridge]. But he did so in the midst of a remarkably busy schedule, one full of the same pastoral priorities that had always governed his life." "Editor's

Four days after the September 1757 death of Aaron Burr (Edwards's son-in-law and the president of the College of New Jersey in Princeton), the College trustees wrote Edwards inviting him to take Burr's place. Edwards would finally become president in February 1758. Just a month later, Edwards died on March 22 due to complications from a smallpox inoculation. He left incomplete his magnum opus, *A History of Redemption*, which he described as a "body of divinity in an entire new method, being thrown into the form of an history, considering the affair of Christian theology, as the whole of it, in each part, stands in reference to the great work of redemption by Jesus Christ, which I suppose is to be the grand design of all God's designs."[13]

Affections in the Later Years

Edwards's affective psychology was vital to his important theological agendas in the later years, especially as part of his arsenal in the apologetic of Calvinist Christianity. The affections were not a convenient category Edwards invented to justify the Awakening. Throughout his later ministry, he emphasized them both in his preaching and published writings. Although the late controversies allowed Edwards the opportunity to develop his thought, his late sermons and writings perpetuated the traditional rubric of the affections he accepted as a young man with remarkable consistency. True religion, original sin, doxology, and morality were among his chief theological concerns later in life, and to all these matters Edwards intricately connected human affectivity.[14]

"Better Pleasures": Edwards's Rubric for Affections

After the Great Awakening, Edwards's understanding of affections and passions changed little. Although one could argue that Edwards's understanding of the revival developed (especially as the situation in Northampton soured), his understanding of the affections did not.

In the sermon *The Peace Christ Gives His True Followers*, the distinction between affections and passions repeated themes from Edwards's earlier sermons.[15] From

Introduction," in Jonathan Edwards, *The "Miscellanies" [Entry Nos. 1153–1360]*, vol. 23 of *The Works of Jonathan Edwards* (New Haven, CT: Yale University Press, 2004), 3. On Edwards as missionary, see Stephen J. Nichols, "Last of the Mohican Missionaries: Jonathan Edwards at Stockbridge," in *The Legacy of Jonathan Edwards*, 47–63 and Rachel M. Wheeler, "Edwards as Missionary," in *Cambridge Companion to JE*, 196–214.

13. *WJE* 16:727–28. See John F. Wilson, "Editor's Introduction," in *WJE* 9:1–109.

14. See Simonson, *Jonathan Edwards*, 22. See Hoopes, "Calvinism and Consciousness from Edwards to Beecher," in *JEAE*, 205–25.

15. Kimnach observes: "Perhaps in a reaction to certain abuses during the Great Awakening, there is a repeated emphasis upon the preeminence of reason as one of the

Jn 14:27, Edwards preached, "That peace which Christ, when he died, left as a legacy to all his true saints, is very diverse from all those things which the men of this world bequeath to their children when they die" (25:540). Christ's peace includes reconciliation with God and peace among other Christians. His grace brings peace to Christian souls through a view of divine beauty, "and to a relish of that good which is a man's proper happiness," leading "the soul to its true center" (25:543). Grace orders the soul, setting "reason on the throne and subjects the senses and affections to its government" (25:544). Edwards said, "Grace tends to tranquility, as it mortifies tumultuous desires and passions, subdues the eager and insatiable appetites of the sensual nature and greediness after the vanities of the world" (25:544). Thereby saints' souls are restored, and peaceful affections reign reasonably over sense passions. This is what Christ leaves his heirs. Humans, however, leave their heirs earthly wealth, pomp, and glory. These empty shadows cannot satisfy the soul the way Christ's peace does. "Christ's peace is a reasonable peace and rest of soul" (25:546). The world blinds and confuses the faculties. The pursuit of earthly pleasures brings only unrest. He who seeks "carnal peace," shuns reason and "[turns] beast as fast as he can" (25:547). Meanwhile, Christ's peace is reason's "great friend" (25:547).

In other sermons, Edwards warned against carnal appetites. In *The Beauty of Piety in Youth*, Edwards urged Northampton's young people to abandon fleshly appetites. "'Tis unreasonable, not becoming a rational creature" for them to indulge "[b]ase and brutish" pleasure that "debases the nature [of man]."[16] Edwards often warned the young people that carnal appetites were strongest in youth.[17] The only

chief results of grace in this life" (*WJE* 25:536–37). Despite this speculation, Kimnach notes, seemingly to the contrary, that Edwards had likely preached the sermon in Northampton sometime earlier, and later corrected it when candidating in Canaan in the summer and fall of 1750, which is the edition of the sermon cited in this paper.

16. *WJE* 25:108. Compare *Youth and the Pleasures of Piety*, in *WJE* 19:82–83.

17. *WJE* 25:108. Compare Edwards's funeral sermon for his own Jerusha, *Youth is Like a Flower That is Cut Down*, in *WJE* 22:324–25. In another sermon from Eccl. 11:9-10, Edwards warned, "When young people will follow their own youthful disposition and indulge themselves in vain mirth & pleasure, God will surely bring 'em into Judgment for those things and they will end in sorrow." 856. Sermon on Eccl. 11:9-10 (February 7, 1746), in *Sermons, Series II, 1747*, vol. 65 of *Works of Jonathan Edwards Online*, ed. Jonathan Edwards Center (New Haven, CT: Yale University, 2008), L.1v, http://edwards.yale.edu/archive?path=aHR0cDovL2Vkd2FyZHMueWFsZS5lZHUvY2dpLWJpbi9uZXdwaGlsby9nZXRvYmplY3QucGw/Yy42Mzo0LndqZW8= (accessed December 4, 2017). Young people, he explained, do not have greater corruption, but "the natural appetites are at the greatest height at that age." Ibid., L.7r. This is not due to their soul as much to "the different state of their bodies" being "more capable of outward pleasures and delights." Edwards warned his hearers that if they indulge their lusts, God will bring sorrow to their hearts and eternal pain to their bodies. Ibid.

way for happiness in youth is to follow Christ. Such "have better pleasures" and "[t]he sweetest gratification of appetites" (25:108–09). Carnal appetites themselves are not sinful, yet they account for human weakness in this world: "much indwelling sin, much temptation, an heavy-molded frail body, and a world of carnal objects" keep saints from Christ (25:231).

Edwards even turned human passions and appetites into a rational argument for the afterlife. In "Misc. 1205," Edwards noted that God provides corresponding means to satisfy all creatures' appetites. For birds and animals, God has given good things "suitable, proportionable and adequate" to fill their appetites. Given the large desires of human soul, God alone can satisfy them.[18] Because God satisfies with sensual good other creatures' appetites, and because human desires are satisfied in God alone, there must be an afterlife: "And will he not make provision for the best, most rational, noble appetites in the world, the desires of virtue and love to God? Would he so order things that, the higher these appetites are, the more disappointment men must suffer, the more must they be crossed, which is the case if there be no future state?" ("Misc. 1205," 23:126).

As for the carnal appetites of humans, Scripture teaches by type that they must be mortified. Both Isa. 28:9 and Ps. 131:2 compare renunciation of the flesh to weaning a child off his mother's milk. "And then the objects of our lust are properly called the milk of our mother's breasts, because 'tis the proper nourishment of that

18. If the whole world were given to a saint, his appetite is large enough that it would still lie unsatisfied. "He would not know how to dispose of it for his own good, as the inferior members of the natural body would not know [how] to dispose of things that the body possesses for their good without the eyes of their head." "Misc. 1072," in Jonathan Edwards, *The "Miscellanies," 833–1152*, vol. 20 of *The Works of Jonathan Edwards*, ed. Amy Plantinga Pauw (New Haven, CT: Yale University Press, 2002), 455–56. In *The Terms of Prayer*, Edwards similarly said, "Men's desires are naturally very large. 'Tis no small matter will satisfy the desires of the soul of man:' tis not all the enjoyments of a finite world will do it. A man must have something of a larger extent than heaven or earth in order to it. And godly men's desires of happiness are no less large than others. Godliness regulates men's desires of happiness, and directs them to right objects; but it don't diminish and confine them, or reduce them to straiter limits. God's people's desires of happiness are exceeding extensive; but as extensive as they are, there is great encouragement in this doctrine to go to God with them. They may expose as large desires as they will, God is ready to hear them. God stands ready to give 'em their hearts' desire. . . . Let 'em open their mouth in their desires and prayers as wide as they will, God stands ready to fill them; yea, he would have them open their mouths wide. Ps. 81:10, 'I am the Lord thy God, which brought thee out of the land of Egypt: open thy mouth wide, and I will fill it'" (*WJE* 19:783–84). On Edwards and prayer, see Peter Beck, "Jonathan Edwards on Prayer and the Triune God," in *Taking Hold of God: Reformed and Puritan Perspectives on Prayer*, eds. Joel R. Beeke and Brian G. Najapfour (Grand Rapids, MI: Reformation Heritage Books, 2011), 187–206.

corrupt nature, which we have by natural generation, the proper satisfaction of the appetite of that flesh, which is born after flesh" ("Misc. 862," 20:88). Likewise the circumcision of the heart is a type of a renunciation of carnal pleasures ("Misc. 862," 20:88). Only the supernatural grace of God can overcome such worldly affections (25:516).

In the late 1740s, Edwards returned to his notebook "The Mind," and drew up a list of "Subjects to Be Handled in the Treatise on the Mind."[19] This list of "Subjects" shows how important the affective psychology explained throughout this book remained to him. In his plans for this treatise (which would remain unwritten), Edwards hoped to argue that "affections or passions" were merely "strong and lively exercises of the will," and to show the effect of these movements "on the animal nature" (6:388). He wished to show "the vast difference between the understanding and the will" and to distinguish "natural appetites and rational desires" (6:387–88). Mere understanding also differs from "the sense of the heart," and Edwards planned to demonstrate how "sense of the heart" differed from the will, noting that "the Scriptures are ignorant of the philosophic distinction of the understanding and the will, and how the sense of the heart is there called knowledge and understanding."[20] He desired to discuss the sense appetites, and how they arouse passions.[21] Edwards also planned to prove that,

19. *WJE* 6:386–93. Brown dates Edwards's "Subjects to be Handled," to the late 1740s or early 1750s. "Edwards, Locke, and the Bible," *Journal of Religion* 79 (1999): 380. Fiering notes the importance of moral thought in Edwards's "Subjects to be Handled." Fiering, *Jonathan Edwards's Moral Thought*, 7. It is unfortunate Edwards never wrote this treatise, for it might have prevented confusion concerning his dependence on Locke, whose thought he wanted to address. It is difficult to determine positively Edwards's thought in this list of "Subjects," because Edwards framed many of the subjects as questions or discussions of the extent to which a given proposition is true without resolving it explicitly.

20. *WJE* 6:389. As argued in chapter 5, this statement is not about the lack of a distinction between understanding and will (something Edwards maintained his entire life), but more about the biblical unity of those two faculties as represented in Edwards's idea of the "sense of the heart."

21. Edwards's described his anticipated discussion of sense appetite to include "How far they consist in some present pain, attended with the idea of ease, habitually connected or associated with the idea of such an object. Whether the sight of food excites the appetite of one who is hungry any other way. By what means persons come to long after a particular thing, either from an idea of pleasure or the removal of pain associated, not immediately after the thing itself, but only the pleasure or removal of pain" (*WJE* 6:390).

although humans share much in their body and instincts with animals, they differ in important ways.[22]

In *Freedom of Will*, Edwards maintained the dictum of *Some Thoughts* and *Affections* that the affections were only the more lively exercises of the will (1:309). Edwards also used the distinction between reason and sense appetite to advance his argument.[23] The "will" is "that by which the mind chooses anything," and the actual faculty "will" is "that faculty or power or principle of mind by which it is capable of choosing: an act of the will is the same as an act of choosing or choice" (1:137). Edwards refused to separate will and desire as "Mr. Locke" did: "A man never, in any instance, wills anything contrary to his desires, or desires anything contrary to his will."[24] Edwards's metaphysics of consent, his Trinitarian theology, and his affective psychology all led to the conclusion that will and desire were inseparable.

For Edwards, the will was determined by the strongest motive, or by whatever in the mind most excites volition. All motives must necessarily be held in the understanding. "[W]hat is wholly unperceived, and perfectly out of the mind's view, can't affect the mind at all" (1:142). Yet all motives must "move or excite the will" before the will actually acts. These objects that make motives are considered "*as good*," and the varying objects considered "good" can be many and diverse in strength. Therefore, "the will is *determined* by the greatest apparent good" (1:144). Edwards recognized the complexity of what makes different objects appear good to different individuals, but insisted that the motives that ultimately determined the will was what the soul concluded was the greatest good under the circumstances (1:147).

Traditionally, intellectualists held that the understanding controlled the will, and voluntarists believed that the will was not bound by reason or the understanding. Touching on this debate, Edwards conceded that the will in a sense follows the last dictate of the practical understanding, but, only as the "practical understanding" means the "whole faculty" of apprehension, not merely reason or judgment. Reason can declare something good that the soul does not deem "most agreeable," all things considered. Although the practical understanding is one of many things "put into the scales" in moving the will, it is very difficult to distinguish the mind's

22. *WJE* 6:391–92. Though the soul differs from the body, the soul is typified in nature (*WJE* 6:390).

23. Suggesting reasons people determine good and evil, Edwards said, "It is most agreeable to some men, to follow their reason; and to others, to follow their appetites: to some men, it is more agreeable to deny a vicious inclination, than to gratify it; others it suits best to gratify the vilest appetites" (*WJE* 1:147).

24. *WJE* 1:139. Edwards had previously expressed this disagreement with Locke. See chapter 4.

view of the greatest good from the mind's choosing.[25] For Edwards, the will did not, properly speaking, determine or choose. The will is the "the soul willing."[26]

The will distinguished human beings from animals. "The brute creatures are not moral agents." A moral agent has a "moral faculty," the ability to discern good and to act accordingly (1:165). God is the moral agent of "the greatest possible perfection," understanding good and evil, discerning its worth, and so choosing according to that understanding. The *imago Dei*—that which separates humans from animals—is "in those faculties and principles of nature, whereby he is capable of moral agency" (1:166). Humans lie between God and animals; like animals, they have a body with sense appetites. Like God, humans have intellect and will, rendering them moral creatures.

"New Relish and Appetite": Affections and Religion

Edwards's concern over the role of affections in religion did not stop with the conclusion of the Awakening. In his publications and sermons, he continued to argue for the necessity of divinely given affections distinct from the wild raptures of enthusiasm. He also maintained that true conversion marries a right understanding of the gospel to the heart's sense of the beauty of the holy glory of God.

Edwards's post-Awakening sermons show his continued concern for religious affections. At the 1744 ordination of Robert Abercrombie, Edwards preached

25. *WJE* 1:148, 144. Edwards avoided a full discussion of influence of the practical understanding on the will (*WJE* 1:141). Wilson observes, "Edwards clearly means to eschew then the self-sovereignty implied in the intellectualist maxim 'that the will always follows the last dictate of the understanding.'" *Virtue*, 202. On the relationship of the will and practical understanding, see Mastricht, *Regeneration*, 40–42; Richard Baxter, *The Saint's Everlasting Rest*, in *Works* 23:31–33; Cherry, *Theology*, 34–39; Muller, *The Unaccommodated Calvin*, 159–73; Reinhold Seeberg, "Scholasticism," in *The New Schaff-Herzog Encyclopedia of Religious Knowledge*, ed. Samuel Macauley Jackson (New York: Funk and Wagnalls Co., 1911); and William J. Courtenay, "Voluntarism," in *The Westminster Dictionary of Christian Theology*, eds. Alan Richardson and John Bowden (Philadelphia, PA.: The Westminster Press, 1983).

26. *WJE* 1:172. "When we say, the understanding discerns, we mean the soul in the exercise of that faculty. So when it is said, the will decides or determines, the meaning must be, that the person in the exercise of a power of willing and choosing, or the soul acting voluntarily, determines." Richard A. Muller provocatively argues that Edwards radically departed from traditional Calvinism toward determinism in *Freedom of Will*. "Jonathan Edwards and the Absence of Free Choice: A Parting of Ways in the Reformed Tradition," *Jonathan Edwards Studies* 1 (2011): 1–22, http://jestudies.yale.edu/index.php/journal/article/view/63 (accessed December 4, 2017). Wilson contends that Edwards softened Calvinism's view of secondary causes and expanded its notion of the will's freedom. *Virtue*, 146–224.

from Jn 5:35 that ministers are to be a "burning and shining light." Edwards said a "burning light" means that a minister is to have "his heart filled with much of the holy ardor of a spirit of true piety." A minister never leaves God's truth in the "speculative knowledge," or in mere "outward morality or forms of religion." His piety is in the heart "and burns there" (25:91). Edwards urged Abercrombie not only to burn, but also to be a "shining" light, or pure in his doctrine (25:92). These two kinds of light must always go together, for only then are they shown to be "genuine" and "divine."[27]

Those ministers who are learned but impious will not save many souls. "And if, on the other hand, he be driven on with a fierce and intemperate zeal, and vehement heat, without light, he will be likely to kindle the like unhallowed flame in his people, and to fire their corrupt passions and affections; but will make them never the better, nor lead them a step towards heaven, but drive them apace the other way" (25:96). The minister's beauty was in having the light and fire together (25:99). Turning to the congregation, Edwards urged them not to put out their minister's light "by casting dirt upon it." "[D]on't raise another fire of a contrary nature, against it, viz. the fire of your unhallowed passions, reflecting upon and reproaching him for his faithfulness" (25:101).

Edwards repeatedly used his pulpit ministry to teach true religion.[28] Church congregants, he said, should love their pastors "with an holy affection and esteem," not because "their carnal affections" are "moved" through "fleshly principles gratified by a florid eloquence," but because he speaks the Lord's message (25:174). In a 1747 sermon, Edwards reiterated the teaching of *Some Thoughts* and *Affections* that someone can experience "great joys, after great fears . . . great melting . . . great raptures . . . great zeal," yet not have true religion.[29]

In *True Grace, Distinguished from the Experience of Devils*, a sermon preached before the Presbyterian Synod of New York, Edwards conceded that devils, though they have a great sense of a divine things and powerful affections, have no "holy sense" or "holy affections."[30] This sermon, by addressing the sinful affections of

27. *WJE* 25:95. Edwards said that a minister with only "great speculative knowledge and the wisdom of this world" without "spiritual warmth and ardor," the light or knowledge he imparts is "like the light of an *ignis fatuus*, and some kinds of putrefying carcasses that shine in the dark, though they are of a stinking savor." The affections of ministers lacking understanding are "like the heat of the bottomless pit."

28. Edwards's sermons show that concerns aroused by the Awakening persisted. Edwards warned his flock against those "wild people" who said they had received new inspirations (*WJE* 25:294). Those who believed they had received revelations during the Awakening had now come to nothing (*WJE* 25:299–300).

29. 859. Sermon on 1 Cor. 6:11 (March 1747), in *WJEO*, 65:L.13v, http://edwards.yale.edu/archive?path=aHR0cDovL2Vkd2FyZHMueWFsZS5lZHUvY2dpLWJpbi9uZXdwaGls by9nZXRvYmplY3QucGw/Yy42Mzo3LndqZW8= (accessed December 4, 2017).

30. *WJE* 25:610. As argued above, Edwards used the word *sense* analogously to speak of the heart or soul's simultaneous apprehension of and delight in some idea. See Jonathan

spirit beings, is especially instructive. For Edwards, experiences like what the devils experience (as in Jas 2:19) were not holy. "'Tis not the subject that makes the affection, or experience, or quality holy, but 'tis the quality that makes the subject holy" (25:610). That devils can believe and tremble is itself noteworthy, for they not only have no holiness, but cannot experience "common grace" like human beings can (25:611).

Speculative knowledge does not assure true religion. Therefore, "no degree of speculative knowledge of things of religion, is any certain sign of saving grace." Satan, like human beings, has not lost any of his faculties (25:613). Satan remembers the Father's face, has a great amount of speculative knowledge, and is capable of remarkable subtlety in temptation (which again proves his intelligence) (25:614). Moreover, those without grace "may have a very great and affecting sense of many divine things on their hearts" (25:626). Both demons and unregenerate people may "have a kind of conviction" of God's moral and natural attributes (25:627).

No one believes that human beings have all the privileges demons do. The wicked are "in the body, that clogs and hinders the soul, and are encompassed with objects that blind and stupefy 'em" (25:629). Still, there is an important similarity between demons and wicked people in Jas 2:19, showing that they both share an understanding, belief, and affection arising from that belief. Demonic and wicked affections similarly arise from "natural understanding and self-love" (25:631). The key element of gracious faith and affections is the "supreme beauty of the divine nature"—both demons and unbelievers are blind to this.[31]

Edwards believed that true saints behold Christ in holy beauty. Their souls are inclined to God and Christ. In the soul "true desires and longings" are aroused for that which is divinely beautiful, in a free manner and without constraint (25:636). The soul desires Christ with "the desires of appetite; the thirstings of a new nature; as a new-born babe desires the mother's breast" (25:636). The wicked mind has "no higher" affections than those of devils; the affections of both arise from pride and self-love.

When those lacking grace make a showy pretense of having it, the result is disastrous. Offering a sober commentary on the Awakening's ills, Edwards said that "[f]alse religion," by imitating true "inward experimental religion," undermines Christianity and bolster's Satan's desire to "harden . . . hearts" and to increase debauchery, profanity, and "atheism" (25:638).

True religion has the opposite effect. Acknowledging that the Awakening's opponents cast the blame on affections *per se*, Edwards maintained that holy affections are essential. Reiterating the 2 Pet. 1:4 connection to affections, Edwards noted, "yea, this is spoken of in Scripture, as a communication of something of God's own beauty and excellency, 'a participation of the divine nature'" (25:639).

Edwards, *Original Sin*, vol. 3 of *The Works of Jonathan Edwards*, ed. Clyde A. Holbrook (New Haven, CT: Yale University Press, 1970), 242.

31. *WJE* 25:633. Christ's divine beauty will be hid from wicked persons even at the judgment day.

This holy affection is that for which Christ died, "the most excellent token of his everlasting love; the chief fruit of his great labors, and the most precious purchase of his blood" (25:639). With such affections, people glorify God, bless others, and live in the comfort of holy peace and joy. When ministering to the Stockbridge Mahicans, Edwards repeated similar themes.[32] It is by holy affections, above all else, that people bring glory to God.

Edwards echoed the Reformed teaching that justifying faith includes affection for God. Saving faith is a supernatural thing, much different from the natural faith exercised by unregenerate people (25:501). Saving faith differs from "common faith" in two ways. First, the foundation of saving faith is a spiritual knowledge of the truth believed. Second, saving faith receives that truth believed with the heart or will (25:510–11). Faith unites the understanding and affections (21:461). New Testament words for faith "signify affiance or trusting, which implies an act of the will as well as [of] the understanding."[33] According to Heb. 3:6, faith is an act of the "whole soul," including the judgment, will, and affections.[34] "See to it that you not only assent to the truth, but that you receive the love of the truth:

32. For example, see Edwards, "131. Sermon on 1 Pet. 1:8(a) (July 1757)," in *Sermons, Series II, 1729*, vol. 44 of *The Works of Jonathan Edwards Online*, ed. Jonathan Edwards Center (New Haven, CT: Yale University, 2008), http://edwards.yale.edu/archive?path=aHR0cDov L2Vkd2FyZHMueWFsZS5lZHUvY2dpLWJpbi9uZXdwaGlsby9nZXRvYmplY3QucGw/ Yy40MjozMS53amVv (accessed December 4, 2017). First Pet. 1:8 teaches that "they live the Happiest life in this world that live a life of Love to Jesus Christ, beholding him with an eye of faith." Ibid., L. 2r. The only way to a happy union between two intelligent beings is love. "Love & Joy are affections of the soul that in their nature are very near akin." Ibid., L. 3r. Love is the soul's agreeableness to another object. Joy is that beloved object in possession. If only faith in Christ can make one happy, why are some saints unhappy? The problem is not with Christianity. Faith and love do not cause unhappiness, but contrary principles exploit the weakness of holy principles. "Leave a vain Pursuit of happiness in other things" and to seek Christ. Ibid., L. 10r. "Earthly things however tempting they appear, however fair an outside they have, if we seek happiness in them we shall surely be disappointed. [T]hey only are happy . . . whose hearts have Left the [world] & whose life is hid with [Christ] in G[od]." Ibid. This doctrine comes from God, the Creator of human beings who knows what will make him happiest. He made man's senses and the abilities to perceive and enjoy things.

33. *WJE* 25:512–13. Edwards encouraged his congregation to test their faith and determine if it was saving or common. The tests for faith look (1) at the ground of faith, that it is a spiritual knowledge of Christ and the gospel; (2) at the seat of faith, that the whole soul, both understanding and will, is receiving Christ; and (3) at the effects of faith, that holy practice flows from it (*WJE* 25:515).

34. *WJE* 21:463. Faith is "the whole soul . . . assenting to the truth and embracing it. There is an entire yielding of the mind and heart to the revelation, and a closing with it and adhering to it with the belief and with the inclination and affection" (*WJE* 21:424). Compare 21:444; Baxter, *The Saint's Everlasting Rest*, in *Works* 22:193; 23:31–33; and Mastricht, *Regeneration*, 13.

that you are not only persuaded [of the truth], but do embrace [it]," Edwards said (25:515). Only saving faith, as supernatural, results in true Christian practice, for only something supernatural can overcome natural depravity. "Our worldly affections and inclinations are natural to us, and nothing can overcome nature but what is supernatural" (25:516). Saving faith works by love to rise above the world and its lusts.[35]

35. *WJE* 25:519–21. Compare "Misc. 218," in *WJE* 13:344–45. For more on Edwards's doctrine of faith, see Cherry, *Theology*, 12–88; McClymond and McDermott, *Theology of Jonathan Edwards*, 366–71. Since the last half of the twentieth century, Jonathan Edwards's understanding of justification itself has not been without controversy. Thomas Schafer famously argued in 1951 that "there are important elements in Edwards's religious thought which cause the doctrine of justification to occupy an ambiguous and somewhat precarious place in his theology." Jonathan Edwards and Justification by Faith," *CH* 20 (1951): 57. Schafer argued that for Edwards sanctification preceded justification. Edwards made love anterior to faith, and thus "the reader cannot help feeling that the conception of 'faith alone' has been considerably enlarged—and hence practically eliminated." Ibid., 60. George Hunsinger more recently sounds different alarms: Edwards, in believing that justifying faith was both fitting for God to reward as well as virtuous in Christ's righteousness alone, moved "closer to Thomas [Aquinas] than the Reformation." "Dispositional Soteriology: Jonathan Edwards on Justification by Faith Alone," *WTJ* 66 (2004): 110. For Hunsinger, if one brings a "soft focus" to Edwards, he sounds like a Reformer; "[i]f one brings a crisper focus, however, . . . to the whole range of his texts, his picture comes out rather differently." Ibid., 119. Also see Brandon Withrow, "Jonathan Edwards and Justification by Faith," *Reformation and Revival Journal* 11 (Spring 2002): 93–109 and 11 (Summer 2002): 98–111; Gerald R. McDermott, "Jonathan Edwards on Justification by Faith Alone—More Protestant or Catholic?" *Pro Ecclesia* 17 (2008): 92–111; and McClymond and McDermott, *The Theology of Jonathan Edwards*, 389–404. A careful reading of chapter 3 shows that many Reformed divines linked affection and faith. The task at hand does not permit these issues to be addressed fully, so the question of Edwards's continuity with the Reformed tradition must be tabled, only noting that Jeffrey Waddington's answer to Schafer (and, briefly, to Hunsinger) adequately answers many of these objections. Waddington argues (among other things) that Edwards's emphasis on love or "spiritual knowledge" in faith does not make him an accidental papist, for the love of which Edwards speaks is not meritorious. "While love always accompanies true faith for the Protestant, it is not meritorious in any sense of the word." "Jonathan Edwards's 'Ambiguous and Somewhat Precarious' Doctrine of Justification," *WTJ* 66 (2004): 369. Waddington observes, "There does seem to be a tendency in recent Edwardsian scholarship . . . to pit the forensic nature of the doctrine of justification against the transformational nature of regeneration/sanctification/practice/disposition as though they stood in opposition to one another. The Reformed tradition has never understood the matter this way. They are complementary. The problem has always been, so it seems to us, either to pit one against the other, as here, or to confuse the one with the other." Ibid., 372. Also see Josh Moody's excellent article "Edwards and Justification

Edwards's publication of *David Brainerd* also shows his continued concern over right affections. In many ways, *David Brainerd* was originally a book more related to the Awakening than to missions, as Edwards made immediately plain in the preface to his publication of Brainerd's personal writings.[36] There Edwards noted that God not only teaches people the nature of true religion, but he provides examples to them of those who had it. David Brainerd is one such example, experiencing an inner change "in his mind and disposition" by the Holy Spirit, and "how it continued," with the resulting "inward frames, thoughts, affections and secret exercises" (7:91).

The inner life of Brainerd was imperfect, and he was uncommonly inclined to "melancholy" (7:91). Nevertheless, Brainerd's "extraordinary devotion" was not simply due to "a warm imagination."[37] He was of "penetrating genius" and "close reasoning," and sound in doctrine.[38] Brainerd carefully distinguished "between

Today," in *Jonathan Edwards and Justification*, ed. Josh Moody (Wheaton, Ill.: Crossway, 2012), 17–44.

36. *Pace* Wilson, who believes that Edwards compiled *David Brainerd* in response to the communion controversy. *Virtue*, 274–76. Throughout Brainerd's writings, one sees similar emphases and ideas of the human soul to those of his mentor, Jonathan Edwards. Of some interest is Brainerd's entry on February 3, 1744, where he noted that he had recorded some thoughts on the "different whispers of the various powers and affections of a pious mind, exercised with a great variety of dispensations" (*WJE* 7:236). Edwards found this document and thought it fitting to include it in the publication of Brainerd's diary. In his meditation, Brainerd presented the role of the different faculties in coming to God. The understanding sees that only God can satisfy the appetite for happiness. The will then chooses "this God for its supreme happiness and only portion" (*WJE* 7:477). Thereafter comes "Ardent Love, or Desire, introduced, as passionately longing to please and glorify the divine being, to be in every respect conformed to him, and in that way to enjoy him" (*WJE* 7:477). Such "Ardent Love," Brainerd noted, is not built upon self-love or terror of God's wrath "nor yet from hopes of feeling the sweetness of that tender and pleasant passion of love in one's own breast," but from beholding the beauty of the Object loved. Brained continued to describe the actions of the different faculties as the soul approaches God. On the influence of *David Brainerd*, see Conforti, *Jonathan Edwards, Religious Tradition*, 62–86 and Andrew F. Walls, "Missions and Historical Memory: Jonathan Edwards and David Brainerd," in *Jonathan Edwards at Home*, 248–65.

37. *WJE* 7:91. Edwards noted that Brainerd's melancholy is further evidence of the genuineness of his affections for God. Normally, those who are melancholic are not characterized by "vehement impetuous affections" (*WJE* 7:91). Brainerd's holy affections had another source.

38. Edwards's sermon at Brainerd's funeral highlighted the rational affections of the young missionary: "And the light let into his mind at conversion, and the influences and exercises that his mind was subject to at that time, appear very agreeable to reason, and the gospel of Jesus Christ; the change very great and remarkable, without any appearance of strong impressions on the imagination, sudden flights and pangs of the affections, and

real solid piety and enthusiasm, between those affections that are rational and scriptural, having their foundation in light and judgment, and those that are founded in whimsical conceits, strong impressions on the imagination, and those vehement emotions of the animal spirits that arise from them" (7:92). Brainerd keenly knew the havoc wreaked by such extreme religion. His piety was never tainted by "lively images formed in his imagination," unlike so many of the enthusiasts (7:93). Yet, as with all saints in this life, Brainerd's religious affections had both natural and spiritual elements (7:95).

Edwards distinguished Brainerd's religion from that of the recent "high pretenders of religion" overcome "by vehement emotions of mind." The revival extremists are like those whom Rom. 10:2 condemns for having a "zeal, not according to knowledge" (7:502). What marked Brainerd's religion was a sense of the beauty of God: "It appears plainly and abundantly all along, from his conversion to his death, that that beauty, that sort of good, which was the great object of the new sense of his mind, the new relish and appetite given him in conversion, and thenceforward maintained and increased in his heart, was holiness, conformity to God, living to God, and glorifying him" (7:506).

Brainerd's great experiences had the desired effects: his conscience remained tender, he maintained his duties, and refused "compliance with carnal appetites" (7:507). He was not like those who only have their "rapture and mighty emotions" when others are around; "his warmest affections and their greatest effects on animal nature, and his sweetest joys, were in his closet devotions and solitary transactions between God and his own soul."[39] Moreover, Brainerd's affections tended "to practice."[40]

Even Edwards's position in the communion controversy flowed from his theology of affections.[41] Edwards's shift on the proper participants in the Lord's Table is built on several theological axioms: (1) true religion consists in the heart's affection for God given by the Holy Spirit, (2) the true church consists of those

vehement emotions in animal nature; but attended with proper intellectual views of the supreme glory of the divine being, consisting in the infinite dignity and beauty of the perfections of his nature; and of the transcendent excellency of the way of salvation by Christ" (*WJE* 25:244).

39. *WJE* 7:509. Edwards's mention of "emotions" refers to affections' effect on the "animal nature."

40. *WJE* 7:510. For Edwards, Brainerd's remains proved that Edwards's theoretical distinctions between true and false religion were valid. In fact, Brainerd's life shows that in revivals, there are genuine religious affections amidst all the enthusiasm (*WJE* 7:517).

41. In his preface to *An Humble Inquiry*, Edwards observed, "I have the same opinion concerning the religion and inward experiences chiefly in vogue among [the enthusiasts] as I had when I wrote my *Treatise on Religious Affections*, and when I wrote my observations and reflections on Mr. Brainerd's life" (*WJE* 12:171). Hall observes, "In the context of the controversy that erupted . . ., it is crucial to note that Edwards regarded practice as indissolubly connected to the affections." "Editor's Introduction," in *WJE* 12:57.

who had such holy affections, and (3) although mere humans cannot prove that this holy affection exists in others, the visible church is only made up of those who at least profess to have this affection (12:182–83, 237). When the early church converts were baptized, the faith they professed was not merely "a historical or doctrinal faith . . . or any common faith." Their faith contained both a doctrinal profession and a promise of future obedience. "True faith in Christ includes in its nature an acceptance of him as our Lord and King, and devoting ourselves to his service: but a profession of historical faith implies no profession of accepting Christ as our King, nor engagement to submit to him as such" (12:210).

If those who do not profess true faith in Christ may enter the church, Christian fellowship is wounded. The New Testament commanded Christians to love other saints, and such love "must have some apprehension of the understanding . . . for its foundation." Otherwise, a church composed of both the outwardly regenerate and unregenerate paralyzes true Christian charity. Therefore, no Christian love can exist without a visible representation to the lover that the beloved is a true Christian.[42]

For Edwards, the Lord's Table symbolized the affections between Christ and saints. Therefore, the Lord's Supper, representing "the two parties transacting the covenant of grace," is only provided for true Christians.[43] If people come and partake of the sacrament while believing that they do not participate in this covenantal relationship, it "is a very absurdity."[44]

42. Edwards said, "In order to a real and fervent affection to another, on account of some amiableness of qualification or relation, the mind must first judge there is that amiableness in the object" (*WJE* 12:254).

43. *WJE* 12:256. Edwards said, "Christ, by the speeches and actions of the minister, makes a solemn profession of his part in the covenant of grace: he exhibits the sacrifice of his body broken and his blood shed; and in the minister's offering the sacramental bread and wine to the communicants, Christ presents himself to the believing communicants, as their propitiation and bread of life; and by these outward signs confirms and seals his sincere engagements to be their Savior and food, and to impart to them all the benefits of his propitiation and salvation. And they in receiving what is offered, and eating and drinking the symbols of Christ's body and blood, also profess their part in the covenant of grace: they profess to embrace the promises and lay hold of the hope set before them, to receive the atonement, to receive Christ as their spiritual food, and to feed upon him in their hearts by faith" (*WJE* 12:256). McClymond and McDermott observe that for Edwards, "the Supper is not only a memorial that helps prevent our forgetting; it also 'revives' our affections of admiration and delight for Christ and what he did for us." *Theology*, 489.

44. *WJE* 12:258. For more on Edwards's theology of the Eucharist, see Graham S. Harrison, "Jonathan Edwards and the Terms of Admission to Communion," in *The Good Fight of Faith: Papers Read at the Westminster Conference 1971* (London: Evangelical Press, 1971): 51–71; R. David Rightmire, "The Sacramental Theology of Jonathan Edwards in the Context of Controversy," *Fides et Historia* 21 (1989): 50–60; Danaher, "By Sensible Signs," 261–87; and McClymond and McDermott, *Theology*, 487–93.

In his sermons, his publication of *David Brainerd*, and his theology amidst the communion controversy, Edwards taught that holy affections are necessary for true Christianity. He remained concerned with those who deemed affections in religion unfashionable, as well as those who built their religion on natural movements of the affections and passions.

"Absolute Masters of the Heart": Affections and Sin

Edwards's posthumously published book *The Great Christian Doctrine of Original Sin Defended* is an example of how Edwards's understanding of affections was used to defend the Reformed faith. Edwards's main opponent in *Original Sin* was the notorious "arch-heretic" John Taylor of Norwich (1694–1761), whose teachings denying the doctrine were already making inroads in the colonies.[45]

Edwards built his case in *Original Sin* in part on his ethics, that there is no moral good without an affection for God behind it.[46] For Edwards, all people existed in order that they might have affection for God. The evidence for humanity's ruin is that the "passions and affections" run more strongly to lesser things, and that, even when people have love for God, that love "has justly more wrong than right" (3:140). Love for God ought to "swallow up all other affections, like a deluge" (3:142). Instead, human affection for God is often cold. Human affections are distorted and ill proportioned. Gratitude for God is often mean compared with the heated anger people have against others (3:143).

True virtue, Edwards explained in *Original Sin*, has a proper regard for everything proportioned to its essence. Therefore, people ought to love God for who he is in himself. "If God be infinitely excellent in himself, then he is infinitely

45. John Taylor was an English "Arminian" (read: proto-liberal or progressive) whose works were highly influential in the eighteenth century American colonies. Taylor not only authored an Hebrew-English concordance (1754), but also an epochal work against original sin (1740), the latter provoking responses from other luminaries (besides Edwards), including Isaac Watts and John Wesley. Original sin was not the only doctrine Taylor, one of the "more liberal-minded Dissenting divines," was reworking; he was (like others) also questioning traditional views of the Trinity, the atonement, and justification. See John Taylor, *The Scripture Doctrine of Original Sin Proposed to Free and Candid Examination* (London: J. Wilson, 1740); Isaac Watts, *The Ruin and Recovery of Mankind* (London: R. Hett and J. Brackstone, 1740); and John Wesley, *The Doctrine of Original Sin: According to Scripture, Reason, and Experience* (Bristol: E. Farley, 1757). For more on Taylor, see G. T. Eddy, *Dr Taylor of Norwich: Wesley's Arch-heretic* (Werrington, U.K.: Epworth, 2003) and Holbrook, "Editor's Introduction," in *WJE* 3:68–70. Also see Marsden, *Jonathan Edwards*, 447–58.

46. Edwards said, "[W]ithout the heart, man's external acts are no more than the motions of the limbs of a wooden image: have no more of the nature of either sin or righteousness. It must therefore needs be so, that love to God, or the respect of the heart, must be the sum of the duty required towards God in his law" (*WJE* 3:140).

lovely on that account; or in other words, infinitely worthy to be loved" (3:144). Edwards challenged his readers to observe for themselves how few people actually directed "disinterested love" toward the true God. Instead, most people love God out of pure self-interest, which is not love at all. True "divine affection" is rare.[47]

Edwards's notion of original sin does not include the idea that God positively gave evil passions or a corrupted nature to humankind. Instead, as he did in his early "Miscellanies," Edwards explained original sin to be God's withdrawal of the special divine influence originally given to Adam and Eve. Consequently, "self-love" and "natural appetite" were left to themselves in humanity, leading to their corruption "without occasion for any positive influence at all."

For Edwards, God created humans with two principles: an inferior, natural principle and a superior, spiritual principle. The inferior principle includes all self-love, "natural appetites and passions," and love for liberty. These principles, when left to themselves, are what the Bible calls "the flesh."[48] The spiritual principles endowed in the first parents were above nature and positively from the "divine nature." The Bible names this principle the "spirit." The divine nature made possible Adam and Eve's communion with God and the Holy Spirit. The absence of divine principles does not make human nature any less human, Edwards insisted. Human beings were created to have the divine nature rule over the natural. "And while things continued thus, all things were in excellent order, peace and beautiful harmony, and in their proper and perfect state" (3:382).

God withdrew the supernatural principle when Adam and Eve sinned, leaving only "flesh" and no "spirit." Thereby "[t]he inferior principles of self-love and natural appetite, which were given only to serve, being alone, and left to themselves, of course became reigning principles; having no superior principles to regulate or control them, they became absolute masters of the heart" (3:382). This

47. *WJE* 3:144. Most people love the Lord far less than their earthly pleasures. For Edwards, the strength of passions and the animal appetite over the higher faculties proved the doctrine of original sin. Edwards repeatedly returns to this doctrine. See, for example, *WJE* 3:201–04.

48. *WJE* 3:381. Compare "Misc. 301," 13:387–88. See chapter 5. Edwards did not believe that when the Bible condemned the "flesh" that it referred exclusively to the animal appetites of human beings. He accepted without question the influence of animal appetites, and believed that they should be controlled, but he did not believe, contrary to his opponents, that the biblical notion of "flesh" referred to them. Instead, the Bible used flesh to refer to evil inclinations (*WJE* 3:277). Here Edwards echoed the thought of Calvin (see chapter 3). The biblical word *flesh* refers to more than mere "inordinate appetites of the body, and their indulgences," but "the whole body of sin," including those sins that are "furthest from any relation to the body," including pride and envy (*WJE* 3:278). Depravity, Edwards argued, is not called "the flesh" because of animal appetites, but because it belongs "to mankind, or the race of Adam, as they are in themselves" (*WJE* 3:279). The word *flesh* designates all humanity, and, because all are depraved, the word has come to refer to that depravity. The word *spirit* similarly came to refer to the new nature working in people.

turned human beings upside down. Natural appetites ruled in God's stead. The absence of the divine principle does not curb God's requirements, however. He still demands worship and the conformity of "inferior passions" to his law. By this conflict, a perpetual war rages within people. "Thus 'tis easy to give an account, how total corruption of heart should follow on man's eating the forbidden fruit, though that was but one act of sin, without God's putting any evil into his heart, or implanting any bad principle, or infusing any corrupt taint, and so becoming the author of depravity" (3:383). As God withdrew from Adam, so he withdraws from all his posterity, so that all are born "under the government of natural and inferior principles; and so become wholly corrupt" (3:383).

For Edwards, passions were not sinful in and of themselves. When rightly subordinate to divine love, they serve people well for life. Adam's original sin, however, ruined his children and their affections. People are overcome by affections and passions through a radical principle of selfishness that taints them. In order to extinguish this sinfulness, one must have divine love rekindled by the Holy Spirit. This divine love is the only way to bring glory to God and live a life of true virtue.

"Pure Love" and "Self-Love": Affections and Ethics

As early Enlightenment thinkers moved further from Christian thought, they were forced to account for a system of good and evil that filled the void left by theological systems, now regarded as implausible.[49] For centuries—including the early eighteenth century—ethics were concerned with the relationship of human passions and affections and the will or reason.[50] Moral philosophers, such as Joseph Butler and George Turnbull, proposed that virtue could be grounded in universal human "moral tastes" (or conscience). Paul Ramsey has shown that Edwards intended *True Virtue* to refute these ideas.[51] *True Virtue* is the second of Edwards's

49. Marsden sums it up well: "In the broadest terms, the British moralists since the time of John Locke were attempting to establish a new moral philosophy as a science equivalent to the new natural philosophy, or natural science. True to the spirit of the age, modern thinkers were striving to establish firm foundations for knowledge that would be universally valid for all humans." Marsden, *Jonathan Edwards*, 464. See Taylor, *Sources*, 248–65.

50. Scientism's artificial construction of humanity as mere biological organism and the resulting collapse of categories like "passions," "emotions," and "will" (among others), has a resulted in a crisis in ethics. In a world without metaphysics, there is no real good and evil. See Alasdair MacIntyre, "Moral Philosophy: What Next?" in *Revisions: Changing Perspectives in Moral Philosophy*, eds. Stanley Hauerwas and Alasdair MacIntyre, Revisions 3 (Notre Dame, IN: University of Notre Dame Press, 1983), 1–15; Cochran, *Receptive*, 6–11; and Richard M. Weaver, *Ideas Have Consequences* (Chicago: University of Chicago Press, 1948).

51. Ramsey, "Edwards on Moral Sense," in *WJE* 8:689–705. See "'Controversies' Notebook: The Nature of True Virtue," in *WJE* 21:314–27. Ramsey strongly denies Fiering's argument that Edwards's *True Virtue* is primarily response to Francis Hutcheson. *Jonathan*

Two Dissertations, which were published seven years after his death, in 1765. The first of *Two Dissertations* is *The End for Which God Created the World*. Together, the two works represent the culmination of Edwards's thought on affections.[52]

Edwards's ethics in *True Virtue* was an attempt to recover the Christian meaning of good and evil in an age scurrying after secularization. His definition of good and evil is implicitly Biblical and Reformed, erected upon a theocentric understanding of the affections. Edwards showed that Jesus's account of morality in Mt. 22:38-39 was clearly embedded in the nature of reality.[53] As such, *True Virtue* deals repeatedly with affections.

Edwards's Moral Philosophy, 256–57, 337. McClymond and McDermott write, "Jonathan Edwards lived in an eighteenth-century world dominated by 'benevolism'—the idea that human beings are naturally benevolent because of their inherent altruism or 'moral sense.'" *Theology*, 533. See idem, *Theology*, 528–48 and Marsden, *Jonathan Edwards*, 464–71. In "Misc. 1003," (written sometime after 1740), Edwards showed that true virtue must come from God's grace: "true virtue and holiness, *which is the highest and most noble of all the qualifications gifts and attainments of the reasonable creature*, and is the crown and glory of the human, and that by which he is nearest to God and does partake of his image and nature, and is the highest beauty and glory of the whole creation, and is as it were the life and soul of the soul, that is given in the new creation or new birth, should be what God don't leave to the power of second causes, or honor any arm of flesh or created power or faculty to be the proper instrument of, but that he should reserve it in his own hands to be imparted more immediately by himself, in the efficacious operation of his own Spirit" (*WJE* 20:328).

52. Surprisingly, Edwards cited no Scripture in *True Virtue*. Yet, he intended to publish *True Virtue* alongside *The End*, which cites much Scripture. As such, *True Virtue* is not purely rational. Edwards's ideas of grace, the will, affections, and spiritual sense show that he deemed naked reason unable to bestow divine grace. On the unity of *Two Dissertations*, see William C. Spohn, "Sovereign Beauty: Jonathan Edwards and the Nature of True Virtue," *TS* 42 (1981): 394–421; Ramsey, "Editor's Introduction," in *WJE* 8:5–7; Murray, *Jonathan Edwards*, 427–28; Marsden, *Jonathan Edwards*, 460; and Strobel, *Theology*, 78–83.

53. Edwards's definition of virtue as "consent to Being in general," which consists primarily in love to God and secondarily in love to other persons, not only resembles biblical "ethics" (see Mt. 22:38-39), but also the Westminster Shorter Catechism (1647). The Catechism defined humanity's duty as "obedience to [God's] revealed will," which is in the "moral law," "summarily comprehended in the ten commandments," which are, in sum, "To love the Lord our God with all our heart, with all our soul, with all our strength, and with all our mind; and our neighbor as ourselves." Joel R. Beeke and Sinclair B. Ferguson, eds., *Reformed Confessions Harmonized: With an Annotated Bibliography of Reformed Doctrinal Works* (Grand Rapids, MI: Baker Books, 1999). Edwards told his friend, the Scottish minister John Erskine (1721–1803) that he could ascribe to the "substance" of the Westminster Confession and encouraged his protégé Joseph Bellamy to teach it to Indians (*WJE* 16:355, 688). Morris says Thomas Manton's dictum that affection for God is different from "the most refined unregenerate *Morality*" resonates with Edwards's teaching in *True Virtue*. *Young Jonathan Edwards*, 251–52. The connection drawn here between Edwards

Edwards began by tying virtue to beauty—particularly to the beauty of moral things. Virtue does not consist in speculation, but in "disposition and will," or the "heart" (8:539). What makes a given act of the heart beautiful? True virtue, in a given "*heart* of an intelligent being," has a general and comprehensive beauty, a (spiritual) beauty seen when considered with respect everything else to which it relates.[54] "True virtue most essentially consists in benevolence to Being in general. Or perhaps to speak more accurately, it is that consent, propensity and union of heart to Being in general, that is immediately exercised in general good will" (8:540). The heart is the seat of virtue, which is concerned with the heart's affections and especially its *love*. "Virtue consists in love" (8:543). Love in virtue is tied to universal existence in general, and not to particulars.[55] As Wilson explains, by "benevolence to Being in general," Edwards had in mind the saints' love to "the entire creation as participating in and in some cases forwarding God's ends for it."[56]

For Edwards, true virtue was a benevolent love. In other words, virtuous love desires the happiness of the beloved rather than the beauty perceived in him.[57] Virtue consists in "'absolute Benevolence' . . . to Being in general" (8:544). "The *first* object of a virtuous benevolence is Being, simply considered: and if Being, *simply* considered, be its object, then Being *in general* is its object; and the thing it has an ultimate propensity to, is the *highest good* of Being in general," Edwards

and the words of Jesus was observed independently from Philip L. Quinn, who also notes it in "The Master Argument of *The Nature of True Virtue*," in *Jonathan Edwards: Philosophical Theologian*, eds. Paul Helm and Oliver D. Crisp (Burlington, VT: Ashgate, 2003), 96.

54. McClymond and McDermott observe, "[N]o one else in Western Christian thought seems to have made God's beauty so integral to Christian theology and to Christian ethics." McClymond and McDermott *Theology*, 548. Using Edwards, Roland A. Delattre rightly challenges his readers: "Somebody must rescue aesthetics from the philosophers, art historians, art critics, and the fashion industry, and restore its relevance to religious ethics." "Aesthetics and Ethics: Jonathan Edwards and the Recovery of Aesthetics for Religious Ethics," *JRE* 31 (2003): 277. Yet, he does not use Edwards well to accomplish that objective.

55. Wilson rightly observes: "Edwards is quite precise in affirming that expressions of supernatural charity can be distinguished from its many natural semblances by its unique motive structure." Wilson, *Virtue*, 49.

56. Wilson, *Virtue*, 75. Compare Cochran, *Receptive*, 41.

57. On this point, Edwards introduced the distinction between love of benevolence and love of complacence. Love of benevolence is the heart's affection to a being, desiring in its happiness, irrespective of its beauty. God (the "Divine Being") is not only the ground of beauty, but the ground of all being; it is God's love of benevolence that inclines him "to give being, beauty, and happiness" (*WJE* 8:542). Love of complacence, on the other hand, is a delight in beauty, or the individual loved for beauty's sake. Virtue does not consist in love to particular beings because of what they have done to us. This would make virtue circular. No, virtue consists in "'absolute Benevolence' . . . to Being in general" (*WJE* 8:544).

said.[58] Edwards also noted that if Being in general is the object of benevolence, then the Being "who has *most* of Being" will be the greatest object of a person's love. Toward the greatest Being people ought to direct "the *greatest* share of the propensity and benevolent affection of the heart" (8:546).

The second object of virtuous benevolence is benevolent being. In other words, benevolence delights in—"attaches his heart to"—other benevolent beings. Those who "consent to Being" will necessarily agree with those who "consent to Being" (8:547). Such consent is true spiritual beauty. The more benevolence and the more "degree of being," the more valuable is such virtue (8:548). Edwards contended that people cannot "*relish*" other benevolent beings unless they are benevolent themselves (8:549). In sum, "From what has been said, 'tis evident that true virtue must chiefly consist in love to God; the Being of beings, infinitely the greatest and best of beings" (8:550).

One cannot claim to have true virtue without loving God first and foremost. God, as the most excellent Being, has not only revealed his beauty to human beings, but has also equipped them with "faculties" adequate to discover his beauty. Therefore, all virtue necessarily consists in a "supreme love to God" (8:551). God is the source of all being, and, consequently, any benevolence to Being in general must be grounded in the God of perfect beauty. Undoubtedly, "love or benevolent affection" is due to God (8:552).

Edwards contended against those moralists who excluded or downgraded devotion to God in their ethics. Some philosophers included an element of respect to God, but this too was inadequate. "If true virtue consists partly in a respect to God, then doubtless it consists *chiefly* in it" (8:553). For Edwards, it was irrational for moralists to extol "love" for others and yet diminish love for God. God is at once "head" of, "chief" of, and "infinitely more" than the whole of the system of being. Therefore, "unless we will be atheists," virtue chiefly consists in love to God; "where this is wanting, there can be no true virtue."[59]

For Edwards, virtue is not idiosyncratic. Put another way, a virtuous person does not love another individual or even group of individuals, *apart from the entire system of being*. Such idiosyncratic affections are "*private affections*" that limit benevolence to a subset of beings, independent of the system as a whole. Edwards believed that private affections were opposed to general benevolence (8:555). If one opposes "Being in general" (through private affections), one opposes God himself, the supreme Being who is the source of all being. Private affections oppose the object of chief benevolence.

In his excursus on private affections, Edwards rejected all systems of morality that are not primarily theocentric. A system of virtue where God is not the supreme object of affections undermines benevolence to Being in general. This is anti-virtue. "[N]o affection whatsoever to any creature, or any system of created

58. *WJE* 8:545. Why does virtue not begin with love to particular beings? Virtue cannot be in any way tinged by selfishness or radical self-love.

59. *WJE* 8:554. Compare *WJE* 2:418–19.

beings, which is not dependent on, nor subordinate to a propensity of union of the heart to God, the Supreme and Infinite Being, can be of the nature of true virtue."[60]

If true virtue includes the *necessity* of affection for God then virtue is *grounded* in a love of God. Any truly virtuous love for others is tempered by a supreme love to God (8:558–59). He who truly loves God will "seek the *glory of God* and make this his supreme, governing, and ultimate end" (8:559). The love of true virtue regards others with reference to God first, pursuing the good of others for God's sake. "And no other disposition or affection but this is the nature of true virtue."[61]

Chapter 3 of *True Virtue* explains the relationship of inferior beauty to virtue. Humanity's aesthetic pleasure is not essential to virtue, but was a shadow of the primary beauty of true virtue. Edwards reiterated that true virtue renders a moral agent beautiful "in the eyes of him that perfectly sees all things as they are." Humans often incorrectly judge as virtuous others' "sensations, propensities and affections of mind." The consent of a moral agent to Being in general is "primary beauty." Edwards defined secondary beauty as "a mutual consent and agreement of different things in form, manner, quantity, and visible end or design."[62] Consent is also known as harmony or symmetry. Secondary beauty is found in many places, from inanimate objects to moral agents.[63]

Why do people find secondary beauty to be beautiful? Edwards believed people see secondary beauty as an "image of true beauty," a type of "being's consent to being, or the union of minds or spiritual beings in a mutual propensity and affection of heart" (8:564). God has created the "external," material world to be an "analogy" of spiritual reality.[64] For example, musical harmony represents the consent of mind between beings, and its secondary beauty can evoke in virtuous people a "sense of spiritual beauty" (8:565).

Edwards distinguished between moral or "cordial" beauty, consisting in "union of mind and heart" (which he regarded as "primary" beauty), and natural,

60. *WJE* 8:556–57. Danaher underscores that Edwards believed that for saints friendship and marriage should be grounded in eternal life. For Edwards, the incarnation has ensured that human friendships are subordinate to love for God, for Christ, as incarnate, is the best possible friend. Because of the incarnation, the friendship saints have with other saints is grounded in eternal life. Danaher, *Trinitarian Ethics*, 99–100, 102–03. Therefore, Edwards said, "This should move us to lay religion and virtue in the foundation of all our friendships, and to strive that the love we have to our friends be a virtuous love, duly subordinated to divine love" ("Misc. 639," in *WJE* 18:172–73).

61. *WJE* 8:560. Compare Spohn, who says: "God is not the only object of virtuous affection, but only if other beings are integrated into the love of God can they be loved virtuously." Spohn, "Sovereign Beauty," 402.

62. *WJE* 8:561. In his *True Virtue* "Controversies" notebook, Edwards noted that even animals have a sense of external secondary beauty (*WJE* 21:316–17).

63. Edwards offered examples of immaterial secondary beauty: an orderly society, wisdom, and justice (*WJE* 8:568–69).

64. *WJE* 8:564; compare *WJE* 11:152.

secondary beauty, consisting in consent of such things as symmetry and form. God has given humans an "*instinct*" whereby they perceive secondary beauty (8:565). Yet, individuals who perceive secondary beauty may not understand how God made it beautiful to them; they may not understand that it is in fact representing to them an image of primary beauty (8:566).

All other things being equal, the greater the object of secondary beauty, the greater the effect on the mind (8:567). The secondary beauty of spiritual objects have the capacity of affecting the mind more than material beauty (8:568). For this reason, justice, although a spiritual reality, still has but a secondary beauty to it, consisting in different things relating to others appropriately. Consent to Being in general still exceeds this beauty (8:571). Virtuous persons delight in justice because it *agrees* with the will of God and results in glory to God and good toward others, but a person can delight in secondary beauty without having true virtue. Simply because folks delight in a nice tune does not mean they are virtuous. The same would be true of justice. By insisting that justice is merely secondary beauty, Edwards was able to exclude the unregenerate from having any claim to true virtue. The moralists were wrong on this point; a recognition of secondary beauty does not prove a "naturally implanted" virtue in human beings (8:574).

In chapter 4 of *True Virtue*, Edwards turned to the question of love and self-love. Does all love come from self-love? Self-love is "generally defined" as "a man's love of his own happiness" (8:575). Self-love can be understood in two different ways. First, self-love can refer to people loving what pleases them. In this sense, the term speaks merely of "our capacity of loving, or hating; . . . which is the same thing as a man's having a faculty of will" (8:575–76). To reject this self-love is to say a person should not be inclined to anything at all, which is clearly impossible. The second (and normal) understanding of self-love is that it refers to "a man's regard to his confined *private self*, or love to himself with respect to his private interest." Edwards had in mind an individual's *private* regard for "external beauty" and satisfying his own "sensitive appetites and aversions" (8:577). Note the connection to the animal passions, which Edwards stressed: "[a]nd as God has constituted our nature, self-love is exercised in no one disposition more than in this" (8:578). Private self-love cannot be virtuous, for in it there is no love to Being in general.

Furthermore, self-love is the root behind the passions of gratitude and anger. Here Edwards wrestled with Francis Hutcheson and other moralists who argued that these passions were caused by an inward sense of moral good and evil (8:579–83). Edwards considered humanity to be much more disordered than that. If the passion of anger arose from a "moral sense" of what is good, then the most benevolent would be those who were most often angry.[65] Humans by nature are

65. *WJE* 8:538. In his notebook on *True Virtue*, Edwards observed that if anger is evidence of a moral sense, then animals also have a moral sense. "But allowing this [anger], such a moral sense, if it be proper to call it by that name, is in some degree in many of the beasts, as they have such a thing as anger. . . . So there are appearances of gratitude in some of the brute creatures" (*WJE* 21:317).

uneasy when they oppose themselves, but this is precisely what pure love requires. When persons have "pure love for others" (not self-love), they unite themselves to *others* and act as if they were united to them. Self-love, on the other hand, acts out of *self*-interest and *self*-unification (8:589). Pure love (true virtue) creates an "inward war" with the self (8:590).

Edwards understood the moralists' notion of the universal inward sense of moral good and evil to be the conscience. The question, then, is whether the conscience proves that humans have a natural bent toward moral goodness. Edwards said that one can approve of human actions for two different reasons, either because of self-love or because those actions agree with a disposition toward Being in general. Against the moralists, he contended that behind the conscience is a principle of self-love. Edwards argued that the conscience is the mental uneasiness in people arising because they cannot consent to the actions they themselves have directed toward others or that others have directed toward them.[66]

Edwards, however, still needed to explain how the conscience judges the *mental* acts of others. To answer this question, Edwards suggested that people remember their own inner acts—"acts, passions, sensations, volitions, etc.,"—and project them into other minds. "'Tis thus in all moral things that we conceive of in others, which are all mental and not corporeal things; and everything that we conceive of, belonging to others, more than shape, size, complexion, situation, and motion of their bodies" (8:591). Similarly, people conceive of the understanding and will of God by abstracting their own internal motions. "Knowing what they are by consciousness, we can add degrees, and deny limits, and remove changeableness and other imperfections, and ascribe them to God. Which is the only way we come to be capable of conceiving of anything in the Deity" (8:591–92).

By nature, the conscience judges the morality of actions between oneself and others from expectations of the treatment one deserves to receive. Note, again, that self-love is crucial to conscience. Conscience also has a "sense of desert," that actions toward others are harmonious with reward and punishment.[67] On the Judgment Day, all human consciences will see clearly whether all their actions conform with true virtue, unhindered "from being stupefied by sensual objects and appetites" (8:595). In sum, contrary to the moralists, there is no universal moral sense in humans. Human conscience is not the same thing as an actual disposition to do what the conscience demands.

In chapter 6, Edwards addressed human instinct. On this point, Edwards showed how the passions relate to true virtue. God created humans with certain inclinations related to the preservation and comfort of life. Natural appetites are *personal* instincts, while other instincts, like the mutual inclination between the

66. *WJE* 8:589. For more on Edwards and the conscience, see Fiering, *Jonathan Edwards's Moral Thought*, 62–67; Ramsey, "Edwards on Moral Sense," in *WJE* 8:689–705; Danaher, *Trinitarian Ethics*, 56–59; and Cochran, *Receptive*, 158–61.

67. *WJE* 8:592–93. Edwards said the conscience should not only judge the morality of actions, but the conscience's response as well.

sexes, are more *social*. Both personal and social instincts can be sensitive and external, like the desire for food and the "inclinations of the sexes towards each other" (8:600). Instincts can also be internal and mental, when humans have "affections" toward others, such as in benevolence and jealousy. These (apparently benevolent) affections, Edwards noted, are not truly virtuous. Familial affections come ultimately from private self-love. They are not evil in themselves, but as they arise from self-love, they do not amount to virtue. Affections between spouses, although not necessarily arising from mere "sensitive desires," but "kind affections" instinctive to human nature, are not virtuous either (8:605).

Because virtue is based in love, Edwards insisted that natural instincts cannot be virtuous.[68] Again, familial affections are restrictive and grounded in self-love. People regard familial affections as virtuous because "they are so ready to leave the Divine Being out of their view" (8:610). Sometimes people regard actions to be virtuous because those actions lack moral evil. Edwards blamed the tendency to regard instincts as virtuous on the fact that the world of sense can overwhelm people so that they forget God altogether:

> But no wonder that by a long continued worldly and sensual life men more and more lose all sense of the Deity, who is a spiritual and invisible Being. The mind being long involved in, and engrossed by sensitive objects, becomes sensual in all its operations, and excludes all views and impressions of spiritual objects, and is unfit for their contemplation. (8:614)

Habitual wickedness impairs the soul. When indulging "sensuality, or the increase of sensual appetites," the soul cannot consider "anything else"—the "appetites take up the whole soul" (8:615).

Some people mistakenly reckon natural, "inferior affections," to be virtuous because they are "of the same denomination" as virtuous affections (8:616). Pity or benevolence rooted in virtue "guides and regulates" the remaining natural instincts (8:617). "Genuine virtue prevents that increase of the habits of pride and sensuality, which tend to overbear and greatly diminish the exercises of the forementioned useful and necessarily principles of nature" (8:618). True benevolence rightly uses "the gentler natural instincts" in the proper channel, in the most fitting manner, to the best ends.[69]

68. *WJE* 8:609. On this point Edwards reiterated the distinction between benevolence and complacence. Virtuous love primarily delights in the object loved for its own sake (benevolence), and only secondarily delights in the happiness that the beloved brings to the lover (complacence) (*WJE* 8:609).

69. *WJE* 8:618. Phil C. Zylla argues that *True Virtue* proves that after Northampton Edwards softened the previous posture he had held against Puritan taboos, but Zylla fails to take into account Edwards's admonitions in *True Virtue* against sensitive appetites, the ground of Edwards's earlier preaching. See Phil C. Zylla, *Virtue as Consent to Being*:

The final chapter of *True Virtue* addresses the extent to which moral good is a principle of sentiment. If virtue is based in beauty, is it fundamentally irrational? Beautiful things have a quality in themselves that is agreeable or comely to the mind. Beauty is not determined by argument, but "by immediate sensation of the gratefulness of the idea" (8:619). Therefore, Edwards conceded, virtue is, in a sense, "founded in sentiment and not in reason," since the beauty of moral good is perceived in the mind or by "a certain spiritual sense given them of God." Since virtue is consent to Being in general, and those who are virtuous "relish" in this consent, those "whose temper is to love Being in general" enjoy virtue (8:620).

Therefore, virtue, being love, is seated in the will or heart. Love comes, not from argument, but from a certain kind of will. Edwards argued for the rationality of his idea of virtue with four arguments. First, virtue is a consent of being to Being; it would be ridiculous for a being to be opposed to general existence (8:620). Second, if God gives the sentiment whereby virtue is relished, then such a gift is agreeable to God's own nature. Third, intelligent beings can be united only by a love for Being in general. Fourth, people can live consistently and not oppose themselves when they have a love for Being in general (8:621). The conscience is not arbitrary, but given by God with respect to the "necessary nature of things" (8:623).

Stephen A. Wilson chastens Ramsey and Delattre for placing Edwards's center for true virtue too close to secular—rather than Calvinist—thought, while at the same time faulting Cherry for limiting Edwards's vision as too Calvinistic. He presents Edwards's sources as a "highly variegated puzzle" of the Sentimentalists, Cambridge Platonists, Protestant Scholasticism, and Separatist ecclesiology.[70] In sum, Edwards was a "catholick theologian" (the term is Holifield's): a Calvinist generally who slightly modified Calvinistic doctrine and widened its terms to make room for "natural causes and moral virtues."[71] Some modern ethicists and philosophers attempt to disentangle Edwards's moral thought from his theological agenda. Philip Quinn, for example, thinks that by separating these two strands of Edwards's thought, his moral thought remains relevant. Wilson cautions strongly against this attempt.[72]

A Pastoral-Theological Perspective on Jonathan Edwards's Construct of Virtue, McMaster Divinity Studies Series (Eugene, OR: Pickwick Publications, 2011), 33–36.

70. Wilson, "Jonathan Edwards's Virtue: Diverse sources, Multiple Meanings, and the Lessons of History for Ethics," *JRE* 31 (2003): 217. Also see Wilson, *Virtue*, 325–26. Compare Ramsey, "Editor's Introduction," in *WJE* 8 and Delattre, *Beauty and Sensibility*. On the influence of the Cambridge Platonists' ethics on Edwards, see Cochran, *Receptive*, 22–28 and 40–61.

71. Wilson, *Virtue*, 16; Holifield, *Theology in America*, 80–83.

72. Philip L. Quinn, "Honoring Jonathan Edwards," *JRE* 31 (2003): 300–03. Wilson, "Jonathan Edwards's Virtue," 219–22. Quinn supposes that he can downgrade Edwards's insistence that the consent of true virtue must be between intellectual beings to include consent to "inanimate natural objects of great beauty." Here Quinn illustrates how some

To Quinn, as to Ramsey and Delattre, Edwards's ethics cannot stand apart from his theological concerns. Edwards's ethics were rooted in his understanding of affections. Though informed by a complex of other sources (as Wilson argues), his moral philosophy was bound to Jesus's two great commandments and addressed the necessary affections behind actions for them to be virtuous. Indeed, looming behind *True Virtue* is the maxim of *Affections*, "True religion in great part consists of holy affections."[73] Firmly believing that an opposition between revealed Christianity and reason was impossible, Edwards tried to prove that an air-tight rational defense of biblical ethics could be made. Edwards showed that ethics must both account for humanity's obligation to God himself and acknowledge the disordered results of self-love (sin) that naturally mars every child of Adam.

"An Infinite Fullness of All Possible Good": Affections and Doxology

Edwards's emphasis on God's glory is well known, but how this emphasis intertwines with his understanding of affections is less studied.[74] In *The End for Which God Created the World*, the first of the *Two Dissertations*, Edwards argued that God, who loves his own glory above all else, created the world to glorify himself. Edwards's God was infinitely happy, and needed nothing to improve that happiness (8:420). God loves his own glory, for it is only fitting that God would value that which has "ultimate value" (8:421). God's love for his own glory is what makes him morally good. Edwards argued: "The moral rectitude and fitness of the disposition, inclination or affection of God's heart does chiefly consist in a respect or regard to himself infinitely above his regard to all other beings: or, in other words, his holiness consists in this" (8:422).

For Edwards, the impassible God was a God of holy affections, principally with affections for (or a heightened inclination toward) his glory.[75] Edwards regarded it

scholars miss Edwards's emphasis on the distinction between the spiritual and the sensual. Quinn, "Master Argument," 86.

73. *WJE* 2:95. See Danaher, *Trinitarian Ethics*, 151–56. In *Justification by Faith Alone*, Edwards said, "[T]here are many things that accompany and flow from faith, that are things with which justification shall be, and without which it will not be, and therefore are found to be put in Scripture in condition propositions with justification and salvation in multitudes of places: such are 'love to God,' and 'love to our brethren'" (*WJE* 19:152).

74. For Edwards's emphasis on doxology, see, for example, Holmes, *God of Grace*, 54–62; John Piper, "A God-Entranced Vision of All Things: Why We Need Jonathan Edwards 300 Years Later," in *A God-Entranced Vision of All Things*, 21–34; Piper, *God's Passion for His Glory*; Owen Strachan and Doug Sweeney, *Jonathan Edwards on Beauty*, The Essential Edwards Collection (Chicago, IL: Moody, 2010); Strobel, *Theology*, 73–104. On the Enlightenment move away from doxology, see Taylor, *Sources*, 266–84.

75. Edwards said, "[A]s 'tis fit that God should love and esteem his own excellence, 'tis also fit that he should value and esteem the love of his excellency" (8:432). Edwards said God's love of himself and his benevolent love cannot be distinguished (8:455).

fitting that human affection for God is the end of human faculties, for God is the one who made the faculties, and God loves his own glory.[76] God created human beings, that they might—like God—glorify God. Consequently, the Bible depicts holy people (who are "the best part of the moral world"), when in their best states, giving "vent to the virtuous and pious affections of their heart," and glorifying God (8:482).

God's ultimate end in creation was to bring himself glory. That glory is God's fullness. That is, God's glory is evident in that he is "an infinite fullness of all possible good," a "fullness of every perfection, of all excellency and beauty, and of infinite happiness" (8:432–3). When God exercises his perfections, he does so in order to glorify himself, or to display this fullness. In creation, the internal glory of God that was his before creation is displayed to the minds of creatures so that they will have a "high esteem of God" (8:527). Therefore, God's acting so that a person gives him glory does not differ from the "communication of [God's] fullness" to that person (8:527).

For Edwards, the internal glory of God was held in the divine "understanding" and "will." The object of God's understanding—what God knows—is his own glory. The object of God's will—God's "holiness and happiness"—is again God's glory. God's glory consists in his infinite knowledge, holiness, and happiness.[77]

In communicating his fullness to his creatures, God shares these three aspects (knowledge, holiness, and happiness) with them. When God gives a knowledge of himself to people's minds, he communicates divine self-knowledge to them. Thereby, God reveals to his creatures his perfection and excellence. When God communicates his holiness to them, he communicates the love he has for himself.[78] Likewise, when God communicates his "happiness and joy" to creatures, he communicates the happiness he has in himself (8:528). These three things "in the

76. "Understanding and will are the highest kind of created existence" (*WJE* 8:454). Edwards once reminded his congregation, the "end of our faculties" is to glorify God. "948. Sermon on Prov. 6:22(a), (Feb.Jan.1749/50)," in *Sermons, Series II, 1750*, vol. 68 of *The Works of Jonathan Edwards Online*, ed. Jonathan Edwards Center (New Haven, CT: Yale University, 2008), L.9v. http://edwards.yale.edu/archive?path=aHR0cDovL2Vkd2FyZHMueWFsZS5lZHUvY2dpLWJpbi9uZXdwaGlsby9nZXRvYmplY3QucGw/Yy42NjoxLndqZW8= (accessed December 4, 2017).

77. All God's attributes are related to these three aspects of God's glory. "We have no conception of God's power, different from the degree of these things, with a certain relation of them to effects. God's infinity is not so properly a distinct kind of good in God, but only expresses the degree of the good there is in him" (*WJE* 8:528). God's eternity speaks to how long his goodness endures.

78. Edwards said, "And thus we see how, not only the creature's seeing and knowing God's excellence, but also supremely esteeming and loving him, belongs to the communication of God's fullness" (*WJE* 8:528).

emanation of his internal glory" comprise God's glory, yet there is but one internal glory of God.[79]

Edwards understood the internal glory of God to be seated in both the divine understanding and will. The holiness and happiness of God are together the will of God in relation to his own glory. God's external glory is really the "emanation" of his internal glory. This explains why God fashioned human faculties as he did. If God's internal glory is in the divine understanding and will, then humans were made with an understanding and will to receive the external outflow of God's glory. "God communicates himself to the understanding of the creature, in giving him the knowledge of his glory; and to the will of the creature, in giving him holiness, consisting primarily in the love of God: and in giving the creature happiness, chiefly consisting in joy in God" (8:529). The Bible calls the communication of God's glory to the understanding "truth" and to the will "grace."[80] Although left unstated in *End*, the truth of God communicated to the understanding of saints is the *logos*—or Word—Jesus Christ, who is excellent or beautiful in himself.[81] As Stephen Holmes notes, Edwards's view of God's glory informed his psychology.[82]

God created the world to bring glory to himself. When God communicates his external glory to people, he does so for their good, yet with a "supreme regard to himself," because it is God's own delight in himself that he communicates to them:

> The emanation or communication of the divine fullness, consisting in the knowledge of God, love to God, and joy in God, has relation indeed both to God and the creature: but it has relation to God as its fountain, and it is an emanation from God; and as the communication itself, or thing communicated, is something divine, something of God, something of his internal fullness; as the water in the stream is something of the fountain; and as the beams are of the sun.[83]

For Edwards, an understanding and love for God's glory was a communication of God to the creature.[84] God is not only the source whereby people taste his glory, but he is the object of that glory (as he is in his internal glory). Edwards continued:

79. The language of emanation is what McGiffert uses to find pantheism in Edwards (*Edwards*, 180). Compare Louis Berkhof, *Systematic Theology* (Grand Rapids, MI: Wm. B. Eerdmans, 1996), 171; and George S. Claghorn, "Introduction," in *WJE* 8:631–35. On Edwards as a panentheist, see Oliver D. Crisp, *Jonathan Edwards on God and Creation* (Oxford: Oxford University Press, 2012), 140–51.

80. Edwards cited Jn 1:14.

81. See, for example, Edwards, *The Excellency of Christ*, in *WJE* 19:563–94.

82. Holmes, *God of Grace*, 180–84.

83. *WJE* 8:531. Also see Cochran, *Receptive*, 47–49.

84. In *The Most High a Prayer-Hearing God*, Edwards argued that God answers prayer in communicating himself to saints. God does not hear prayer to "be informed of our wants or desires," but so to show mercy, which is most fittingly a communication of himself (*HW*

> In the creature's knowing, esteeming, loving, rejoicing in, and praising God, the glory of God is both exhibited and acknowledged; his fullness is received and returned. Here is both an *emanation* and *remanation*. The refulgence shines upon and into the creature, and is reflected back to the luminary. The beams of glory come from God, and are something of God, and are refunded back again to their original. So that the whole is *of* God, and *in* God, and *to* God; and God is the beginning, middle and end in this affair. (8:531)

Edwards wanted to hold two paradoxical things together. God exhibits his own glory for his own glory, yet, at the same time, God exhibits his glory to bring creatures the greatest benefit. Edwards urged that these apparently conflicting ends not be pressed too greatly. God's heart is not divided. His intent in creating the world was something that saw all these aspects of his glory at once. Although God has never needed humans to bring him glory, God knew he would emanate his glory, communicate himself, and that it would be returned to him.[85] From the beginning, this was God's plan for bringing himself glory. God loves his own glory, and so he loves "the image," which is the creature's delight in the glory of God (8:532). Moreover, it is exactly because God delights in himself that he delights in his creature's happiness as found in him. From this, "'tis easy" to understand how God, in seeking to bring himself glory, also seeks humanity's good, for people's greatest happiness is found in God's beauty. God's making his glory his chief end and the creature's good are not opposed:

> God's respect to the creature's good, and his respect to himself, is not a divided respect; but both are united in one, as the happiness of the creature aimed at is happiness in union with himself. The creature is no further happy with this happiness which God makes his ultimate end than he becomes one with God. The more happiness the greater the union. (8:533)

Throughout eternity, human happiness in God will perpetually increase as the union perfects, "nearer and more like to that between the Father and the Son" (8:533). The most perfect union a creature can have with God is infinitely higher than anything experienced in this world, and throughout eternity, the union of the saint with God moves increasingly upwards. Because God intended this union,

2:115). "While they are praying, he gives them sweet views of his glorious grace, purity, sufficiency, and sovereignty; and enables them, with great quietness, to rest in him, to leave themselves and their prayers with him, submitting to his will, and trusting in his grace and faithfulness" (*HW* 2:114). Compare *Praying for the Spirit* in *WJE* 22:213–23.

85. Doug Sweeney says it well: "That Christians magnify but do not increase God's fullness is only the most poignant of Edwards' several paradoxes. (Others: the notion that our actions are both free and morally necessary; the notion that sinners are able and unable to convert.) He was a both/and thinker, who tried to speak persuasively to the many paradoxes of life." *Jonathan Edwards*, 162 n34.

and is the object of the creature's increasing perfection, even here, "if God be this center, then God aimed at himself."[86]

Conclusion

In his later years, Jonathan Edwards was still concerned with affections. As a young man, he had defined "being" to be consent. In his mature thought, Edwards continued to use the same metaphysical framework to confront the early modern tendencies away from the God of excellence. God loved his own glory in a Trinity of love. He created human beings to reflect that glory back to him through true affections for God given by the Holy Spirit.[87]

To his death, Edwards maintained the conceptual distinction between the soul's higher affections and the passions of the body's appetites. He continually stressed that Spirit-wrought affections were necessary in true religion. Given that humans were created with rational faculties to bring glory to God, sin itself was a distortion of the created order in radical self-love, seen both in affections toward oneself (as in pride) and in the abuse of the passions. Consequently, true virtue is not found in an optimistic notion that all humans naturally love, but in "consent to Being in general," first in love to God and then toward fellow humans. The Triune God who is infinitely joyful in beholding and loving his own glory wants his creatures to share in that happiness that can only be found in him.

The first chapter of this book cited several evangelical and charismatic authors, as well as other scholars, who sustain the notion that the affections Edwards discussed are emotions. Affections are not emotions. First, pre-modern and early modern models of human affectivity seated affections and passions in the soul. While Christian thinkers recognized the *effect* these movements had on the body, they distinguished the cause (affections) from these effects. Second, earlier models of human affectivity generally viewed the affections and passions of the soul as mere inclinations and aversions. The focus was not on corporeal feelings, but on the desires and repulsions behind them. Third, Christian theologians traditionally distinguished between the movements of the higher soul and those movements connected with the lower soul and the appetites of the body. Indeed, Edwards had a concept of the corporeal effects of the affections and passions, and he refused to include those effects with his idea of affections.

86. Edwards continued: "And herein it appears that as he [God] is the first author of their being and motion, so he is the last end, the final term, to which is their ultimate tendency and aim" (*WJE* 8:535).

87. Ronald Story observes, "Love pervades Jonathan Edwards's ministry and writing, a point often overlooked given his lingering reputation as a preacher of damnation." Ronald Story, *Jonathan Edwards and the Gospel of Love* (Amherst: University of Massachusetts Press, 2012), 98.

Furthermore, at least four problems often arise with many of the theologians and scholars who identify Edwards's concept of affections with emotions: (1) a lucid definition of emotion is often absent from their discussion; (2) Edwards explicitly rejected the idea that affections are intrinsically corporeal; (3) Edwards strongly cautioned against making much of the bodily effects of affections—although these effects nearly always occur in embodied souls, they are deceptive and to be avoided; and (4) the various accounts often fail to appreciate the importance the distinction between affections and passions played in Edwards's thought.

Edwards believed that the affections of embodied souls always have bodily effects, but those bodily effects are not, strictly speaking, part of or necessary to affections.[88] So, although John Piper is right to insist that Edwards married heart and head, at times he goes too far in saying that corporeal feelings attend Edwards's idea of affections.[89] It is noteworthy that Piper's exposition of emotions and religion in other discussions is more in line with Edwards's thought.[90]

Gerald McDermott's definition of affections as "*strong inclinations of the soul that are manifested in thinking, feeling and acting*" is helpful, but he nevertheless confuses the matter when he says emotions are necessary to all affections.[91] Sam Storms distinguishes affections and emotional feelings, yet adds confusion by insisting that affections must be "emotional" and involve "intense feelings."[92] Borgman's definition of emotions as the expression of values is a step in the right direction, but even this "cognitive view" of emotions—that he associates with the category of affections in Edwards—does not match affections as love or heightened movements of the will.[93]

Furthermore, those evangelicals who defend highly manipulative forms of worship in the name of Edwards's idea of affections not only misunderstand the category affections, but the whole point of Edwards's theology of affections. Similarly, John White, Jack Deere, and Guy Chevreau seem to have actually taken Edwards's concept of "passions" to defend their idea of religious emotion.

88. Affections always affect the body. Edwards said: "So subject is the body to the mind, and so much do its fluids, especially the animals spirits, attend the motions and exercises of the mind, that there can't be so much as an intense thought, without an effect upon them. Yea, 'tis questionable, whether an embodied soul ever so much as thinks one thought, or has any exercise at all, but that this is some corresponding motion or alteration of motion, in some degree, of the fluids, in some part of the body" (*WJE* 2:132).

89. John Piper, *Desiring God*, 79, 298–9n1.

90. See John Piper, *When I Don't Desire God*, 179–82.

91. Gerald R. McDermott, *Seeing God*, 32. Similar analysis could be made of Mark Talbot's article "Godly Emotions."

92. Sam Storms, *Signs of the Spirit*, 45.

93. Brain S. Borgman, *Feelings and Faith*, 19–27.

Edwards's category of passions should not be equated with contemporary emotions either.[94] It is true that passions relate to the sense appetite and the corporeal body—they have their "seat in animal nature" (4:297). Yet they are not mere feelings of the body. Passions arise from natural instincts and sensitive desires (8:565, 595). In *Charity*, Edwards described the passion of anger as a movement that bypasses reason (8:277). In any case, the modern category "emotions," in its ambiguity, may be used more broadly to mean something other than mere physiological feelings.

The greatest clarity can be found in Dixon and McClymond's works.[95] McClymond is right when he says: "Edwards says little on the metaphysical issue of how soul and body interact, though he seems to imply that changes in either the soul or the body may affect the other." "Seems to imply," however, is too weak a description. Edwards did, in fact, insist that the body could have a profound influence on the soul as well as the inverse. A passion could never cause a *religious affection* in the sense that Edwards meant by that concept, but the means of grace, in all their externality, could be used by the Spirit of God to give more divine love for the glory of God.

94. *Pace* Sailer, *The Soul in Paraphrase*, 4–14; Aniol, *Worship in Song*, 52–54; Hotz and Matthews, *Shaping the Christian Life*, 13–14; and Lucas, *God's Grand Design*, 92.

95. Dixon, *From Passions to Emotions*; McClymond, "Jonathan Edwards," in *OHRE*, 404–17. One can only applaud someone like McClymond who has the audacity to say, in a book about "religion and emotion," that Edwards really did not talk about emotion.

Chapter 8

TOWARD A THEOLOGY OF AFFECTIONS

O hide this self from me, that I
No more, but Christ in me, may live;
My vile affections crucify,
Nor let one darling lust survive;
In all things nothing may I see,
Nothing desire, or seek, but Thee.

— Gerhard Tersteegen, tr. John Wesley

The goal of this book has been to describe Edwards's affective psychology, and to find its points of contact and discordance with modern emotions.

The introduction showed that many explanations of Edwards—ranging from those by American evangelicals and Charismatics, to other scholars—equate affections (as Edwards understood them) and emotions. Another frequent charge is that Edwards derived his psychology from John Locke.

Citing the research of Thomas Dixon and others, the introduction also showed that emotions are actually a modern category rising from the influence of science in the nineteenth century. By the late twentieth century, there were many competing definitions of emotions—thereby making their continuity with the past even more difficult to determine. Proposing that emotions be defined as "a class of feelings, differentiated from sensation or proprioceptions by their experienced quality," the argument of this book has been that Edwards's idea of affections was not only in line with traditional Christianity, but also quite distinct from what often are considered emotions today.

To defend the position that Edwards shared great continuity with traditional Christian understandings of human affectivity, it is necessary to understand those traditional ideas. The study of these ideas in the second and third chapters produced the following conclusions: (1) traditionally, Christian theologians understood affections and passions as movements of the soul; (2) they saw these movements to be inclinations or aversions; (3) the authors distinguished the soul's higher and lower appetites and their accompanying movements; (4) the distinction between affections and passions is illustrated in the simultaneous approbation of divine impassibility and love; and (5) they often saw passions affecting the body, although this influence was distinguished from the passion itself. Puritans and Reformed

Scholastics interpreted the affections as movements of the soul, connected with the will. God is the object of the will and affections of saints. God alone can change peoples' affections, which are by nature depraved.

In his formal education, Edwards received this traditional Christian understanding of human affectivity. Despite his enjoyment of Locke, Edwards rejected the philosopher's affective psychology on almost every point. He learned the traditional Puritan model of affections. Ames, Turretin, Stoddard, and other Reformed authors taught Edwards that the faculties of the soul are not distinct entities. He also learned of the close relationship of the will and love to affections, another common view in Reformed literature.

Edwards's early writings and sermons demonstrate that he accepted these teachings. In his definition of being as consent, Edwards made affections a crucial underpinning to his metaphysics. The Triune God, although impassible, was a God of affections. The Holy Spirit, the Triune person of divine love, is the bond that unites the Father and the Son. The Spirit is also the divine love graciously bestowed to believers, and thereby holy affections toward the spiritual beauty of divine reality dwell within the saints. Holy affections are a "sense of the heart," a marriage of ideal apprehension and the will, directed toward the spiritual beauty of divine holiness.

Edwards also acknowledged lower desires arising from sense pleasure and pain. Although Edwards did not always distinguish *affections* and *passions* by name, he did so conceptually. Affections are the actions of the will, while passions are violent movements arising out of self-love corresponding to the sensitive appetite. Edwards permitted holy affections to be unhindered, but he urged that passions be controlled by reason. To be ruled by the passions is to lower oneself to the level of animals. To be controlled by holy affections shows the influence the Holy Spirit.

When the Great Awakening rolled over New England, Edwards found himself addressing affections again. Not only was he called upon to help spiritually guide newly "affected" converts, but he found himself defending the importance of holy affections against the revival's opponents. Most notable among the Awakening's detractors was Charles Chauncy, who said that high affections amounted to enthusiasm. He saw affections as lower movements to be controlled by reason. Edwards rejected this. Leaning upon his Puritan heritage, his metaphysics and theology, and the Bible itself, Edwards argued that affections are not only important, but crucial: "True religion, in great part, consists in holy affections" (2:95). Edwards pointed out that affections were different from passions. Nevertheless, Edwards did not endorse everything done in the name of affections amidst the revival. Holy affections were absolutely supernatural. He carefully distinguished gracious affections, natural affections, passions, and their bodily effects.

Edwards maintained these emphases on affections until his untimely death. He perpetuated his rubric for affections, distinguishing them from movements of the sense appetites. He emphasized divinely given holy affections in religion as distinct from the false affections of extremists. Against the increasingly secular mores of his epoch, Edwards's understanding of human affectivity looms large in his project to defend Calvinist Christianity from its moralistic and Arminian foes. He reiterated that (1) humans by nature have an innate problem with sinful affections and passions, (2) true virtue lies not in mere external behavior but in a fundamental reorientation of affections toward God and fellow humans, and (3) God's final end for all creation is that human wills and affections reflect back to God the glory that he graciously communicates to them. Affections lie near the heart of Edwards's entire theological system.

Edwardsean studies have not paid due attention to Edwards's distinction between affections and passions. The conversation has so focused on Locke and "sense of the heart" that other important aspects of Edwards's theological anthropology have gone all but overlooked. Nevertheless, the distinction between body and soul, spiritual and sense appetites, and affections and passions were crucial for Edwards. He never abandoned these traditional Christian notions of humanity, and he used them powerfully in his sermons and writings. Although the distinction between affections and passions is not, in itself, absolutely central in Edwards's thought, the neglect in scholarship of this important theme has hindered a right understanding of Edwards. The tendency to reinterpret him for our own time has also dimmed the colors of the portrait. By replacing affections with emotions (often done to make Edwards more intelligible and contemporary), interpreters have left readers with a distorted Edwards. Edwards did not conceive of affections as corporeal feelings at all, but as strong movements of the will.

This study suggests other possible scholarly pursuits. For one, it asks for a refreshed understanding of all pre-modern Christian thought on affections and passions and chastens those who equate these categories with emotions. More study could be done on how Cartesian thought on the passions influenced Edwards and his Puritan fathers. With respect to Edwards, additional work could be done to understand his relationship to John Norris (first) and Nicholas Malebranche in the specific realm of human affectivity. A thorough look at John Owen's influence on Edwards would likely bear much fruit. Finally, it is quite common today for theologians to reject the traditional doctrine of the impassibility of God.[1] This study encourages all theologians to return to the primary sources and struggle to understand the intent of the impassibility doctrine before rejecting it outright.

Joseph Conforti recounts that during the "Second Great Awakening" one of the important questions of the "paper wars" between Finney and the New

1. For example, see Wayne Grudem, *Systematic Theology: An Introduction to Biblical Doctrine* (Grand Rapids, MI: Zondervan Publishing House, 1994), 165–66; Stanley J. Grenz, *Theology for the Community of God* (Grand Rapids, MI: Zondervan Publishing House, 2000), 91; John S. Feinberg, *No One Like Him: The Doctrine of God*, Foundations of Evangelical Theology (Wheaton, IL: Crossway Books, 2001), 277, 239–43, 264–76, 325–37. Compare Weinandy, *Does God Suffer?*; Michael Horton, *The Christian Faith: A Systematic Theology for Pilgrims on the Way* (Grand Rapids, MI: Zondervan, 2011), 242–53; and James E. Dolezal, *All That is in God: Evangelical Theology and the Challenge of Classical Christian Theism* (Grand Rapids, MI: Reformation Heritage Books, 2017).

England revivalists was the role of affections in revivals.[2] This paper hints that it may be necessary to reinvestigate and perhaps qualify those interpretations of Edwards and American thought that argue that Edwards gave sanction to emotion for his heirs.[3] Furthermore, no work has yet charted and explained the erosion of Edwardsean thought on affections among the New England theologians and especially in Charles Finney, who confused Edwards's notion of *affections* with bodily "emotions."[4]

In conclusion, it is fitting to address a few questions that may have come up while reading this book. Several emphases in Edwards's thought merit careful reevaluation. Generally speaking, Edwards's system is compelling. His teachings on God's glory, affections for God, the distinction between affections and passions, the nature of true religion, the difference between humans and animals, the role of the Word in the affections, the Trinity, the image of God, ethics, and the work of the Spirit are—especially as united together—an elegant way of putting the Christian faith together.

A return to the traditional Christian notion of human affectivity is likely impossible. Even a large movement of people determined not to speak of emotions,

2. Conforti, *Jonathan Edwards, Religious Tradition*, 11–35, 36–61. See Lyman Beecher and Asahel Nettleton, *Letters of the Rev. Dr. Beecher and Rev. Mr. Nettleton on the "New Measures" in Conducting Revivals of Religion* (New York: G. & C. Carvill, 1828), 64, 79; William Buell Sprague, *Lectures on the Revivals of Religion* (Glasgow: William Collins, 1832); Samuel Miller, *Lives of Jonathan Edwards and David Brainerd*, ed. Jared Sparks, Library of American Biography 8 (Boston: Hilliard, Gray, and Co., 1837); Charles G. Finney, *Lectures to Professing Christians* (New York: John S. Taylor, 1837); Also see, William H. Channing, "Edwards and the Revivalists," *Christian Examiner* 43 (1847): 374–94; Conforti, *Jonathan Edwards, Religious Tradition, & American Culture* (Chapel Hill: University of North Carolina Press, 1995); and Mark Noll, *America's God.*

3. Norman Grabo, "Colonial American Theology: Holiness and the Lyric Impulse," in *Essays in Honor of Russel B. Nye*, ed. Joseph Waldheim (East Lansing: Michigan State University Press, 1978), 74–91; Suzanne Geissler, *Jonathan Edwards to Aaron Burr, Jr.: From the Great Awakening to Democratic Politics*, Studies in American Religion 1 (Lewiston, NY: Edwin Mellen, 1981); Wayne Proudfoot, "From Theology to a Science of Religions: Jonathan Edwards and William James on Religious Affections," *Harvard Theological Review* 82 (1989): 149–68.

4. Charles G. Finney, "Love Worketh No Ill," *Oberlin Evangelist* 3, no. 5 (March 3, 1841), 35. But compare his *Lectures to Professing Christians*, 313. Also see Joseph Bellamy, *True Religion Delineated* (1750; repr., Morris-town, NJ: Henry P. Russell, 1804); Samuel Hopkins, *The System of Doctrines*, 2 vols. (Boston: Isaiah Thomas & Ebenezer T. Andrews, 1793); Jonathan Edwards (Jr.), *Remarks on the Improvements Made in Theology by his Father, President Edwards*, in *The Works of Jonathan Edwards, D.D., Late President of Union College*, ed. Tryon Edwards (Boston: Doctrinal Tract and Book Society, 1850), 1:481–92; and Sweeney and Guelzo, eds., *The New England Theology.*

but only clearly of affections and passions, is both unlikely and problematic.[5] Even so, the category emotions is bankrupt, for people rarely speak understandingly of them. This is a difficult issue. If people insist on addressing modes of human affectivity as emotions, they should avoid the notion that emotions are corporeal. Understanding people as human beings rather than mere matter is more intelligible and true. The images from brain scans that show visual representations of the intellect and affections do not prove that these acts are material any more than facial expressions do. Christians, like Edwards, should believe that God has given to his image-bearers a spiritual capacity of apprehension and love.

From a Christian point of view, the word *emotions* does not provide clarity to our understanding of ourselves, our God, or the Scriptures, especially if the most common definition is applied. Christians should attempt to reintroduce the distinctions, and to recognize the differences, among God, humans, and animals, and between affections and passions. Like Edwards, Christian thinkers should define terms, and this is especially true for a word like *emotions*, which has so many competing definitions.[6] It is unnecessary to refer to human affections as emotions, and it would be beneficial (although no panacea) to resurrect the more traditional concepts *and language* of affectivity, especially in service of Christian theology.[7]

Human beings, and especially Christians, are not better off having forgotten these distinctions. Christian churches, in the name of Jesus Christ, habitually exploit the appetites and passions to win converts. Edwards's thought calls believers to return to *spiritual* affections as the cornerstone of Christian piety. Many people find all human passions self-justifying. Consequently, few have the courage, even on rational grounds, to forbid even the basest human desires. Edwards's thought also calls for a return to ethics and morality, and for those systems to consider the

5. Indeed, there are points of continuity between emotions and affections. Love (another term whose currency is hazarded through abuse), joy, and anger are all considered affections and emotions. As noted in the introduction, analytic philosophy has suggested constructive and improved understandings of emotions, seeking to root them more in traditional or Neo-Stoic thought. Some philosophers purposefully regard emotions as states of the mind or even the soul. Even so, if one redefines emotions as "value judgments," as Martha Nussbaum does, one still lacks the distinction between rational value judgments and sensitive value judgments. In other words, redefining *emotions* (the ambitious goals of such a project aside) still tends toward collapsing the pre-modern categories.

6. For many reasons, Paul Lewis's proposal of using Edwards's notion of affections to "reconceive of emotions as the unity of the self" is an example of the dead-end in using emotions as a fill-in for affections. If one includes both affections and passions as emotions, in that sense Edwards did not conceive of human affectivity as bringing unity to the self. It is also questionable if he regarded mere affections as bringing unity to the self as Lewis proposes. Through self-love, passions and natural affections often warred against gracious affections. See "Springs of Motion," 293–94.

7. For example, see Alvin Plantinga's discussion of affections (interacting with Edwards) in *Warranted Christian Belief* (Oxford: Oxford University Press, 2000), 294–304.

distinction between higher and lower desires. Because of his rigid commitment to the Word of God, Edwards had the audacity to assert that Christian morality and aesthetics are revealed in nature and are most reasonable. Christians today would do well to model such courage and clarity of thought.

Edwards, like many Christians before him, rightly believed that human beings were fundamentally creatures of inclination and desire. Love is a fundamental aspect of existence. Truly, the loves of the higher, rational aspect of humanity transcend the passions of lower sensuality, and, as creatures endowed with a rational soul, those higher loves ought to govern and moderate the pursuit of sensual pleasures that arise from self-love. Ultimately, those rational pleasures ought to be inclined toward the only thing that can satisfy the infinite appetite of the immaterial soul: the Triune God. This can only happen by the grace of God.

The dark truth is that by nature humanity universally recoils from their Creator. As punishment for original sin, God has withdrawn the principles of divine grace originally given to our first parents, and self-love now reigns like a despot. Human desires are unbridled, immoderate, and base. Even those who have the appearance of real virtue are often rooted in sordid self-love principles such as pride and vainglory. Yet, Jesus Christ, the Son who displays the fullness of the excellency of the Father, died to reconcile humanity to God, and his death made affections or consent between the creature and Creator possible. This is the love of God for his creation on display.

In Christ humans see God's glory. For those who believe on him, which itself is a form of consent to this excellent Christ and God, God gives the Spirit of love, who works supernatural principles of divine love in the human heart, bringing holy affections that see the glorious beauty of holiness in the Triune God. Consequentially, this is true virtue, for human beings to love the Lord their God with all their heart, soul, mind, and strength, and their neighbor as themselves. True religion, in great part, consists in holy affections.

BIBLIOGRAPHY

Yale Works of Jonathan Edwards

Edwards, Jonathan. *Freedom of the Will.* Vol. 1 of *The Works of Jonathan Edwards.* Edited by Paul Ramsey. New Haven, CT: Yale University Press, 1957.

Edwards, Jonathan. *Religious Affections.* Vol. 2 of *The Works of Jonathan Edwards.* Edited by John E. Smith. New Haven, CT: Yale University Press, 1959.

Edwards, Jonathan. *Original Sin.* Vol. 3 of *The Works of Jonathan Edwards.* Edited by Clyde A. Holbrook. New Haven, CT: Yale University Press, 1970.

Edwards, Jonathan. *The Great Awakening.* Vol. 4 of *The Works of Jonathan Edwards.* Edited by C. C. Goen. New Haven, CT: Yale University Press, 1972.

Edwards, Jonathan. *Apocalyptic Writings.* Vol. 5 of *The Works of Jonathan Edwards.* Edited by Stephen J. Stein. New Haven, CT: Yale University Press, 1977.

Edwards, Jonathan. *Scientific and Philosophical Writings.* Vol. 6 of *The Works of Jonathan Edwards.* Edited by Wallace E. Anderson. New Haven, CT: Yale University Press, 1980.

Edwards, Jonathan. *The Life of David Brainerd.* Vol. 7 of *The Works of Jonathan Edwards.* Edited by Norman Pettit. New Haven, CT: Yale University Press, 1985.

Edwards, Jonathan. *Ethical Writings.* Vol. 8 of *The Works of Jonathan Edwards.* Edited by Paul Ramsey. New Haven, CT: Yale University Press, 1989.

Edwards, Jonathan. *A History of the Work of Redemption.* Vol. 9 of *The Works of Jonathan Edwards.* Edited by John F. Wilson. New Haven, CT: Yale University Press, 1989.

Edwards, Jonathan. *Sermons and Discourses, 1720–1723.* Vol. 10 of *The Works of Jonathan Edwards.* Edited by Wilson H. Kimnach. New Haven, CT: Yale University Press, 1992.

Edwards, Jonathan. *Typological Writings.* Vol. 11 of *The Works of Jonathan Edwards.* Edited by Wallace E. Anderson and Mason I. Lowance, Jr., with David H. Watters. New Haven, CT: Yale University Press, 1993.

Edwards, Jonathan. *Ecclesiastical Writings.* Vol. 12 of *The Works of Jonathan Edwards.* Edited by David D. Hall. New Haven, CT: Yale University Press, 1994.

Edwards, Jonathan. *The "Miscellanies" (Entry Nos. a–500).* Vol. 13 of *The Works of Jonathan Edwards.* Edited by Thomas A. Schafer. New Haven, CT: Yale University Press, 1994.

Edwards, Jonathan. *Sermons and Discourses, 1723–1729.* Vol. 14 of *The Works of Jonathan Edwards.* Edited by Kenneth P. Minkema. New Haven, CT: Yale University Press, 1997.

Edwards, Jonathan. *Notes on Scripture.* Vol. 15 of *The Works of Jonathan Edwards.* Edited by Stephen J. Stein. New Haven, CT: Yale University Press, 1998.

Edwards, Jonathan. *Letters and Personal Writings.* Vol. 16 of *The Works of Jonathan Edwards.* Edited by George S. Claghorn. New Haven, CT: Yale University Press, 1998.

Edwards, Jonathan. *Sermons and Discourses, 1730–1733.* Vol. 17 of *The Works of Jonathan Edwards.* Edited by Mark Valeri. New Haven, CT: Yale University Press, 1999.

Edwards, Jonathan. *The "Miscellanies" (Entry Nos. 501–832).* Vol. 18 of *The Works of Jonathan Edwards.* Edited by Ava Chamberlain. New Haven, CT: Yale University Press, 2000.

Edwards, Jonathan. *Sermons and Discourses, 1734–1738.* Vol. 19 of *The Works of Jonathan Edwards.* Edited by M. X. Lesser. New Haven, CT: Yale University Press, 2001.

Edwards, Jonathan. *The "Miscellanies," 833–1152*. Vol. 20 of *The Works of Jonathan Edwards*. Edited by Amy Plantinga Pauw. New Haven, CT: Yale University Press, 2002.

Edwards, Jonathan. *Writings on the Trinity, Grace, and Faith*. Vol. 21 of *The Works of Jonathan Edwards*. Edited by Sang Hyun Lee. New Haven, CT: Yale University Press, 2003.

Edwards, Jonathan. *Sermons and Discourses, 1739–1742*. Vol. 22 of *The Works of Jonathan Edwards*. Edited by Harry S. Stout and Nathan O. Hatch. New Haven, CT: Yale University Press, 2003.

Edwards, Jonathan. *The "Miscellanies" (Entry Nos. 1153–1360)*. Vol. 23 of *The Works of Jonathan Edwards*. Edited by Douglas A. Sweeney. New Haven, CT: Yale University Press, 2004.

Edwards, Jonathan. *The "Blank Bible."* Vol. 24 of *The Works of Jonathan Edwards*. 2 vols. Edited by Stephen J. Stein. New Haven, CT: Yale University Press, 2006.

Edwards, Jonathan. *Sermons and Discourses, 1743–1758*. Vol. 25 of *The Works of Jonathan Edwards*. Edited by Wilson H. Kimnach. New Haven, CT: Yale University Press, 2006.

Edwards, Jonathan. *Catalogues of Books*. Vol. 26 of *The Works of Jonathan Edwards*. Edited by Peter J. Thuesen. New Haven, CT: Yale University Press, 2008.

Edwards, Jonathan. *The Works of Jonathan Edwards Online*. Vols. 27–73. Edited by Jonathan Edwards Center. New Haven, CT: Jonathan Edwards Center at Yale University, 2008. http://edwards.yale.edu/

Other Works by Jonathan Edwards

Edwards, Jonathan. *The Blessing of God: Previously Unpublished Sermons of Jonathan Edwards*. Edited by Michael D. McMullen. Nashville, TN: Broadman and Holman Publishers, 2003.

Edwards, Jonathan. *Charity and Its Fruits; or, Christian Love as Manifested in the Heart and Life*. Edited by Tryon Edwards. New York: Robert Carter & Brothers, 1852.

Edwards, Jonathan. Sermon on Mt. 24:12. Folder 501. Box 7. Jonathan Edwards Papers. Beinecke Rare Book and Manuscript Library. New Haven, CT: Yale University Press, 1742.

Edwards, Jonathan. *The Experience that Counts!* Edited by Nicholas R. Needham. London: Grace Publications Trust, 1991.

Edwards, Jonathan. *The Glory and Honor of God: Volume 2 of the Previously Unpublished Sermons of Jonathan Edwards*. Edited by Michael D. McMullen. Nashville, TN: Broadman & Holman, 2004.

Edwards, Jonathan. *True and False Christians (On the Parable of the Wise and Foolish Virgins)*. Vol. 1 of *Sermons by Jonathan Edwards on the Matthean Parables*. Edited by Kenneth P. Minkema, Adriaan C. Neele, and Bryan McCarthy. Eugene, OR: Cascade Books, 2012.

Edwards, Jonathan. *The Works of Jonathan Edwards*. 2 vols. Edited by Edward Hickman. Edinburgh: Banner of Truth Trust, 1974.

Faust, Clarence H., and Thomas H. Johnson. *Jonathan Edwards: Representative Selections, with Introduction, Bibliography, and Notes*. Rev. ed. New York: Hill and Wang, 1962.

Howard, Leon. *"The Mind" of Jonathan Edwards: A Reconstructed Text*. Berkeley: University of California Press, 1963.

Other Primary Sources

Addison, Joseph. *The Spectator, Vol. III.* 12th ed. London, 1739.

Ames, William. *The Marrow of Theology.* 1968. Reprint, Grand Rapids, MI: Baker Books, 1997.

Ames, William. *The Substance of Christian Religion: or, A plain and easie Draught of the Christian Catechisme.* London: T. Mabb for T. Davies, 1659.

Anselm of Canterbury *St. Anselm: Basic Writings.* Translated by S. N. Deane. LaSalle, IL: Open Court, 1962.

Anselm of Canterbury. *The Prayers and Meditations of Saint Anselm with the Proslogium.* Translated by Benedicta Ward. Penguin Classics. New York: Penguin Books, 1973.

Augustine of Hippo. *Answer to the Pelagians III.* Vol. 25 of *The Works of Saint Augustine.* Translated by Roland J. Teske. New York: New City Press, 1999.

Augustine of Hippo. *St. Augustine, of the Citie of God: with the Learned Comments of Ioannes Lodovicus Vives.* Translated by J. H. N.P.: George Eld, 1610.

Augustine of Hippo. *The City of God.* Translated by Marcus Dods. New York: The Modern Library, 1993.

Augustine of Hippo. *Confessions.* Edited by W. H. D. Rouse. 2 vols. Loeb Classical Library 26–27. Cambridge, MA: Harvard University Press, 1977.

Augustine of Hippo. *De Civitate Dei.* In *Sancti Aurelii Augustini, Hipponensis Episcopi, Opera Omnia, Tomus Septimus,* edited by the Monks of the Order of Saint Benedict, 13–804. Vol. 41 of *Patrologiæ Latina,* J. -P. Migne. Paris, 1864.

Augustine of Hippo. *The Happy Life, Answer to Skeptics, Divine Providence and the Problem of Evil, and Soliloquies.* Vol. 1 of *The Writings of Saint Augustine.* Edited by Ludwig Schopp. Fathers of the Church 5. New York: CIMA Publishing, 1948.

Augustine of Hippo. *On Marriage and Concupiscence.* In *Saint Augustin's Anti-Pelagian Works,* translated by Peter Holmes, Robert Ernest Wallis, and Benjamin B. Warfield, 257–308. Nicene and Post-Nicene Fathers, First Series 5. 1887. Reprint, Peabody, MA: Hendrickson Publishers, 1994.

Augustine of Hippo. *The Trinity* (De Trinitate). Translated by Edmund Hill. *The Works of Saint Augustine,* Part I, Vol. 5. Edited by John E. Rotelle. Hyde Park, NY: New City Press, 1991.

Baxter, Richard. *The Practical Works of The Rev. Richard Baxter with a Life of the Author, and a Critical Examination of his Writings.* 23 vols. Edited by William Orme. London: James Duncan, 1830.

Baxter, Richard. *The Reasons of the Christian Religion. The First Part, of Godliness: Proving by Natural Evidence the Being of God, the Necessity of Holiness, and a future Life of Retribution; the Sinfulness of the World; the Desert of Hell; and what hope of Recovery Mercies intimate. The Second Part, of Christianity: Proving by Evidence Supernatural and Natural, the certain Truth of the Christian Belief: And Answering the Objections of Unbelievers.* London: R. White for Fran. Titon, 1667.

Beecher, Lyman, and Asahel Nettleton. *Letters of the Rev. Dr. Beecher and Rev. Mr. Nettleton on the "New Measures" in Conducting Revivals of Religion.* New York: G. & C. Carvill, 1828.

Bellamy, Joseph. *True Religion Delineated.* 1750. Reprint, Morris-town, NJ: Henry P. Russell, 1804.

Bernard of Clairvaux. *Life and Works of Saint Bernard, Abbot of Clairvaux.* Edited by John Mabillon. Translated by Samuel J. Eales. 4 vols. London: John Hodges, 1889–96.

Bernard of Clairvaux. "Of the Three Ways in Which We Love God (Sermon XX on the Song of Songs)." In *Late Medieval Mysticism*, edited by Ray C. Petry, 66–73. Library of Christian Classics 8. Philadelphia: Westminster Press, 1957.

Bernard of Clairvaux. *Saint Bernard on the Love of God*. Translated by Marianne Caroline and Coventry Patmore. London: C. Kegan Paul, 1881.

Bernard of Clairvaux. *Sermones in Cantica canticorum*. In *S. Bernardi, Claræ-Vallensis Abbatis Primi, Opera Omnia, Sex Tomis*, edited by John Mabillon, 785–1198. Vol. 183 of *Patrologiæ Latina*, edited by J. -P. Migne. Paris, 1862.

Bernard of Clairvaux. *Treatises II*. Vol. 5 of *The Works of Bernard of Clairvaux*. Translated by Robert Walton. Cistercian Fathers Series 13. Washington, DC: Consortium Press, 1974.

Boston, Thomas. *Human Nature in Its Fourfold State of Primitive Integrity, Entire Depravity, Begun Recovery, and Consummate Happiness or Misery*. Carlisle, PA: The Banner of Truth Trust, 1964.

Brown, Thomas. *Lectures on the Philosophy of the Human Mind*. 2 vols. Hallowell: Glazier, Masters and Smith, 1839.

Calvin, John. *Commentaries on the First Twenty Chapters of the Book of the Prophet Ezekiel*. Translated by Thomas Myers. Grand Rapids, MI: Baker Book House, 1979.

Calvin, John. *The Epistles of Paul the Apostle to the Galatians, Ephesians, Philippians and Colossians*. Translated by T. H. L. Parker. Calvin's Commentaries 11. Grand Rapids, MI: William B. Eerdmans, 1965.

Calvin, John. *The Epistle of Paul The Apostle to the Hebrews and The First and Second Epistles of St Peter*. Translated by William B. Johnston. Calvin's Commentaries 12. Grand Rapids, MI: William B. Eerdmans, 1963.

Calvin, John. *In Evangelium Ioannis*. Vol. 3 of *Novum Testamentum Commentarii*. Edited by August Tholuck. Berlin: Gustav Eichler, 1833.

Calvin, John. *The Gospel according to St John 11-21 and The First Epistle of John*. Translated by T. H. L. Parker. Calvin's Commentaries 5. Grand Rapids, MI: William B. Eerdmans, 1959.

Calvin, John. *A Harmony of the Gospels: Matthew, Mark and Luke Volume III and the Epistles of James and Jude*. Calvin's Commentaries 3. Translated by A. W. Morrison. Grand Rapids, MI: William B. Eerdmans, 1972.

Calvin, John. *Institutes of the Christian Religion*. Edited by John T. McNeill. Translated by Ford Lewis Battles. Library of Christian Classics 20-21. Philadelphia: Westminster Press, 1960.

Calvin, John. *Institutio Christianae Religionis*. Edited by August Tholuck. Berlin: Gustav Eichler, 1834.

Calvin, John. *Writings on Pastoral Piety*. Edited by Elsie Anne McKee. Classics of Western Spirituality. Mahwah, NJ: Paulist Press, 2001.

Chambers, Ephraim. *Cyclopedia: or an Universal Dictionary of Arts and Sciences; containing the Definitions of the Terms, and Accounts of The Things Signify'd Thereby, in the Several Arts, both Liberal and Mechanical, and the Several Sciences, Human and Divine*. London: n.p., 1728.

Charnock, Stephen. *The Works of Stephen Charnock*. Edited by Thomas Smith. 5 vols. Edinburgh: James Nichol, 1864–65.

Chauncy, Charles. *Enthusiasm, Described and Caution'd Against*. Boston: J. Draper, 1742.

Chauncy, Charles. *Seasonable Thoughts on the State of Religion in New-England, A Treatise in Five Parts*. Boston: Rogers and Fowle, 1743.

Chauncy, Charles. *The Wonderful Narrative: Or, a Faithful Account of the French Prophets, Their Agitations, Extasies, and Inspirations.* Glasgow: Robert Foulis, 1742.

The Church Fathers—Ante-Nicene Fathers. Edited by Alexander Roberts and James Donaldson. 10 vols. 1885–87. Reprint, Peabody, MA: Hendrickson Publishers, 1994.

The Church Fathers—Nicene and Post-Nicene Fathers. Series 1. Edited by Philip Schaff. 14 vols. 1886–89. Reprint, Peabody, MA: Hendrickson Publishers, 1994.

The Church Fathers—Nicene and Post-Nicene Fathers. Series 1. Edited by Philip Schaff and Henry Wace. 14 vols. 1890–1900. Reprint, Peabody, MA: Hendrickson Publishers, 1994.

Clement of Alexandria. *Stromata, or Miscellanies.* In *Fathers of the Second Century: Hermas, Tatian, Athenagoras, Theophilus, and Clement of Alexandria (Entire)*, edited by A. Cleveland Coxe, 299–568. Ante-Nicene Fathers 2. 1885. Reprint, Peabody, MA: Hendrickson Publishers, 1994.

Clement of Alexandria. *Stromata.* In *Clementis Alexandrini Opera Quæ Exstant Omnia*, edited by Nicolai le Nourry, 9–602. Vol. 9 of *Patrologiæ Græcæ*, edited by J. -P. Migne. Paris, 1857.

Crousaz, Jean-Pierre de. *A New Treatise of the Art of Thinking; or, A Compleat System of Reflections, Concerning the Conduct and Improvement of the Mind.* 2 vols. London: Tho. Woodward, 1724.

Day, Jeremiah. *An Inquiry Respecting the Self-Determining Power of the Will or Contingent Volition.* New Haven: Herrick & Noyes, 1838.

Descartes, René. *The Passions of the Soul.* Translated by Stephen H. Voss. Indianapolis: Hackett, 1989.

Donne, John. *John Donne's Poetry.* 2nd ed. Edited by Arthur L. Clements. Norton critical edition. New York: Norton, 1992.

Edwards Jr., Jonathan. *Remarks on the Improvements Made in Theology by his Father, President Edwards.* In *The Works of Jonathan Edwards, D.D., Late President of Union College*, edited by Tryon Edwards, 481–92. Vol. 1. Boston: Doctrinal Tract and Book Society, 1850.

Fenner, William. *A Treatise of the Affections; or The Souls Pulse.* London: A.M., 1650.

Fiddes, Richard. *Theologia Speculativa: or, The First Part of a Body of Divinity Under that Title. Wherein are explain'd the Principles of Natural and Reveal'd Religion.* London: W. Bowyer, 1718.

Finney, Charles G. *Lectures to Professing Christians.* New York: John S. Taylor, 1837.

Finney, Charles G. "Love Worketh No Ill." *Oberlin Evangelist* 3, no. 5 (March 3, 1841): 33–36.

Gregory of Nyssa. *De Anima et Resurrectione Dialogus.* In *Gregorii, Episcopi Nysseni Opera Quæ Reperiri Potuerunt Omnia*, edited by J. -P. Migne, 11–160. Vol. 46 of *Patrologiæ Græcæ*, edited by J. -P. Migne. Paris, 1863.

Gregory of Nyssa. *Dogmatic Treatises, Etc.* Edited by William Moore and Henry Austin Wilson. Nicene and Post-Nicene Fathers, Second Series 5. 1893. Reprint, Peabody, MA: Hendrickson Publishers, 1994.

Gregory of Nyssa. *On the Soul and the Resurrection.* Translated by Catharine P. Roth. Popular Patristic Series. Crestwood, NY: St. Vladimir's Press, 2002.

Hopkins, Samuel. *The System of Doctrines.* 2 vols. Boston: Isaiah Thomas & Ebenezer T. Andrews, 1793.

Hutcheson, Francis. *An Essay on the Nature and Conduct of the Passions and Affections. With Illustrations upon the Moral Sense.* 3rd ed. Glasgow: Robert & Andrew Foulis, 1769.

Lewis, C. S. *The Great Divorce.* New York: Macmillan, 1946.

Locke, John. *An Essay Concerning Human Understanding.* Edited by Alexander Campbell Fraser. Great Books of the Western World 35. Chicago, IL: Encyclopædia Britannica, Inc., 1952.

Malebranche, Nicholas. *The Search after Truth: With Elucidations of The Search after Truth.* Edited by Thomas M. Lennonand Paul J. Olscamp. Cambridge Texts in the History of Philosophy. Cambridge: Cambridge University Press, 1997.

Manton, Thomas. *One Hundred and Ninety Sermons on the Hundred and Nineteenth Psalm.* 3 vols. London: William Brown, 1842.

Mastricht, Peter van. *Theoretico-Practica Theologia, qua Per singula capita Theologia, pars exegetica, dogmatica, elenchtica & practica, perpetua successione conjugantur.* Utrecht: W. Van de Water, J. v. Poolsum, J. Wagens, G. v. Paddenburg, 1724.

Mastricht, Peter van. *A Treatise on Regeneration.* Edited by Brandon Withrow. 1769. Reprint, Morgan, PA: Soli Deo Gloria Publications, 2002.

Mather, Increase, and Solomon Stoddard. *Increase Mather vs. Solomon Stoddard: Two Puritan Tracts.* Research Library of Colonial America. New York: Arno Press, 1972.

Melanchthon, Philip. *De Arte Concionandi Formulae ut Breves, Ita Doctae & Piae.* Basil: n.p., 1540.

Melanchthon, Philip. *Die Loci Communes.* Edited by D. Th. Kolde. Erlangen: George Böhme, 1890.

Melanchthon, Philip. *Loci Communes Theologici.* In *Melanchthon and Bucer*, edited by Wilhelm Pauck, 18–152. Library of Christian Classics 19. Philadelphia: Westminster Press, 1969.

Miller, Samuel. *Lives of Jonathan Edwards and David Brainerd.* Edited by Jared Sparks. Library of American Biography 8. Boston: Hilliard, Gray, and Co., 1837.

Nemesius of Emesa. *On the Nature of Man.* In *Cyril of Jerusalem and Nemesius of Emesa*, edited by William Telfer, 203–453. Library of Christian Classics 4. Philadelphia, PN: The Westminster Press, 1955.

Norris, John. *A Collection of Miscellanies: Consisting of Poems, Essays, Discourses, & Letters, Occasionally Written.* 3rd ed. London: S. Manship, 1699.

Owen, John. *The Works of John Owen.* Edited by William Goold. 23 vols. 1850–53. Reprint, Carlisle, PA: Banner of Truth Trust, 1966.

Pascal, Blaise. *Blaise Pascal: Thoughts and Minor Works.* Harvard Classics 48. Translated by O. W. Wright. New York: P. F. Collier and Son, 1938.

Pascal, Blaise. *Pensées.* Translated by A. J. Krailsheimer. New York: Penguin Books, 1966.

Pascal, Blaise. *Pensées.* Translated by Roger Ariew. Indianapolis, IN: Hackett, 2004.

Patrologia latina. Edited by J. -P. Migne. 217 vols. Paris, 1844–1864.

Patrologia graeca. Edited by J. -P. Migne. 162 vols. Paris, 1857–1886.

Petry, Ray C., ed. *Late Medieval Mysticism.* Library of Christian Classics 8. Philadelphia: Westminster Press, 1957.

Preston, John. *The Breast-Plate of Faith and Love.* Edited by Richard Sibbes and John Davenport. 6th ed. London: George Purflow, 1651.

Preston, John. *The Golden Sceptre Held Forth to the Humble.* London: Religious Tract Society, 1837.

Priestly, Joseph. *Hartley's Theory of the Human Mind, on the Principle of the Association of Ideas; with Essays relating to the Subject of It.* London: J. Johnson, 1775.

Reynolds, Edwards. *Treatise on the Passions and Faculties of the Soul.* Vol. 6 of *The Works of Edward Reynolds.* Edited by Alexander Chalmers. 1826. Reprint, Morgan, PA: Soli Deo Gloria, 1996.

Sibbes, Richard. *The Works of Richard Sibbes*. 7 vols. Edited by Alexander Balloch Grosart. Edinburgh: James Nichol, 1862.
Shepard, Thomas. *The Parable of the Ten Virgins Opened and Applied*. 1659. Reprint, Orlando, FL: Soli Deo Gloria Publications, 1990.
Smith, John. *Select Discourses*. 3rd ed. London: Rivingstons and Cochran, 1821.
Sprague, William Buell. *Lectures on the Revivals of Religion*. Glasgow: William Collins, 1832.
Stewart, Dugald. *The Works of Dugald Stewart*. 7 vols. Cambridge: Hilliard and Brown, 1829.
Stoddard, Solomon. *A Guide to Christ, or The Way of Directing Souls That Are under the Work of Conversion. Compiled for the Help of Young Ministers, and May Be Serviceable to Private Christians, Who are Enquiring the Way to Zion*. Northampton: Andrew Wright, 1816.
Stoddard, Solomon. *The Safety of Appearing at the Day of Judgment in the Righteousness of Christ, Opened and Applied*. Northampton: Thomas M. Pomroy, 1804.
Tappan, Henry. *A Treatise on the Will*. Glasgow: Lang, Adamson, & Co., 1857.
Taylor, John. *The Scripture Doctrine of Original Sin Proposed to Free and Candid Examination*. London: J. Wilson, 1740.
Thomas Aquinas. *The Emotions (1a2ae. 22–30)*. Vol. 19 of *Summa Theologiae*. Edited by Eric D'Arcy. New York: McGraw-Hill Book, 1967.
Thomas Aquinas. *Introduction to Saint Thomas Aquinas*. Edited by Anton C. Pegis. New York: The Modern Library, 1948.
Thomas Aquinas. *On Evil*. Translated by Richard Regan. Edited by Brian Davies. New York: Oxford University Press, 2003.
Thomas Aquinas. *Summa Theologica Editio Altera Romana ad Ementatiores Editiones Impressa et Noviter Accuratissime Recognita: Pars Prima*. Rome: Ex Typographia Forzani, 1894.
Thomas Aquinas. *The Summa Theologica of St. Thomas Aquinas*. 2nd ed. Translated by the Fathers of the English Dominican Province. 1920. http://www.newadvent.org/summa (accessed December 4, 2017).
Thomas Aquinas. *The Treatise on Human Nature: Summa Theologiae 1a, 75–89*. Edited by Robert Pasnau. Indianapolis, IN: Hacket, 2002.
Thomas Aquinas. *St. Thomas Aquinas: Philosophical Texts*. Edited by Thomas Gilby. New York: Oxford University Press, 1960.
Turretin, Francis. *Institutes of Elenctic Theology*. Translated by George Musgrave Giger. Edited by James T. Dennison, Jr. Phillipsburg, NJ: P&R Publishing, 1994.
Turretin, Francis. *Institutio Theologiæ Elencticæ*. 3 vols. Geneva: Samuelem de Tournes, 1679–86.
Watson, Thomas. *A Body of Practical Divinity, in a Series of Sermons on the Shorter Catechism*. Aberdeen: George King and Robert King, 1838.
Watts, Isaac. *The Ruin and Recovery of Mankind*. London: R. Hett and J. Brackstone, 1740.
Wesley, John. *The Doctrine of Original Sin: According to Scripture, Reason, and Experience*. Bristol: E. Farley, 1757.
Williams, Solomon. *The True State of the Question Concerning the Qualifications Necessary to Lawful Communion in the Christian Sacraments*. Boston: S. Kneeland, 1751.
Wolleb, John. *The Abridgement of Christian Divinitie*. 3rd ed. Translated by Alexander Ross. London: T. Mabb, 1660.

Biography

Allen, Alexander Viets Griswold. *Jonathan Edwards*. New York: Houghton Mifflin, 1889.

Gura, Philip F. *Jonathan Edwards: America's Evangelical*. New York: Hill and Wang, 2005.

Hopkins, Samuel. *The Life and Character of the Late Reverend, Learned, and Pious Mr. Jonathan Edwards*. Boston: S. Kneeland, 1765.

Marsden, George M. *Jonathan Edwards: A Life*. New Haven, CT: Yale University Press, 2003.

McGiffert, Jr., Arthur Cushman. *Jonathan Edwards*. Philosophy in America. 1932. Reprint, New York: Harper & Row, 1980.

Miller, Perry. *Jonathan Edwards*. 1949. Reprint, Lincoln: University of Nebraska Press, 2005.

Murray, Iain. *Jonathan Edwards: A New Biography*. Carlisle, PA: Banner of Truth, 1987.

Nichols, Stephen J. *Jonathan Edwards: A Guided Tour of His Life and Thought*. Phillipsburg, NJ: P&R Publishing, 2001.

Tracy, Patricia J. *Jonathan Edwards, Pastor: Religion and Society in Eighteenth-Century Northampton*. New York: Hill and Wang, 1980.

Winslow, Ola Elizabeth. *Jonathan Edwards, 1703–1758: A Biography*. New York: The Macmillan Company, 1940.

Secondary Sources: Books and Dissertations

Aniol, Scott. *Worship in Song: A Biblical Approach to Music and Worship*. Winona Lake, IN: BMH Books, 2009.

Arendt, Hannah. *Love and Saint Augustine*. Edited by Joanna Vecchiarelli Scott and Judith Chelius Stark. Chicago, IL: University of Chicago Press, 1996.

Arnold, Magda. *The Nature of Emotion: Selective Readings*. New York: Penguin, 1968.

Bainton, Roland H. *Here I Stand: A Life of Martin Luther*. New York: Mentor, 1950.

Beecher, Edwards. "The Works of Samuel Hopkins." *Bibliotheca Sacra* 10 (1853): 66–67.

Beeke, Joel R. *Puritan Reformed Spirituality: A Practical Theological Study from our Reformed and Puritan Heritage*. Darlington, England: Evangelical Press, 2006.

Beeke, Joel R., and Randall J. Pederson. *Meet the Puritans: With a Guide to Modern Reprints*. Grand Rapids, MI: Reformation Heritage Books, 2006.

Beeke, Joel R., and Sinclair B. Ferguson, eds. *Reformed Confessions Harmonized: with an Annotated Bibliography of Reformed Doctrinal Works*. Grand Rapids, MI: Baker Books, 1999.

Berardino, Angelo di, ed. *The Golden Age of Latin Patristic Literature from the Council of Nicea to the Council of Chalcedon*. Vol. 4 of *Patrology*. Translated by Placid Solari. Westminster, MD: Christian Classics, 1991.

Berkhof, Louis. *Systematic Theology*. Grand Rapids, MI: Wm. B. Eerdmans, 1996.

Beza, Theodore. *The Life of John Calvin*. Translated by Henry Beveridge. Philadelphia: Westminster Press, 1909.

Biehl, Craig. *Reading* Religious Affections: *A Study Guide to Jonathan Edwards' Classic on the Nature of True Christianity*. Birmingham, AL: Solid Ground Christian Books, 2012.

Blight, James George. "Gracious Discoveries: Toward an Understanding of Jonathan Edwards' Psychological Theory, and an Assessment of his Place in the History of American Psychology." PhD diss., University of New Hampshire, 1974.

Borgman, Brian S. *Feelings and Faith: Cultivating Godly Emotions in the Christian Life*. Wheaton, IL: Crossway, 2009.
Bouwsma, William J. *John Calvin: A Sixteenth Century Portrait*. New York: Oxford University Press, 1988.
Brown, Peter. *Augustine of Hippo: A Bibliography*. Rev. ed. London: Faber and Faber, 1967.
Brown, Robert E. *Jonathan Edwards and the Bible*. Bloomington: Indiana University Press, 2002.
Bushman, Richard L., ed. *The Great Awakening: Documents on the Revival of Religion, 1740–1745*. Documentary Problems in Early American History. New York: Atheneum, 1970.
Chadwick, Owen. *The Reformation*. Grand Rapids, MI: Wm. B. Eerdmans, 1964.
Coulter, Dale M., and Amos Young, eds. *The Spirit, the Affections, and the Christian Tradition*. Notre Dame, IN: University of Notre Dame Press, 2016.
Dexter, Franklin Bowditch, ed. *Documentary History of Yale University: Under the Original Charter of the Collegiate School of Connecticut 1701–1745*. New Haven, CT: Yale University Press, 1916.
Dexter, Franklin Bowditch, ed. *Sketch of the History of Yale University*. New York: Henry Holt and Co., 1887.
Dorrien, Gary. *The Making of American Liberal Theology: Imagining Progressive Religion, 1805–1900*. Louisville: Westminster John Knox Press, 2001.
Caldwell III, Robert W. *Communion in the Spirit: The Holy Spirit as the Bond of Union in the Theology of Jonathan Edwards*. Studies in Evangelical History and Thought. Eugene, OR: Wipf & Stock Publishers, 2006.
Cassirer, Ernst. *The Philosophy of the Enlightenment*. Translated by Fritz C. A. Koelln and James P. Pettegrove. Princeton, NJ: Princeton University Press, 2009.
Chai, Leon. *Jonathan Edwards and the Limits of Enlightenment Philosophy*. New York: Oxford, 1998.
Cherry, Conrad. *The Theology of Jonathan Edwards: A Reappraisal*. Bloomington: Indiana University Press, 1990.
Chevreau, Guy. *Catch the Fire: The Toronto Blessing: An Experience of Renewal and Revival*. Toronto: HarpersPerennial, 1994.
Clapper, Gregory S. *John Wesley on Religious Affections: His Views on Experience and Emotion and Their Role in the Christian Life and Theology*. Pietist and Wesleyan Studies 1. Metuchen, NJ: The Scarecrow Press, 1989.
Clark, Gordon. *The Biblical Doctrine of Man*. Jefferson, MD: Trinity Foundation, 1984.
Cochran, Elizabeth Agnew. *Receptive Human Virtues: A New Reading of Jonathan Edwards's Ethics*. University Park: Pennsylvania State University Press, 2010.
Conforti, Joseph A. *Jonathan Edwards, Religious Tradition, & American Culture*. Chapel Hill: University of North Carolina Press, 1995.
Corrigan, John. *Business of the Heart: Religion and Emotion in the Nineteenth Century*. Berkeley: University of California Press, 2002.
Corrigan, John. *Religion and Emotion*. New York: Oxford University Press, 2004.
Corrigan, John, ed. *The Oxford Handbook of Religion and Emotion*. New York: Oxford University Press, 2008.
Crampton, W. Gary. *Meet Jonathan Edwards: An Introduction to America's Greatest Theologian/Philosopher*. Morgan, PA: Soli Deo Gloria Publications, 2004.
Crapps, Robert W. *An Introduction to Psychology of Religion*. Macon, GA: Mercer University Press, 1986.

Crisp, Oliver D. *Jonathan Edwards on God and Creation*. Oxford: Oxford University Press, 2012.

Crisp, Oliver D., and Douglas A. Sweeney, eds. *After Jonathan Edwards: The Courses of the New England Theology*. New York: Oxford University Press, 2012.

Damasio, Antonio. *Descartes' Error: Emotion, Reason, and the Human Brain*. New York: Penguin Books, 1994.

Danaher, Jr., William J. *The Trinitarian Ethics of Jonathan Edwards*. Columbia Series in Reformed Theology. Louisville, KY: Westminster John Knox, 2004.

Davidson, Edward H. *Jonathan Edwards: The Narrative of a Puritan Mind*. Riverside Studies in Literature. Boston: Houghton Mifflin, 1966.

Deere, Jack. *Surprised by the Power of the Spirit: A Former Dallas Seminary Professor Discovers that God Speaks and Heals Today*. Grand Rapids, MI: Zondervan, 1993.

Delattre, Roland A. *Beauty and Sensibility in the Thought of Jonathan Edwards: An Essay in Aesthetics and Theological Ethics*. Jonathan Edwards Classic Studies Series 4. 1968. Reprint, Eugene, OR: Wipf and Stock Publishers, 2006.

Dever, Mark. *Richard Sibbes: Puritanism and Calvinism in Late Elizabethan and Early Stuart England*. Macon, GA: Mercer University Press, 2000.

Dixon, Thomas. *From Passions to Emotions: The Creation of a Secular Psychological Category*. Cambridge: Cambridge University Press, 2003.

Dolezal, James E. *All That is in God: Evangelical Theology and the Challenge of Classical Christian Theism*. Grand Rapids, MI: Reformation Heritage Books, 2017.

Eddy, G. T. *Dr Taylor of Norwich: Wesley's Arch-heretic*. Werrington, U.K.: Epworth, 2003.

Edwards, Dwight. *Revolution Within: A Fresh Look at Supernatural Living*. Colorado Springs, CO: Waterbrook Press, 2002.

Ekman, Paul, and Richard J. Davidson, eds. *The Nature of Emotion: Fundamental Questions*. New York: Oxford University Press, 1994.

Elliott, Matthew A. *Faithful Feelings: Rethinking Emotion in the New Testament*. Grand Rapids, MI: Kregel Academic & Professional, 2006.

Engle, Paul E., and Paul A. Basden, eds. *Exploring the Worship Spectrum: Six Views*. Grand Rapids, MI: Zondervan, 2004.

Erdt, Terrence. *Jonathan Edwards and the Sense of the Heart*. Amherst: University of Massachusetts Press, 1980.

Eustace, Nicole. *Passion is the Gale: Emotion, Power, and the Coming of the American Revolution*. Chapel Hill: University of North Carolina Press, 2008.

Faulkner, Quentin. *Wiser than Despair: The Evolution of Ideas in the Relationship of Music and the Christian Church*. Contributions to the Study of Music and Dance 40. Westport, CT: Greenwood Press, 1996.

Feinberg, John S. *No One Like Him: The Doctrine of God*. Foundations of Evangelical Theology. Wheaton, IL: Crossway Books, 2001.

Fiering, Norman S. *Jonathan Edwards's Moral Thought and Its British Context*. Chapel Hill: University of North Carolina Press, 1981.

Fiering, Norman S. *Moral Philosophy at Seventeenth-Century Harvard: A Discipline in Transition*. Chapel Hill: University of North Carolina Press, 1981.

Gaustad, Edwin Scott. *The Great Awakening in New England*. New York: Harper & Brothers, 1957.

Gaustad Edwin S., and Mark A. Noll, eds. *A Documentary History of Religion in America to 1877*. 3rd ed. Grand Rapids, MI: William B. Eerdmans, 2003.

Geissler, Suzanne. *Jonathan Edwards to Aaron Burr, Jr.: From the Great Awakening to Democratic Politics*. Studies in American Religion 1. Lewiston, NY: Edwin Mellen, 1981.

Goen, C. C. *Revivalism and Separatism in New England, 1740–1800: Strict Congregationalists and Separate Baptists in the Great Awakening.* Middletown, CT: Wesleyan University Press, 1987.

Green, Bradley G., ed. *Shapers of Christian Orthodoxy.* Downers Grove, IL: InterVarsity Press, 2010.

Grenz, Stanley J. *Theology for the Community of God.* Grand Rapids, MI: Zondervan Publishing House, 2000.

Griffin, Edward M. *Old Brick: Charles Chauncy of Boston, 1705–1787* Minnesota Monographs in the Humanities. Minneapolis: University of Minnesota Press, 1980.

Grudem, Wayne. *Systematic Theology: An Introduction to Biblical Doctrine.* Grand Rapids, MI: Zondervan Publishing House, 1994.

Gustafson, James M. *Can Ethics Be Christian?* Chicago: University of Chicago Press, 1975.

Haroutunian, Joseph. *Piety versus Moralism: The Passing of the New England Theology.* 1932. Reprint, Hamden, CT: Archon Books, 1964.

Hart, D. G., ed. *Reckoning with the Past: Historical Essays on American Evangelicalism from the Institute for the Study of American Evangelicals.* Grand Rapids, MI: Baker Books, 1995.

Hart, D. G., Sean Michael Lucas, and Stephen Nichols, eds. *The Legacy of Jonathan Edwards: American Religion and the Evangelical Tradition.* Grand Rapids, MI: Baker Academic, 2003.

Hatch, Nathan O., and Harry S. Stout, eds. *Jonathan Edwards and the American Experience.* New York: Oxford University Press, 1988.

Haykin, Michael A. G. *Jonathan Edwards: The Holy Spirit in Revival: The Lasting Influence of the Holy Spirit in the Heart of Man.* Webster, NY: Evangelical Press USA, 2005.

Heimert, Alan, and Perry Miller, eds. *The Great Awakening: Documents Illustrating the Crisis and its Consequences.* Indianapolis, IN: The Bobbs-Merrill Company, 1967.

Heinze, Rudolph W. *Reform and Conflict: From the Medieval World to the Wars of Religion, A.D. 1350–1648.* Baker History of the Church 4. Grand Rapids, MI: Baker Books, 2005.

Helm, Paul, and Oliver D. Crisp, eds. *Jonathan Edwards: Philosophical Theologian.* Burlington, VT: Ashgate, 2003.

Hoadly, Benjamin. *Sixteen Sermons Formerly Printed, Now Collected into One Volume. To which are added, Six Sermons upon Public Occasions, Never before Printed.* London: John and Paul Knapton, 1754.

Holbrook, Clyde A. *The Ethics of Jonathan Edwards: Morality and Aesthetics.* Ann Arbor: The University of Michigan Press, 1973.

Holifield, E. Brooks. *The Covenant Sealed: The Development of Puritan Sacramental Theology in Old and New England, 1570–1720.* New Haven, CT: Yale University Press, 1974.

Holifield, E. Brooks. *Theology in America: Christian Thought from the Age of the Puritans to the Civil War.* New Haven, CT: Yale University Press, 2003.

Holmes, Stephen R. *God of Grace & God of Glory: An Account of the Theology of Jonathan Edwards.* Grand Rapids, MI: William B. Eerdmans, 2001.

Honderich, Ted, ed. *The Oxford Companion to Philosophy.* New York: Oxford University Press, 1995.

Hoopes, James. *Consciousness in New England: From Puritanism and Ideas to Psychoanalysis and Semiotic.* Baltimore, MD: The John Hopkins University Press, 1989.

Horton, Michael. *The Christian Faith: A Systematic Theology for Pilgrims On the Way.* Grand Rapids, MI: Zondervan, 2011.

Hotz, Kendra G., and Matthew T. Mathews. *Shaping the Christian Life: Worship and the Religious Affections.* Louisville, KY: Westminster John Knox, 2006.

Houston, James M. *Religious Affections: A Christian's Character before God.* Minneapolis, MN: Bethany House, 1996.

Immink, Gerrit, and Reinder Bruinsma. *Faith: A Practical Theological Reconstruction.* Translated by Reinder Bruinsma. Grand Rapids, MI: Eerdmans, 2005.

Jackson, Samuel Macauley, ed. *The New Schaff-Herzog Encyclopedia of Religious Knowledge.* New York: Funk and Wagnalls Co., 1911.

James, Susan. *Passion and Action: The Emotions in Seventeenth-Century Philosophy.* Oxford: Clarendon Press, 1997.

Jensen, Robert. *America's Theologian: A Recommendation of Jonathan Edwards.* Oxford: Oxford University Press, 1988.

Lippy, Charles H. *Seasonable Revolutionary: The Mind of Charles Chauncy.* Chicago, IL: Nelson-Hall, 1981.

Kapic, Kelly M. *Communion with God: The Divine and the Human in the Theology of John Owen.* Grand Rapids: Baker Academic, 2007.

Kapic, Kelly M., and Randall C. Gleanson, eds. *The Devoted Life: An Invitation to the Puritan Classics.* Downers Grove, IL: InterVarsity Press, 2004.

Karant-Nunn, Susan C. *The Reformation of Feeling: Shaping the Religious Emotions in Early Modern Germany.* New York: Oxford University Press, 2010.

Kidd, Thomas S. *The Great Awakening: The Roots of Evangelical Christianity in Colonial America.* New Haven, CT: Yale University Press, 2009.

Kimnach, Wilson H., Caleb J. D. Maskell, and Kenneth P. Minkema, eds. *Jonathan Edwards's* Sinners in the Hands of an Angry God: *A Casebook, Including the Authoritative Edition of the Famous Sermon.* New Haven, CT: Yale University Press, 2010.

Kling, David W., and Douglas A. Sweeney. *Jonathan Edwards at Home and Abroad: Historical Memories, Cultural Movements, Global Horizons.* Columbia: University of South Carolina Press, 2003.

Knight, Janice. *Orthodoxies in Massachusetts: Rereading American Puritanism.* Cambridge, MA: Harvard University Press, 1994.

Knight III, Henry H. "True Affections: Biblical Narrative & Evangelical Spirituality." In *The Nature of Confession: Evangelicals & Postliberals in Conversation,* edited by Timothy R. Phillips and Dennis L. Okholm, 193–200. Downers Grove, IL: InterVarsity Press, 1996.

Knuutila, Simo. *Emotions in Ancient and Medieval Philosophy.* Oxford: Clarendon Press, 2004.

Koch, G. Adolf. *Religion of the American Enlightenment.* New York: Thomas Y. Crowell, 1968.

Kuklick, Bruce. *A History of Philosophy in America, 1720–2000.* Oxford: Clarendon Press, 2001.

Lambert, Frank. *Inventing the "Great Awakening."* Princeton, NJ: Princeton University Press, 1999.

Larsen, Dale, and Sandy Larsen. *Jonathan Edwards: Renewed Heart.* Downers Grove, IL: InterVarsity, 2002.

Lee, Sang Hyun. *The Philosophical Theology of Jonathan Edwards.* Princeton, NJ: Princeton University Press, 1988.

Lee, Sang Hyun, ed. *The Princeton Companion to Jonathan Edwards.* Princeton, NJ: Princeton University Press, 2005.

Lesser, M. X. *Reading Jonathan Edwards: An Annotated Bibliography in Three Parts, 1729–2005.* Grand Rapids, MI: William B. Eerdmans, 2008.
Lester, Andrew D. *The Angry Christian: A Theology for Care and Counseling.* Louisville, KY: Westminster John Knox Press, 2003.
Levi, Anthony. *French Moralists: The Theory of the Passions 1585 to 1649.* Oxford: Clarendon Press, 1964.
Lewis, Charlton T., and Charles Short. *A New Latin Dictionary.* New York: American Book Company, 1907.
Lewis, Donald M., ed. *Dictionary of Evangelical Biography, 1730–1860.* 2 vols. 1995. Reprint, Peabody, MA: Hendrickson, 2004.
Lucas, Sean Michael. *God's Grand Design: The Theological Vision of Jonathan Edwards.* Wheaton, IL: Crossway, 2011.
Lutz, Catherine A. *Unnatural Emotions: Everyday Sentiments on a Micronesian Atoll & Their Challenge to Western Theory.* Chicago: University of Chicago Press, 1988.
Lystra, Karen. *Searching the Heart: Women, Men, and Romantic Love in Nineteenth-Century America.* New York: Oxford University Press, 1989.
May, Henry. *The Enlightenment in America.* New York: Oxford University Press, 1976.
McClymond, Michael J. *Encounters with God: An Approach to the Theology of Jonathan Edwards.* New York: Oxford University Press, 1998.
McClymond, Michael J., and Gerald R. McDermott. *The Theology of Jonathan Edwards.* New York: Oxford University Press, 2012.
McCollum, David C. "A Study of Evangelicals and Revival Exercises from 1730–1805: Tracing the Development of Exercise Traditions through the First Great Awakening to the Southern Great Revival." PhD diss., Southeastern Baptist Theological Seminary, 2009.
McDermott, Gerald R. *The Great Theologians: A Brief Guide.* Downers Grove, IL: IVP Academic, 2010.
McDermott, Gerald R. *Jonathan Edwards Confronts the Gods: Christian Theology, Enlightenment Religion, and Non-Christian Faiths.* New York: Oxford University Press, 2000.
McDermott, Gerald R. *One Holy and Happy Society: The Public Theology of Jonathan Edwards.* University Park: The Pennsylvania State University Press, 1992.
McDermott, Gerald R. *Seeing God: Twelve Reliable Signs of True Spirituality.* Downers Grove, IL: InterVarsity Press, 1995.
McKim, Donald K., ed. *Dictionary of Major Biblical Interpreters.* Downers Grove, IL: IVP Academic, 2007.
McNeill, John T. *The History and Character of Calvinism.* London: Oxford University Press, 1954.
Miller, Perry. *Errand into the Wilderness.* Cambridge, MA: Harvard University Press, 1984.
Miller, Perry. *The New England Mind.* New York: The Macmillan Company, 1939.
Miller, Perry. *The Young Jonathan Edwards: A Reconstruction.* Jonathan Edwards Classic Studies Series 1. 1991. Reprint, Eugene, OR: Wipf & Stock Publishers, 2005.
Miner, Robert. *Thomas Aquinas on the Passions: A Study of* Summa Theologiae *1a2ae 22–48.* Cambridge: Cambridge University Press, 2009.
Moody, Josh. *Jonathan Edwards and the Enlightenment: Knowing the Presence of God.* Lanham, MD: University Press of America, 2005.
Moody, Josh, ed. *Jonathan Edwards and Justification.* Wheaton, IL: Crossway, 2012.
Morgan, Chris. *Jonathan Edwards & Hell.* Ross-shire, Scotland: Christian Focus Publications, 2004.

Morimoto, Anri. *Jonathan Edwards and the Catholic Vision of Salvation*. University Park, PA: Pennsylvania State University Press, 1995.

Morris, William Sparkes. *The Young Jonathan Edwards: A Reconstruction*. Chicago Studies in the History of American Religion 14. Brooklyn NY: Carlson Publishing, 1991.

Muller, Richard A. *The Unaccommodated Calvin: Studies in the Foundation of a Theological Tradition*. Oxford: Oxford University Press, 2000.

Nadler, Steven, ed. *The Cambridge Companion to Malebranche*. Cambridge: Cambridge University Press, 2000.

Neele, Adriaan Cornelis. *The Art of Living to God: A Study of Method and Piety in the* Theoretico-Practica Theologia *of Peter van Mastricht (1630–1706)*. Perspectives on Christianity, 8th ser., vol. 1. Pretoria: University of Pretoria, 2005.

Nelson, James M. *Psychology, Religion, and Spirituality*. New York: Springer, 2009.

Nichols, Stephen J. *An Absolute Sort of Certainty: The Holy Spirit and the Apologetics of Jonathan Edwards*. Phillipsburg, NJ: P&R Publishing, 2003.

Noll, Mark. *America's God: From Jonathan Edwards to Abraham Lincoln*. Oxford: Oxford University Press, 2002.

Noll, Mark. *The Rise of Evangelicalism: The Age of Edwards, Whitefield, and the Wesleys*. A History of Evangelicalism: People, Movements and Ideas in the English-Speaking World 1. Downers Grove, IL: InterVarsity Press, 2003.

Nussbaum, Martha C. *The Therapy of Desire: Theory and Practice in Hellenistic Ethics*. Princeton, NJ: Princeton University Press, 1994.

Nussbaum, Martha C. *Upheavals of Thought: The Intelligence of Emotions*. Cambridge: Cambridge University Press, 2001.

Nuttall, Geoffrey F. *The Holy Spirit in Puritan Faith and Experience*. Chicago: University of Chicago Press, 1992.

O'Connell, Robert J. *St. Augustine's Early Theory of Man, A.D. 386–391*. Cambridge, MA: Harvard University Press, 1968.

Olson, Roger. *Westminster Handbook to Evangelical Theology*. Louisville, KY: Westminster John Knox Press, 2004.

Ortlund, Dane. *A New Inner Relish: Christian Motivation in the Thought of Jonathan Edwards*. Ross-shire, Scotland: Christian Focus Publications, 2008.

Oviatt, Edwin. *The Beginnings of Yale (1701–1726)*. New Haven: Yale University Press, 1916.

Pauw, Amy Plantinga. *The Supreme Harmony of All: The Trinitarian Theology of Jonathan Edwards*. Grand Rapids, MI: William B. Eerdmans Publishing Company, 2002.

Pettit, Norman. *The Heart Prepared: Grace and Conversion in Puritan Spiritual Life*. New Haven, CT: Yale University Press, 1966.

Pinto, Vivian de Sola. *Peter Sterry: Platonist and Puritan 1613–1672: A Biographical and Critical Study with passages from his Writings*. Cambridge: Cambridge University Press, 1934.

Piper, John. *Desiring God: Meditations of a Christian Hedonist*. Sisters, OR: Multnomah Books, 1996.

Piper, John. *God's Passion for His Glory: Living the Vision of Jonathan Edwards with the Complete Text of* The End for Which God Created the World. Wheaton, IL: Crossway Books, 1998.

Piper, John. *When I Don't Desire God: How to Fight for Joy*. Wheaton, IL: Crossway Books, 2004.

Piper, John, and Justin Taylor, eds. *A God Entranced Vision of All Things: The Legacy of Jonathan Edwards*. Wheaton, IL: Crossway Books, 2004.

Plantinga, Alvin. *Warranted Christian Belief.* Oxford: Oxford University Press, 2000.
Platner, John Winthrop. *Exercises Commemorating the Two-Hundredth Anniversary of the Birth of Jonathan Edwards, Held at Andover Theological Seminary, October 4 and 5, 1903.* Andover, MA: Andover Press, 1904.
Pope, Robert G. *The Half-Way Covenant: Church Membership in Puritan New England.* Princeton, NJ: Princeton University Press, 1969.
Postman, Neil. *Amusing Ourselves to Death. Amusing Ourselves to Death: Public Discourse in the Age of Show Business.* New York: Penguin, 1985.
Quasten, Johannes. *Patrology.* 3 vols. Utrecht: Spectrum Publishers, 1953–66.
Randall, Jr., John Herman. *The Making of the Modern Mind: A Survey of the Intellectual Background of the Present Age.* Rev. ed. Cambridge, MA: Houghton Mifflin, 1954.
Richardson, Alan, and John Bowden, eds. *The Westminster Dictionary of Christian Theology.* Philadelphia, PA: The Westminster Press, 1983.
Rivett, Sarah. *The Science of the Soul in Colonial New England.* Chapel Hill: University of North Carolina Press, 2011.
Roberts, Robert C. *Spiritual Emotions: A Psychology of Christian Virtues.* Grand Rapids, MI: William B. Eerdmans, 2007.
Sailer, Don E. *The Soul in Paraphrase: Prayer and the Religious Affections.* New York: The Seabury Press, 1980.
Simonson, Harold P. *Jonathan Edwards: Theologian of the Heart.* Reprints of Scholarly Excellence. 1974. Reprint, Macon, GA: Mercer University Press, 1982.
Skirry, Jason. "Malebranche's Augustinianism and the Mind's Perfection." *Publically accessible Penn Dissertations*, Paper 179. PhD diss., University of Pennsylvania, 2010.
Smart, Robert Davis. *Jonathan Edwards's Apologetic or the Great Awakening with Particular Attention to Charles Chauncy's Criticisms.* Grand Rapids, MI: Reformation Heritage Books, 2011.
Smith, Gordon T. *The Voice of Jesus: Discernment, Prayer and the Witness of the Spirit.* Downers Grove, IL: InterVarsity Press, 2003.
Smith, J. Warren. *Passion and Paradise: Human and Divine Emotion in the Thought of Gregory of Nyssa.* New York: Crossroad Publishing, 2004.
Solomon, Robert C. *The Passions: Emotions and the Meaning of Life.* Indianapolis, IN: Hackett, 1993.
Solomon, Robert C., ed. *What Is an Emotion? Classic and Contemporary Readings*, 2nd ed. New York: Oxford University Press, 2003.
Sproul, R. C., and Archie Parrish. *The Spirit of Revival: Discovering the Wisdom of Jonathan Edwards with the Complete, Modernized Text of* The Distinguishing Marks of a Work of the Spirit of God. Wheaton, IL: Crossway Books, 2008.
Starkie, Andrew. *The Church of England and the Bangorian Controversy, 1716–1721.* Studies in Modern British Religious History 14. Woodbridge, Suffolk, UK: Boydell Press, 2007.
Stein, Stephen J. *The Cambridge Companion to Jonathan Edwards.* Cambridge: Cambridge University Press, 2007.
Stein, Stephen J., ed. *Jonathan Edwards's Writings: Text, Context, and Interpretation.* Bloomington: Indiana University Press, 1996.
Storms, Sam. *Signs of the Spirit: An Interpretation of Jonathan Edwards' Religious Affections.* Wheaton, IL: Crossway Books, 2007.
Story, Ronald. *Jonathan Edwards and the Gospel of Love.* Amherst: University of Massachusetts Press, 2012.
Stout, Harry S., ed. *The Jonathan Edwards Encyclopedia.* Grand Rapids, MI: Eerdmans, 2017.

Strachan, Owen, and Douglas Sweeney. *Jonathan Edwards on Beauty*. The Essential Edwards Collection. Chicago, IL: Moody Publishers, 2010.

Strobel, Kyle C. *Jonathan Edwards's Theology: A Reinterpretation*. London: Bloomsbury T&T Clark, 2013.

Sweeney, Douglas A. *Jonathan Edwards and the Ministry of the Word: A Model of Faith and Thought*. Downers Grove, IL: IVP Academic, 2009.

Sweeney, Douglas A., and Allen C. Guelzo, eds. *The New England Theology: From Jonathan Edwards to Edwards Amasa Park*. Grand Rapids, MI: Baker Academic, 2006.

Schweitzer, William M. *God is a Communicative Being: Divine Communicativeness and Harmony in the Theology of Jonathan Edwards*. London: T&T Clark, 2012.

Taylor, Charles. *Sources of the Self: The Making of the Modern Identity*. Cambridge, MA: Harvard University Press, 1989.

Toon, Peter. *God's Statesman: The Life and Work of John Owen: Pastor, Educator, Theologian*. Grand Rapids: Zondervan, 1971.

Trueman, Carl R. *Histories and Fallacies: Problems Faced in the Writing of History*. Wheaton, IL: Crossway Books, 2010.

Trueman, Carl R. *John Owen: Reformed Catholic, Renaissance Man*. Great Theologians Series. Burlington, VT: Ashgate, 2007.

Tulloch, John. *The Cambridge Platonists*. Vol. 2 of *Rational Theology and Christian Philosophy in England in the Seventeenth Century*. Edinburgh: William Blackwood and Sons, 1874.

Turnbull, Ralph G. *Jonathan Edwards the Preacher*. Grand Rapids, MI: Baker Book House, 1958.

Wainwright, William J. *Reason and the Heart: A Prolegomenon to a Critique of Passional Reason*. Cornell Studies in the Philosophy of Religion. Ithaca, NY: Cornell University Press, 1995.

Walker, Williston. *Ten New England Leaders*. New York: Arno Press & The New York Times, 1969.

Walton, Brad. *Jonathan Edwards,* Religious Affections, *and the Puritan Analysis of True Piety, Spiritual Sensation, and Heart Religion*. Studies in American Religion 74. Lewiston, NY: E. Mellen Press, 2002.

Ward, Graham. *How the Light Gets In: Ethical Life I*. New York: Oxford University Press, 2016.

Wawrykow, Joseph P. *The SCM Press A–Z of Thomas Aquinas*. London: SCM Press, 2005.

Weaver, Richard M. *Ideas Have Consequences*. Chicago: University of Chicago Press, 1948.

Weinandy, Thomas G. *Does God Suffer?* Notre Dame, IN: University of Notre Dame Press, 2000.

White, Eugene E. *Puritan Rhetoric: The Issue of Emotion in Religion*. Carbondale: Southern Illinois University Press, 1972.

White, John. *When the Spirit Comes with Power: Signs & Wonders among God's People* Downers Grove, IL: InterVarsity Press, 1988.

White, Morton. *Science and Sentiment in America: Philosophical Thought from Jonathan Edwards to John Dewey*. New York: Oxford University Press, 1972.

Wilson, Stephen A. *Virtue Reformed: Rereading Jonathan Edwards's Ethics*. Brill's Studies in Intellectual History 132. Leiden: Brill, 2005.

Yarbrough, Stephen R., and John C. Adams. *Delightful Conviction: Jonathan Edwards and the Rhetoric of Conversion*. Great American Orators 20. Westport, CT: Greenwood Press, 1993.

Zalta, Edward N., ed. *The Stanford Encyclopedia of Philosophy*. Spring 2010 ed. http://plato.stanford.edu/.

Zylla, Phil C. *Virtue as Consent to Being: A Pastoral-Theological Perspective on Jonathan Edwards's Construct of Virtue*. McMaster Divinity Studies Series. Eugene, OR: Pickwick Publications, 2011.

Secondary Sources: Journal Articles and Essays

Armstrong, Maurice W. "Religious Enthusiasm and Separatism in Colonial New England." *Harvard Theological Review* 38 (1945): 111–40.

Aune, Michael B. "'A Heart Moved': Philip Melanchthon's Forgotten Truth About Worship." *Lutheran Quarterly* 12 (1998): 395–418.

Beck, Peter. "Jonathan Edwards on Prayer and the Triune God." In *Taking Hold of God: Reformed and Puritan Perspectives on Prayer*, edited by Joel R. Beeke and Brian G. Najapfour, 187–206. Grand Rapids, MI: Reformation Heritage Books, 2011.

Blight, James George. "Jonathan Edwards's Theory of the Mind." In *Explorations in the History of Psychology in the United States*, edited by Josef Brožek, 61–119. Cranburg, NJ: Associated University Presses, 1984.

Brockway, Robert W. "Significance of James Davenport in the Great Awakening." *Journal of Religious Thought* 24 (1967–68): 86–94.

Brown, Robert E. "Edwards, Locke, and the Bible." *Journal of Religion* 79 (1999): 361–84.

Channing, William H. "Edwards and the Revivalists." *Christian Examiner* 43 (1847): 374–94.

Clay, Robert E. "James Davenport's Post-Bonfire Ministry, 1743–1757." *Historian* 59 (1996): 59–73.

Copan, Paul. "Jonathan Edwards's Philosophical Influences: Lockean or Malebrachean?" *Journal of the Evangelical Theological Society* 44 (2001): 107–24.

Danaher, Jr., William J. "By Sensible Signs Represented: Jonathan Edwards' Sermons on the Lord's Supper." *Pro Ecclesia* 7 (1998): 261–87.

Darwall, Stephen. *Egoism and Morality*. In *The Oxford Handbook of Philosophy in Early Modern Europe*, edited by Desmond M. Clarke and Catherine Wilson, 381–402. Oxford: Oxford University Press, 2011.

Davidson, Bruce W. "Glorious Damnation: Hell as an Essential Element in the Theology of Jonathan Edwards." *Journal of the Evangelical Theological Society* 54 (2011): 809–22.

Delattre, Roland A. "Aesthetics and Ethics: Jonathan Edwards and the Recovery of Aesthetics for Religious Ethics." *Journal of Religious Ethics* 31 (2003): 277–97.

Dixon, Thomas. "Revolting Passions." *Modern Theology* 27 (2011): 298–312.

Emmons, Robert A. *Sacred Emotion*. In *Soul, Psyche, Brain: New Directions in the Study of Religion and Brain-Mind Science*, edited by Kelly Bulkeley, 93–112. New York: Palgrave MacMillan, 2005.

Fay, Jay Wharton. *American Psychology before William James*. New Brunswick, NJ: Rutgers University Press, 1939.

Fedler, Kyle. "Calvin's Burning Heart: Calvin and the Stoics on the Emotions." *JSCE* 22 (2002): 133–62.

Floyd, Shawn D. "Aquinas on Emotions: A Response to Some Recent Interpretations." *History of Philosophy Quarterly* 15 (1998): 161–76.

Fiering, Norman S. "Will and Intellect in the New England Mind." *William and Mary Quarterly* 29 (1972): 515–58.

Fisher, George P. "The Philosophy of Jonathan Edwards." *The North American Review* 128 (1879): 284–303.

Fulcher, J. Rodney. "Puritans and the Passions: The Faculty Psychology in American Puritanism." *Journal of the History Behavioral Sciences* 9 (1973): 123–39.

Grabo, Norman. "Colonial American Theology: Holiness and the Lyric Impulse." In *Essays in Honor of Russel B. Nye*, edited by Joseph Waldheim, 74–91. East Lansing: Michigan State University Press, 1978.

Hannah, John D. "Jonathan Edwards, The Toronto Blessing, and the Spiritual Gifts: Are the Extraordinary Ones Actually the Ordinary Ones?" *Trinity Journal* 17 (1996): 167–89.

Harrison, Graham S. "Jonathan Edwards and the Terms of Admission to Communion." In *The Good Fight of Faith: Papers Read at the Westminster Conference*, 51–71. London: Evangelical Press, 1971.

Helm, Paul. "Edwards on True Religion." April 1, 2011. *Helm's Deep* (blog). http://paulhelmsdeep.blogspot.com/2011/04/edwards-on-true-religion.html (accessed December 4, 2017)

Helm, Paul. "John Locke and Jonathan Edwards: A Reconsideration." *Journal of the History of Philosophy* 7 (1969): 51–61.

Hessel-Robinson, Timothy and Jonathan Edwards. *Religious Affections*. Pages 269–80 in *Christian Spirituality: The Classics*. Edited by Arthur Holder. New York: Routledge, 2010.

Hoopes, James. "Jonathan Edwards's Religious Psychology." *The Journal of American History* 69 (1983): 849–65.

Hunsinger, George. "Dispositional Soteriology: Jonathan Edwards on Justification by Faith Alone." *Westminster Theological Journal* 66 (2004): 107–20.

Lewis, C. S. Introduction to St. Athanasius, *On the Incarnation: The Treatise* De Incarnatione Verbi Dei. Translated by a religious of C. S. M. V. Crestwood, NY: St. Vladimir's Seminary Press, 1993.

Lewis, Paul. "'The Springs of Motion': Jonathan Edwards on Emotions, Character, and Agency." *Journal of Religious Ethics* 22 (1994): 275–97.

Lowance, Jr., Mason I. "Jonathan Edwards and the Platonists: Edwardsean Epistemology and the Influence of Malebranche and Norris." *Studies in Puritan American Spirituality 2* (1992): 129–52.

Lucas, Sean Michael. "'What is the Nature of True Religion?': *Religious Affections* and Its American Puritan Context." In *All for Jesus: A Celebration of the* 50th*Anniversary of Covenant Theological Seminary*, edited by Robert A. Peterson and Sean Michael Lucas, 117–36. Ross-shire, UK: Mentor, 2006.

MacIntyre, Alasdair. "Moral Philosophy: What Next?" In *Revisions: Changing Perspectives in Moral Philosophy*, edited by Stanley Hauerwas and Alasdair MacIntyre, 1–15. Revisions 3. Notre Dame: IN: University of Notre Dame Press, 1983.

Martin, Ryan J. "'Violent Motions of Carnal Affections': Jonathan Edwards, John Owen, and Distinguishing the Work of the Spirit from Enthusiasm." *Detroit Baptist Seminary Journal* 15 (2010): 99–116.

McClymond, Michael J. "Spiritual Perception in Jonathan Edwards." *The Journal of Religion* 77 (1997): 195–216.

McDermott, Gerald R. "Jonathan Edwards on Justification by Faith Alone–More Protestant or Catholic?" *Pro Ecclesia* 17 (2008): 92–111.

Miller, Michael R. "Aquinas on the Passion of Despair." *New Blackfriars* 93 (2012): 387–96.

Miller, Perry. "Jonathan Edwards on the Sense of the Heart." *Harvard Theological Review* 41 (1948): 123–45.

Miller, Perry. "Solomon Stoddard, 1643–1729." *Harvard Theological Review* 34 (1941): 277–320.

Minkema, Kenneth P. "Chronology of Edwards's Life and Times." Jonathan Edwards Center at Yale University. http://edwards.yale.edu/research/chronology (accessed December 4, 2017).

Minkema, Kenneth P. "Jonathan Edwards in the Twentieth Century." *Journal of the Evangelical Theological Society* 47 (2004): 659–87.

Muller, Richard A. "Jonathan Edwards and the Absence of Free Choice: A Parting of Ways in the Reformed Tradition." *Jonathan Edwards Studies* 1 (2011): 1–22. http://jestudies.yale.edu/index.php/journal/article/view/63 (accessed December 4, 2017).

Oliphint, Scott. "Jonathan Edwards: Reformed Apologist." *Westminster Theological Journal* 57 (1995): 165–86.

Pauw, Amy Plantinga. Review of *Jonathan Edwards and the Limits of Enlightenment Philosophy*, by Leon Chai. *Calvin Theological Journal* 35 (2000): 167–68.

Percy, Martyn. "Adventure and Atrophy in a Charismatic Movement: Returning to the 'Toronto Blessing.'" *Journal of Contemporary Religion* 20 (2005): 71–90.

Piper, John. "Sweet Sorrow: The Happy Root of Holy Living." Lecture, The Jonathan Edwards Institute, Annapolis, Maryland, July 2, 2003. Desiring God Ministries. https://www.desiringgod.org/messages/sweet-sorrow-the-happy-root-of-holy-living (accessed November 24, 2017).

Proudfoot, Wayne. "From Theology to a Science of Religions: Jonathan Edwards and William James on Religious Affections." *Harvard Theological Review* 82 (1989): 149–68.

Quinn, Philip L. "Honoring Jonathan Edwards." *JRE* 31 (2003): 299–314.

Rightmire, R David. "The Sacramental Theology of Jonathan Edwards in the Context of Controversy." *Fides et Historia* 21 (1989): 50–60.

Robbins, Duffy. "Jonathan Edwards, Religious Affections, and Spirituality in the Third Millennium." In *This Way to Youth Ministry Companion Guide: Readings, Case Studies, Resources to Begin the Journey*, edited by Duffy Robbins and Len Kageler, 167–70. El Cajon, CA: Youth Specialties Books, 2004.

Schafer, Thomas. "Jonathan Edwards and Justification by Faith." *Church History* 20 (1951): 55–67.

Smith, John E. "Jonathan Edwards as Philosophical Theologian." *Review of Metaphysics* 30 (1976): 306–24.

Smyth, Egbert C. "Early Writings of Jonathan Edwards A.D. 1714–26." In *Proceedings of the American Antiquarian Society*, 212–47. Worcester, MA: Charles Hamilton, 1895.

Spohn, William C. "Passion and Principle." *Theological Studies* 52 (1991): 69–87.

Spohn, William C. "Sovereign Beauty: Jonathan Edwards and the Nature of True Virtue." *Theological Studies* 42 (1981): 394–421.

Spohn, William C. "Spirituality and Its Discontents: Practices in Jonathan Edwards's *Charity and Its Fruits*." *Journal of Religious Ethics* 31 (2003): 253–76.

Sweeney, Douglas A. Review of *Jonathan Edwards and the Limits of Enlightenment Philosophy*, by Leon Chai. *Theology Today* 56 (1999): 438–41.

Ursula, Brumm. "Passions and Depressions in Early American Puritans." In *La passion dans le monde anglo-américain aux XVIIe et XVIIIe siècles*, 85–96. Paris: Universite de Bourdeaux, 1978.

Vascardi, Christopher J. Review of *Jonathan Edwards and the Limits of Enlightenment Philosophy*, by Leon Chai. *Theological Studies* 60 (1999): 193–94.

Vetö, Miklos. "La Connaissance Spirituelle Selon Jonathan Edwards." *Revue de Theologie et de Philosophie* 111 (1979): 233–51. Translated in Michael J. McClymond. "Spiritual Knowledge according to Jonathan Edwards." *Calvin Theological Journal* 31 (1996): 161–81.

Wannenwetsch, Bernd. "Affekt und Gebot. Zur ethischen Bedeutung der Leidenschaften im Licht der Theologie Luthers and Melanchthon." *Passion, Affekt und Leidenschaft in der Frühen Neuzeit*, 2 vols., 1:203–15. Edited by Johann Anselm Steiger. Wiesbaden, Germany: Harrassowitz Verlag, 2005.

Waddington, Jeffrey C. "Jonathan Edwards's 'Ambiguous and Somewhat Precarious' Doctrine of Justification." *Westminster Theological Journal* 66 (2004): 357–72.

Weaver-Zercher, David L. "Theologies." In *Themes in Religion and American Culture*, edited by Philip Goff and Paul Harvey, 5–37. Chapel Hill: University of North Carolina Press, 2004.

Westberg, Daniel."Emotion and God: A Reply to Marcel Sarot." *The Thomist* 60 (1996): 109–21.

Wilson, John F. Review of *Jonathan Edwards and the Limits of Enlightenment Philosophy*, by Leon Chai. *Church History* 67 (1998): 811–12.

Wilson, Stephen A. "Jonathan Edwards's Virtue: Diverse sources, Multiple Meanings, and the Lessons of History for Ethics." *Journal of Religious Ethics* 31 (2003): 201–28.

Winiarski, Douglas L. "Jonathan Edwards, Enthusiast? Radical Revivalism and the Great Awakening in the Connecticut Valley." *Church History* 74, no. 4 (2005): 683–739.

Withrow, Brandon. "Jonathan Edwards and Justification by Faith [Part 1]." *Reformation and Revival Journal* 11 (Spring) 2002: 93–109.

Woodward, Kenneth L. "The Giggles are from God." *Newsweek* 125 (February 5, 1995): 54.

Zahl, Simeon. "On the Affective Salience of Doctrines." *Modern Theology* 31 (2015): 428–44.

INDEX

Abercrombie, Robert 206–7
The Abridgement of Christian Divinitie (Wolleb) 94 n.15
Adam 42, 44–5, 66, 78, 121, 122 n.31, 152 n.121, 178, 180 n.69, 215–16, 225. *See also* Eve
Adams, John C. 131 n.56
Addison, Joseph 170 n.43
admiration 68, 114–15, 115 n.7
aesthetic pleasure 220
aesthetics 104, 118, 121, 138, 218 n.54, 220, 238
affection(s). *See also* religion
  bodily effects of 184
  Charismatic movement 10–12
  Chauncy on 164–71
  counterfeit 89, 95 n.28, 143, 182, 192
  emotional evangelicalism 5–10
  emotions *vs.* 5–10
  eschatological 36–7, 43 n.61
  gracious (*see* gracious affections)
  nature of 185–6
  "no signs" 186–7
  problem of interpreting 4–5
  rubric for 201–6
  theology 233–8
affections and passions, distinction of 9, 31, 32, 41, 43, 43 n.61, 45, 46, 52–3, 65, 67, 72, 73–4, 80 n.136, 93, 115–6, 142 n.88, 151–3, 159–60, 171, 177, 178–82, 194, 201, 214, 229, 230, 233–7
affective psychology 28, 38, 91, 95, 98, 111
  description 23
  early Enlightenment 67–74
  "The Mind" 112–17
  Puritans and Reformed thought 74–88
  synthesis of Edwards's 172–84
  understanding of 106–10
"Affekt und Gebot. Zur ethischen Bedeutung der Leidenschaften im Licht der Theologie Luthers and Melanchthon" (Wannenwetsch) 60 n.2
agape 127, 174 n.51
Allen, Alexander Viets Griswold 14, 14 n.50
American evangelicalism 5–10
American Heritage Dictionary 21
Ames, William 74–5, 92, 93, 93 n.14, 94, 95, 96, 103, 109, 110, 128, 234
amor 54
Amusing Ourselves to Death: Public Discourse in the Age of Show Business (Postman) 5 n.3
Anderson, Wallace 4 n.1, 106 n.108–9, 112 n.1–3, 115 n.9, 116 n.13, 120 n.24
angels 25, 41, 52, 54, 116, 122 n.31, 143, 154, 175
anger 19 n.78, 32–3, 35–6, 54 n.118, 80, 214, 221, 221 n.65
  concept 152
  as irascible passion 153
  irrational 152–3
  as sinful 153
  unjustified 152, 152 n.122
  unsuitable 152
animals
  appetites 116
  vs. humans 36 n.28, 48, 65 n.34, 78, 81, 116, 138–42, 139 n.78, 142 n.85, 152, 155, 156 n.134, 188, 221 n.65
  minds 116
Anselm of Canterbury 46, 46 n.73
Answer to the Pelagians III (Augustine of Hippo) 42 n.57
apatheia 45
Apocalyptic Writings (Edwards) 162 n.2

appetites
carnal (*see* carnal appetite)
divine 55–6
God satisfying 203
as inclination 51
intellectual 51–6
natural 50 n.99, 116, 193, 202 n.17, 204, 215–16, 222–3
sensory (*see* sensual/sensory appetite)
soul and 50
Aquinas, Thomas 2, 19 n.79, 25, 29, 30, 31, 37, 46, 49–57, 63 n.19, 73, 81 n.138, 82 n.145, 93, 108, 109, 153, 210 n.35
"Aquinas on Emotions: A Response to Some Recent Interpretations" (Floyd) 52 n.108, 56 n.125
Aquinas on the Emotions: A Religious-Ethical Inquiry (Cates) 56 n.125
Arendt, Hannah 40 n.45, 43 n.61
Aristotle 53, 76 n.102, 135 n.64
Aristotelianism 92
Aristotelian philosophers 41
"Arminianism" 164–5
Armstrong, Maurice W. 183 n.75
Arnold, Magda 18 n.76, 20 n.82, 21 n.91, 22 n.97
atheism 208
Augustine of Hippo 2, 25, 29, 31, 35 n.22, 37–47, 54, 56, 75, 92–3, 93 n.14, 109
Augustine of Hippo: A Bibliography (Brown) 38 n.36
Aune, Michael B. 61 n.5
aversions 8, 26, 30, 31, 40, 45, 66, 111, 113, 160, 194

Bach, Johann Sebastian 3, 138 n.74
Bainton, Roland H. 59 n.1
baptism 198
Basden, Paul A. 9 n.22
Baxter, Richard 92, 94–5, 95 n.25, 109, 128, 168, 206 n.25
beasts. *See* animals
beauty
moral 220
physical 112, 113
secondary 220–1
spiritual beauty (*see* spiritual beauty)
virtue (*see* virtue)
The Beauty of Piety in Youth (Edwards) 202–3
Beck, Peter 203 n.18
Beecher, Edwards 96 n.32, 201 n.14
Beecher, Lyman 236 n.2
Beeke, Joel R. 13 n.44, 63 n.17, 74 n.88, 81 n.138, 81 n.139, 203 n.18, 217 n.53
being. *See also* virtue
benevolent 219
consent to 113–15
Being in general 218–19
Bellamy, Joseph 171 n.86, 217 n.53, 236 n.4
benevolent being 219
Berardino, Angelo di 40 n.46
Berkhof, Louis 227 n.79
Bernard of Clairvaux 46, 47, 47 n.78, 48 n.83–5, 49 n.90, 93
Beveridge, Henry 62 n.17
Beza, Theodore 62 n.17
Bianco da Siena 3
Bible 24, 30–1, 33, 43, 60, 63, 86 n.71, 95 n.28, 127, 137, 147, 152, 159, 162, 173, 175, 186–7, 215, 215 n.48, 226, 227, 234
The Biblical Doctrine of Man (Clark) 24 n.106
Biblical interpretation 119
Biehl, Craig 184 n.77
Blaise Pascal: Thoughts and Minor Works (Pascal) 69 n.62
The "Blank Bible" (Edwards) 137 n.72
blessedness 44, 45, 108, 123, 189 n.91
The Blessing of God: Previously Unpublished Sermons of Jonathan Edwards (Edwards) 138 n.74, 140 n.79, 180 n.69
Blight, James George 14–15, 14 n.54, 15 n.55
blind/blindness 119, 128, 129 n.49, 149–50, 190, 202, 208
A Body of Practical Divinity, in a Series of Sermons on the Shorter Catechism (Watson) 86 n.162

Bolton, Robert 168
"*bonum formosum*" 189
Borgman, Brian S. 9, 9 n.19, 10, 22, 22 n.93
Boston, Thomas 82, 82 n.146, 86, 95
Bouwsma, William J. 63 n.17
Bowden, John 206 n.25
Bradshaw, William 103
brain 116
Brainerd, David 211–14
Brattle Street Church, Boston 148
The Breast-Plate of Faith and Love (Preston) 80 n.136
Brockway, Robert W. 158 n.139
Brožek, Josef 14–15 n.54
Brooks, Thomas 104
Brown, Peter 38 n.36
Brown, Robert E. 137 n.72, 144 n.98, 204 n.19
Brown, Thomas 17–18, 18 n.70, 26, 26 n.118
Burgersdicius 92, 117 n.17
"burning light" 207
Burr, Aaron 201
Bushman, Richard L. 162 n.3, 163 n.7
Butler, Joseph 216

Caldwell, John 165 n.14
Caldwell, Robert W., III 127 n.46
Calvin, John 60, 62–6, 78, 81 n.138, 83, 89, 132 n.57, 178, 215 n.48
The Cambridge Companion to Jonathan Edwards (Stein) 4 n.1
Cambridge Platonists 67, 70, 93, 98, 104, 107, 107 n.110, 131, 183
The Cambridge Platonists (Tulloch) 107 n.110
carnal affections 70–1, 75
carnal appetite 141. *See also* sensual/sensory appetite
  Jesus Christ 123
  young people 202–4
carnality 70 n.66, 154, 155
carnal love 47–9
carnal man 42
carnal peace 202
Cassirer, Ernst 100 n.53
"Catalogue" (Edwards) 71 n.77
Catalogues of Books (Edwards) 81 n.138
Catch the Fire: The Toronto Blessing: An Experience of Renewal and Revival (Chevreau) 11 n.36
Cates, Diana 56, 56 n.125
"catholick theologian" 224
Chadwick, Owen 60 n.1
Chai, Leon 15 n.54, 99, 99 n.49
Chambers, Ephraim 190 n.93
Channing, William H. 236 n.2
Charismatic movement 10–12
Charity and Its Fruits; or, Christian Love as Manifested in the Heart and Life (Edwards) 15 n.54, 119 n.22, 148–55, 231
Charnock, Stephen 168, 168 n.29
Chauncy, Charles 12–13, 16 n.59, 30 n.2, 91, 97, 98, 102, 160, 161, 163, 164–71, 173, 174, 179, 183 n.75, 185, 186, 190–1 n.94
Cherry, Conrad 13, 13 n.44, 14–15 n.54, 98, 130–1 n.56, 183 n.75, 224
Chevreau, Guy 11–12, 12 n.39, 230
Christian
  fortitude 192
  love 149–52
    humility 150
    indwelling Spirit 150–1
  meekness 192
  morality and aesthetics 238
  New Testament 209, 213
  "noble mind" 141
  obedience 193
  peace 202
  self-denial 191
The Christian Faith: A Systematic Theology for Pilgrims on the Way (Horton) 235 n.1
Christian Happiness (Edwards) 138–9
churches 237
The Church of England and the Bangorian Controversy (Starkie) 171 n.43
Cicero 41
The City of God (Augustine of Hippo) 38, 38 n.36
Clapper, Gregory S. 28 n.126, 185 n.77
Clark, Gordon 24, 24 n.106
Clarke, Desmond M. 72 n.81
Clay, Robert E. 158 n.139

Clement of Alexandria 31, 32–4, 34 n.19–21, 36, 36 n.32
Cochran, Elizabeth Agnew 190 n.93, 216 n.50, 218 n.56, 222 n.66, 224 n.70, 227 n.83
cognition 8, 20, 22–3, 22 n.98, 27, 51–2, 56, 56 n.125, 60, 230
  and appetite 51–6
Coleman, Benjamin 148, 149
A Collection of Miscellanies: Consisting of Poems, Essays, Discourses, & Letters, Occasionally Written (Norris) 71 n.77
College of New Jersey in Princeton 198, 201
Collegiate School of Connecticut 92
"Colonial American Theology: Holiness and the Lyric Impulse" (Grabo) 236 n.3
Commentaries on the First Twenty Chapters of the Book of the Prophet Ezekiel (Calvin) 65 n.34
Communion in the Spirit: The Holy Spirit as the Bond of Union in the Theology of Jonathan Edwards (Caldwell) 127 n.46
Communion with God: The Divine and the Human in the Theology of John Owen (Kapic) 76 n.102, 76 n.104, 77 n.124, 78 n.125
concupiscible capacity 51, 52–3
Confessions (Augustine of Hippo) 38, 38 n.36, 39–40, 44 n.65, 93
Conforti, Joseph A. 5 n.3, 211 n.36, 235 n.56, 236 n.2
Conscience 84 n.152, 113 n.5, 143, 212, 216, 222, 224
  morality of actions 222
  self-love 222
consent 100, 112–14, 117, 146, 159, 173, 205, 217 n.53, 218–24, 229, 234
  to being 113–15
  as harmony or symmetry 220
  importance of 113
  theory of 112
"Contemporary Music-Driven Worship" (Horness) 9, 9 n.22
Copan, Paul 132 n.57
Corrigan, John 15 n.54, 17 n.62, 18 n.74, 21 n.90, 22 n.100, 26 n.119, 45, 45 n.68
Coulter, Dale M. 7 n.11
covenantal relationship 213
The Covenant Sealed: The Development of Puritan Sacramental Theology in Old and New England (Holifield) 199 n.4
Crampton, W. Gary 4 n.1
Crapps, Robert W. 9, 9 n.27
Crisp, Oliver D. 218 n.53, 227 n.79
Crousaz, Jean-Pierre de 114–15, 115 n.7
Cyclopedia: or an Universal Dictionary of Arts and Sciences (Chambers) 190 n.93

Damasio, Antonio 90 n.21
Danaher, Jr., William J. 15 n.54, 28 n.126, 99, 99 n.50, 113 n.5, 114 n.6, 116 n.12, 125 n.40, 127 n.46, 129 n.49, 132 n.57, 135 n.64, 173 n.46, 176 n.55, 184 n.77, 199 n.5, 213 n.44, 220 n.60, 222 n.66, 225 n.73
D'Arcy, Eric 19 n.79, 27 n.121, 56
Darwall, Stephen 72 n.81
Davenport, James 157–8, 158 n.139
Davenport, John 80 n.136, 158 n.139
Davidson, Bruce W. 141 n.83
Davidson, Edwards H. 114 n.6, 131 n.56
Davidson, Richard J. 17 n.62
Day, Jeremiah 14, 14 n.48
De Anima et Resurrectione Dialogus (Gregory of Nyssa) 32 n.12
De Arte Concionandi Formulae ut Breves, Ita Doctae & Piae (Melanchthon) 62 n.16
debauchery 208
Deere, Jack 11, 11 n.34, 12, 230
Delattre, Roland A. 98, 98 n.41, 213 n.4, 218 n.54, 224, 224 n.70, 225
Delightful Conviction: Jonathan Edwards and the Rhetoric of Conversion (Yarbrough and Adams) 131 n.56
demonic affections 208
Dennison, James T., Jr. 82 n.145

depravity 61, 64, 66, 78, 106 n.109, 215 n.48
Descartes, René 67–9, 73, 178 n.60, 179, 179 n.66
Descartes' Error: Emotion, Reason, and the Human Brain (Damasio) 21 n.90
Desiring God: Meditations of a Christian Hedonist (Piper) 5–6, 5 n.4, 6 n.8, 27 n.121
Dever, Mark 84 n.153, 85 n.156
Dexter, Franklin Bowditch 92 n.2
Ðíåõìáôïëïãéá (Owen) 76 n.105, 77 n.111
diary (Edwards) 118–19. *See also* personal writings
Die Loci Communes (Melanchthon) 60 n.3
dilectio 54
Discourse on the Trinity (Edwards) 126 n.42, 127 n.46, 128
disposition 37, 64, 78, 80, 84, 113, 127, 129, 144, 147, 149, 218, 220, 221–2
dissension 114
The Distinguishing Marks of a Work of the Spirit of God (Edwards) 10, 11, 158–9, 163, 172, 184, 186
A Divine and Supernatural Light (Edwards) 130, 144–6
divine appetite 55–6
divine light. *See* light
divine love 46, 48, 88, 114, 123 n.37, 135, 136 n.64, 125–6, 154 n.126, 218, 225, 225 n.75, 234
  affection of 155
  Holy Spirit 126–8, 153 n.125, 234
  natural affection *vs.* 151
divinity 34 n.19, 80 n.138, 86 n.71, 107 n.110, 201
Dixon, Thomas 1, 2 n.2, 17–19, 25–6, 29, 45, 50 n.95, 56, 179, 231, 233
The Doctrine of Original Sin: According to Scripture, Reason, and Experience (Wesley) 214
Documentary History of Yale University: Under the Original Charter of the Collegiate School of Connecticut 1701–1745 (Dexter) 92 n.2
Does God Suffer? (Weinandy) 30 n.4, 235 n.1
Dolezal, James E. 235 n.1
Donne, John 197, 197 n.1
Dorrien, Gary 165 n.11, 170 n.42
dove 126 n.44
doxology 225–9
"Dummer Collection" 92, 93, 96
duty 139, 157, 176 n.57, 187, 187 n.85, 212, 217 n.53

Ecclesiastical Writings (Edwards) 199 n.4
Eddy, G. T. 214 n.45
Edwards, Dwight 15 n.54, 176 n.55
Edwards, Jonathan 1, 2. *See also* *specific work*
  affections (*see* affection(s))
  affective psychology (*see* affective psychology)
  College of New Jersey in Princeton 198, 201
  dismissal at Northampton 198–200
  educational background 92–6
  Locke and 96–110
  "The Mind" 101, 112–17, 118, 174 n.51, 204
  revival writings and sermons 137–46, 172
  sermons during Great Awakening 155–9
  Stockbridge, Massachusetts 198, 200–1
  theology of 3–4
Edwards, Jonathan, Jr. 236 n.4
Edwards, Sarah 172 n.45
Edwards, Tryon 149 n.11, 151 n.20, 236 n.4
"Edwards and the Revivalists" (Channing) 236 n.2
"Egoism and Morality" (Darwall) 72 n.81
Ekman, Paul 17 n.62, 21 n.90
Elliott, Matthew A. 15 n.54, 17 n.62, 22 n.97–8, 27 n.121
Emmons, Robert A. 15 n.54

emotion(s). *See also* religion
affections *vs.* 5–10
as a fill-in for affections 237 n.6
hydraulic model 21 n.90
obedience without 11
physiological feelings 8
problem of 23–8
study of 1
as value judgments 20, 237 n.5
emotional evangelicalism 5–10
"Emotion and God: A Reply to Marcel Sarot" (Westberg) 52 n.108
The Emotions (1a2ae. 22–30) (Aquinas) 19 n.79, 27 n.121, 53 n.112
Encyclopedia (Chambers) 190 n.93
The End for Which God Created the World (Edwards) 217–25
Engle, Paul E. 9 n.22
Enlightenment 67–74
Enthusiasm (Chauncy's sermon) 165–6
Enthusiasm, Described and Caution'd Against (Chauncy) 165, 165 n.14
The Epistle of Paul The Apostle to the Hebrews and The First and Second Epistles of St Peter (Calvin) 65 n.34
The Epistles of Paul the Apostle to the Galatians, Ephesians, Philippians and Colossians (Calvin) 63 n.21
Erdt, Terrence 16, 16 n.57, 101–2, 132 n.57
Erskine, John 217 n.53
eschatological affections 36–7, 43 n.61
An Essay Concerning Human Understanding (Locke) 97 n.35, 112
An Essay on the Nature and Conduct of the Passions and Affections (Hutcheson) 72 n.81
Ethical Writings (Edwards) 72 n.82
ethics 28, 31, 41–42, 150, 216–25, 236, 237
Eustace, Nicole 25, 25 n.111–12
evangelical humiliation 191
evangelicalism 5–10
"Evangelical Tradition in America" (Sweeney) 5 n.3
Eve 44, 66, 121, 122 n.31, 215. *See also* Adam
excellency 112
Exercises Commemorating the Two-Hundredth Anniversary of the Birth of Jonathan Edwards, Held at Andover Theological Seminary, October 4 and 5, 1903 (Platner) 96 n.32
The Experience that Counts! (Edwards) 10 n.30, 27 n.121
Exploring the Worship Spectrum: Six Views (Engle and Basden) 9, 9 n.22
external beauty. *See* physical beauty
external worship 157

faculty, defined 23
faculty psychology 12–14, 23, 97–9, 109
faith 209–10
affections of 74–5
properties of 74
saving (*see* saving faith)
A Faithful Narrative (Edwards) 141 n.84, 146–8, 149
false fortitude 192
Faulkner, Quentin 59 n.1
Faust, Clarence H. 12 n.40, 14, 14 n.51
Fay, Jay Wharton 96 n.32
fear of hell 123, 187 n.82
Fedler, Kyle 63 n.19, 66 n.40, 66 n.42
Feelings and Faith (Borgman) 9, 9 n.19
Feinberg, John S. 235 n.1
Fenner, William 81, 81 n.141, 83, 83 n.150, 85, 85 n.159
Ferguson, Sinclair B. 217 n.53
Fiddes, Richard 135–6 n.64
Fiering, Norman S. 30 n.2, 69 n.56, 70 n.70, 72 n.81, 75 n.101, 78 n.125, 81 n.141, 93, 93 n.6, 93 n.11–12, 93 n.14, 95 n.27, 99, 102, 105, 106 n.105, 109, 125 n.40, 170, 204 n.19, 216 n.51, 222 n.66
Finney, Charles G. 235–6, 236 n.2, 236 n.4
Fisher, George P. 3 n.1
flesh 215, 215 n.48
appetite of 203–4

Floyd, Shawn D. 52 n.108, 56 n.125
forgive/forgiveness 122 n.30
fortitude 192
Freedom of the Will (Edwards) 3 n.1, 107 n.114
freedom of will 121
French Prophets 190–1 n.94
"From Theology to a Science of Religions: Jonathan Edwards and William James on Religious Affections" (Proudfoot) 236 n.3
Fulcher, J. Rodney 13, 13 n.44, 81 n.142, 98

Galen 31, 32 n.11
Garden of Eden 122
Gaustad, Edwin Scott 146 n.102, 162 n.2–3, 165, 190 n.94
Geissler, Suzanne 236 n.3
genuine religion 9, 14, 143
"The Giggles are from God" (Woodward) 11 n.35
Gleason, Randall C. 82 n.142, 84 n.153
The Glory and Honor of God: Volume 2 of the Previously Unpublished Sermons of Jonathan Edwards (Edwards) 139 n.77
glory of God 78, 119, 123–4, 155, 188, 206, 220, 225–9, 231
  external 227–8
  internal 227
God is a Communicative Being: Divine Communicativeness and Harmony in the Theology of Jonathan Edwards (Schweitzer) 100 n.55
God's Statesman: The Life and Work of John Owen: Pastor, Educator, Theologian (Toon) 76 n.102
Goen, C. C. 15 n.54, 141 n.84, 146 n.102, 162 n.3, 164 n.14, 176 n.56
The Golden Age of Greek Patristic Literature from the Council of Nicaea to the Council of Chalcedon (Quasten) 31 n.8
The Golden Age of Latin Patristic Literature from the Council of Nicea to the Council of Chalcedon (Berardino) 40 n.46
The Golden Sceptre Held Forth to the Humble (Priestly) 83 n.147
good and evil 216–25
The Good Fight of Faith: Papers Read at the Westminster Conference 1971 213 n.44
Goodwin, Thomas 104, 131
The Gospel according to St John 11–21 and The First Epistle of John (Calvin) 66 n.40
Grabo, Norman 236 n.3
The Grace and Duty of Being Spiritually Minded (Owen) 78–9
gracious affections 95, 119, 134–5, 144, 147, 147 n.105, 159, 164, 179, 179 n.66–7, 181, 208, 234–5
  beautiful symmetry of proportion 192
  change of nature 191–2
  Christ-like characteristics 192
  evangelical humiliation 191
  excellency of divine things 188
  imagination 183
  judgment 191
  mixed religious experience 182–3
  moral excellency 189
  "new sense" doctrine 187–8
  "no signs" 186–7
  obedience 193
  self-love 188
  "sense of the heart" 190
  signs of 187–94
  tenderness of spirit 192
  understanding 189–90
"gracious appetite" 82 n.43
"Gracious Discoveries: Toward an Understanding of Jonathan Edwards' Psychological Theory, and an Assessment of his Place in the History of American Psychology" (Blight) 15 n.55
Great Awakening 2, 6, 12–13, 91, 161–94
The Great Awakening (Edwards) 141 n.84
The Great Awakening: Documents on the Revival of Religion, 1740–1745 (Bushman) 162 n.3
The Great Christian Doctrine of Original Sin Defended (Edwards) 214

The Great Divorce (Lewis) 120 n.23
Green, Bradley G. 49 n.93
Gregory of Nyssa 31–7
Grenz, Stanley J. 235 n.1
Griffin, Edward M. 165, 165 n.11
Grudem, Wayne 235 n.1
Guelzo, Allen C. 5 n.3, 236 n.4
A Guide to Christ (Stoddard) 95 n.28
Gura, Philip F. 15 n.54, 200 n.7
Gustafson, James M. 6 n.4

Half-Way Covenant 198–9
The Half-Way Covenant: Church Membership in Puritan New England (Pope) 199 n.4
Hannah, John D. 11 n.35, 25, 25 n.110, 183 n.75
happiness 226–7
  notions 151
  spiritual 120
A Harmony of the Gospels: Matthew, Mark and Luke Volume III and the Epistles of James and Jude (Calvin) 65 n.36
Haroutunian, Joseph 14, 14 n.51
Harrison, Graham S. 213 n.44
Hart, D. G. 5 n.3, 13, 13 n.46, 98, 98 n.46
Hartley's Theory of the Human Mind, on the Principle of the Association of Ideas; with Essays relating to the Subject of It (Priestly) 23 n.102
Harvard 92
Hatch, Nathan O. 4 n.1, 74 n.88, 106 n.105, 116 n.11, 171 n.44
Haykin, Michael A. G. 25, 25 n.110, 150 n.116, 184 n.77
heart 49, 53 n.114, 64, 75, 84, 108, 115, 116, 148, 149 n.111, 157, 167, 176, 178, 179 n.67, 187, 188 n.90, 191, 192, 206–7, 209 n.34, 213 n.43, 215, 216, 219
  affections of 39, 48 n.86, 59, 60, 62, 64, 76, 77, 81, 85, 85 n.159, 136, 139, 143, 146, 212, 226
  circumcision of 77, 204
  of God 225, 228
  Puritan theology of 16, 85 n.156, 104
  relation of will to 61, 63, 81, 83, 85 n.156, 87, 109, 116, 126, 130, 133, 174–5, 185, 209, 218, 224, 230
  sense 129–37
"'A Heart Moved': Philip Melanchthon's Forgotten Truth About Worship" (Aune) 61 n.5
"heat without light" 128 n.49, 176, 189
heaven 118, 120, 121, 128, 137, 139, 143, 145, 153–5, 175, 180, 183, 189 n.92
Heaven is a World of Love 153–5
heavenly minds 121
heaven's love 153–5
Heimert, Alan 14 n.47, 165 n.14
Heinze, Rudolph W. 59 n.1
hell 141 n.83
  fear of 123, 187 n.82
Helm, Paul 16, 16 n.60, 131 n.56, 218 n.53
Here I Stand: A Life of Martin Luther (Bainton) 59 n.1
Hessel-Robinson, Timothy 25 n.109
Histories and Fallacies: Problems Faced in the Writing of History (Trueman) 28 n.125
The History and Character of Calvinism (McNeill) 62–3 n.17
A History of Redemption (Edwards) 201
A History of the Work of Redemption (Edwards) 136 n.67
Hoadly, Benjamin 167 n.22, 170, 170 n.43
Holbrook, Clyde A. 176 n.56, 208 n.30, 214 n.45
Holifield, E. Brooks 85 n.60, 162 n.3, 199 n.4, 224
holiness 226–7
  affections 11, 143, 154, 157, 174, 176, 185, 185 n.79, 206–14, 225, 234
  conformity of heart to God 143
  spiritual beauty 114, 119
Holmes, Peter 44 n.63
Holmes, Stephen R. 15 n.54, 174 n.51, 225 n.74, 227, 227 n.82

Holy Spirit 126–8, 153 n.125, 234
  gracious work of 144
  light 144–6
  “new sense” doctrine 187–8
  works 145–6
Honderich, Ted 23 n.104
Hooker, Thomas 103
Hoopes, James 102–3, 103 n.76–80, 106 n.107, 125 n.40, 131 n.56, 201 n.14
Hopkins, Samuel 4, 4 n.2, 96 n.32, 100, 106 n.106, 138 n.74, 236 n.4
Horness, Joe 9, 9 n.22
Horton, Michael 235 n.1
Hotz, Kendra G. 25 n.114, 231 n.94
Houston, James 10, 10 n.29
Howard, Leon 106 n.105, 112 n.1, 112 n.2, 117 n.14
How the Light Gets In: Ethical Life I (Ward) 61 n.9
human instincts 222–3
Human Nature in Its Fourfold State (Boston) 82 n.146
humans
  vs. animals 116
  as unintelligent beasts 36 n.28, 48, 65 n.34, 78, 81, 116, 124, 138–42, 139 n.78, 142 n.85, 152, 155, 156 n.134, 188, 221 n.65
An Humble Attempt (Edwards) 198, 198 n.2
humility 150, 150 n.114, 191
Hunsinger, George. 210 n.35
Hutcheson, Francis 72–3, 73 n.85–6, 178 n.60, 190 n.93, 216 n.51, 221
hydraulic model of emotions 21 n.90
hypocrites 193

ideal apprehension 133
ideas 133
Ideas Have Consequences (Weaver) 216 n.50
imagination 147–8, 183
imago Dei 206
immaterialism 105
immaterial soul 38, 50, 137, 160, 238
immaterial world of spiritual realities 115
Immink, Gerrit 9, 9 n.23
immortality 94
immortal soul 139
impassibility 30 n.4, 33–6, 36 n.32, 37, 44, 46–7, 65, 88, 96, 135 n.64, 153, 233, 235
inclinations 111
  appetite as 51
  to good 113
  inferior 121
  mutual 222–3
  natural 121–3
  of reason and judgment 121–2
Increase Mather vs. Solomon Stoddard: Two Puritan Tracts (Mather and Stoddard) 199 n.4
indifference 115 n.7
Indwelling Sin (Owen) 76 n.103, 78 n.123
In Evangelium Ioannis (Calvin) 65 n.33
inferior appetite 94, 122 n.31
inferior inclinations 121
inferior passions 216
inferior powers 188
inferior principle 215–16
“inner man” 38
An Inquiry Respecting the Self-Determining Power of the Will or Contingent Volition (Day) 14 n.48
instincts. *See* human instincts
Institutes of Elenctic Theology (Turretin) 82 n.145
Institutes of the Christian Religion (Calvin) 63, 63 n.18
Institutio Christianae Religionis (Calvin) 63 n.18
“Intellectual Fathers” 103
intellectualism 29–30
intellectual love of God 72
internal worship 157
Introduction to Saint Thomas Aquinas (Aquinas) 49 n.93
irascible capacity/appetite 51, 52–3, 63
irascible passions 153

Jackson, Samuel Macauley 206 n.25
James, Susan 175 n.53
James, Williams 18, 18 n.76
Jensen, Robert 24, 24 n.107

Jesus Christ 28, 34, 36, 40, 76, 78, 80, 82, 85–6, 118, 120, 123, 128, 141, 147, 148, 150, 153 n.125, 156–7, 168 n.32, 190, 192, 201–3, 208–9, 209 n.32–3, 211 n.38, 213 n.43, 227, 237–8
  account of morality 217
  carnal appetite 123
  conformity of heart to 143
  death 238
  divine light 144–6
  "dying love" 181
  exercise of delight in 143
  fleshly love for 49
  as God's glory 238
  gracious affections 192
  incarnate 65–6
  Lord's Table 199, 212–13
  love for 48–9
  passionate love of 135–6
  true faith in 62, 213
  words to Peter in Mt. 16:17 144
John Calvin: A Sixteenth Century Portrait (Bouwsma) 63 n.17
John Donne's Poetry (Donne) 197 n.1
John Owen: Reformed Catholic, Renaissance Man (Trueman) 76 n.102
John Wesley on Religious Affections: His Views on Experience and Emotion and Their Role in the Christian Life and Theology (Clapper) 28 n.126
Jonathan Edwards (Allen) 14 n.50
Jonathan Edwards (McGiffert) 200 n.10, 227 n.79
Jonathan Edwards (Miller) 12 n.40
Jonathan Edwards (Winslow) 14 n.53, 148 n.109, 162 n.3, 200 n.10
"Jonathan Edwards, Enthusiast? Radical Revivalism and the Great Awakening in the Connecticut Valley" (Winiarski) 163 n.4, 183 n.75
Jonathan Edwards, Pastor: Religion and Society in Eighteenth-Century Northampton (Tracy) 98 n.45, 146 n.102, 148 n.109
"Jonathan Edwards, Religious Affections, and Spirituality in the Third Millennium" (Robbins) 7 n.9
Jonathan Edwards, Religious Affections, *and the Puritan Analysis of True Piety, Spiritual Sensation, and Heart Religion* (Walton) 16 n.58
Jonathan Edwards, Religious Tradition, & American Culture (Conforti) 5 n.3, 211 n.36, 236 n.2
Jonathan Edwards: A Guided Tour of His Life and Thought (Nichols) 98 n.47
Jonathan Edwards: A Life (Marsden) 3 n.1
Jonathan Edwards: America's Evangelical (Gura) 15 n.54
"Jonathan Edwards and Justification by Faith" (Schafer) 210 n.35
"Jonathan Edwards and Justification by Faith" (Withrow) 210 n.35
Jonathan Edwards and the Bible (Brown) 137 n.72
Jonathan Edwards and the Gospel of Love (Story) 229 n.87
Jonathan Edwards and the Limits of Enlightenment Philosophy (Chai) 15 n.54, 99 n.49
Jonathan Edwards and the Ministry of the Word: A Model of Faith and Thought (Sweeney) 13 n.44, 138 n.74
Jonathan Edwards: A New Biography (Murray) 13 n.44
"Jonathan Edwards as Philosophical Theologian" (Smith) 98 n.42
"Jonathan Edwards between Church and Academy: A Bibliographic Essay" (Lucas) 5 n.3
The Jonathan Edwards Encyclopedia (Stout) 11 n.35
Jonathan Edwards on Beauty (Strachan and Sweeney) 225 n.74
"Jonathan Edwards on Prayer and the Triune God" (Beck) 203 n.18

Jonathan Edwards: Representative Selections, with Introduction, Bibliography, and Notes (Faust and Johnson) 12 n.40
"Jonathan Edwards's 'Ambiguous and Somewhat Precarious' Doctrine of Justification" (Waddington) 210 n.35
Jonathan Edwards's Theology: A Reinterpretation (Strobel) 126 n.41
"Jonathan Edwards's Virtue: Diverse sources, Multiple Meanings, and the Lessons of History for Ethics" (Wilson) 224 n.70, 224 n.72
Jonathan Edwards's Writings: Text, Context, and Interpretation (Stein) 113 n.5
Jonathan Edwards the Preacher (Turnbull) 138 n.73
Jonathan Edwards to Aaron Burr, Jr.: From the Great Awakening to Democratic Politics (Geissler) 236 n.3
joy 11, 27, 68–9, 77, 120 n.25, 121, 124, 139, 168, 168 n.32, 175n.54, 181, 188–9, 209, 209 n.32, 226–7
  Augustine 42–5
  bodily pleasures 121
  necessity of 30
judgment 191
  inclinations of 121–2
justice 221

Kapic, Kelly M. 76 n.102, 76 n.104, 77 n.114, 78 n.125, 82 n.142, 84 n.153
Karant-Nunn, Susan C. 62 n.15
Kidd, Thomas S. 146 n.102, 158 n.139, 158 n.140, 162 n.3, 165 n.14
Kimnach, Wilson H., 6 n.7, 107 n.10, 138 n.73–4, 142 n.89, 163 n.4, 199 n.6, 201 n.15
Kling, David W. 5 n.3
Knight, Henry H., III 15 n.54
Knight, Janice 103–4, 103 n.83–4
knowledge 226–7
Knuuttila, Simo 27 n.121, 32 n.12, 37 n.35, 47 n.78, 55–6, 56 n.124, 72 n.46
Koch, G. Adolf 165 n.11
Kuklick, Bruce 4 n.1

"La Connaissance Spirituelle Selon Jonathan Edwards" (Vetö) 131 n.56
Lambert, Frank 162 n.3, 183 n.75
Larsen, Dale 9, 9 n.25
Larsen, Sandy 9, 9 n.25
Late Medieval Mysticism (Petry) 48 n.83
laughter 11 n.35, 120 n.22, 181
laws 18, 94, 114, 144 n.97, 150, 180
Lectures on the Philosophy of the Human Mind (Brown) 17–18, 18 n.70, 26 n.118
Lectures on the Revivals of Religion (Sprague) 236 n.2
Lectures to Professing Christians (Finney) 236 n.2, 236 n.4
Lee, Sang Hyun 92 n.2, 126 n.41, 129 n.51, 133 n.59
The Legacy of Jonathan Edwards: American Religion and the Evangelical Tradition (Hart, Lucas and Nichols) 5 n.3, 13 n.46
Lesser, M. X. 1 n.1, 5 n.3, 138 n.74
Lester, Andrew D. 9
Letters and Personal Writings (Edwards) 83 n.146
Letters of the Rev. Dr. Beecher and Rev. Mr. Nettleton on the "New Measures" in Conducting Revivals of Religion (Beecher and Nettleton) 236 n.2
Levi, Anthony 67 n.46, 68 n.55, 69 n.56–7
Lewis, Charlton T. 39 n.42
Lewis, C. S. 2, 2 n.3, 120 n.23
Lewis, Donald M. 158 n.139
Lewis, Paul 15 n.54, 23 n.103, 131 n.56, 237 n.6
The Life and Character of the Late Reverence, Learned, and Pious Mr. Jonathan Edwards (Hopkins) 4 n.2

Life and Works of Saint Bernard, Abbot of Clairvaux (Bernard of Clairvaux) 48 n.84
The Life of David Brainerd (Edwards) 197, 198 n.3, 211–14
The Life of John Calvin (Beza) 62 n.17
light 144–6
Lippy, Charles H. 165 n.11
Littledale, Richard Frederick 3
Lives of Jonathan Edwards and David Brainerd (Miller) 236 n.2
Loci Communes Theologici (Melanchthon) 60, 60 n.2–3, 61 n.10
Locke, John 5, 12–14, 91, 92, 96–110, 112, 112 n.1, 112 n.4, 117, 117 n.14, 117 n.17, 130, 131 n.56, 137, 170, 170 n.41, 179 n.66, 188 n.87, 204 n.19, 216 n.49, 234, 235
logos 127, 174 n.51, 227
longing desires 147
Lord's Supper 213
Lord's Table 199, 212–13
love 111–59. *See also* affection(s); religion; virtue
  Augustine on 40, 43–6
  of benevolence 218 n.57
  carnal 47–9
  Christian 149–52
  of complacence 218 n.57
  divine (*see* divine love)
  heavenly 153–5
  infinite 225–9
  intellectual and passionate 72
  medieval thought 46–57
  necessity of 30
  Owen on 76–80
  passionate love of Christ 135–6
  patristic psychology 33–7
  self-love (*see* self-love)
  spiritual 150–1, 153–5
  voluntarism 29
Love and Saint Augustine (Arendt) 40 n.45, 43 n.61
"Love Worketh No Ill" (Finney) 236 n.4
Lowance, Mason I, Jr. 115 n.9, 132 n.57
Lucas, Sean Michael 5 n.3, 13 n.46, 25, 25 n.114, 104, 104 n.85–6, 231 n.94
lust 19, 35, 36, 42, 123, 127–8, 140
Luther, Martin 59 n.1
Lutz, Catherine A. 21 n.90
Lystra, Karen 15 n.54

MacIntyre, Alasdair 216 n.50
The Making of American Liberal Theology: Imagining Progressive Religion, 1805–1900 (Dorrien) 165 n.11, 170 n.42
Malebranche, Nicholas 72, 73, 99, 102, 132 n.57, 178, 178 n.60–1, 235
man 132 n.58
  body of 180
  desires of happiness 203 n.18
  "inner man" 38
  "natural man" 61, 78
  soul 81–8
  whole man 87, 94, 109
  wise man 115 n.7
Manton, Thomas 81–2, 82 n.143, 83, 84 n.152, 86, 86 n.163, 95, 178, 217 n.53
The Marrow of Theology (Ames) 74–5, 93
Marsden, George 3 n.1, 30 n.2, 92 n.2, 93 n.11, 118 n.18, 119 n.21, 138 n.73, 141 n.42, 146 n.102, 148 n.109, 149 n.110, 158 n.139, 162 n.3, 163 n.4, 163 n.6, 164 n.9, 165 n.11, 165 n.13, 172 n.45, 184 n.77, 199 n.4, 199 n.5, 200 n.10, 214 n.45, 216 n.49, 217 n.51, 217 n.52
Martin, Ryan J. 171 n.44, 183 n.75
Maskell, Caleb J. D. 163 n.4
Mastricht, Peter van 86–8, 95, 104
material appetite 116
material aspects of passions 55
materialism 70, 115
Mather, Cotton 86, 109, 109 n.122
Mather, Increase 199 n.4
Mathews, Matthew T. 25 n.114, 231 n.94
matter 21, 26 n.118, 115 n.10, 119
McCarthy, Bryan 148 n.109

McClymond, Michael J. 3 n.1, 4, 4 n.2, 5 n.3, 10 n.32, 13 n.44, 22, 22 n.100, 26, 92 n.2, 93 n.11, 106 n.108, 106 n.109, 130–1 n.56, 162 n.2, 170, 170 n.41, 171 n.44, 183 n.75, 210 n.35, 213 n.43, 213 n.44, 217 n.51, 218 n.54, 231, 231 n.95
McCollum, David C. 162 n.3
McDermott, Gerald R. 3 n.1, 4, 5 n.3, 6–7, 7 n.11, 10, 10 n.32, 13 n.44, 25 n.110, 26, 49 n.93, 92 n.2, 93 n.11, 100 n.55, 106 n.108, 106 n.109, 114 n.6, 123 n.36, 131 n.56, 162 n.2, 184 n.77, 210 n.35, 213 n.43, 217 n.51, 218 n.54, 230, 230 n.91
McGiffert, Arthur Cushman, Jr. 200 n.10, 227 n.79
McKim, Donald K. 137 n.72
McMullen, Michael D. 138 n.74, 139 n.77
McNeill, John T. 62–3 n.17, 63 n.18
medieval theology 46–57
meditation 39, 78, 120 n.22, 211 n.36
Medulla Theologiae (Ames) 74 n.88, 92, 92 n.1
meekness 192
Meet the Puritans: With a Guide to Modern Reprints (Beeke and Pederson) 13 n.44, 74 n.88, 81 n.138, 81 n.139, 82 n.142
melancholy 118 n.19, 119, 211, 211 n.37
Melanchthon, Philipp 60–2, 66, 78, 83, 93
mental passions 81
mental science 26 n.118
metaphysics 112
Miller, Michael R. 50 n.100
Miller, Perry 3 n.1, 12–13, 14 n.47, 14 n.52, 23 n.10, 67 n.44, 81 n.138, 93 n.11, 96–109, 130–1 n.56, 165 n.14, 182, 199 n.4
Miller, Samuel 236 n.2
mind(s)
  heavenly 121
  human 121
  ideas 133
  sense 129–37
"The Mind" (Edwards) 101, 112–17, 118, 174 n.51, 204
"The Mind" of Jonathan Edwards: A Reconstructed Text (Howard) 106 n.105
Miner, Robert 50 n.99–100, 51 n.105, 53, 53 n.115–16, 55 n.120, 56, 56 n.126
ministers 207
Minkema, Kenneth P. 5 n.3, 130 n.55, 138 n.74, 140 n.81, 145 n.99, 148 n.109, 163 n.4
"Miscellanies" (Edwards) 119–37, 139 n.78, 147, 152 n.121, 197, 203 n.18, 215
"Misc. 3" 124
"Misc. 34" 124
"Misc. 37" 136
"Misc. 81" 136
"Misc. 94" 126
"Misc. 96" 136
"Misc. 98" 126 n.44
"Misc. 99" 124
"Misc. 101" 120–1
"Misc. 105" 137
"Misc. 106" 137
"Misc. 108" 120
"Misc. 123" 128 n.47, 129 n.51
"Misc. 134" 126 n.42
"Misc. 143" 127
"Misc. 146" 127
"Misc. 149" 121 n.26
"Misc. 151" 126 n.43
"Misc. 157" 127
"Misc. 180" 136 n.65
"Misc. 182" 121
"Misc. 189" 136
"Misc. 204" 124 n.38
"Misc. 212" 129 n.50
"Misc. 213" 136 n.66
"Misc. 218" 210 n.35
"Misc. 233" 121 n.27
"Misc. 238" 128, 128 n.48
"Misc. 284" 130 n.52
"Misc. 291" 121–2
"Misc. 301" 121, 123, 152 n.121, 215 n.48
"Misc. 305" 127 n.45
"Misc. 336" 127

"Misc. 341" 127 n.45
"Misc. 355" 127 n.45
"Misc. 359" 136
"Misc. 362" 137 n.71
"Misc. 364" 127 n.45
"Misc. 370" 128
"Misc. 394" 122 n.33
"Misc. 396" 127
"Misc. 397" 129–30, 129 n.51, 130 n.52
"Misc. 436" 122
"Misc. 437" 122 n.31
"Misc. 457" 122–3,
"Misc. 471" 123 n.34
"Misc. 488" 122 n.31
"Misc. 489" 130
"Misc. 507" 129 n.50, 130 n.53
"Misc. 530" 124 n.39, 152 n.121
"Misc. 539" 130 n.54
"Misc. 540" 130 n.53, 130 n.54
"Misc. 637" 137 n.70
"Misc. 639" 137, 220 n.60
"Misc. 669" 122 n.30
"Misc. 679" 124 n.37
"Misc. 683" 128
"Misc. 749" 125–6
"Misc. 782" 101 n.68, 104, 106 n.108, 108 n.119, 130, 130 n.55, 132–5
"Misc. 791" 123
"Misc. 822" 128
"Misc. 862" 204
"Misc. 961" 74 n.88
"Misc. 1003" 217 n.51
"Misc. 1072" 203 n.18
"Misc. 1205" 203
"Misc. a" 119, 141, 143, 155 n.131
"Misc. f" 120
"Misc. w" 120 n.22, 155 n.131
"Misc. x" 120 n.22
"Misc. z" 135
"Misc. aa" 129 n.50
"Misc. gg" 123
"Misc. kk" 123
"Misc. ll" 124
"Misc. tt" 137, 170
Moody, Josh 105, 105 n.98–9, 210 n.35
moral beauty 220
moral faculty 206
moral good 224
morality 237–8
moral philosophy 66–88
  early Enlightenment 67–74
  Puritan and Reformed thought 74–8
Moral Philosophy at Seventeenth-century Harvard: A Discipline in Transition (Fiering) 23 n.103, 30 n.2, 102, 109 n.121
moral sensible knowledge 134–5
Morgan, Chris 141 n.83
Morimoto, Anri 49 n.94, 87 n.175
Morris, William Sparkes 92, 92 n.3–4, 93 n.5, 94 n.15, 99–100, 100 n.56–7, 105, 112 n.1, 112 n.4, 117, 117 n.15–17, 217 n.53
Morrison, A. W. 65 n.36
Muller, Richard A. 30 n.2, 63 n.20, 63 n.21, 64 n.26, 206 n.25, 206 n.26
Murray, Iain 13 n.44, 15 n.54, 92 n.2, 118 n.18, 119 n.21, 138 n.73, 146 n.102, 148 n.109, 162 n.3, 184 n.77, 200 n.7, 200 n.10, 217 n.52
mutual inclination 222–3

Nadler, Steven 178 n.60
The Nakedness of Job (Edwards) 140
natural affection 61, 78, 144, 182–3
  divine love *vs.* 151
  for God 79
  as hysteria 189
  passion as 80 n.136
  spiritual danger of 118–19, 122 n.33
  Stoddard's caution 95
natural appetite 50 n.99, 116, 193, 202 n.17, 204, 215–16, 222–3
natural goodness of religion 183–4
natural inclination 121–3
"natural man" 61, 78
natural sensible knowledge 134
The Nature, Power, Deceit, and Prevalency of the Remainders of Indwelling Sin in Believers (Owen) 76 n.103
The Nature of Emotion: Fundamental Questions (Ekman and Davidson) 21 n.90, 61 n.17

The Nature of Emotion: Selected Readings (Arnold) 18 n.76, 20 n.82, 21. 91
The Nature of True Virtue (Edwards) 48 n.79, 72, 216–25
Neele, Adriaan Cornelis 86 n.171, 87 n.174, 148 n.109
Nelson, James M. 25 n.110
Nemesius of Emesa 31–7, 46, 52
Nettleton, Asahel 236 n.2
The New England Theology: From Jonathan Edwards to Edwards Amasa Park (Sweeney and Guelzo) 5 n.3, 236 n.4
New Light 164, 165 n.14, 167, 169
The New Schaff-Herzog Encyclopedia of Religious Knowledge (Jackson) 206 n.25
"new sense" doctrine 187–8
New Testament 209, 213
A New Treatise of the Art of Thinking (Crousaz) 114–15
New York City 118, 119
Nichols, Stephen J. 5 n.3, 13 n.46, 98–9, 98 n.47, 174 n.51, 184 n.177, 201 n.12
Noll, Mark A. 5 n.3, 24, 24 n.108, 162 n.2, 162 n.3, 236 n.2
Norris, John 71–2, 72 n.78–80, 73–4, 132, 132 n.57, 235
Northampton, Massachusetts 138, 144, 146, 198–200
"no signs" 186–7
notebook. *See* "The Mind" (Edwards)
Notes on Scripture (Edwards) 137 n.72
Nussbaum, Martha 20, 20 n.84–8, 21, 22, 22 n.97, 23, 27, 27 n.121–2, 33 n.14, 43 n.60, 237 n.5
Nuttall, Geoffrey F. 132 n.57

obedience 193
O'Connell, Robert J. 38 n.38, 39 n.43
"Of the Three Ways in Which We Love God (Sermon XX on the Song of Songs)" 48 n.83
Old Light 6, 160, 163 n.7, 164, 165, 173, 187
Oliphint, Scott 14, 14 n.47, 15 n.54, 23 n.103, 98 n.46, 175 n.51
Olson, Roger 9, 9 n.26
One Hundred and Ninety Sermons on the Hundred and Nineteenth Psalm (Manton) 82, 82 n.143
On Evil (Aquinas) 51 n.104
On the Nature of Man (Nemesius of Emesa) 31, 31 n.9
On the Soul and the Resurrection (Gregory of Nyssa) 32–3, 33 n.14, 33 n.18, 36 n.31
original sin 214–16
Original Sin (Edwards) 197, 200, 214–16
Ortlund, Dane 9–10, 10 n.28
Oviatt, Edwin 92 n.2, 94 n.15
Owen, John 76–9, 93, 95, 100, 104, 132, 168 n.32, 235
The Oxford Handbook of Religion and Emotion (Corrigan) 21 n.90, 22 n.100, 26 n.119, 72 n.81

papist 210 n.35
The Parable of the Ten Virgins Opened and Applied (Shepard) 81–2 n.142, 83 n.147, 85 n.160
Parrish, Archie 10, 10 n.31
Pascal, Blaise 69–70
Passion and Paradise: Human and Divine Emotion in the Thought of Gregory of Nyssa (Smith) 33 n.14, 33 n.17, 36 n.31, 37 n.34
"Passion and Principle" (Spohn) 21 n.89
passions 7
  affections and 52–4, 177–82
  definitions 32–3
  eschatological 36–7
  formal and material aspects 55–6
"Passions and Depressions in Early American Puritans" (Ursula) 67 n.44
The Passions: Emotions and the Meaning of Life (Solomon) 17 n.62
The Passions of the Soul (Descartes) 67
patristic theology 31–46
Pauck, Wilhelm 60 n.3
Pauw, Amy Plantinga 93 n.11, 99 n.49, 126 n.41, 203 n.18
peace 34 n.20, 151, 155, 167, 175 n.54, 209, 215, 202

The Peace Christ Gives His True Followers (Edwards) 201–2
Pederson, Randall J. 13 n.44, 74 n.88, 81 n.138, 81 n.139, 82 n.142
Pensées (Pascal) 69–70 n.58–68
perception 18, 22, 24, 26, 52, 67–8, 73, 101, 102, 104, 108, 114, 115 n.10, 117, 125, 128, 170 n.41, 179, 179 n.66
Percy, Martyn 11 n.35
"perfect man" 36
Perkins, William 103, 104
A Personal Narrative (Edwards) 144 n.98, 187 n.84, 188 n.90, 189 n.92, 191 n.95, 191 n.96, 192 n.98
personal writings 118–37
persuasion 77 n.112, 96 n.30, 173, 210
Petry, Ray C. 48 n.83, 49 n.90
Pettit, Norman 131 n.56, 198 n.3
The Philosophy of the Enlightenment (Cassirer) 100 n.53
physical beauty 112, 113, 120–1, 221
physical world 113, 115
Pinto, Vivian de Sola 95 n.25
Piper, John 5–6, 5 n.4, 6 n.8, 7, 8 n.15, 9, 10, 27 n.121, 225 n.74, 230
Plantinga, Alvin 237 n.7
Platner, John Winthrop 96 n.32
Platonic philosophers 41
Platonists 41, 42 n.58–9, 43 n.60. *See also* Cambridge Platonists
pleasure and displeasure 134
pleasure and pain 117
Pope, Robert G. 199 n.4
Postman, Neil 5 n.3
practical understanding 205–6
The Practical Works of The Rev. Richard Baxter with a Life of the Author, and a Critical Examination of his Writings (Baxter) 95 n.25
praise 33, 36, 37, 118, 147, 155, 187
The Prayers and Meditations of Saint Anselm with the Proslogium (Anselm of Canterbury) 46 n.73–4
preaching 3, 75, 91, 95, 166–9, 175–6
  disturbances during 167
  on justification by faith 146
  "whining tone" in 120 n.22
Presbyterians 82, 138, 162
Presbyterian Synod of New York 207–8
Preston, John 80–1 n.138, 80 n.136, 83, 83 n.147–8, 85, 85 n.157, 103
pride 44, 122, 155, 157, 182–3, 188, 192, 208, 223
Priestly, Joseph 23 n.102
Princeton 198, 201
profanity 143, 208
Prophets, French 190–1 n.94
proportion 55, 112–14, 121, 124, 181, 183, 192, 203
Protestant Scholasticism 92
Proudfoot, Wayne 236 n.3
psychology. *See also* affection(s); emotion(s)
  affective (*see* affective psychology)
  described 23
  faculty 12–14, 23, 97–9, 109
pure love 216–25. *See also* self-love; virtue
Puritan and Reformed thought 74–88, 91
Puritan Reformed Spirituality: A Practical Theological Study from our Reformed and Puritan Heritage (Beeke) 63 n.17
Puritan Rhetoric: The Issue of Emotion in Religion (White) 16 n.56, 96 n.30, 109 n.122–3

Quasten, Johannes 31 n.6, 31 n.8–9, 32 n.10
Quinn, Philip L. 218 n.53, 224, 224 n.72, 225

Ramsey, Paul 3 n.1, 72 n.82, 97 n.37, 148 n.109, 149 n.110, 149 n.111, 151 n.20, 216–17 n.51, 222 n.66, 224, 224 n.70, 225
Ramus 92
Randall, John Herman, Jr. 59 n.1
rationalism 12, 105, 161
rational passions 81

Reading Religious Affections: A Study Guide to Jonathan Edwards' Classic on the Nature of True Christianity (Biehl) 184 n.77
reality 91, 113, 123, 167, 191, 217, 220–1
reason 13–6, 17, 29–30, 32–6, 41, 44, 45 n.69, 46, 48, 50–1, 54–54, 55, 63–6, 68, 69, 81, 94, 97, 100, 116, 119, 127, 132 n.58, 142, 145, 152–3, 155, 165–6, 167–71, 176 n.56, 191, 194, 201 n.15, 202, 205, 216, 217 n.52, 221, 224, 231, 234
  inclinations of 121–2
  self-evident 143
  sinners 139–40
Reason and the Heart: A Prolegomenon to a Critique of Passional Reason (Wainwright) 131 n.56
The Reasons of the Christian Religion (Baxter) 94, 94 n.22
Receptive Human Virtues: A New Reading of Jonathan Edwards's Ethics (Cochran) 190 n.93
redemption 145, 188 n.90, 201
The Reformation (Chadwick) 60 n.1
The Reformation of Feeling: Shaping the Religious Emotions in Early Modern Germany (Karant-Nunn) 62 n.15
Reformed Confessions Harmonized: With an Annotated Bibliography of Reformed Doctrinal Works (Beeke and Ferguson) 217 n.53
Reformed Scholasticism 97
Reformed theology. *See* Puritan and Reformed thought
Reformed tradition 83
Reformers 59–66, 83
  Calvin 62–6
  Melanchthon 60–2
regeneration 76–7, 77 n.111, 84, 86–7, 87 n.175, 96, 122 n.33, 127 n.46, 146, 154, 170, 192, 193, 199
religion
  Chauncy on 164–71
  Edwards on 182–94, 206–14
  genuine 9, 14, 143
  true religion (*see* true religion)
Religious Affections (Edwards) 4 n.2, 6 n.8, 8, 9, 10, 14, 24, 28 n.126, 79 n.126, 81 n.138, 101, 104, 130, 149, 164, 176, 177, 182, 184–7
"Religious Enthusiasm and Separatism in Colonial New England" (Armstrong) 183 n.75
relish 78, 79, 79 n.126, 128, 189 n.91, 190, 202, 206–14
Remarks on the Improvements Made in Theology by his Father, President Edwards (Edwards, Jr.) 236 n.4
repentance 64 n.26, 94, 118
"Resolutions" (Edwards) 118, 118 n.18
revelations 141, 144, 146, 170 n.41, 183 n.75, 190, 209 n.34
Review of *Jonathan Edwards and the Limits of Enlightenment Philosophy* by Leon Chai (Pauw) 99 n.49
Review of *Jonathan Edwards and the Limits of Enlightenment Philosophy* by Leon Chai (Sweeney) 99 n.49
Review of *Jonathan Edwards and the Limits of Enlightenment Philosophy* by Leon Chai (Vascardi) 99 n.49
Review of *Jonathan Edwards and the Limits of Enlightenment Philosophy* by Leon Chai (Wilson) 99 n.49
Reynolds, Edwards 81–8
rhetoric 3, 96–7, 103
Richardson, Alan 206 n.25
Rightmire, R. David 213 n.44
Rivett, Sarah 92 n.2, 188 n.87
Robbins, Duffy 7 n.9
Roberts, Robert C. 15 n.54, 21, 21 n.89, 27 n.121
Roth, Catharine P. 32 n.10, 32 n.12
The Ruin and Recovery of Mankind (Watts) 214 n.45

"The Sacramental Theology of Jonathan Edwards in the Context of Controversy" (Rightmire) 213 n.44

sacraments 199, 213
The Safety of Appearing at the Day of Judgment in the Righteousness of Christ, Opened and Applied (Stoddard) 95 n.28
Sailer, Don E. 24, 24 n.105, 25, 231 n.94
Saint Bernard on the Love of God (Bernard of Clairvaux) 48 n.85
saints 71, 141, 180–92
 affection 74–5, 76, 77, 234
 glorified bodies of 121
 God's delight in 123 n.37
 heavenly 137, 153–5
 Holy Spirit 127–8, 129
 joy 192
 Lord's Table 213
 love of glorified 137
 peach left by Christ to 201–2
 resurrected 37
 spiritual love 150–1, 153–5
sapientia 38
saving faith 64, 66, 85, 93, 136, 149, 209–10
Schafer, Thomas 119 n.21, 130 n.52, 210 n.35
Schweitzer, William M. 100 n.55
science 18, 23, 92 n.2, 216 n.49, 233
Science and Sentiment in America: Philosophical Thought from Jonathan Edwards to John Dewey (White) 4 n.1
scientia 38
Scientific and Philosophical Writings (Edwards) 4 n.1
The SCM Press A-Z of Thomas Aquinas (Wawrykow) 50 n.98
The Scripture Doctrine of Original Sin Proposed to Free and Candid Examination (Taylor) 214 n.45
Scriptures 11, 24, 31, 32, 33, 40, 41–2, 43, 48, 60, 63, 70, 78, 114, 116, 119, 126–8, 136, 137, 144 n.98, 156, 173, 175, 185, 190, 193–4, 199, 203–4, 208, 217 n.52, 237
The Search after Truth (Malebranche) 73 n.85, 178, 178 n.60–1
Seasonable Thoughts on State of Religion in New England (Chauncy) 164–5, 165 n.13, 166–71
secondary beauty 220–1
 defined 220
 moral *vs.* 220–1
 spiritual objects 221
"Second Great Awakening" 235–6
secularism 224, 234
secularization 217
self-knowledge 226
self-love 40, 69–71, 221–2. *See also* virtue
 concept 221
 conscience 222
 gracious affections 188
 "inordinate" nature 152 n.121
 sinful 113, 122–3
sensations 12, 22–3, 38, 73, 99, 101, 101 n.68, 104–5, 107–8, 125 n.40, 132 n.57, 133, 180, 188, 189, 220
"sense of the heart" 129–37, 145, 190
sensible knowledge 133–5
 natural *vs.* moral 134–5
sensitive passions 81
sensual/sensory appetite 51, 52–6, 61, 71, 75, 78, 104, 122–3, 139–42, 156, 223
sentiment 224
sermon(s). *See also specific sermon*
 during Great Awakening 155–9
 revival 137–46, 172
Sermon on Mt. 24:12 (Edwards) 157 n.138
Sermons and Discourses (Edwards) 6 n.7, 74 n.88, 107 n.110, 125 n.40, 138 n.74, 199 n.6
shadows 115, 120, 202, 220
Shepard, Thomas 81–2 n.142, 83 n.147, 85, 85 n.160–1, 95, 104
Sibbes, Richard 80, 80 n.136–7, 81 n.138, 83 n.147, 84–5 n.153–156, 95, 103–4
signs 132–3
Signs of the Spirit: An Interpretation of Jonathan Edwards' Religious Affections (Storms) 8 n.17, 10

Simonson, Harold P. 101, 101 n.61, 201 n.14
simple idea 98, 106, 108
sin 143, 214–16
enslavement to 139–40
sincerity 193
singing 75, 146 n.104, 168 n.32
Sinners in the Hands of an Angry God (Edwards) 118, 118 n.18, 163
Sketch of the History of Yale University (Dexter) 92 n.2
Skirry, Jason 178 n.60
Smart, Robert Davis 16, 16 n.59, 162 n.2, 162 n.3, 164 n.9, 184 n.77
Smith, Gordon T. 15 n.54
Smith, John 4, 4 n.2, 24–5, 70–1, 71 n.73, 71 n.76, 73, 74 n.88, 81 n.138, 98, 98 n.42, 98 n.43, 104, 107, 107 n.110, 130 n.55, 131, 132 n.57, 183–4, 184 n.76–7
Smith, J. Warren 33 n.14, 33 n.17, 36 n.31, 37 n.34
Smith, Thomas 168 n.29
Smyth, Egbert C. 92 n.2
Solari, Placid 40 n.46
Solomon, Robert C. 17 n.62, 20–1, 21 n.90, 22 n.96, 23
"Some Early Writings of Jonathan Edwards. A. D. 1714–1726" (Smyth) 92 n.2
Some Thoughts (Edwards) 11–12, 158, 161, 163–5, 169, 172, 172 n.45, 174, 174 n.50, 175 n.54, 177, 182, 184, 205, 207
soul 32–3
appetites (*see* appetites)
body and 67–74
immaterial 38, 50, 137, 160, 238
man 81–8
patristic distinctions between movements of 34–7
Sources of the Self: The Making of the Modern Identity (Taylor) 66 n.40
"Sovereign Beauty: Jonathan Edwards and the Nature of True Virtue" (Spohn) 217 n.52
"sovereign love" 70
The Spectator (Addison) 170, 170 n.43
speculation 133
speculative knowledge 207, 208
The Spirit of Revival: Discovering the Wisdom of Jonathan Edwards with the Complete, Modernized Text of The Distinguishing Marks of a Work of the Spirit of God (Sproul and Parrish) 10 n.31
"spiritual appetite" 82 n.43
spiritual beauty 112–14, 119, 121, 190, 218, 219, 220, 234
Spiritual Brethren 103
spiritual consent 115
spiritual conviction 191
spiritual deformity 114
Spiritual Emotions: A Psychology of Christian Virtues (Roberts) 15 n.54, 21 n.89, 27 n.121
spiritual happiness 120
spirituality 113, 120
"Spirituality and its Discontents: Practices in Jonathan Edwards's *Charity and its Fruits*" (Spohn) 15 n.54
"spiritual man" 39
spiritual principles 215
spiritual realities 132
spiritual sensation 104–5
spiritual sense 129–35
spiritual sensible knowledge 134–5
spiritual understanding 190, 191
Spohn, William C. 15 n.54, 21 n.89, 217 n.52, 220 n.61
Sprague, William Buell 236 n.2
"'The Springs of Motion': Jonathan Edwards on Emotions, Character, and Agency." 15 n.54, 23 n.103, 131 n.6, 237 n.6
Sproul, R. C. 10 n.31
The Stanford Encyclopedia of Philosophy (Zalta) 17 n.65, 72 n.81
St. Anselm: Basic Writings (Ames) 75 n.75
Starkie, Andrew 171 n.43
St. Augustine, of the Citie of God: with the Learned Comments of Ioannes Lodovicus Vives (Augustine of Hippo) 41 n.50

Stein, Stephen J. 4 n.1, 113 n.5, 137 n.72, 153 n.124, 162 n.2, 198 n.2
Stewart, Dugald 3 n.1
Stockbridge, Massachusetts 198, 200–1, 209
Stoddard, Solomon 93, 95–6, 96 n.29–30, 109, 110, 121 n.28, 138, 145 n.99, 146, 178, 198, 199, 199 n.4, 234
Stoics 41
Storms, Sam 7, 8, 8 n.17–18, 10, 184 n.77, 230, 230 n.92
Story, Ronald 229 n.87
Stout, Harry S. 4 n.1, 11 n.35, 13 n.44, 74 n.88, 106 n.105, 116 n.11, 162 n.2, 171 n.44
Strachan, Owen 225 n.74
Strobel, Kyle C. 99 n.48, 126 n.41, 129 n.49–50, 130 n.53, 176 n.55, 185 n.77, 217 n.52, 225 n.74
Stromata, or Miscellanies (Clement of Alexandria) 31, 32
St. Thomas Aquinas: Philosophical Texts (Aquinas) 49 n.93
"Subjects to Be Handled in the Treatise on the Mind" (Edwards) 204–5
The Substance of Christian Religion: Or, A Plain and easie Draught of the Christian Catechisme (Ames) 74 n.90, 75 n.100
Summa Theologica Editio Altera Romana ad Ementatiores Editiones Impressa et Noviter Accuratissime Recognita: Pars Prima (Aquinas) 52 n.108
The Summa Theologica of St. Thomas Aquinas (Aquinas) 54 n.118
Surprised by the Power of the Spirit (Deere) 11, 11 n.34
Sweeney, Douglas A. 5 n.3, 99 n.49, 118 n.18, 137 n.72, 138 n.74, 200 n.12, 225 n.74, 228 n.85, 236 n.4
Systematic Theology (Berkhof) 227 n.79
Systematic Theology: An Introduction to Biblical Doctrine (Grudem) 235 n.1
The System of Doctrines (Hopkins) 236 n.4
tabula rasa 106 n.109
Taking Hold of God: Reformed and Puritan Perspectives on Prayer (Beeke and Najapfour) 203 n.18
Talbot, Mark 7–8, 8 n.16, 9, 9 n.19, 10, 230 n.91
Tappan, Henry 14, 14 n.49
taste 48, 79, 80 n.137, 190 n.93
  "moral tastes" 216
  "spiritual taste" 189, 190
Taylor, Charles 66 n.40, 216 n.49, 225 n.74
Taylor, John 214, 214 n.45, 236 n.2
Taylor, Justin 8 n.15
Telfer, William 31 n.8, 32 n.11
temper 127, 129, 151, 181–2, 192
temperament 122, 164
Tennent, Gilbert 162
Ten New England Leaders (Walker) 14, 14 n.51, 165 n.11
Tersteegen, Gerhard 29, 233
Theologia Speculativa: or, The First Part of a Body of Divinity Under that Title. Wherein are explain'd the Principles of Natural and Reveal'd Religion (Fiddes) 135 n.64
"Theologies" (Weaver-Zercher) 15 n.54
theology. *See also* Christian
  affections 233–8
  medieval 46–57
  patristic 31–46
The Theology of Jonathan Edwards (McClymond and McDermott) 3 n.1
The Theology of Jonathan Edwards: A Reappraisal (Cherry) 13 n.44
Theoretico-Practica Theologia (Mastricht) 86–8
Toon, Peter 76 n.102
Tracy, Patricia J. 98, 98 n.45, 146 n.102, 148 n.109, 199 n.5
Trapé, Agostino 40 n.46, 45 n.69
A Treatise Concerning Religious Affections (Edwards) 93 n.9, 95 n.26, 106 n.106, 106 n.108, 128 n.49, 132 n.57, 133 n.59, 142 n.88, 143 n.90, 150 n.115, 150 n.118,

161, 164, 170 n.42, 173 n.46, 173–84, 184–94, 199 n.6, 219 n.59, 225, 230 n.88, 234
A Treatise of the Affections; or The Souls Pulse (Fenner) 81 n.141
The Treatise on Human Nature: Summa Theologiae 1a, 75–89 (Aquinas) 49 n.93
A Treatise on Regeneration (Mastricht) 86 n.171
A Treatise on the Passions and Faculties of the Soul of Man (Reynolds) 81–8
A Treatise on the Will (Tappan) 14 n.49
Treatises II (Bernard of Clairvaux) 47 n.78
Trinity 111, 121, 126 n.41–2, 127–9, 137, 173
The Trinity (De Trinitate) (Augustine of Hippo) 38 n.37
Triune God 113, 117, 146, 153, 173, 186, 229, 234, 238
True and False Christians (On the Parable of the Wise and Foolish Virgins) (Edwards) 148 n.109
True Grace, Distinguished from the Experience of Devils (Edwards) 207–8
Trueman, Carl R. 28 n.125, 76 n.102
True Nobleness of Mind (Edwards) 140–4
true religion 4, 5, 9, 12, 16, 28, 71 n.76, 98, 185–6, 191, 201, 207–8, 225, 234, 236
True Religion Delineated (Bellamy) 236 n.4
The True State of the Question Concerning the Qualifications Necessary to Lawful Communion in the Christian Sacraments (Williams) 200 n.9
true virtue. *See* virtue
truth 114
Tulloch, John 107 n.110
Turnbull, George 216
Turnbull, Ralph G. 14 n.54, 138 n.74
Turretin, Francis 82, 82 n.145, 86, 86 n.168, 86 n.171, 95, 104, 108, 108 n.120, 109, 110, 131, 132 n.57, 234
Two Dissertations (Edwards) 197, 200, 217, 225
Typological Writings. (Edwards) 115 n.9

understanding 29, 81–7, 83 n.148, 94, 97, 100, 107–8, 109, 109 n.120, 117, 129, 129 n.50, 130 n.52, 132 n.58, 133, 146, 156, 159, 166, 169, 173, 174, 174 n.51, 176, 180, 188, 208, 209, 227. *See also* affection(s)
  affective psychology 106–10
  divine 126 n.42, 128, 128–9 n.49, 226–7
  gracious affections 189–90
  practical 87 n.175, 205–6
  spiritual 190, 191
  will 30, 63–4, 67, 100 n.57, 101–2, 117, 125, 126 n.42, 130, 133, 139, 140 n.78, 140 n.81, 146, 173, 176 n.55, 204, 205–6, 209 n.33, 222
Unnatural Emotions: Everyday Sentiments on a Micronesian Atoll & Their Challenge to Western Theory (Lutz) 21 n.90
unregenerate 64, 121–2, 128, 150, 189, 208, 209, 213, 221
Ursula, Brumm 67 n.44

Valeri, Mark 144
value judgments, emotions as 20, 237 n.5
The Value of Salvation (Edwards) 139
Vascardi, Christopher J. 99 n.49
vehemence 12, 181, 182–3, 212
Vetö, Miklos 131 n.56
Vineyard movement 10–11
"'Violent Motions of Carnal Affections': Jonathan Edwards, John Owen, and Distinguishing the Work of the Spirit from Enthusiasm" (Martin) 171 n.44, 173 n.75
virtue 216–25
  beauty 218, 224
  benevolence to Being 218–19
  devotion/love to God 219–20
  human instincts 222–3
  love in 218

self-love 221–2
sentiment 224
Virtue as Consent to Being: A Pastoral-Theological Perspective on Jonathan Edwards's Construct of Virtue (Zylla) 223–4 n.69
Virtue Reformed: Rereading Jonathan Edwards's Ethics (Wilson) 27 n.124
virtuous benevolence 218–19
virtuous person 36, 219–21
The Voice of Jesus: Discernment, Prayer and the Witness of the Spirit (Smith) 15 n.54
voluntariness 123–8
voluntarism 29–30, 93, 102, 109, 170

Waddington, Jeffrey C. 210 n.35
Wainwright, William J. 131 n.56
Walker, Williston 14, 14 n.51, 165 n.11
Walton, Brad 16, 16 n.58, 75 n.100, 76 n.102, 82 n.142, 84 n.153, 94 n.21, 95 n.26, 99, 104–5, 107, 184 n.77
Walton, Robert 47 n.78
Wannenwetsch, Bernd 60 n.2
Ward, Benedicta 46 n.73
Ward, Graham 61 n.9, 62 n.15
Warranted Christian Belief (Plantinga) 237 n.7
Watson, Thomas 85, 86 n.162, 95, 95 n.26
Watters, David H. 115 n.9
Watts, Isaac 59, 162 n.2, 179 n.65, 214 n.45
Wawrykow, Joseph P. 50 n.98
Weaver, Richard M. 216 n.50
Weaver-Zercher, David L. 15 n.54
Weinandy, Thomas G. 30 n.4, 235 n.1
Wesley, Charles 161
Wesley, John 14 n.53, 28 n.126, 29, 111, 214 n.45, 233
Westberg, Daniel 52 n.108
Westminster Catechism 92
Westminster Confession 217 n.53
The Westminster Dictionary of Christian Theology (Richardson and Bowden) 206 n.25
Westminster Handbook to Evangelical Theology (Olson) 9 n.26
Westminster Shorter Catechism 217 n.53
Wetzel, James 41 n.51
What Emotions Really Are: The Problem of Psychological Categories (Griffiths) 21 n.90
What Is an Emotion? Classic and Contemporary Readings (Solomon) 21 n.90
When the Spirit Comes with Power: Signs & Wonders among God's People (White) 11 n.33
Whichcote, Benjamin 107 n.110
White, Eugene E. 15, 16 n.56, 96 n.30, 109 n.22
White, John 10–11, 11 n.33, 230
White, Morton 4 n.1
Whitefield, George 158 n.139, 160, 162, 162 n.2
whole man 87, 94, 109
wicked affections 208
wicked men/people 36, 139–43, 145–6, 208
Wicked Men's Slavery to Sin (Edwards) 139
wicked will 121
will 30, 42, 44, 51–2, 60–2, 63–4, 65, 109, 120–3, 205–6, 227
affections and 40, 43, 47, 52, 75, 76, 81, 83–4, 85 n.159, 87, 93, 116–7, 147, 166, 173–6, 177, 185, 216
Aquinas on 51–4
as consent 112–2
desire and 205
divine 55, 72–3, 126, 128, 129–30, 173, 227
Locke's theory of 117, 137
motives 205
understanding 109, 117, 133, 204, 205–6
Williams, Don 9, 9 n.22
Williams, Solomon 200, 200 n.9
Wilson, Catherine 72 n.81
Wilson, John F. 99 n.49, 201 n.13, 239, 258

Wilson, Stephen A. 27 n.124, 127 n.46, 218, 224–5
Windsor, Connecticut 92
Winiarski, Douglas L. 163 n.4, 183 n.75, 258
Winslow, Ola Elizabeth 14, 14 n.53, 148 n.109, 162 n.3, 199 n.7, 200 n.10
wise man 115 n.7
Withrow, Brandon 86 n.171, 210 n.35, 244, 258
Wolleb(Wollebius), John 92, 94–5, 96
The Wonderful Narrative: Or a Faithful Account of the French Prophets, their Agitations, Extasies, and Inspirations (Chauncy) 191 n.90
Woodward, Kenneth L. 11 n.35
"The Word of God" 143–4
work of grace 39, 122 n.33, 168 n.29, 182
The Works of Dugald Stewart (Stewart) 3 n.1
The Works of John Owen (Owen) 76 n.104
The Works of Richard Sibbes (Sibbes) 80 n.135
"The Works of Samuel Hopkins" (Beecher) 96 n.32
The Works of Stephen Charnock (Charnock) 168 n.29
worship 5–6, 9, 120–1, 216
  bodily 120–1
  external 157
  internal 157
  inward affection 75
  "manner of expression" 120
  regulative principle 119
Worship in Song: A Biblical Approach to Music and Worship (Aniol) 25 n.114
writings of Edwards 118–37
Writings on Pastoral Piety (Calvin) 63 n.17
Writings on the Trinity, Grace, and Fath (Edwards) 126 n.41

Yale College 163
Yale Edition of the *Works of Jonathan Edwards* 239–40, xiii
Yarbrough, Stephen R. 131 n.56, 254
Young, Amos 7 n.11, 247
The Young Jonathan Edwards: A Reconstruction (Morris) 92 n.3, 94 n.15, 94 n.21, 112 n.1, 117 n.15–17

Zahl, Simeon 60 n.2, 61 n.5, 62 n.14
Zalta, Edward N. 17 n.65, 72 n.81, 255
zeal 77 n.111, 156 n.135, 181, 182
Zylla, Phil C. 223 n.69, 255